CITIZEN COUNTESS

Sofia Panina AND THE FATE
OF REVOLUTIONARY RUSSIA

ADELE LINDENMEYR

The University of Wisconsin Press

The University of Wisconsin Press
728 State Street, Suite 443
Madison, Wisconsin 53706
uwpress.wisc.edu

Gray's Inn House, 127 Clerkenwell Road
London EC1R 5DB, United Kingdom
eurospanbookstore.com

Printed in the United States of America

This book may be available in a digital edition.

Library of Congress Cataloging-in-Publication Data
Names: Lindenmeyr, Adele, author.
Title: Citizen countess: Sofia Panina and the fate of revolutionary Russia / Adele Lindenmeyr.
Description: Madison, Wisconsin: The University of Wisconsin Press, [2019] | Includes bibliographical references and index.
Identifiers: LCCN 2019008124 | ISBN 9780299325305 (cloth: alk. paper)
Subjects: LCSH: Panina, Sofiia Vladimirovna, grafinia, 1871–1956.
| Women philanthropists—Russia—Biography.
| Women politicians—Russia—Biography.
| Russia—History—Nicholas II, 1894–1917—Biography.
| Russia—History—February Revolution, 1917—Biography.
| Saint Petersburg (Russia)—History—Revolution, 1917–1921—Biography.
Classification: LCC DK254.P275 L56 2019 | DDC 947.084/1092 [B]—dc23
LC record available at https://lccn.loc.gov/2019008124

ISBN 978-0-299-32534-3 (pbk.: alk. paper)

To the women of Russia,
past and present

Contents

Illustrations

Acknowledgments

The project that became *Citizen Countess* originated in New York City, in the tranquil reading room of Columbia University's Rare Book and Manuscript Library, where I first discovered Sofia Panina's papers among the many treasures of the Bakhmeteff Archive. While I did not realize it at the time, my quest to find as much surviving evidence about her life as possible would lead me to many similar institutions in Russia, Europe, and elsewhere in the United States. One of the great joys of writing this book has been working in these remarkable places, near and far, and meeting their dedicated librarians and archivists. Some let me stay beyond working hours or provided a photograph or photocopy at short notice; others offered tea and cookies at the end of an exhausting day. All were unfailingly knowledgeable and helpful. My thanks go to the staff of the Bakhmeteff Archive; Yale University's Sterling Memorial Library (Historical Manuscripts and Archives Department); and the Hoover Institution Archives at Stanford University for their kind assistance. I am especially grateful to the librarians and archivists at the Russian institutions that managed to preserve documents from Sofia Panina's long and interrupted life: the State Archive of the Russian Federation, the Russian State Archive of Ancient Acts, and the Russian State Library's Manuscript Division, all in Moscow; and in St. Petersburg, the Central State Historical Archive of St. Petersburg, the Institute of Russian Literature of the Russian Academy of Sciences, the Russian Institute for the History of Art, the Manuscript Collection at the State Museum of the History of St. Petersburg, the Manuscript Division of the Russian Public Library, and the extraordinary photograph collection at the Central State Archive of Film, Photography, and Sound. The Bibliothèque de Documentation Internationale Contemporaine, now called La Contemporaine, at the University of Paris-Nanterre yielded still more treasures, as did the manuscript collections at the British Library. Thanks also go to the staff in the Interlibrary Loan Department at Villanova University's Falvey Memorial

Library for their remarkable ability to locate and deliver any book or article, no matter what its language.

I was fortunate to receive funding for these archival explorations from Villanova University, the American Philosophical Society, and the Dmitry S. Likhachev International Charitable Foundation in St. Petersburg. A research fellowship from the National Endowment for the Humanities (grant FB-53760-08) provided me with a precious year of leave that enabled me to organize this book and write more than half of it. *Citizen Countess* simply would not exist without the generous support of these great institutions and organizations.

Another great joy in writing this book has come from the many new friends and acquaintances I made in the course of my research. First and foremost, I am deeply grateful to Sofia Panina's descendants, Vlad and Olga Lehovich. Unfailingly supportive, they placed their trust in me and waited patiently for the completion of what must have seemed an endless project. Their willingness to share family photographs, documents, and recollections with me has made this book much richer and better. I owe an enormous debt of gratitude to the late Boris Strelnikov of St. Petersburg—World War II veteran, retired teacher, local historian, and the first person to retrieve and rehabilitate the memory of Sofia Panina in post-Soviet Russia. Boris Nikolaevich welcomed me—a total stranger from America—into his circle and rejoiced at my interest and familiarity with her life. He dedicated whole days to guiding me around Sofia's St. Petersburg during my visits in the 1990s, introducing me to the historical and archival discoveries he had previously made. The Likhachev Foundation in St. Petersburg provided not only financial and logistical support for my research but also introductions to new people and sources; thank you, Alexander Kobak, Oleg Leikind, and Elena Vitenberg. I also benefited from the knowledge of the historian-preservationists Alexander Margolis, of the International Charitable Foundation for the Renaissance of Petersburg-Leningrad, and Alexander Kalmykov, of the State Museum of Political History of Russia in St. Petersburg.

As I began working on Sofia Panina's life in emigration, I received valuable assistance from the historian Marina Sorokina and her institution, the Alexander I. Solzhenitsyn Institute for Russia Abroad in Moscow. Another historian who generously shared her expertise is Galina Ulyanova of the Institute of History in Moscow; her incomparable knowledge of the history of Russian charity, entrepreneurship, and the city of Moscow has greatly enriched my own over the course of our long friendship. Mikhail Gorinov and the late Sergei Dundin provided expert research assistance in locating new sources within the vast labyrinth that is the State Archive of the Russian Federation in Moscow. I am also indebted to the late Michelle Lamarche Marrese for her help with sources in the Russian State Archive of Ancient Acts; she is missed by her colleagues in Russian women's history. I will always remember my first visit to Marfino on a brilliant June day in 1998, accompanied by the architectural historian Natalia Datieva and literary scholar Alexander Pankin, who shared their knowledge of Marfino's history, their wonder at its unique natural and architectural beauty, and a delicious picnic. Marfino's and Sofia Panina's legacy could have no better protectors than the resourceful sisters Elena and Victoria Kashirtseva, creators and curators of the "Internet Museum of Countess Sofia Panina." My sincere gratitude goes to all of these individuals still living; to those no longer with us, I will never forget you.

I have been equally fortunate in the advice and encouragement I received from friends and colleagues who read all or parts of *Citizen Countess*. While the shortcomings of this book are all my own, I happily acknowledge the many contributions to its merits made by these readers and friends. My greatest debt of gratitude goes to Seth Koven of Rutgers University, this project's most avid supporter and wisest guide. Throughout the many years of research and writing, Seth gently but persistently spurred me to take my analysis deeper, make my interpretations more nuanced, and use a comparative lens to illuminate Sofia Panina's life and times. That our friendship survived and thrived while my labor of love remained under his sharp critical gaze testifies to his intellectual generosity and kindness. My colleagues at the long-running Delaware Valley Russian History Seminar graciously spent several Sunday afternoons discussing and critiquing various chapters of *Citizen Countess*; these discussions always added historical depth and insight to my work. I am particularly grateful to my friends Laurie Bernstein and Bob Weinberg for sharing their deep knowledge of Russian history (and English grammar) to make the manuscript as good as it could be. Marion Roydhouse read the entire manuscript as well, enriching it with her extensive knowledge of American women's history. Elizabeth Block and Laura Jackson gave me the benefit of their perspective as perceptive, well-informed nonspecialist readers. Other friends, along with my history colleagues at Villanova University and my sister Louise Lindenmeyr, kept my morale high and my progress steady while offering helpful insights and suggestions. Finally, my heartfelt gratitude goes to

Natalia Smirnova for her friendship and hospitality during my many visits to her city since we first met in Leningrad in 1977.

I was fortunate to have considerable assistance from several colleagues at Villanova University as I put together the final version of the manuscript. Lorraine McCorkle of Creative Services expertly handled the preparation of the illustrations and helped me create the Panin family tree. Eric Wagner generously contributed his time and expertise to create the map. Jutta Seibert of Falvey Memorial Library guided me through the maddening intricacies of *The Chicago Manual of Style* as she helped me assemble the bibliography. Sarah Keith wrangled the disparate parts of the manuscript into the required submission format. Finally, it has been a pleasure to work with the University of Wisconsin Press. Laura Engelstein's thorough reading and insightful critique of *Citizen Countess* as one of the manuscript reviewers resulted in numerous improvements; the two other anonymous readers made a number of useful recommendations as well. I especially thank Gwen Walker, executive editor; Anna Muenchrath, acquisitions assistant; managing editor Adam Mehring; and Judith Robey, the copyeditor who did such a meticulous review of the manuscript. Versions of a few chapters were previously published: chapter 4 in *The Journal of Modern History* 84 (March 2012); parts of chapters 7 and 8 in *The Journal of Russian History and Historiography* 9 (2016); and chapter 9 in *The Russian Review* 60 (October 2001).

A Note on Names and Dates

I have chosen to use first names for Sofia Panina and her close family members and friends (including her parents, husband Alexander Polovtsov, and partner Nikolai Astrov) and last names for all other persons. For transliterating Russian I employ the Library of Congress system, although some first names are Anglicized (Alexander instead of Aleksandr), and last names are simplified. For example, I use Kerensky, Obolensky, and Vernadsky instead of Kerenskii, Obolenskii, and Vernadskii, and I use Maltsov instead of Mal'tsov, as well as familiar spellings of well-known Russians such as Tolstoy and Gorky.

Russia officially used the Julian calendar until February 1, 1918, when the Soviet government converted to the Gregorian calendar, used in Europe and the United States. The Julian calendar ran twelve days behind the Western calendar in the nineteenth century and thirteen days behind in the twentieth. Thus, for example, the February Revolution against the Russian monarchy took place in March according to the Gregorian calendar, and the Bolsheviks seized power in October in Russia but in November in the West. Educated Russians such as Sofia Panina often wrote both dates, for example in letters written from abroad. Unless otherwise indicated, dates before 1918 are according to the Julian calendar. When both dates are given, the date according to the Julian calendar precedes the date in the Gregorian calendar.

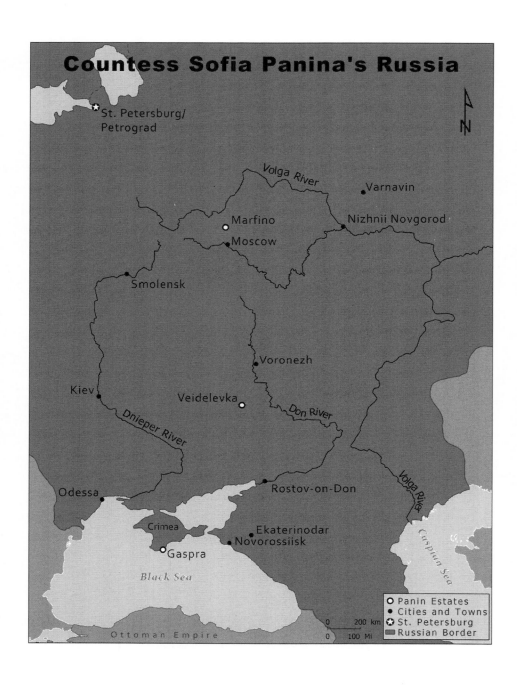

Countess Sofia Panina's Russia

St. Petersburg/
Petrograd

Volga River

Varnavin

Marfino

Nizhnii Novgorod

Moscow

Smolensk

Voronezh

Kiev

Veidelevka

Don River

Dnieper River

Odessa

Rostov-on-Don

Crimea

Ekaterinodar

Volga River

Novorossiisk

Gaspra

Caspian Sea

Black Sea

Ottoman Empire

N

○	Panin Estates
•	Cities and Towns
✪	St. Petersburg
▬	Russian Border

0   200 km

0   100 Mi

Countess Sofia Vladimirovna Panina
Family History

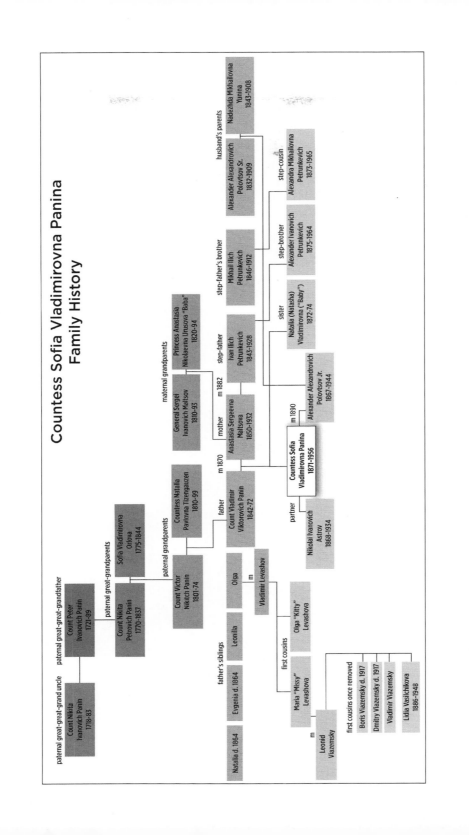

CITIZEN COUNTESS

Introduction

In November 1991 I traveled to Russia to look for traces of the life of a woman named Sofia Panina. Born in 1871, descended from the Russian aristocracy's highest ranks, and heiress to one of its great fortunes, Countess Panina won the admiration of progressive contemporaries for her work to expand access to education and culture for the working class before World War I. Early in the revolutionary year of 1917, after the monarchy fell and a provisional government took over Russia's deteriorating military front and collapsing economy, she moved onto the political stage and attracted national and international attention as the first woman in world history to occupy a ministerial position in a government. After a second revolution toppled that government in October, the liberal countess became an "enemy of the people." In December 1917, "Citizen Panina," charged with stealing government funds, faced the Bolsheviks' new revolutionary tribunal in their first trial of a political opponent. Yet few works by Western historians have mentioned her name, and her remarkable life has never been written. I had only learned about her in the course of research for a book on the history of Russian charity. Were Russians equally unaware, I wondered, of a woman who once counted among the best-known members of her generation?

3

Although I had visited Russia and lived there numerous times before, never had the country seemed as dark as it did that November. Light fixtures with missing or low-watt bulbs barely illuminated the airport, railroad station, and other public places. Anger and anxiety darkened the public mood as well. Chaos and rebellion are imminent, a fearful Moscow acquaintance warned. There is nothing to eat and nothing to buy, a cab driver complained bitterly, not even underwear. A Petersburg friend was concerned about my welfare; there is rationing in the city and the shops are empty, she advised, and I don't know how you will eat. In Red Square on November 7, the recently abolished holiday commemorating the Bolshevik Revolution, I watched irate citizens arguing with each other over whether the Communists, the West, or the Jews had stolen Russia's wealth. A few weeks after my departure, on Christmas Day 1991, President Mikhail Gorbachev announced the dissolution of the Union of Soviet Socialist Republics to a shocked populace. As the hammer-and-sickle was lowered over the Kremlin, the new flag of the Russian Federation, adapted from the Romanovs' imperial tricolor, rose above the capital and the country. Thus began one of the most troubled eras in Russian history, a decade characterized by political disarray, the loss of international power and prestige, failed economic reforms, corruption, and widespread suffering.

Yet amid the pessimism that darkened those November days there were unmistakable signs of resilience, energy, and initiative. In June 1991 Leningrad residents had voted to renounce the city's revolutionary past by restoring the name it had proudly possessed before World War I as the capital of one of history's great empires—St. Petersburg. The vote symbolically expressed the efforts by countless Russians to bring to light forgotten chapters and individuals from twentieth-century history, heroes as well as villains. For the group of St. Petersburg activists I met that November, one of those heroes was Countess Sofia Vladimirovna Panina.

Toward the end of my stay in the city, I took a tram to a gritty industrial neighborhood, searching doubtfully for surviving remnants of the Ligovsky People's House, the educational and cultural institution Sofia Panina built for workers in 1903. I was astonished to discover an imposing complex of well-designed brick buildings, wholly intact and immediately recognizable from prerevolutionary photographs. Remarkably, Sofia Panina's people's house, known since the 1920s as the Railroad Workers' Palace of Culture, still graced its nondescript surroundings, having survived the October 1917 socialist revolution, the siege and

Entrance to the Railroad Workers' Palace of Culture (formerly the Ligovsky People's House), November 1991. (photograph by the author)

bombings of World War II, and Soviet-era attempts to erase imperial history. Installed above foundation walls marked with graffiti—unheard of in Soviet times—two plaques outside the main door spoke to the institution's dual past. The older one, marble with gold lettering, proclaimed its distinguished status in the Soviet era as one of the "Lenin Places" (*Leninskie mesta*), sites made sacred by having been visited by the founder of the USSR. "In this building on May 9/22 1906," the plaque announced, "V. I. Lenin gave a speech before a popular assembly on the tactics of the RSDWP with respect to the State Duma. The assembly adopted the resolution proposed by V. I. Lenin."[1] The second, less imposing plaque—new, small, and placed lower than its companion—employed elements of Art Nouveau design to convey a simpler message: "Ligovsky People's House, founded April 20, 1903."

Inside the building the institution's prerevolutionary importance was on full display. In the center of the spacious main hall hung an oil portrait of its aristocratic founder, a copy of the one painted in 1909 by Ilya Repin, the eminent realist artist and Sofia Panina's personal friend. On the walls an exhibit celebrated the prerevolutionary origins and history of the people's house, while accentuating continuities with

Soviet-era cultural institutions. The Ligovsky People's House was the predecessor of today's Palace of Culture for Railroad Workers, the exhibit explained, and the origins of Leningrad's beloved Theater for Young Audiences may be traced to the theater that occupied the second floor. Before the revolution the people's house "accomplished significant work in educating and enlightening the working class," one display asserted, "and enjoyed the love and respect of the common people and cultural figures." The Ligovsky People's House even won a medal, the exhibit claimed proudly if erroneously, at the Brussels International Exhibition in 1915.

The inspiration behind the reclamation of the institution's prerevolutionary past, I soon learned, came from its director, staff, and volunteers. The members of this small but ardent group, composed of students on internships and professionals experienced in the running of workers' clubs, local historians and retired teachers, amateur poets and artists, were united by a mission to preserve, reinvigorate, and reinvent an outmoded and financially struggling Soviet institution, the ubiquitous palace of culture.[2] One way to move forward, they believed, was to look back to the ideals embraced by the institution's founder, Countess Panina, and to study its pre-Soviet record of cultural uplift and educational advancement among some of St. Petersburg's poorest and most culturally deprived inhabitants.

Though surprised by my unannounced visit, Kim Nikolaevich Izmailov, the institution's director, and local historian Boris Nikolaevich Strelnikov welcomed me enthusiastically and bombarded me with questions, information, and anecdotes. Did I know exactly when Sofia Vladimirovna was born, and where she died? Where was her grave— Paris? Prague?[3] Two years earlier, I was told, as plans to resurrect the institution's history got underway, they had commissioned an artist to paint the copy of Repin's portrait and hung it on the wall opposite the obligatory bust of Lenin in the main hall.[4] The countess and the Communist stared at each other for a while until eventually the staff decided it was safe to take Lenin away entirely, though they only dared to put it into storage; his bust was still somewhere in the building. Boris Nikolaevich recounted two tales that he insisted were true: that she hid Lenin from the police during the 1905 Revolution and that he in turn saved her from a second arrest and trial in late 1917. Countess Panina's institution, I was assured, still radiated its own unique "spirit," originating in the high ideals of class unity, progress, and democracy advanced by its aristocratic founder. These activists hoped to bring what

Countess Sofia Vladimirovna
Panina by Ilya Repin, 1909.
(courtesy of the Russian Museum, St. Petersburg)

they regarded as her special qualities of simplicity, sincerity, and commitment to cultural progress back into the work of the workers' palace. By animating one small corner of St. Petersburg with her democratic ideals, they hoped to advance the political, cultural, and spiritual renewal of their liberated but imperiled nation.

Twenty years later I traveled to Russia to participate in two consecutive conferences, one in Moscow and the second in St. Petersburg, devoted to the life and legacy of Countess Sofia Panina. Russia had transformed itself in the intervening two decades. In 2011 high speed trains connected the two cities, which gleamed with rebuilt roads, new construction, extensive historical restoration, and a plethora of shops, cafes, and restaurants. Russians now enjoyed social stability and access to a once unimaginable range of consumer goods. Employment had risen, as had the country's international influence. The crisis of 1991 was now only a bitter memory, but the search for a usable past to help guide the post-Communist future continued. Hopes of the 1990s for a democratic evolution had not been fulfilled. While a majority of the population credited the government, especially the increasingly authoritarian but still popular Vladimir Putin, with restoring domestic order and international muscle, many were angered by rising corruption and diminishing civil liberties. The two conferences in 2011 brought together professionals from a variety of fields—history, museum and archive administration, science, sociology, law, and philosophy. Some devoted their presentations to different aspects of Sofia Panina's life; others explored historical problems illuminated by her story that still resonate in the present: social solidarity, the responsibilities of wealth, and the viability of political liberalism and civil society.[5] In 2011 as in 1991, the lives of individuals from the prerevolutionary past offered Russians the opportunity to question historical inevitabilities, to imagine different narratives, and to find new sources of national identity.

If Russia's need for a usable past and its search for forgotten heroes were the only reasons for a biography of Sofia Panina, then this book probably should have been written by a Russian, for Russians. What first drew me to this project was less her relevance for post-Soviet history than her own remarkable capacity for self-reinvention in the face of both opportunity and necessity. Like their European and American sisters, Russian women of Sofia Panina's generation faced unprecedented opportunities along with numerous obstacles when they ventured into public roles. Men dominated the political realm, civic associations, and the professions; legal and social norms reinforced gender inequality. But movements for women's emancipation and equal rights in the late nineteenth and early twentieth centuries increasingly challenged these boundaries and stereotypes. The "New Women" of the *fin de siècle*—independent, adventurous, and determined to lead their lives according to their talents and desires rather than society's rules—became feminism's symbol. In certain important aspects, Sofia Panina's life is their story, and many undertook the same project of self-reinvention that repeatedly defined her life.

A child of privilege and one of St. Petersburg society's most eligible brides, Sofia emancipated herself from the expectations of her class and gender. Once the pawn in a struggle between her mother and grandmother over custody and her inheritance, she grew up to become an independent woman thirsting for higher education and a social purpose. More important, she liberated herself from the traditions of the stereotypical Lady Bountiful. Inspired by the Russian intelligentsia's commitment to using social service to effect a more just society, Sofia channeled her great wealth and passion to be useful into ambitious, comprehensive projects aimed at producing permanent improvement in the lives of workers and poor women and educating them for citizenship. Thus her story contributes a new chapter to the history of charity and progressive social reform in the modern era. The nature and goals of her philanthropic work place her among such well-studied contemporaries as Jane Addams of Hull House and Frances Perkins, Franklin Roosevelt's Secretary of Labor; other comparable figures include Muriel Lester, the founder of London's radically egalitarian Kingsley Hall settlement house, and the social worker and suffragist Eleanor Rathbone, one of the first female members of the British Parliament.

Unlike their American or British counterparts, however, Russians who undertook social initiatives such as hers took on no small measure of political risk. The expansion of civil society proceeded under the tsarist regime's strict yet unpredictable censorship policies, police surveillance, and, until 1906, prohibitions against any kind of political association. Although Sofia strenuously rejected any political affiliation before the revolution, the nature of her work among the working class of St. Petersburg linked her to the liberal opposition movement; some contemporaries even labeled her the "red countess." During World War I it became difficult for her to maintain this apolitical stance. Along with millions of other Russians, Countess Panina found an outlet for her patriotism in the efforts to aid the war's victims on the home front. Her organizational talents quickly elevated her to ever greater responsibilities in public relief organizations in Russia's capital, work that took on distinct political overtones as the tsarist government's own war efforts faltered. When the Romanov dynasty fell in early 1917, she displayed little attachment to the old regime. Instead, Countess Panina boldly transformed herself yet again, this time from social worker into one of the few women to take a leading political role in the Russian Revolution. The Petrograd City Council elected her in March as one of its first female deputies. Shortly thereafter the leading liberal party, the Constitutional Democrats, or Kadets, voted for her to join its central committee, one of only two women. She also took her place as the only woman in the new Provisional Government when she was appointed assistant minister, first of state welfare and later of education. Even the Bolshevik commissar who arrested her in late November of 1917 paid tribute to the one he termed "the First Woman of Russia."

Sofia Panina's striking personal reinvention paralleled Russia's own self-reinvention in the late imperial and revolutionary eras. She belonged to the remarkable generation of Russians that came of age in the last two decades of Romanov rule, a period she once characterized as a time of "spiritual effervescence and creative vigor." Members of this generation directed Russia's industrial enterprises, extended its railroads across Siberia, established its first political parties, and created its brilliant *fin-de-siècle* artistic and intellectual culture. They led their nation in war and revolution, then witnessed its agonies in the civil war that ravaged the country from 1918 to 1920. Those who remained in Soviet Russia enlisted, willingly or unwillingly, in the great project to remake the country into the first socialist society. Others like Sofia fled Russia and experienced, as she termed it, "all the bitterness of the loss of one's own fatherland."[6] While mourning their incalculable losses, she and her fellow exiles went on to create a "Russia Abroad" in émigré colonies around the globe in their effort to preserve the prerevolutionary culture and values they believed Soviet rule had betrayed.

Embarking on this book, I sought to discover what enabled Sofia Panina not only to survive the cataclysms of her era but also to recreate a purposeful life—in wartime and revolutionary Petrograd, in southern Russia with the anti-Bolshevik White Army, and in exile in Geneva, Prague, and New York. Russia's revolutionary history has seldom been told from a perspective such as hers. In most accounts, women appear in the historical narrative primarily as working-class and peasant housewives and soldiers' wives, who as instigators of bread riots sparked political protests but never led them, and who neither constituted an organized force nor exerted a decisive influence on the revolution. Recently historians have begun the important work of uncovering and analyzing Russian women's immense contributions to their country during World War I, and their struggle to attain political rights and civil equality in 1917.[7] The voices of individual women, however, are still all but absent in most accounts of Russia's revolution. To most Russian historians during the Soviet era there seemed to be little point in writing about those like Sofia Panina who landed on the revolution's losing side, except in the cause of exposing the hypocrisy of their liberal values. When it comes to biography, it is the ill-fated Empress Alexandra or revolutionaries such as the Bolshevik feminist Alexandra Kollontai who have attracted most of the attention. The American journalist Louise Bryant, who attended Sofia's trial in Petrograd in December of 1917, established the precedent in her book about the revolution *Six Red Months in Russia*. Bryant draws a somewhat forced parallel between Sofia, whom she misidentifies as the former "minister of welfare" in the liberal Provisional Government, and Kollontai, who stepped into power as Commissar of Social Security after the October Revolution. While Kollontai, Bryant claims, was "much loved" by the masses, Panina "has been swept aside in the public regard after the harsh test of revolution."[8]

But to interpret Sofia Panina's life solely within the historical parameters of modern female emancipation or the Russian Revolution is to miss the complexities of her personality, the contradictions of her choices, and the ways that her life simultaneously conformed to and deviated from contemporary norms and historians' generalizations. Historical patterns do not fully explain her decisions or provide insight into her inner life. Rather than fitting her into established categories, I have tried during the course of my research to be attentive to her individuality and to hear her distinctive voice. In doing so I have learned that writing biography requires both intimate proximity to one's subject and critical distance. In these respects, Sofia Panina has been an enormously sympathetic but also frustratingly uncooperative biographical subject.

First of all, she intentionally shaped and revised the record she left behind. Of course, she was not thinking of the convenience of her future biographer when she left virtually everything she possessed to flee Russia and the Bolsheviks in 1920. An unknowable number of records were lost or destroyed. The sources on her life before the revolution that did survive are fragmentary and scattered in numerous archives and libraries in Russia, Europe, and the United States. Like many of her fellow refugees, Sofia began to assemble her personal papers and reflect on her life while living as an émigré. She turned to those tasks in earnest after she resettled for the last time in the United States, where she arrived from Nazi-threatened Prague in early 1939. There she composed the only memoir she allowed to be published, posthumously, in New York in 1957. Detailed and eloquent in its account of the establishment and operation of the Ligovsky People's House, it modestly attributes the initiative and ideas behind the institution to others, wholly omits her childhood and youth, and reveals virtually nothing about her private life in adulthood. She also wrote a short reminiscence about her school years, which she did not publish; though personal and emotional in tone, it ends abruptly in a two-sentence paragraph.

Invited to donate her papers to the Bakhmeteff Archive at Columbia University, Sofia Panina was deliberate in selecting what she wished to preserve for future historians. What truly mattered, in her opinion, was not documenting her personal life but preserving historical records related to her country's fate in the twentieth century: the failed liberal alternative to revolution to which she committed her life and fortune, and the catastrophe that befell her nation when it came under Soviet rule. She also destroyed documents as a way to relieve the pain of memory. "I am burning everything that is personal and dear," she confessed to her step-cousin Alexandra Petrunkevich in 1953.[9] Indeed, her archive at Columbia University contains a scant five pieces of correspondence from her beloved mother, and nothing at all written either to or from Nikolai Astrov, the man she lived with from 1918 to his death in Prague in 1934.

During the early stages of this project, I sometimes despaired of finding sufficient source material for the kind of in-depth analysis of Sofia Panina as an individual that I wished to undertake. Given what seemed to be a dearth of personal records and her own resistance, I feared that my research would produce yet another example of the "just add women and stir" approach to women's history: a two-dimensional reconstruction of the life of a worthy woman unjustly ignored by historians. But as I continued my search, exciting discoveries began to fill in the gaps. Buried in the personal archive of a high-ranking tsarist official was a trove of more than fifty letters Sofia wrote in her twenties to her childhood friend Varya Volkova. The voluminous files of Russia's state surveillance agencies yielded their own surprises, such as police reports on her activities and the petition her mother wrote to Emperor Alexander III, asserting her loyalty in the face of charges of revolutionary sympathies and begging him not to take eleven-year-old Sofia away from her. A particularly exciting discovery came when I joined one of her descendants in opening her battered, water-stained leather valise, left in a New York apartment after her death, to find several richly detailed handwritten reminiscences amid a jumble of pen nibs, cemetery receipts, recipes, and yellowed photos.

A still greater challenge to writing a biography of Sofia Panina has to do with her many admirable qualities. As a girl and young woman, she faced heartbreak and adversity with empathy and resilience. In prison and on trial she defended her principles and values. Once one of Russia's wealthiest women, she spent the last thirty-six years of her life as an émigré living frugally but without complaint on her own meager earnings. Feeling a bit guilty and unfair, Sofia's biographer must try to look past her charm and accomplishments in order to achieve a balanced interpretation. This is the dilemma encountered by "historians who love too much," as described by historian and biographer Jill Lepore. "Finding out and writing about people, living or dead, is tricky work," she points out. You must "balance intimacy with distance while

Sofia's valise, 2011.
(photograph by the
author)

at the same time being inquisitive to the point of invasiveness."[10] There
is the danger of getting too close to one's subject, and becoming too fond
of her. At the same time, there is the other risk of not getting to know
one's subject well enough by being too respectful, and insufficiently
nosy, intrusive, and critical.

It has often been difficult, I confess, to overcome the influence of this
charismatic, warm, energetic woman with her passionate commitment to
human betterment. Moreover, it is virtually impossible to find a single
negative opinion of her in the surviving records. Family and friends
adored her. According to the recollections of one relative who spent
time as a child in New York City with the countess, "Aunt Sophie" was
"a warm, cozy figure who got along famously with her much younger
niece, my mother, and had a close and affectionate rapport with my
father." With her "smiling face and a parcel of questions," she had "an
utterly uncondescending way" of talking and "an engaging way of
entertaining us."[11] Even journalist Louise Bryant, though harsh in her
judgments about Sofia Panina's principles and actions, responded to
the charm of the woman she described as "gay and amusing," who
loved to tell "funny anecdotes" about the revolution.[12]

Countess Panina also connected with her social inferiors. No dour
do-gooder, she provided not only literacy classes and science lectures

to St. Petersburg's downtrodden but also opportunities to have fun and experience joy. Captivated by her personal warmth, energy, and dedication to social progress, those who worked at the people's house and many of its working-class visitors deeply admired, even worshipped her. In the highly contested social and political terrain of prerevolutionary Russia, contemporaries ignored the contradictions of her life in order to see her as a symbol of self-sacrificing Russian womanhood, or the promise of class harmony and liberal democracy.

Nevertheless, those contradictions constitute an important part of Sofia Panina's story. I have sought to discern alternatives to the ways she represented herself, as well as to the ways others represented her. Although in her memoirs she depicts herself as defiantly hostile toward the values of the elite girls' school she attended, in actuality Sofia quickly conformed to the institution's demands and excelled there. The future "red countess" followed the standard script for a young heiress of the aristocracy when her debut into high society culminated in marriage at age eighteen to a wealthy, handsome, and well-connected officer. Self-emancipation came about gradually, greatly aided by the autonomy that her considerable wealth made possible. I have also tried to penetrate the riddles of Sofia's closest personal relationships. Her mother's reckless, defiant behavior as a young widow, for example, led to the tragedy of their forced separation, yet Sofia seems to have harbored no resentment against Anastasia or the stepfather who competed for her mother's love. The nature of the relationship Sofia constructed after 1917 with Nikolai Astrov, her political partner and life companion, is also puzzling, at least to the modern observer; friends treated the virtually inseparable pair as husband and wife, yet they never married.

Other contradictions in Sofia's life arise out of collisions between the worlds that she inhabited. The woman whom contemporaries considered a democrat or even a quasi-socialist insisted that the Ligovsky People's House was above politics; and her refusal to acknowledge the political implications of her social activism before and during the Great War seem naïve if not frankly disingenuous. Her faith in the liberal values of individual freedom, self-determination, civil rights, and citizenship obstructed her understanding of demands for economic and social justice. Despite the many years she spent interacting with workers, she does not seem to have understood the deep wells of their anger and resentment against the upper classes that exploded in 1917. At the forefront of revolutionary events during 1917, Sofia alternated between hope and despair as she imagined Russia's future. By the time she and

Astrov found a safe harbor in Western Europe, she had lost any remaining illusions. Unlike some fellow exiles, who discerned some positive aspects in the Soviet system, she considered the Russia she loved to be lost forever but refused to denounce publicly the regime she despised.

My hope is that readers will understand these contradictions and get to know the qualities of Sofia Panina's soul: her modesty and pride; the cheerfulness and gaiety that sometimes masked deep anguish; the ways she both resisted and expressed the prejudices of her class; the extraordinary generosity she extended to others, even when she possessed barely more than the less fortunate who received her aid; and finally, her courage and resilience. The aristocratic society into which Countess Panina was born may be extinct, but the competing currents of her time still resonate with us and influence contemporary history: the conflict between philanthropy and economic justice, and between gradual reform and violent revolution. Her story reminds us of the contingency of history. The kind of progress to which she dedicated her life before the Great War was not necessarily doomed. It was a combination of personal choices and historical events, not fate, which condemned the countess to living the last third of her life as a stateless refugee. Long consigned to the dustbin of history in favor of Communists like Alexandra Kollontai, Sofia Panina made a dramatic reentry into historical memory in post-Soviet Russia, reminding us that we can never know how history ends.

1

A Fairy-Tale Childhood

In a short reminiscence written long after she had fled Soviet Russia, Sofia remembered a "carefree, joyful childhood, entirely imbued with my mother's warmth and love," a childhood she characterized as a "fairy tale."[1] Viewing her life through the prism of age, after experiencing revolution, imprisonment, civil war, and exile, she understandably idealized her early years. Yet the comparison of her childhood to a fairy tale is apt. Like many fairy tales, hers began with early losses—the death of her father when she was not yet one year old, followed by the death of her only sibling, a younger sister. Despite her grief over the deaths of her husband and baby daughter, Sofia's mother, Anastasia, provided both security and freedom to her cherished only child. Sofia had been sickly as a baby and toddler, but she turned into an active and daring little girl. "I was physically very dexterous and strong," she recalled; "I climbed trees like a squirrel and performed head-spinning gymnastics." More like a boy in her tastes and games, she rejected dolls in favor of modeling herself after two idealized, romantic images: "redskinned Indians, moving stealthily, all-seeing, all-hearing and always noble … and courageous and enterprising seafarers."[2]

As in many fairy tales, Sofia's early years also proceeded under the shadow of powerful though distant external forces. Some resulted from unique family circumstances, accidents of birth, death, and personality. Others originated in her status as the child of two powerful noble families, the Panins and the Maltsovs, whose history incorporated contradictory currents of loyalty and rebellion, great wealth and commitment to economic modernization, adherence to aristocratic convention and rejection of it in the name of self-determination and progress. Still other threats to Sofia's fairy-tale childhood arose from deeper historical changes that began in the mid-nineteenth century. By the time Sofia was born in 1871—one year after Vladimir Lenin—the Russian nobility had begun to lose its hold on supremacy. The abolition of serfdom and other reforms enacted by Emperor Alexander II in the 1860s undermined the nobility's economic foundations along with its political and social status. The nobility's social and cultural preeminence also gave way to the progressive social goals and political vision that inspired members of the "generation of the sixties"—the cohort of idealistic young men and women such as Sofia's parents, who came of age during the 1860s and 1870s. Many young people from the nobility sought to create new identities for themselves, ones untainted by the legacy of serf ownership and class privilege. Despite their social status and wealth, Sofia's father, Count Vladimir Panin, and her mother, Anastasia Maltsova, embraced their generation's faith in progress, commitment to individual freedom, and opposition to political and social repression.

Both the Panins and the Maltsovs belonged to the highest stratum of the nobility and ranked among its wealthiest. Sofia could be proud of the contributions made by her grandfathers on both sides to Russia's legal and economic modernization, as well as their relatively enlightened treatment of their serfs and workers. The families differed sharply, however, in the routes they took to achieve wealth and power, the relationships they formed with the Russian monarchy, and the values and priorities by which they defined themselves.

The Panins had always been closely, and sometimes dangerously, entwined with the Russian monarchy. Their dedication to serving tsar and state brought privileges and material rewards but also made them dependent on imperial favor and vulnerable to factional intrigues at court. Family legend traced their origins to an Italian from Lucca named "Pagnini" who immigrated to Muscovy in the fifteenth century. The Panins took pride in their supposed Italian ancestry (a claim the historian David Ransel regards with skepticism).[3] Originally members of the Muscovite service nobility, the family began its ascent to wealth and power in the early eighteenth century under Peter the Great. Ivan Panin

(1673–1736) achieved the rank of lieutenant-general and was appointed to Peter's Senate, in addition to making an advantageous marriage to a relative of Peter's close friend Prince Alexander Menshikov.

General Ivan Panin's two sons, Nikita and Peter, attained positions of great influence early in the reign of Catherine the Great (1762–96), only to lose the empress's favor as a result of their political intrigues and arrogance. Peter Panin led the Russian army to victory during the Seven Years' and First Turkish Wars. Then in 1774 he was called by Catherine to crush the Cossack rebellion led by Emelian Pugachev. Only the death of the original commander and the peril to the state that the rebellion presented could have persuaded Catherine to call upon a man she deeply distrusted. Their relationship had become so rancorous that she came to consider him her "first enemy," and he had resigned his commission in 1770. The relationship between Peter's brother Nikita (1718–83) and Catherine was equally troubled. In 1760 Nikita became the tutor to her eight-year-old son Paul, the acknowledged heir of her husband Grand Duke Peter. The position provided Nikita with material rewards and brought him into daily contact with Catherine. At the time she was the spurned wife of the heir to the throne, who made his intentions to divorce her clear when he became Emperor Peter III in late 1761. As a close adviser to Catherine, Nikita Panin played a major role in the conspiracy that resulted in Peter III's overthrow and murder in 1762. Nikita's aim had been to place his pupil Paul on the throne, but Catherine had a different plan—to occupy it herself. After Catherine became empress, Nikita, a highly educated man and political theorist as well as the leader of one of the most powerful court factions, retained influence at her court into the 1770s. But his support for her son Paul, along with the intrigues of rival factions, led to a steady deterioration in his relations with the empress, who finally forced him into retirement in 1780; he died soon thereafter.[4]

The thorny relationship between the Panins and their sovereign continued in the next generation, following the same trajectory of rapid rise and precipitous fall. Peter Panin's son and Nikita's nephew, also named Nikita (1770–1837), rose quickly in the diplomatic service, thanks to talent and great ambition. In 1797 Emperor Paul I, who finally attained the throne after his mother's death in 1796, appointed Nikita Panin ambassador to Berlin. But the emperor's erratic personality, combined with his irritation with Nikita's arrogant manner, soon turned favor into disgrace, and like his father, Peter, and his uncle Nikita, he was dismissed from service. Echoing the conspiratorial role played by his uncle, the younger Nikita joined a coup d'état to overthrow Emperor Paul in favor of his son Alexander in 1801; but the success of the plot, which resulted in Paul's death, did not endear him to the new monarch. Nikita spent a brief six months back in imperial service before Alexander I banished the "imperious" and outspoken young man permanently to his distant estate of Dugino in western Smolensk province. Forbidden to enter St. Petersburg or Moscow, Sofia's great-grandfather spent the rest of his life at Dugino as the potentate of his own kingdom, devoting himself to its management and beautification.[5]

Although the younger Nikita's rise in state service came to an abrupt end, it was he and not his father or uncle who was responsible for increasing the family's material fortunes. His marriage to Sofia Vladimirovna Orlova (1775–1844) transformed the Panins into one of the richest aristocratic families in nineteenth-century Russia. Sofia was the daughter of Vladimir Orlov, the youngest of the five brothers who had helped Catherine seize the throne in 1762 (and who constituted the Panin brothers' rival faction at court). Catherine rewarded the brothers with forty-five thousand serfs and millions of rubles in cash and valuables during the first twenty years of her reign. But the five brothers among them left no sons and only two daughters who married and had descendants. Since women in tsarist Russia enjoyed inheritance and property rights, roughly half of the Orlov fortune descended to Vladimir's daughter Sofia Panina née Orlova. The vast wealth that she brought into the Panin family when she married Nikita passed to her sons, Alexander and Victor, and became the foundation of the fortune that her great-granddaughter and namesake Sofia eventually inherited at the end of the nineteenth century.[6]

Sofia and Nikita's son Victor (1801–74) grew up in his father's exile kingdom of Dugino, where he was thoroughly educated in the upper-class tradition of his age and class. His classical training earned the highly intelligent and talented young man a reputation as one of the most learned members of his generation. Victor studied Greek and Latin and acquired fluency in German and French; like many members of the nobility, he conducted all family correspondence in French. A passionate bibliophile, he amassed one of the great private libraries of the nineteenth century, which he donated upon his death to the Moscow Public and Rumiantsev Museums — institutions that eventually became the Lenin Library, now the Russian State Library.[7] At Dugino Victor was also educated in the history of his family's complicated and troubled relationship with the Russian throne. "Panin went through life," writes

historian Richard Wortman, "burdened by the sense that he had inherited a disgrace ordained for disobedience."[8] As the most talented
and promising of the banished Nikita's five surviving children, Victor
became his parents' hope for attaining political redemption and restoring the Panin family to imperial favor.

Victor fulfilled those hopes and redeemed his family's honor by
serving three emperors with unswerving loyalty over the course of
more than fifty years. He entered state service in 1819 at the Ministry of
Foreign Affairs, but in 1832 he moved to the Ministry of Justice, becoming minister of justice in 1842. In 1834 Victor married Countess Natalia
Pavlovna Tizengauzen (1810–99), his second cousin and the daughter
of a distinguished though impoverished family from the German Baltic nobility.[9] Unsociable and eccentric, Victor was not well liked in St.
Petersburg society, and he acquired a reputation as an unbending supporter of absolutism, serfdom, and the old order.[10] When Emperor Alexander II appointed him to be the chairman of the Editing Commission
that was preparing the legislation to abolish serfdom, supporters of
emancipation were appalled, seeing in him an archetypal defender of
serfdom. As he had throughout his career, however, Victor remained
devoted to implementing the tsar's will and did not obstruct or delay
the emancipation of 1861, despite his personal opposition. In the often
corrupt world of court politics Sofia's paternal grandfather stood out
for his loyalty, honesty, refusal to engage in intrigue, and commitment
to compliance with statute law.[11]

Victor Panin's enormous income came from the old regime's twin
assets, land and enserfed peasants. According to the historian Dominic
Lieven, he owned 15,325 male serfs on the eve of emancipation, placing
him at number eleven on the list of the sixty-three greatest serf-owners
in the empire.[12] As the owner of other human beings, he completely
eclipsed American plantation masters in the antebellum South, fewer
than 3 percent of whom owned more than fifty enslaved people on the
eve of the American Civil War.[13] Victor's annual income fell between
127,000 and 136,000 rubles—more than ten times the statutory salary for
a minister in the tsarist government—all of which he spent.[14] In addition
to the Panin mansion on the Fontanka River in St. Petersburg and Dugino,
his father's estate in Smolensk that he co-owned with his brother, Victor
owned at least eleven separate serf estates and additional unsettled
land across European Russia.[15] The abolition of serfdom in 1861 had no
discernible impact on his fortune. His two surviving daughters, Sofia's
aunts Olga and Leonilla, who married in the early 1860s, received some

of his property as their dowries. Victor retained ownership of eight estates located in the provinces of Moscow, Voronezh, Kostroma, Yaroslavl, Nizhny Novgorod, and Tver. A total of more than ten thousand
male peasant adults lived on these estates—ex-serfs newly emancipated
from serfdom but still obligated to pay dues to the Panins.[16] He also
owned Gaspra, a neo-Gothic castle on the Black Sea coast in the Crimea,
which he bought in 1867 after retiring from state service.

The Panin estates were exceptional not only for their extent but
for their diversity and income-producing capabilities. Mstera in Vladimir province, for example, was a proto-industrial village of prosper-
ous icon painters and skilled artisans, who paid annual dues to Panin;
when it became part of Leonilla's dowry in 1864, Mstera was valued at
167,200 rubles.[17] Veidelevka, a huge estate in agriculturally rich Voronezh province, took up almost half of one district of the province, with
26,000 desiatins (more than 70,000 acres) devoted to raising racehorses
and purebred livestock.[18] Although he opposed the abolition of serfdom, Victor reportedly treated his peasants relatively well. His serfs
mainly paid annual money dues instead of the more onerous labor service many serfs owed their masters.[19] He even gave his former serfs on
the Veidelevka estate part of their postemancipation land allotment as
a gift.[20]

In his will Victor left the life interest in his enormous estate to his
widow and instructed that upon her death everything was to be transferred directly to his only son, Vladimir (Sofia's father). Although Victor
died two years after his son's death, he did not change his will. Vladimir does not appear to have made a will, and what his own assets were
is unknown. But by Russian law his widow, Anastasia, and his only
child, Sofia, were his coheirs.[21] In other words, Vladimir's heirs, Anastasia and Sofia, were also coheirs to Victor Panin's estate, although the
latter remained the property of Countess Natalia Panina, Sofia's paternal
grandmother, during her lifetime. When the old Countess Panina died,
Sofia would inherit the bulk of Victor Panin's considerable fortune.[22]

Thus Sofia inherited from the Panins not only great wealth but also
a complex history of service to the Russian monarchy. Although she
probably had no memory of her grandfather Victor, who died in Nice
when she was three, she doubtless heard a great deal about the Panin
family's history of imperial favor and disgrace from her grandmother
Natalia, who took great pride in the Panin lineage and continued Victor's
efforts to rebuild its reputation for loyalty to the throne. Sofia never renounced her aristocratic origins. Throughout her life, even while living

in America in her final years, she used the title "Countess," suggesting that she was proud of the Panin name and her ancestors' distinguished service to Russia, along with their reputation for learnedness, integrity, and incorruptibility. Despite his personal opposition to abolishing serfdom, her grandfather Victor had played a critical role in the emancipation. Victor's great-uncle Nikita Panin had formulated a plan under Catherine the Great for the separation of legislative and juridical powers and the creation of an Imperial Council; had they been implemented, his proposals might have created a foundation for the constitution sought by Russian liberals a century and a half later.

Sofia's mother, Anastasia, also grew up in wealth and privilege, although the sources of the Maltsov fortune differed dramatically from those of the Panins. Anastasia's father, Major-General Sergei Ivanovich Maltsov (1810–93), was a millionaire industrialist and entrepreneur who contributed enormously to Russia's economic transformation from an agrarian into an industrial power in the second half of the nineteenth century. Sofia's maternal grandfather bears a greater resemblance to Americans like Andrew Carnegie than to such peers as Victor Panin, who followed careers in state service and lived off the income from the serfs who farmed their estates. Some called Sergei Maltsov's extensive industrial empire "America in Russia," an indication of its uniqueness in the Russia of his day.[23] The Maltsov fortune originated in glassworks that Sergei's merchant ancestors had established over the course of the eighteenth century. In addition to bottles, sheet glass, and other everyday items, the Maltsov glassworks produced fine crystal, the Russian equivalent of Baccarat, which continues to be manufactured in Russia today by the successor firm Diatkovo Crystal. While glass and fine crystal remained the heart of the family enterprises, Sofia Panina's great-grandfather Ivan Akimovich Maltsov began expanding into other branches of manufacturing in the early decades of the nineteenth century, including the production of beet sugar, cast iron, cotton, and rails for Russia's first railroads. Along the way he acquired vast holdings of land and control over thousands of free and enserfed workers. In contrast to the Panins, members of the Russian nobility since the sixteenth century, the Maltsovs succeeded in shedding their merchant origins and acquiring noble status only in 1775, thanks to a grant from Empress Catherine. The move was dictated by economic necessity. Like other Russian manufacturers they relied on enserfed peasants and workers legally assigned to their factories. That labor supply was threatened when Catherine, seeking to bolster support from the nobility by granting them a monopoly on serf ownership, deprived merchants of that right. The Maltsovs seem to have assimilated with ease into the nobility, acquiring its tastes and habits; Ivan Akimovich served in the army, married a noblewoman, and raised his son Sergei in a manner befitting a rich young nobleman.[24]

Thus Anastasia's father (Sofia's maternal grandfather) received an excellent and unusually broad education at home, becoming proficient in several languages and in various branches of science. While Victor Panin chose the Russian civil service, Sergei entered military service, and as a member of an elite Guards regiment rose in the ranks without, it seems, ever coming close to a battlefield. Sergei could easily have chosen the idle, pleasure-seeking life of a Guards officer, supported by his father's already considerable wealth. But he was fascinated by the nineteenth century's rapid industrial progress and committed to furthering his country's economic development. He traveled in England and Europe to learn about the latest industrial technology and was even reported to have joined workers there at the factory bench or furnace. He retired from the military while still in his thirties with the rank of major general, and from 1849, when his father handed him control of the Maltsov enterprises, to the mid-1880s he devoted himself to the expansion and modernization of his factories and mills.[25]

The Maltsov industrial complex was unique in Russia not only in its breadth and diversity, but also in the treatment of its workers. On the eve of emancipation Sergei owned more than seven thousand five hundred male adults, the thirty-fourth highest number of serfs owned by any Russian landowner. Victor Panin, in comparison, owned enough serfs to position him as number eleven. While roughly half of Sergei's serfs worked in agriculture, the rest toiled in his factories and workshops. A paternalistic employer *par excellence*, Sergei built schools, hospitals, and churches and provided housing and free medical care. Literacy rates among his workers were higher than average. Those who worked in particularly difficult jobs enjoyed an eight-hour day; disabled and elderly workers received pensions. Sergei distributed holiday gifts of beer, sugar, and tea to his workers, and even free seltzer water in hot weather. Although work in the Maltsov factories and mills was demanding and dangerous, his workers and their families enjoyed a level of welfare that was rare elsewhere in Russia.[26]

At its peak in the 1860s and 1870s the sprawling Maltsov industrial complex covered six thousand square kilometers in three provinces in south-central Russia.[27] Much of the land in this region was unproductive for farming but endowed with excellent water transportation and natural resources such as timber, coal, and clay and sand for the porcelain and glass factories. As many as 25 large factories and more than 100 smaller enterprises employed between 13,000 and 15,000 skilled workers, who produced steam locomotives, freight cars and rails, steamboats, and agricultural machinery. Always ready to try out the latest technology, Sergei Maltsov connected his factories, sawmills, glassworks, workshops, and worker settlements with a narrow-gauge railway, telegraph lines, and eventually a telephone network.[28]

Sergei's paternalism and entrepreneurship had a darker side, however. His solicitude for his workers notwithstanding, he was a "philanthropic despot," according to his daughter Maria. A man of robust health, iron character, and immense energy, he "exhausted literally everyone he employed and outlived quite a lot of generations of workers." "If he had lived in another time," Maria continued bitterly, "he would have been a Torquemada burning bodies in order to save souls, or a tyrannical reformer like Peter the Great, except for the genius."[29] Like Victor Panin, Sergei opposed emancipation, particularly if it granted ex-serfs land allotments. Emancipation coupled with land rights would undermine Russian peasants' respect for private property, he insisted, and would encourage them to demand yet more concessions from the government. Accustomed to dominating every aspect of his workers' lives, he adjusted with greater difficulty, it seems, than Victor Panin to the changes that emancipation and the other reforms of the 1860s introduced.[30]

Sergei Maltsov was as domineering as a husband and father as he was as an employer. When he married the beautiful Princess Anastasia Urusova (1820–94) in 1837, the rich, well-connected, and dashing Guards officer must have seemed a good match. His bride was still in her teens; as she told her daughter Maria (Sofia's aunt) years later, she was completely inexperienced and scarcely cognizant of the importance of the step she was taking. Yet one can scarcely imagine any experience that would have prepared even an older woman for marriage to Sergei. He expected his entire family to follow his rules and orders without question and sought to control every aspect of their lives as he controlled every aspect of his economic empire. His children rejoiced when their father was not home because when he was around, he berated them from morning to night. Calling him "our despot," Maria relates how he taught his children to swim by taking them out to the middle of a pond and throwing them in.[31]

The former Princess Urusova pined for the glittering social world of the capital during the long periods when her husband forced her and the children to live at Diatkovo, his mansion at the center of the Maltsov economic empire. Surrounded by smoking factories and workshops, model workers' cottages, and deep forests, Diatkovo was literally and figuratively distant from anything resembling urban life and culture. As the years passed, relations between the spouses worsened. According to Maria, her father was "irritated by everything that gave my mother pleasure" and did nothing to accommodate her preferences and tastes. She recalled the "terrible scenes" that erupted when, for example, Sergei, who rose at 3:00 in the morning and never stopped working the entire day, refused to take an evening promenade with his wife in the mansion park. Sergei, who had ordered all his workers to don a pseudo-folk costume of his own design, allegedly never forgave his wife for refusing to wear it herself.[32]

After fifteen years of marriage the couple separated permanently. Princess Anastasia took their children back to live in St. Petersburg, while her husband, now permanently alienated from most of his children, remained in Diatkovo with a succession of peasant housekeeper-mistresses.[33] In Petersburg Anastasia Maltsova reentered high society and acquired significant influence at court as the best friend and confidante of Empress Maria Alexandrovna, the wife of Alexander II. While the older Anastasia controlled access to the empress, her daughter Anastasia, Sofia's mother, played with the imperial couple's younger children.[34] Twenty years passed before Sergei and Anastasia Maltsova saw each other again, an accidental meeting while strolling along the Rue de Rivoli in Paris. "Eh bien pardonne," she remarked when she recognized him, "nous sommes maintenant des vieux"; "pardonne aussi," he replied, "nous ne nous reverrons plus." ("Well, pardon me, we are now old." "Pardon me as well, we will not see each other again.")[35]

As her parents' second youngest child, Sofia's mother was far less affected than her siblings by her father's domineering ways. The younger Anastasia was only a few years old when her parents separated in the early or mid-1850s, and she had little contact with her father after that. Unlike her widowed sister, Maria, who depended on her father's remittances, she escaped his iron rules and regimentation (and pseudo-folk costume) and had more freedom to explore her personality and develop into the girl Maria called "our playful scamp" (*notre folâtre polissonne*).[36] Anastasia enjoyed a girlhood spent in imperial palaces and the favorite European playgrounds of the Russian nobility, the security of seemingly unlimited financial resources, and influential relatives in high government positions. Her mother provided a model of self-determination, having left her husband after fifteen years of marriage in spite of legal and social norms that demanded wives' unquestioned obedience to their husbands. These aspects of the younger Anastasia's free and privileged upbringing fostered those characteristics of pride and self-assurance that would eventually lead to defiance of social conventions, conflict with her Panin in-laws, and loss of custody over her only child.

Sofia's mother was still in her teens and eight years younger than her future husband when she became engaged to Count Vladimir Panin in late 1869. Like her tree-climbing daughter Sofia, Anastasia was a tomboy. Recalling a time when they were visiting the Austrian Alps, her older sister Maria described the seventeen-year-old "Nastya" as a "true child," lively and happy in demeanor. She hiked in the mountains, rode horseback, and drove a team of four horses. "In a word," Maria remembered, she was "more like a playful little boy than a young girl, and at the same time she was very kind, very intelligent. . . . I wished my young daughters to be like my sister Nastya at that time."[37] Vladimir Panin's early life and upbringing were far more conventional and constrained. Dutiful, unemotional letters written in French by the teenaged "Volodya" to his mother describe travels to Europe and visits with his father to their serf estates, where peasant elders greeted them with bread and salt, the traditional offerings of hospitality.[38] Meeting her sister's fiancé for the first time shortly before their wedding, Maria described him as "extremely tall, thin, pale, not handsome, but intelligent and good." Others knew him as a cultivated and studious young man, who despite his shyness enjoyed playing with children.[39]

The scholarly, subdued Vladimir and the vivacious Anastasia must have seemed an unlikely couple. Moreover, by the time they married in January 1870 he was dying of tuberculosis. Two of his four sisters had died of the same disease while in their twenties.[40] During the wedding festivities, Maria recollected, "Vladimir Panin looked so sick that against my will I feared for the future of my sister."[41] Given his grave condition, the sad fate of his two sisters, and the concern expressed by members of her own family, one wonders why Anastasia embarked on such a marriage. In part her choice may reflect the fact that tuberculosis was a common disease at the time, a feature of almost everyone's experience, and she may have underestimated the seriousness of his condition. Or she may have persuaded herself that a cure could be found in

Countess Leonilla Panina and Count Vladimir Panin, before 1870. (private collection)

the spas of Europe or on the sunny shores of France or Italy, where so many others had found respite. In the end, however, the explanation may simply lie in the fact that Anastasia and Vladimir deeply loved each other, attracted by qualities that they had missed in their own parents. Anastasia's energy and passion contrasted radically with the conventionality and cold formality of her in-laws, Count Victor Panin, the imperial minister of justice; his wife, Natalia, a lady-in-waiting at the imperial court; and their two surviving daughters, Olga and Leonilla. Anastasia, in turn, found in her kind, gentle Vladimir the exact opposite of her father, General Sergei Maltsov, whose dictatorial ways and erratic behavior alienated his wife and aroused fear in his children.

Another source of their affectionate bond was the couple's shared commitment to the ideals and goals of the generation of the sixties. Vladimir enjoyed a reputation as a liberal who associated with members of the progressive intelligentsia such as physicians, professors, and local government activists.[42] He exerted considerable intellectual and moral influence over his younger wife during their brief marriage. "[Well] educated like all the Panins," his great-niece Lidia Vasilchikova asserted, "my Great-uncle Vladimir considered the knowledge of his young wife insufficient, and he set about to improve her level of education." Deeply in love with her husband, Anastasia proved to be easily swayed and "advocated fairly progressive views up to her death."[43] Embracing the liberal ethos of her husband and her generation, Anastasia adhered to their moral principles of honesty and defiance of convention throughout her life. These parental values guided their daughter Sofia through the numerous personal challenges she experienced beginning in her childhood years and gave her strength to withstand the historical upheavals she faced in Russia's tumultuous twentieth century.

The couple's first child, Sofia was born in Moscow on August 23, 1871, and baptized on September 9, with grandparents Victor Panin and Anastasia Maltsova serving as her godparents.[44] Although Vladimir and Anastasia spent much of their brief marriage in the mild climate of Italy, the refuge of so many nineteenth-century consumptives, his health continued to decline. When they visited Anastasia's sister Maria in Florence in the winter of 1872, his face "bore the stamp of death." Soon thereafter, on a voyage to Constantinople, he caught a cold that accelerated the course of the disease. Failing fast, and wishing to die in Russia, he hastened with his pregnant wife and one-year-old Sofia to the Panin estate of Marfino, north of Moscow. There he died in Anastasia's arms in July 1872. He was only thirty years old. His twenty-two-year-old widow gave birth to a second daughter, Natalia, known as Natasha, a few months after his death.[45]

Anastasia's profound grief intensified her fears for her daughters' health during the first years of her widowhood. Shaken by the premature deaths of her young husband and his two sisters, she worried constantly about the Panin family's susceptibility to tuberculosis. Hereditary frailty seemed to threaten her little girls. Sofia was prone to fevers and other illnesses, and she was slow in learning to talk. When Maria visited her sister in Nice, she thought the baby Natasha looked weak and dangerously anemic. In addition to an English baby nurse, Anastasia employed a full-time doctor who traveled with her and her daughters. In 1873 and 1874 they spent the summer at the Panina estate of Marfino but otherwise avoided Russia's harsh climate in favor of European locations thought to be healthy, such as Nice and Switzerland.[46]

Motivated in part by a desire to honor her husband's memory, Anastasia still found time to show interest in one of the major social issues of the day, popular education. Schools for peasants were rare and rudimentary at this time, and the literacy rate was extremely low. The abolition of serfdom in 1861, and the introduction of elected local government councils called zemstvos in the countryside in 1864, brought the issue of elementary education for the newly emancipated peasants to the forefront of public debate. The reforms inspired individual and collective social action by members of the generation of the sixties; a typical example was the primary school for peasant children that the Panins supported at Marfino.

Anastasia became interested in the school, which had been founded by her father-in-law in 1871, during the summer she spent with her daughters at Marfino in 1873. Her actual involvement appears at first glance superficial; like a typical lady of the manor, she attended the pupils' final examinations and distributed prizes, tea, and cakes to the graduates, and unlike some progressive noblewomen, she took no direct part in teaching. Nonetheless, her letters to her mother-in-law devote considerable attention to the school, suggesting a genuine interest in its pedagogical approach and actual results. The school is making remarkable progress, she wrote, thanks to a new system of teaching reading and writing adopted on Vladimir's advice. She expressed particular pleasure at learning that boys who entered school the previous October could already read with comprehension and write legibly and accurately. She also visited another school in the district to compare it to Marfino and acquire new ideas.[47]

Anastasia's first priority, however, was to safeguard the fragile health of her own children. Yet wealth and privilege could not protect them from the epidemics and childhood diseases rampant during the nineteenth century. Despite her best efforts, Anastasia suffered a second devastating loss when Natasha, not quite two years old, died in early September 1874. "Baby," as family members called her, had been ill for two months, first with scarlet fever, then typhus; she died, finally, of meningitis. According to Maria, who lost a young daughter herself at about the same time, "poor Nastya" changed completely; the loss of her husband and younger daughter "took away my sister's youth and joy, casting a shadow over her entire life."[48] Natasha was buried in the family tomb at Marfino, next to her father. A restored white marble monument to father and daughter stands today, a witness to Anastasia's dual losses. The new widow was not yet twenty-five years old.

After "Baby's" death Anastasia concentrated her intense love and anxiety on three-year-old Sofia. Spending extended periods of time in Europe, they led a life even more nomadic than before. "For the entire first eleven years of my life," Sofia later recalled, "my mother and I

Panin family graves at Marfino, May 2011. The horizontal stone commemorates "Vladimir Panin, 1842–1872, and his daughter, infant Natalia, 1872–1874." (photograph by the author)

constantly moved from one place to another. . . . We did not have a set-tled life, a home, a 'nest.'" Sofia describes her mother at this time as "an unusual, incomparable beauty" with the "irresistible charm of an im-petuous temperament and a fiery, lofty and passionate heart."[49] In fact, the attractive young widow—traveling across Europe and Russia with-out a chaperone and in the company of a young child, a nursemaid, and a private physician—was skirting the boundaries of propriety. Even before her younger daughter's death, as Anastasia was preparing to leave Marfino for Europe with her two daughters, her behavior pro-voked criticism from her straight-laced sister-in-law Leonilla. "A young widow of her age should not travel by railroad alone," Leonilla com-plained to her mother, but "Nastya does not understand anything about life and the difficulties of her position." According to another Panin relative, every doctor whom Anastasia employed fell in love with her.[50]

Anastasia's independent and nomadic life distanced Sofia from the influence of the rigid, conventional Panins and freed her from many of the restrictions and expectations of the class into which she had been born. Her childhood, despite her mother's grief, was full of adventure and fun. Sofia explored the Bavarian mountains with her Maltsov cousins, went swimming in the Atlantic Ocean, and spent long periods of time in the European and Russian countryside. When she and her mother lived for a time in Kiev, the children of her mother's "kind-hearted and lazy" Ukrainian servant Luke became her "best friends." They spent the summer of 1877 with Sofia and her mother in a simple peasant house in a Ukrainian village, where the children fed milk to hedgehogs and grass snakes with a spoon.[51] In Moscow mother and daughter occupied a house opposite the notorious Butyrki prison; Sofia remembers how she trembled as she watched the "endless lines of prisoners being led or carted away in shackles" on their way to Siberia. In Moscow Sofia met the novelist Ivan Turgenev, with his "blindingly white" hair, during his last visit to Russia. She also heard his one-time literary adversary Fedor Dostoevsky give his famous speech on Alexander Pushkin and Russian national identity when the new monument to Pushkin was erected in 1880.[52]

These early years laid the foundation for a lifelong relationship of mutual love and respect between mother and daughter. Sofia credits her mother with creating a "spiritual atmosphere" that influenced her personality and moral development "forever." Left alone with each other, the pair made what Sofia describes in her memoirs as an unspoken "pact" based on "courage, honesty, responsibility, and always a heroic element." The incident she chose to illustrate her mother's moral influence was Anastasia's gift to her of a marble statuette of George Washington as a boy, "sitting with a little axe in his hand next to the little tree he had cut down." "Little George," she remembers her mother telling her, had disobeyed his father's orders by cutting down this special cherry tree. But he "openly and honestly confessed his crime to his father and did not conceal his guilt, he did not stay silent, nor did he tell a tale on someone else." In Sofia's memory, her mother's gift symbolized the importance of courage and truth.[53]

Thus Sofia's recollections of her early years with her mother describe a childhood that combined adventure with moral lessons about honesty, freedom, and the moral responsibilities of high social rank. Representing herself as an imaginative, physically active, and daring girl whose ideals were American Indians and George Washington, she creates the impression of a self-confident child. If she encountered any strictures on how to behave, they go unmentioned; active play and exploration of the natural world were encouraged and nurtured by her mother. Another striking feature of Sofia's memories of her childhood is the fairy-tale motif she employs. It shapes her description of her maternal grandmother, for example, during a visit to the now elderly Anastasia Maltsova at her home in Tsarskoe Selo, a park-like suburb of aristocratic mansions outside St. Petersburg. Baba, as Sofia called her, was "a slender, miniature lady, with little graying curls framing her lovely face." When Baba took gold tweezers and removed one of her "thin little cigarettes, as slender and miniature as she," from the box on her table, and then blew "an aromatic, rapidly expanding ringlet of smoke," she seemed to have the power to keep any evil away from "the charmed kingdom that was created by her caress, her laugh, her beauty." On the emerald green front lawn Sofia remembered her merry Uncle Seryozha—Uncle Joker, as she called him—throwing a boomerang. "[N]either the Forest King nor Chernomor [the wicked sorcerer who kidnaps the maiden in the fairy tale *Ruslan and Liudmila*] could kidnap me from Baba's magical kingdom, from the protection of the flying boomerang."[54] Reminiscences like these vividly convey the security, freedom, and magic that Sofia, raised with love and blessed by good fortune, felt she experienced as a girl. This environment helped to build the foundation for the independence of thought and action that Sofia came to display as an adult.

Like all autobiographies, however, Sofia's memories of her childhood are colored by her own nostalgia and influenced by the experiences of her generation. Although her various and brief reminiscences of her early years are undated, they were all written sometime after the death of her beloved mother in Prague in 1932. By then more than a decade had passed since revolution and civil war had forced her, her mother, and countless friends and relatives to leave Russia forever. The enchanted world of her childhood—and the entire world of the prerevolutionary Russian nobility—had perished. Returning to Russia was out of the question, and besides, beloved places like the Panin estate at Marfino were in ruins or in the hands of the Soviet government. While nostalgia for a lost world of childhood is common in autobiographies, the revolutionary violence, destruction, and separation that Sofia and others of her generation experienced as adults made their childhood seem all the more precious and ideal.

Sofia's mother was considerably more complex, however, than the figure portrayed by her loving daughter. Anastasia was a strong-willed woman, willing to risk her reputation and defy social convention and the powerful Panin family for the sake of autonomy, love, and political ideals. Still young and very beautiful, and encouraged by her late husband to engage with the progressive ideas and initiatives of the day, the widowed Anastasia increasingly looked outside her aristocratic social circle for friendship and purpose. The decisive moment, as Sofia later termed it, occurred when she and her mother were living in Kiev, during the Russo-Turkish War of 1877–78. While Anastasia worked in a hospital, six-year-old Sofia had her first formal lessons with a tutor in his late twenties named Irodion Alexeevich Zhitetsky, the son of a rural priest. He was a "most captivating teacher," Sofia recalled, who not only taught her to read and write but also led her into the "magical world of nature." Teacher and pupil conducted physics experiments together and, joined by her mother, went on delightful excursions to the countryside, collecting plants and insects.[55] But Zhitetsky was more than a gifted teacher: he was also a radical Ukrainian nationalist. Expelled from Kiev University in 1878 for his participation in student demonstrations, he was sent into internal exile from Kiev the following year for belonging to a revolutionary group and possession of illegal literature.[56]

Heedless of the risks such associations posed both to her reputation and to custody over her cherished only daughter, Anastasia became increasingly involved in the liberal and radical opposition movements of the late 1870s. One sees traces of the imperious Sergei Maltsov in Anastasia, with her "impetuous" temperament and "fiery, lofty and passionate heart." Like her father, young Anastasia was stubborn. The tragedy of losing both a husband and a baby while still in her early twenties made the once playful and carefree Anastasia more serious and kept her tied to the Panins for a time. But as the attractive and wealthy widow traveled unchaperoned around Russia and Europe with Sofia, she freed herself from that dependence. Anastasia Panina's self-confidence grew into self-assertion and, eventually, a kind of independence even stronger than her mother's, making a collision with her mother-in-law, the cautious, conservative Countess Natalia Panina, inevitable. Both Anastasias, mother and grandmother, provided Sofia with examples of women who defied social convention in their pursuit of self-determination. But her mother's strong will, her grandmother's magical smoke rings, and her Uncle Joker's boomerang all lacked the power to prevent the girl from being "kidnapped" by real-life evil sorcerers, who snatched her away from her childhood of freedom.

2

The Battle for Sofia

Sofia Panina's fairy-tale childhood came to an abrupt end on Sunday, October 24, 1882, in the suite she and her mother were sharing at St. Petersburg's exclusive Hotel de l'Europe during one of their occasional visits to the capital. Before leaving for church, Anastasia told her daughter to sew a button back on her shoe. As Sofia bent over her task, she glimpsed an unfamiliar and unexpected visitor in military uniform who entered the adjoining room and began talking with her mother. A few minutes later Anastasia returned in tears. "Sofyushka, get dressed," she remembers her mother saying; "we are going immediately to the Catherine Institute." Turning to the man in uniform, Anastasia firmly declared, "I'll take her there myself."[1] Later that day Anastasia and Sofia walked into the institute, an elite girls' school located in the heart of the imperial capital, where the eleven-year-old child was formally separated from her mother by personal order of Emperor Alexander III.

Though written many years later, Sofia's account of her arrival at the Catherine Institute still reverberates with hurt and anger. "Everything around me was a hateful enemy," she recalled, from the pompous servant wearing red livery and carrying a mace who escorted them to the headmistress's office, to the school's "new and alien" culture.[2] When Sofia parted from her mother that day, she left a childhood infused with the progressive values and idealism of her parents' generation and entered an insular world of moral conformism and social privilege.

The stranger who visited her mother that Sunday with the emperor's order was Major-General P. A. Gresser of the St. Petersburg Police.[3] The drastic and cruel separation he was charged with carrying out, precipitated by Anastasia's marriage two months earlier to a leader of liberal opposition to the imperial regime, marked the culmination of ten years of conflict between the impetuous young widow and her Panin in-laws. Anastasia first attracted their concern during the 1870s by her conduct as Sofia's custodian and cotrustee of the little girl's substantial inheritance. From 1879 to 1882 her deepening relationship with Ivan Petrunkevich, a man the Panins and the government regarded as a dangerous political criminal, cast further suspicion on her moral reputation and political loyalties. As the conflict escalated, both the Panins and Anastasia accused each other of harming Sofia's health and well-being. Both sides drew upon their respective allies at the imperial court to attempt to influence the emperor to intervene on their behalf, but when Anastasia married Ivan in October 1882, she lost the fight for her daughter.

The fierce battle between the Panins and Anastasia over custody of Sofia was the decisive event of Sofia's early life. It not only tore her from the mother she adored but also entangled her in dramatic historical events, including turmoil within the imperial family over the personal conduct of Alexander II and the unprecedented upsurge in opposition to the state that culminated in Alexander's assassination by terrorists in 1881. At the age of eleven Sofia fell victim to the struggle between Russia's autocratic government and the movements for political reform and revolution that would dominate the last decades of Romanov rule. Contrary to the Panins' hopes, the struggle only strengthened Sofia's commitment to her mother's principles and values.

Anastasia's battle for exclusive control over her daughter and her daughter's inheritance began a few years after her husband's premature death in 1872. Vladimir Panin had left his widow a very wealthy woman. In addition to a share of her husband's estate, she received a generous annual allowance from her mother-in-law for Sofia's support, which equaled or even surpassed the entire salary of a high-ranking state bureaucrat.[4] Anastasia also exercised guardianship over Sofia's large inheritance from her father, consisting of former serf estates in several provinces, bonds, and interest-bearing securities. In addition, as Vladimir's heirs she and Sofia were in line to inherit her father-in-law's estate after the death of his widow, Countess Natalia Panina. Anastasia also enjoyed a steady if comparatively small income from her shares in her father's industrial enterprises.[5]

Russian law, along with the size of the Panin estate and the family's noble status, dictated that the highest levels of the imperial government, along with the St. Petersburg Nobility's Board of Guardians, would become involved in Sofia's affairs after the death of her father and grandfather. Several months after Vladimir's death in 1872, the Imperial Senate appointed a cotrustee, Senator Nikolai Miagkov, to serve as coguardian with Anastasia over Sofia and her inheritance. When Victor Panin died two years later, Sofia became the ward of the Board of Guardians, which supervised trusts for orphaned minors from the nobility, with her mother and Miagkov acting as coguardians and trustees. Shortly thereafter another imperial decree entrusted the board with managing the little heiress's trust. At about this time, however, Miagkov requested to be removed from his position, and no guardian was named in his place. Anastasia quickly interpreted this to mean that she now possessed sole control over her daughter's person and property.[6] But she still found aspects of the guardianship arrangement restrictive and unjust. In April 1877 Anastasia complained to the board that she used all of the sixteen thousand-ruble allowance she received from her mother-in-law just for her daughter's housing and travel, and had to dip into her own funds in order to cover additional expenses necessary for Sofia's support and education. She should have the right, she argued, to spend her mother-in-law's allowance without having to submit receipts and reports. Meanwhile, Anastasia's actions indicated that she intended to act as she wished. In both 1877 and 1878 she overspent the allowance by several thousand rubles, without providing the Board of Guardians with any explanation of where or how she had used the additional funds. Pointing out that Sofia was only six or seven years old at this time, the board was understandably puzzled and suspicious about Anastasia's lavish spending on the little girl and her refusal to provide accounts or receipts.[7]

Anastasia's continued willful conduct as Sofia's guardian and trustee invited yet more government intervention. In March 1879 the Senate, acting upon instructions from Emperor Alexander II, decreed that if Countess Natalia Panina, then in her late sixties, died while Sofia was still a minor, two guardians would be appointed along with her mother to administer the girl's trust.[8] Two months later the Board of Guardians made several decisions intended to subject Anastasia to greater control. It asked Miagkov to resume the position of coguardian of Sofia's person and property. Re-imposing a strict limit on the allowance for Sofia's support, the board insisted that Anastasia was authorized to spend only this amount and must return to the estate any amount she had over-spent. Henceforth, she must submit annual budgets to the board, along with all receipts and other documents on both income and expenditure. Finally, the board insisted on being informed about "where . . . Sofia is located at the present time, what is the condition of her health, and in general how she is being brought up."[9]

Anastasia reacted to these attempts to limit her autonomy with irri-tation and defiance. By law and imperial decree, she insisted, guardian-ship over Sofia and her property belonged "exclusively to me as her mother without the participation of any outside persons." The board had no right to appoint Miagkov as coguardian. It had no right to limit what she spent on Sofia's support and education. "I have the right," she declared, "to spend the entire sum of income [from Sofia's property] that I consider necessary for the good of my daughter, with the only condition that I provide the Guardians with proof of the actuality and expediency of that expenditure, which I intend to do shortly." (The archive contains no evidence that she did.) Faced with her refusal to comply with its decisions, in November 1879 the board requested help from the provincial governor, who in turn asked Minister of Justice Dmitrii Nabokov (the novelist Vladimir's grandfather) for his interpre-tation of Anastasia's rights as guardian.[10]

The escalating involvement—Anastasia would call it intrusion—of the Senate, the minister of justice, and even the emperor in the matter of one little rich girl and her obstinate, free-spending mother indicates that more than control over Sofia's inheritance was at stake. In fact the state security police, responsible for ferreting out political dissent, had been investigating Anastasia's conduct for several years. According to information they obtained, she maintained contacts with people "of dubious political reliability" after settling with her daughter in Kiev in the mid-1870s. Testimony from an unnamed "state criminal" about underground activities in southern Russia, for example, had identified Anastasia as an acquaintance of a known revolutionary, whose clan-destine meetings she reportedly attended. She also was suspected of giving money to university students in Kiev who had been exiled for participating in demonstrations. The most damning information con-cerned the private physician she employed, Gavrilov. The doctor had ties to members of secret political societies and at one time also ran a carpentry workshop in Kiev "with criminal aims" that the police believed Anastasia helped to finance. They also suspected that more than shared political sympathies lay behind the attractive widow's "extremely close relations" with her private physician.[11]

These accusations against Anastasia must be regarded with caution. The gendarmes, as members of the political police were called, relied on informers and the confessions of individuals already arrested for alleged revolutionary activity—sources that could be either reliable or highly dubious, depending on the case. Anastasia was clearly sympathetic toward radical causes, as suggested by her choice of the Ukrainian radical Zhitetsky as Sofia's tutor. But evidence of any direct ties between her and anti-government circles in Kiev before December 1878 rested mostly on guilt by association. Moreover, the tsarist government's definition of "revolutionary" and "criminal" activities could be quite expansive. Gavrilov's carpentry workshop could have attracted police attention because it served as a cover for socialist propaganda and plots against the government—or because it brought workers together with members of educated society. The truth of the police report's implication that Anastasia and her doctor were lovers is impossible to determine; by the time the report was written in 1882, Gavrilov was dead. Thus it seems difficult to establish whether Anastasia's early associations with oppositionists in Kiev amounted to more than the fact that she employed young men with radical sympathies.[12]

Any uncertainty about whether Anastasia held oppositionist sympathies disappeared at the end of 1878, when she met Ivan Ilich Petrunkevich. Born in 1843 and several years older than Anastasia, Ivan had returned to the Ukrainian countryside after finishing university in Kiev to help manage his family's large estate, Plysky. There he threw himself into the unprecedented opportunities to engage in civic life that opened to educated Russians in the 1860s. Still only in his mid-twenties, he entered the zemstvo, the new institution of representative local government introduced in 1864, as a deputy in the zemstvo assembly of his district, then won election to the zemstvo assembly of the entire Chernigov province. From 1869 to 1879 Ivan also served as a justice of the peace, an office introduced in 1864 to handle small civil claims and minor criminal offenses, and was elevated by his fellow justices to the position of president of their district conference.[13]

Ivan's definition of his generation perhaps best expresses his own political beliefs and aims. Inspired by government reforms of the early 1860s—the abolition of serfdom, the introduction of representative local government, and the modernization of the judicial system—the

"people of the sixties . . . were passionately devoted to the idea of re-
newing Russia." Of course, he continued, "they saw and recognized all
the flaws of the reforms—their obvious insincerity, the fear of giving
more than was absolutely necessary and inevitable, their illegality and
inconsistency." Nevertheless many in Ivan's generation took advantage of every opportunity the reforms offered to become involved for
the first time in "socially useful work"; such work, he believed, would
inevitably "move the boundaries established by the government, and
prepare the country for the broadest possible self-government."[14]

Ivan was not exaggerating his generation's social commitment. As a
rural government leader he knew personally many of the educated
young idealists who moved to the countryside to help advance social
progress. The schools and clinics being opened by zemstvos in the 1860s
and 1870s provided these men and women with new means to better
the lives of the recently emancipated yet still downtrodden peasants,
while also spreading dissent and socialist ideas among them. Ivan first
fell under government suspicion for protecting and assisting such radicals. According to the local police authorities, he used his position as
chairman of the district school board to hire teachers "with extreme
views and anti-government tendencies." The local gendarmes came to
consider Plysky as a notorious headquarters of revolutionaries, whom
Ivan welcomed into his home and to whom he lent "tendentious" books
from his library. The adult evening classes he established, they feared,
enabled "unreliable" teachers to spread their "harmful teachings"
among the local peasantry.[15]

Ivan never shared the socialist principles and revolutionary dreams
held by some members of his generation. He charted a route toward a
different outcome, believing that the new institutions of representative
local government could exert sufficient pressure on the monarchy to
force it to grant a constitution and civil rights. By the late 1870s opposition against the Russian state had splintered. As more cautious zemstvo
activists balked at demanding further reforms from the government,
Ivan and his fellow liberals grew impatient. On the left, the idealists of
the earlier part of the decade, men and women like Ivan's young associates who worked to spread enlightenment and socialism among the
populace in the Ukrainian countryside, had been decimated by arrests,
prison, and hard labor. In their place arose underground organizations
of single-minded revolutionaries who believed that terrorist acts
against the government were the only viable means left to achieve political freedom and social justice.

The year 1878 opened with a shocking act that marked the beginning of an intensifying cycle of violence and retaliation by revolutionaries and their government adversaries: a young woman named Vera Zasulich, enraged by the beating of a young and ill political prisoner, walked into the office of the St. Petersburg chief of police and shot him point blank, though not fatally. Zasulich was acquitted by a jury at her trial two months later, a decision hailed by such liberals as Ivan as a rebuke to a government that now relied entirely on violence and other extralegal means to deal with dissent. Terrorists, for their part, began targeting other high government officials. In August 1878 they succeeded in assassinating General Nikolai Mezentsev, chief of the state security police. In the growing atmosphere of crisis within the government, those who advocated reconciliation with liberal public opinion battled proponents of intensified repression against all forms of dissent. Reeling from the shock of Mezentsev's assassination, the official government newspaper printed a most unusual appeal to the population for its help in fighting against "sedition." In November 1878 the emperor himself gave a speech that similarly urged society to cooperate with the government in combating terrorism.

By this time Ivan Petrunkevich had emerged as a leader of a growing political movement that included like-minded advocates of moderate political reform from zemstvo assemblies in his own province of Chernigov and other parts of Russia. While focusing their main efforts on building a national constitutional movement, the liberals also sought to build a bridge with revolutionaries. One such effort occurred on December 3, 1878, when Ivan met with representatives from both the Ukrainian nationalist movement (including Sofia's tutor Zhitetsky) and terrorist organizations in Kiev. Ivan begged the radicals to "temporarily suspend all terrorist acts." This, he argued, would enable zemstvo liberals to organize a national "open protest" against the government and in support of fundamental reforms, including a constitution, popular participation in government, and "freedom and the inviolability of individual rights." Although Ivan later admitted that his discussion with the radicals did not lead to anything definite, he left the meeting encouraged by what he regarded as their tacit support for the liberals' public campaign of protest.[16]

While his political hopes proved to be unfounded, the meeting produced an outcome of enormous personal significance—his introduction to Anastasia. With her ties to two of Russia's richest aristocratic families, Anastasia would seem to be a most unlikely and unwelcome guest at a

Anastasia Panina-Petrunkevich's locket, with photos of her and the date of her first meeting with Ivan Petrunkevich; photographed 2011. (photograph by the author)

clandestine and risky gathering of sworn opponents of the imperial regime. Ivan's own account of her presence raises as many questions as it answers. He emphasizes how grave the consequences would have been if the police learned about the meeting, yet apparently the conspirators relied solely upon the tutor Zhitetsky's word in permitting a wealthy young countess to be an "accidental and unknown witness," in Ivan's words, to their secret negotiations. Anastasia's reputation in Kiev for radical sympathies and financial support of students may have opened the door to her on this occasion. Her behavior at the meeting, where she listened but did not participate, apparently raised no concerns over her trustworthiness, for Ivan later welcomed her offer to use her Kiev apartment for future meetings.[17]

Although its political consequences were inconclusive, the meeting completely transformed Ivan's and Anastasia's lives. A gold locket given by Ivan to Anastasia and inscribed simply "December 3, 1878," commemorates the beginning of their life together. Lovingly preserved, one of the few possessions the elderly couple managed to carry out of Russia when they fled the Revolution, this treasured memento remains in the possession of Anastasia's descendants today. The date inaugurated a personal and political partnership between two passionate advocates of the rule of law and civil rights that ended only when Ivan died in Prague in 1928. Dedicating his memoirs to Anastasia, Ivan called her "my true and priceless friend," whose devotion to the truth and "limitless love, selflessness, and goodness" guided him throughout their decades together. A close friend of the couple called them two bodies with one soul.[18]

For Sofia, although she could not yet know it, the meeting in Kiev in late 1878 resulted in the loss of her monopoly on Anastasia's love. Many years later Sofia perceptively characterized Ivan and his political cause as her rivals. From the time her mother met Ivan, Sofia wrote, "*struggle* entered my mother's life as the fundamental leitmotiv of her whole existence: struggle for her love and her happiness, struggle for political and social ideals, then struggle for me." Anastasia succeeded in attaining only her first goal, Sofia continued, but the kind of love and happiness she found with Ivan "rarely falls to humans' lot."[19] Although Sofia pointedly places herself last in the list of her mother's struggles, there is no rancor evident in her words. She appears never to have blamed Anastasia for the actions that led to their forced separation in 1882, when she was only eleven. To a modern observer the absence of any recriminations in Sofia's recollections or surviving letters seems suspect. Progressive-minded Russians of Sofia's generation, however, expected to subordinate their private interests, joys, and sorrows to the far greater cause of Russia's emancipation from tyranny and backwardness. Sofia modeled herself on her mother and Ivan's ideals and no doubt found it impossible to criticize her mother for jeopardizing her childhood security when Anastasia was working for the greater good of her country.

Anastasia threw herself completely into Ivan's life and cause. When he sought greater publicity for his liberal opposition movement, she traveled with him to St. Petersburg to help him make contacts with influential journalists she knew. When he returned to his estate of Plysky in April 1879, she rented an estate just a few miles away. By early 1879 Ivan had moved out of the shadows of private, conspiratorial discussions into the limelight of public protest. Delegated by the Chernigov zemstvo to write an address to the throne calling for reform, he composed a draft that attributed terrorism to the government's denial of freedom and civil rights. When he read the denunciation to the Chernigov assembly, it raised such a furor that the governor closed down the meeting. The provincial authorities finally concluded that Ivan was a dangerous radical whose influence was growing and whose aims were "indisputably of an anti-government character." On April 27, 1879, five gendarmes on horseback arrived at Plysky and placed him under arrest. Ivan was promptly sent under police guard out of Ukraine and far to the east, to the provincial city of Kostroma. There he was informed that he was being exiled to the remote town of Varnavin, where he would live under surveillance.[20]

Ivan's new status as a political criminal proved to be only a temporary obstacle to his deepening relationship with Anastasia. A much more serious impediment was the fact that he was already married. Ivan had wed Anna Petrovna Kandyba in 1866, while still in his early twenties, and the couple had five surviving children.[21] Revealingly, upon his arrest Ivan left instructions to inform Anastasia first, and then his wife, Anna, and their children, who were living in Kiev at the time. It was Anastasia, not Anna, who visited him in Kostroma in the company of his brother, Mikhail.[22] Although only a few months had passed since Ivan and Anastasia's first meeting, she seems already to have replaced Ivan's wife as his confidante and partner.

A divorce was extremely difficult to obtain in Russia at this time. Only the Orthodox Church could dissolve a marriage, and the only acceptable grounds were adultery, prolonged disappearance, sexual incapacity, or exile to Siberia. A spouse who admitted to adultery was forbidden to remarry. Many decades later Alexander Petrunkevich, Ivan and Anna's second youngest child and a renowned entomologist at Yale University, explained how Ivan overcame this formidable obstacle by asking his wife not only to agree to a divorce, but to accept responsibility for the dissolution of the marriage. "Since my father wished to remarry," Alexander recalled, "the charge of adultery had to be placed on my mother, and it was a mark of greatness on my mother's part to accept publicly the blame for an act she did not commit."[23] This story provides both a glimpse into Ivan's magnetic, egotistical personality and a striking instance of the self-sacrifice that Russian women of this time were expected to exemplify.

As Ivan and Anastasia began the long wait for the church to approve his divorce, the newly accused political criminal started his sentence of exile in the remote town of Varnavin in the summer of 1879. Located amid vast and thick forests on the Vetluga River, the town had all of three streets and six hundred inhabitants. Anastasia made the arduous journey to Varnavin several times, including once when she took eight-year-old Sofia along together with Ivan's eldest son, and three times in the depths of winter. After a year in Varnavin, Ivan was allowed to move to the western provincial city of Smolensk in the summer of 1880, where he spent another three years under surveillance. He was forbidden to visit either Moscow or St. Petersburg, a ban that was lifted only in the 1890s.[24]

Anastasia's deepening relationship with Ivan intensified the concerns of the Panins and the government about her financial mismanagement, questionable morality, and dangerous political associations. She had firmly and boldly rejected the Board of Guardians' authority to impose conditions on her actions as her daughter's trustee and guardian. For at least two years she had associated with young men whom the police suspected of anti-government activity. From late 1878 she had conducted a public relationship with a married man and political criminal, whom she regularly visited at his place of exile—including at least one time with Sofia. She had been under police surveillance since at least July 1879. In addition, despite attempts to impose fiscal control over Sofia's trust, in 1880 Anastasia enjoyed an enormous income of approximately forty-two thousand rubles.[25] Countess Natalia Panina, Sofia's grandmother, grew increasingly alarmed by the possibility that Anastasia was using that income to fund opposition movements. Battle lines were now drawn between Anastasia and her mother-in-law, as the old countess began to take steps to keep both Panin family money and her granddaughter out of the hands of revolutionaries.

Relations between Anastasia and Natalia had not always been hostile. Anastasia named her second daughter, born after her husband's death, after her mother-in-law. There is also little sign of the future conflict between the two women in the surviving letters Anastasia wrote to "chère Maman" from the Panins' estate of Marfino during the spring and summer of 1873, and during the fall and following spring from southern France. The letters show Anastasia to be a grieving widow, a devoted mother, and a grateful and affectionate daughter-in-law.[26] What accounts for her transformation from dutiful daughter-in-law to political and moral rebel? Widowhood followed by years of living in Europe and Ukraine and increasingly infrequent visits to St. Petersburg or Marfino distanced Anastasia and her daughter from her late husband's family. Her powerful love for Ivan, in whom she found personal fulfillment and purpose, separated her still further from the Panins' aristocratic values and staunch monarchist loyalties. Anastasia's independence also reflected the pride and self-assurance of her class; inherited wealth and privilege provided her with the means to exert her autonomy. In rejecting the authority of the Board of Guardians, in associating with young radicals in Kiev and then with Ivan, she demonstrated a firm belief in her own judgment and her right to do exactly as she pleased. One detects at least a trace of her domineering father, with his unshakable confidence in his own judgment.

Countess Natalia Panina's background and character made her disapproval of her daughter-in-law's behavior inevitable. Born in 1810 to an impoverished but noble Baltic German family, the petite and beautiful young Countess Natalia von Tizengauzen had been the toast of the aristocratic salons of St. Petersburg. The social customs of the 1820s and 1830s continued to govern her views for the rest of her life. She never learned to speak proper Russian, according to Sofia, but communicated almost exclusively in French; "she never became truly RUSSIAN," but was a "typical representative of that international aristocracy whose fatherland was Europe."[27] The old countess was a "hard and cold woman," her great-granddaughter Lidia Vasilchikova recalled, "who instilled into her own children a sense of deferential timidity, and I can still remember quite well the frozen expression of my grandmother [Natalia Panina's daughter Olga] whenever the old lady was present." The contrast in personality between Sofia's mother and her grandmother could scarcely have been greater. "Great-grandmamma [Natalia Panina] had neither sympathy nor understanding for her daughter-in-law's [Anastasia's] impetuous but basically good-hearted nature," continued Lidia.[28] Natalia Panina was also determined to uphold her family's loyalty to the Russian throne. After the deaths of her husband, only son, and two of her four daughters, she saw herself as the head of a great but dwindling aristocratic family, guardian of its reputation and wealth. Anastasia threatened the Panin family's honor as well as its fortune. Her daughter-in-law's involvement with political opposition movements was reminiscent of the involvement of earlier Panins in conspiracies against Peter III and Paul I that had resulted in the murder of both emperors.[29] Anastasia's liaison with the married Ivan, along with her financial conduct and political affiliations, extinguished whatever affection or respect the deeply conservative, elderly Countess Panina may have had for the widow of her only son.

The growing conflict between the two women unfolded during a period historians used to call the "revolutionary situation of 1879–81," as terrorists made repeated and daring attempts on the life of Alexander II. In 1880, for example, a group planted a bomb under the dining room of the Winter Palace. The bomb missed injuring the imperial family by seconds when it exploded. The crisis undoubtedly played a role in hardening Natalia Panina's attitudes and actions against her daughter-in-law. According to a story she confided to Sofia's future father-in-law ten years later, Anastasia appeared at the Panin family offices at this time and demanded her daughter's entire capital, amounting to several hundred thousand rubles. The old Countess allegedly became extremely alarmed, certain now that her "hated" daughter-in-law had joined the revolutionaries. Regardless of whether this incident in fact happened, in 1880 Natalia Panina wrote a letter to Alexander II requesting another guardian for her granddaughter.

Although Countess Panina enjoyed powerful connections at court, her appeal ran into opposition from Sofia's other grandmother, "Baba" Anastasia Maltsova, lady-in-waiting and the closest friend of Empress Maria Alexandrovna. "Baba" Maltsova begged the empress to intervene. Maria Alexandrovna, though extremely ill and estranged from Alexander II at this time, extracted a promise from the emperor on her deathbed that he would stop any attempt to take Sofia away from her mother.[30] The dying empress's plea explains why, when the government did act in July 1880, the restrictions imposed on Anastasia were relatively mild. Alexander II appointed two senators to serve as cotrustees of Sofia's property but kept Anastasia as both cotrustee and the little girl's sole guardian.[31] But Anastasia soon lost her powerful protectors. Empress Maria Alexandrovna, her mother's close friend, died in 1880; and on March 1, 1881, terrorists finally succeeded in assassinating Alexander II.

For a time Anastasia appears to have suspended the activities that had alarmed the Panins and the authorities. While Ivan settled into his term of exile in Smolensk in the summer of 1880, she took her daughter for reasons unknown to live in the remote countryside of Tambov province. There Sofia fell ill with typhoid fever and almost died. When she recovered, Anastasia took her to Italy, where they spent the winter and spring of 1880–81. But upon her return to Russia Anastasia resumed her relationship with Ivan. In June 1881 she moved to Smolensk, where she rented a house for herself, Sofia, three of Ivan's children, and their governess.[32] Although Ivan lived in separate quarters, he and Anastasia set up a household in accordance with the agreement Ivan had made with his wife, Anna: three of their children would live with their father, while two stayed with their mother. "But we visited back and forth," their son Alexander recalled, "and in a manner of speaking I had two mothers." Anastasia evidently won not only Ivan's heart, but his children's as well. "I cannot with honesty say which I loved the more,"

Alexander reflected. "Both were noble women in the best sense of the word," he continued, "and in each home we were equally loved."[33]

These arrangements placed Anastasia's custody over Sofia in extreme jeopardy. The reports of the gendarmes were unequivocal: Anastasia repeatedly exposed her daughter to the influence of political criminals, first with Gavrilov, and now with the even more dangerous Petrunkevich.[34] To be sure, police surveillance over Anastasia and Ivan in Smolensk had its comical elements. In the summer of 1881, shortly after Anastasia had established her household in the town, several provincial officials, including the governor and the head of the local gendarmes, received anonymous letters urging them to disobey the new emperor, Alexander III. Governor Lev Tamara accused Ivan of dictating these seditious letters to Anastasia, which he claimed were written in her handwriting. He denounced the couple's efforts to stir up revolution to his superior, the minister of the interior, and recommended that Ivan be exiled to Siberia. Conducting his own investigation into the letters, Colonel Esipov, the chief of gendarmes, noticed similarities between the handwriting of the anonymous letters and letters the governor had written to his mistress. The resemblance convinced the alert Esipov that Governor Tamara himself had written the anonymous letters. But why? Esipov recalled a bibulous dinner at the mayor's, at which Tamara had stated that "it would be good to marry Countess Panina." The mayor commented that she was going to marry Petrunkevich. "Well," Tamara reportedly answered, "Petrunkevich can be taken away to Siberia," and Panina could be held in Smolensk; "that can be arranged." Esipov and the local prosecutor became convinced that the letters were part of the governor's amorous pursuit of the beautiful and wealthy Anastasia. After they reported their suspicions to their respective ministers, Tamara was transferred to another province.[35]

This time a relatively honest gendarme colonel protected the couple from being subjected to intensified persecution (and Anastasia from the governor's romantic attentions). But tolerance for Anastasia's liaison with a married political criminal was dwindling after the assassination of Alexander II. His son Alexander III, a model of marital fidelity, and the new empress, Maria Feodorovna, had strongly disapproved of Alexander II's flagrantly open relationship with his mistress, Princess Dolgorukaya, with whom he had three children. Alexander III blamed his father's scandalous adultery for what he and his wife regarded as a rise of dissolute behavior in high society, which Alexander II himself had seemed to condone.[36] At their new imperial court Anastasia's liaison with Ivan represented not only a political threat but also a glaring example of moral decline.

In the battle for custody over Sofia, the assassination of Alexander II in March 1881 and the new moral order at the imperial court tipped the balance in Countess Natalia Panina's favor. In February 1882 Alexander III, at the elderly countess's request, removed Anastasia as Sofia's guardian and named Natalia and her son-in-law, Lieutenant-General Vladimir Levashov, in her place. The Ministry of the Interior's summary of the case exposes the family pride, financial interest, and political tension that combined to drive the Panins' and the government's intervention into the relations between mother and daughter. Replacing Anastasia as guardian was necessary, the report argued, because of legitimate fears that young Sofia, the "last scion" of the eminent and loyal Panin family, and her "very large financial resources" would fall under the influence of politically dangerous ideas and persons.[37] Henceforth Sofia's grandmother and uncle would make the decisions about her upbringing, not her mother.

Ivan and Anastasia had one remaining ally in Count Nikolai Ignatiev, the minister of the interior and head of the security police, who was Anastasia's cousin. Thanks to his intervention Anastasia was not physically separated from her daughter in early 1882. But Countess Panina and Levashov ordered Anastasia to remove her daughter from Smolensk and Ivan's pernicious influence immediately. Anastasia moved to Odessa in February 1882. There Sofia, who had previously been educated at home, entered her first educational institution, a private gymnasium for girls. Keeping Anastasia under surveillance, the gendarmes in Odessa interpreted her conduct there as more evidence of her political disloyalty. Once again they established her guilt through a chain of associations: Anastasia, they alleged, kept company with people who acquired their reputation for political unreliability through their own acquaintance with others suspected of anti-government sentiments. The gendarmes regarded her choice of a school for Sofia, for example, as evidence of her oppositionist sympathies: they considered its director to be a person with an "anti-government frame of mind" who associated with other young people arrested for crimes against the state. It was not merely Anastasia's associations that caused concern, but also persistent suspicions that she was funding anti-government groups out of her daughter's inheritance.[38]

The final act in the battle for Sofia commenced in the summer of 1882. Having finally received a divorce, Ivan married Anastasia in

Smolensk in August. The timing was unfortunate for Anastasia; her cousin Ignatiev had been dismissed as minister of the interior in May, and his replacement, the arch-conservative Count Dmitry Tolstoy, had no reason to intercede with Alexander III on Anastasia's behalf. News of Anastasia's marriage horrified the Panin family. Countess Panina wrote to Minister of the Interior Tolstoy, begging him to help "save" her granddaughter. She accused Anastasia of violating the conditions Sofia's guardians had imposed and endangering the child. In Odessa, she claimed, Sofia did not go to church, take communion, or receive religious instruction. Instead of cooperating with the governess that Sofia's two guardians had chosen, Anastasia treated her as a spy for the Panin family (which in all likelihood she was!). She accused Anastasia of repeatedly abandoning her daughter for weeks at a time and leaving Sofia with the children of servants. Because of Anastasia's hostility toward the entire Panin family, the old countess complained that she had not seen her granddaughter in several years. Anastasia's marriage to a man whom "the government has long known as a dangerous political agitator," and whose divorce was a scandal, was the final blow. As a grandmother and the head of the Panin family, the old countess declared that it was her "sacred duty" to defend Sofia against her stepfather's harmful influence, and to keep the Panin fortune out of the hands of revolutionaries. Unwilling to sacrifice herself for the good of her daughter, Anastasia was not a fit mother. The only recourse, Countess Panina concluded, was to appeal to the emperor to remove Sofia from her mother completely, and to place her in one of the boarding schools for noble girls.[39]

Deprived of her allies at court, at this point Anastasia's only hope was to plead her case directly to the throne. In a long petition addressed to Alexander III, she revealed the conflicting passions that had brought her to the brink of losing her daughter completely—her love for Ivan, her embrace of his political cause, and her no less ardent devotion to her only child. The petition opens with a scathing critique of the Panins, whom Anastasia accused of acting out of malice toward her, and whose demands endangered Sofia's life. Three of Countess Panina's children— Sofia's father and his two sisters—died early of tuberculosis, Anastasia pointed out, and the children of the two surviving sisters either died or grew up puny and sickly. Despite this potentially fatal hereditary propensity, her guardians ordered Sofia and her mother to move to Odessa, notorious for its unhealthy climate. Now they were trying to tear Sofia from her mother's arms by sending her to school in St. Petersburg,

exposing the little girl to the indifferent care of strangers and the capital's deadly winters. The dying Vladimir Panin had tried to protect his
infant daughter from his cold, emotionally distant mother, Anastasia
told the emperor; "when the father of my daughter designated me her
sole guardian before his death, he probably remembered his sad childhood and wished to spare his daughter contact with the oppressive
conditions of domestic life that helped bring his sisters to the grave!"[40]

In addition to attacking the Panins, Anastasia wrote eloquently in
her own defense. For her daughter's entire life, she assured the emperor,
she had done everything possible to protect Sofia's physical and moral
health. Yet even as she appealed to Alexander III as a distraught mother
in need of his protection, Anastasia could not resist advocating for the
principles of law, truth, and justice that she and Ivan supported so passionately. The family bond is the foundation of legality and the state,
Anastasia boldly reminded the emperor, and it was in defense of that
principle that she dared to seek his protection. Her "enemies" the Panins
used her marriage to Ivan as proof of her lack of love for Sofia, and as
the justification for their efforts to take her daughter away. "But my
conscience is clear," Anastasia declared, "as both a loyal subject and a
mother I did not violate my duty." Moreover, she continued, Ivan did
nothing to deserve his sentence of exile, and his persecution was unjust.
She asked the emperor to submit his case and Anastasia's to a fair, im-
partial judge, whose examination, she was sure, would uncover the
truth and "dispel all the slander following us." "If my husband and I
are so criminal that we deserve such an unusual punishment as taking
a child away, a punishment that is not imposed by law even on a criminal going to Siberia, then punish us, but at least we will know why we
are suffering." But a fair investigation would vindicate them, Anastasia
confidently asserted.[41]

Anastasia's passionate and defiant petition is a striking combination
of protestations of loyalty and impertinent, even seditious demands directed at Russia's absolute sovereign. But it reached the emperor too
late. It is dated October 15, 1882—the same day that the minister of the
interior brought Countess Natalia Panina's request to Alexander III's
attention. The emperor, who may not have even read Anastasia's appeal, immediately approved his minister's recommendation that Sofia
be taken from her mother and placed in the Catherine Institute, one of
the boarding schools for noble girls in St. Petersburg.[42]

The decision against Anastasia seems inevitable. Victor Panin's record
of irreproachably loyal service to three Russian emperors undoubtedly

strengthened Countess Natalia Panina's hand, while Anastasia undermined her position as her daughter's guardian by forming suspect political associations as well as sexually improper relationships. She could count on little more than her own connections at court for protection, and after Alexander II's death, they were considerably weakened. Moreover, the tension that pervaded government circles in the aftermath of the assassination of Alexander II elevated a family dispute between Anastasia and her mother-in-law to a matter of state security.

The battle for Sofia generated so much anger and distress on both sides that emotions still colored accounts written long afterward. The Panin side, as one would expect, emphasized Anastasia's responsibility for losing her daughter. More than a century later one Panin descendant blamed Anastasia and her "crazy," impulsive personality as solely responsible for the family "catastrophe." After all the efforts Victor and Natalia Panin had devoted to restoring the family's reputation for loyalty to the throne, the Panins were understandably protective of the family's honor. In a time of extreme political tension and repeated terrorist attacks, they might also be forgiven for failing to distinguish between Ivan Petrunkevich's liberal constitutionalism and the terrorists' revolutionary socialism. Writing years after the 1917 Revolution, Lidia Vasilchikova, whose grandparents Olga and Vladimir Levashov played major roles in the Panins' battle for custody of Sofia, does draw that distinction. In the late 1870s and 1880s, she wrote, Ivan Petrunkevich's activities were considered "highly subversive." But to those like her who experienced the 1917 Revolution "Petrunkevich, as compared to the Bolsheviks, does not seem to have been 'radical' at all." Nevertheless, she maintained, dissidents like Anastasia and Ivan still exerted a harmful influence on Russia's political destiny. "It stands beyond doubt that the destructive activity of the 'radicals' of the seventies contributed to shake the foundations of the Empire and made it easier for more extremist elements later to strike the fatal blow."[43] At the same time, it is not difficult to sympathize with Anastasia's anguish over the emperor's decision to take her daughter away, a decision Ivan called "a crime against not only all human laws but God's as well."[44]

It is striking that none of the adults in this dispute mentions how they thought the separation might affect the little girl at its center. Completely engrossed in the political ramifications of this family struggle, Ivan, Anastasia, and Countess Panina seem to have paid scant attention to its emotional impact on Sofia. Up to that point Sofia had enjoyed an extremely close relationship with her mother, who had been "my whole life, my family, my love, the whole meaning of my existence."[45] The conditions of the separation were especially harsh; her guardians allowed Anastasia to see Sofia at the school only a limited number of times per month, and their meetings had to take place at the headmistress's apartment in the presence of school personnel.[46] Sofia may have been too young to understand the complex family history, personal animosities, and political events behind the forced separation from her mother, but its severity and injustice were not lost on her. During her first months at the institute she made no attempt to disguise her outrage or accommodate herself to her new circumstances. She refused to speak to her grandmother when she visited. "I sat like a stone," she remembered, and "gave no answers whatever when grandmother questioned and addressed me." Sofia grew indignant when a schoolmistress chastised her with a warning that if she continued to be stubborn, her grandmother might disinherit her. Claiming that at the time she understood little about her inheritance or "money in general," Sofia recalled years later how "the notion that my feelings could be 'bought' by a threat of this kind deeply offended me," and made her despise the school even more.[47]

Sofia found other ways to demonstrate her allegiance to her mother and rejection of her grandmother. All conversation at the institute was conducted in French, and the girls were required to call the headmistress *maman*. Sofia refused. "That I would call her mother . . . —not for anything in the world!" The "obnoxious, high-breasted" headmistress, "tightly buttoned into a bright blue dress (that any minute, it seems, would burst open)," personified "the evil power that took my mother from me. . . . So to the end of my stay at the institute she was called Madame by me, with special emphasis on this 'impertinence.'"[48] Sofia spent her first Christmas at school, unable to be with her mother and refusing to go to her grandmother's. Countess Panina sent a Christmas tree to the institute with gifts for Sofia and six other girls who remained there for the holiday. Sofia regarded this as yet another affront to her moral principles. "I remember how keenly I suffered from being put in the privileged position of giving gifts to my mates, who did not have the material possibility of reciprocating to me," she later wrote. Standing in a corner during the entire party while her "simple-hearted" schoolmates enjoyed themselves, she refused to have anything to do with her grandmother's candle-lit Christmas tree and gifts. Her recollections reveal not only a streak of stubborn pride—she herself refers to her "complex psychology"—but also her confusion over how to relate to the other girls at school, compared to whom she felt different, even morally superior.[49] Sofia began to speak with her grandmother only after several months, when her mother ordered her to do so.

Reflecting Anastasia's propensity for claiming moral superiority, Sofia also found the school's culture and mores offensive. The headmistress and other staff treated girls from wealthy families much better than poorer girls, she noticed, while she had been raised to believe in equality and justice. A surprise visit by the institute's patroness, Empress Maria Feodorovna, gave the new pupil another occasion to demonstrate that she was Anastasia's daughter. As the small, gracious figure of the empress processed between two rows of girls in their white school pinafores, they curtsied deeply. Curious, no doubt, to meet the object of such a bitter custody battle, the empress headed straight for Sofia, and extended her hand to the girl. "I curtsy, having firmly mastered this first rule of courtesy," Sofia remembered, "but I absolutely do not know what to do with the Imperial hand extended to me!" So she shook it. The handshake caused a sensation. The blue dresses of the headmistress and other staff "almost burst" from their barely suppressed indignation, Sofia recalled, while the other girls gasped in amazement. "Kiss the hand," hissed the headmistress; "leave her in peace," responded the empress. The school administration regarded Sofia's behavior as a defiant political act attributable to her mother's influence, while her schoolmates interpreted the handshake as evidence of her intimacy with the imperial family.[50]

But was her handshake with the empress as unintentional as she represents, the result of a childhood spent with the nonconformist Anastasia in ignorance of society's rules? It seems improbable that at the age of eleven Sofia was unaware of such a basic social convention— that imperial hands are to be kissed, not shaken. Sofia's dramatic account of her rebellious first months at the Catherine Institute should be read with caution. It was written many decades after the events it describes, and was no doubt tinged by the years Sofia dedicated to progressive social causes and the liberal political movement to which her mother and stepfather devoted their lives. Just as she probably exaggerated her ignorance of the aristocratic conventions that ruled the institute, her recollections stress the hostility she felt toward her grandmother. But the memoirs of the old countess's great-granddaughter Lidia, who often visited the Panin mansion on the Fontanka, tell a more nuanced story. Lidia never observed any tension between Sofia and her grandmother. Sofia understood, Lidia claimed, that her grandmother had acted only according to what she believed was her granddaughter's best interests. As for Countess Panina, her granddaughter's entry into her life mellowed the stern, emotionally distant old lady, and Sofia became the only person she ever truly loved. "She had adopted [Sofia] out of a sense of duty; later she could not do without her." The competition between her mother and grandmother for her allegiance and affections may not have been as bitter as Sofia described. According to Lidia, Sofia maintained a tender, close relationship with Anastasia after their separation "without ever having to go behind her grandmother's back."[51] As for Anastasia, she disapproved of Sofia's disrespectful conduct toward her grandmother, and ordered her to stop the silent treatment.[52]

Nevertheless, Sofia's adjustment to the institute was undoubtedly painful. It must have been difficult to reconcile the sharp differences between the principles behind the progressive upbringing she had received from her mother and the institute's elitist culture. Torn from parents passionately committed to political reform, Sofia now found herself in a deeply conservative institution founded on unquestioned devotion to the throne. In addition, Sofia's recollections suggest that Anastasia had raised her to have little awareness of how privileged she really was. Her grandmother's gifts and the institute's favoritism toward rich girls like her brought Sofia face-to-face with this fact. Far from enjoying her newfound status, she reacted to this surprising and unpleasant discovery with confusion over how to behave and antipathy toward those whose snobbery elevated her above the other girls.

Sofia's reaction to her first months in the institute reveals other aspects of her personality and character. Raised by a mother who took orders from no one, Sofia too could be strong-willed, even stubborn. These traits shaped her actions when she first entered the institute—the refusal to call the headmistress *maman*, for example, or to enjoy her grandmother's Christmas tree. Even in the shock of separation from her mother, Sofia found recourse in defiance rather than despair. In standing up to both her grandmother and the headmistress, she demonstrated the qualities of independence and courage that she drew upon again and again in the future dramas and tragedies of her life. But after the first months of anger and resistance, Sofia proved her essential fairness and understanding by reconciling with her grandmother. Equally revealing of Sofia's character is her relationship to her mother. It strains credulity that Sofia felt no jealousy or resentment at all toward Anastasia for her share of responsibility for their separation. Nevertheless she remained devoted throughout her life to both her mother and the principles of justice and integrity she claimed Anastasia taught her. In the end, Sofia adapted quite well to the institute's routines and expectations, and she thrived for more than a decade in an environment very different from the one she had known as a child—Countess Natalia Panina's world of the St. Petersburg aristocratic elite.

3

"The Richest Marriageable Girl in Russia"

The elegant neoclassical building of the School of the Order of St. Catherine was constructed at the beginning of the nineteenth century according to the plans of Italian architect Giacomo Quarenghi, a follower of the Renaissance master Palladio. Sofia lived there for five years, graduating in 1887 a few months before her sixteenth birthday. Although the Catherine Institute, as it was commonly known, was located in the heart of the imperial capital, Sofia and her privileged schoolmates spent little time outside its grounds. A tall iron fence with spikes separated their building from city traffic on the embankment. The girls took their exercise in a tree-shaded garden that extended behind the building, and they attended church in the institute's own chapel in the magnificent Hall of Columns. The institute was one of thirty educational institutions in the empire for girls from the nobility. Although other kinds of secondary institutions for girls opened after the mid-nineteenth century, elite families like the Panins preferred the "institutes for noble girls" because of the schools' close association with the imperial family, their selective reputation, and their pervasive monarchist ethos.[1]

Throughout its long history Sofia's school, which opened in 1798, played second fiddle to the more prestigious Smolny Institute, founded

The St. Petersburg School of the Order of St. Catherine. (Tsentral'nyi gosudarstvennyi arkhiv kinofotofonodokumentov g. Sankt-Peterburga, A2325)

in 1764. "These two institutes were destined to be eternal rivals in all areas," Sofia dryly remarked in her recollections of her school years, "although to everyone except 'Catherine girls' it was perfectly clear that this competition was won by the 'Smolny girls' from the very 'starting line.'"[2] Yet the rival schools pursued the same mission of helping to prop up Russia's dominant class by educating its daughters to take their place at the top of the social hierarchy. The Catherine Institute's massive edifice announced the nobility's political and social supremacy and the stability of the dynasty it served. Behind the grand entrance, however, conditions inside the institute hinted at the cracks and strains within the nobility as it encountered modernity in the late nineteenth century.

The Panins' choice of the Catherine Institute for Sofia testifies to the close supervision they intended to maintain over her upbringing now that they had won custody of the girl from her mother. The building was located almost directly across the Fontanka River from her grandmother's mansion. Sofia's cousin Olga Levashova, or "Kitty," as she was known, was also an "*institutka*" there and became her close friend.[3] The exclusive school with its tradition-bound customs and ties to the throne—the empress was its patroness—was an eloquent symbol of Sofia's removal from the influence of her defiantly unconventional mother and politically unreliable stepfather. With her granddaughter now under close observation, the elderly Countess Panina could be sure that Sofia would receive an education aligned with the monarchist values of the capital's aristocracy.

When Sofia entered the institute's imposing premises in late October 1882, there were approximately three hundred and fifty girls in seven grades, all of whom belonged to the nobility, a legally defined social class in Russia.[4] Her grandmother insisted that she live not in the dormitory but with one of the inspectresses, a woman Sofia immediately detested. This arrangement "poisoned my existence," Sofia recalled, because her schoolmates suspected that she would snitch on them to the administration. But she soon dispelled these suspicions; "I hated the 'exceptionality' of my position so sincerely and was so oppressed by it, and I was, by contrast, so permeated by the spirit of fidelity to that unique order called 'schoolfellowship,' that without doubt I would have sooner endured the worst tortures than give away the 'secrets' of our class life."[5] These special living arrangements may have been prompted by more than her grandmother's snobbery, however. Although the institute was one of the most prestigious schools in Russia, it was a remarkably unhealthy place.

Sanitary conditions in Quarenghi's seventy-five-year-old building were deplorable. Fetid air rose up the broad staircase from the basement. The large classrooms were drafty, and the third-floor dormitories were crowded. The institute used the city water supply, which in the 1880s was drawn from contaminated rivers and canals. Toilets were "of the old type," made from wooden planks; their smell permeated the corridors. The bathrooms were also cold, with temperatures ranging from 48 to 55 degrees Fahrenheit. The girls were frequently ill, and epidemic disease was a recurring problem. Girls made daily "pilgrimages" to the doctor's office, bringing complaints of gastro-intestinal illnesses, inflammations of the throat and chest, fevers and bronchial diseases, coughs, joint pains, and muscle aches. In addition to almost 1,300 outpatient visits, there were almost 700 admissions to the institute's infirmary in 1883—that is, on average, every girl was a patient there twice. The infirmary was too small to isolate infectious cases; girls with measles, scarlet fever, and diphtheria were carried through the entire building to two small rooms on the same floor as the classrooms, and treated all together.[6]

A survey done by the school physician in 1883 revealed that almost half of the girls were anemic. The majority were also below normal weight for their age. The physician speculated that the cause lay in the fact that girls were underfed, especially the older ones, who received the same amount of food as the younger *institutki*. He also faulted the school's bizarre meal schedule. Girls received only tea and a roll at 8 p.m. before going to bed. There was no breakfast. When their next meal finally came at noon, sixteen hours after the bedtime snack, the ravenous girls devoured every crumb. Their next meal came just a few hours later, at 4 p.m., when the girls, still full from the midday meal, only picked at their food. Although the administration made some improvements during Sofia's time there, disease continued to plague the institute. A full-blown epidemic of typhoid fever broke out in the fall of Sofia's third year, followed by outbreaks of influenza and diphtheria in the winter of 1886.[7]

These appalling conditions seem surprising in an institution that served Russia's social elite, but their origins lay in several almost intractable circumstances. The old building occupied by the Catherine Institute was difficult and expensive to maintain and modernize. St. Petersburg's northerly location, polluted rivers and canals, and extreme climate made it one of Europe's unhealthiest cities, with extremely high rates of tuberculosis, cholera, and other diseases. At the time, neither medicine nor science could do much to ameliorate the effects of the city's inhospitable location. Another reason may have been a lack of funds. With their modest tuition and many scholarship students, the institutes could not be self-supporting. In a symbolic sense the decaying building, illness-stricken students, and straitened finances of the Catherine Institute in the late nineteenth century mirrored the declining status of the landowning nobles and high-ranking state servitors who sent their daughters there.

The schools for noble girls were also widely considered to be hopelessly out of date. With their embittered, badly paid teachers, dangerous sanitary conditions, and superficial educational program, one critic charged, the schools were "not only harmful but simply pernicious," producing graduates who knew nothing about the real world.[8] The institutes owed much of this poor reputation among progressive Russians to their heavy emphasis on patriotism and reverence for the imperial family. Although the French language dominated over Russian within their walls, a major component of the institutes' mission was the creation of loyal daughters of the Russian fatherland. Portraits of emperors and empresses past and present adorned their walls. (At the Irkutsk Institute for Noble Girls the students clung to a superstition that the ghost of one empress stepped out of the frame of her portrait and stalked the corridors at night.[9]) The reigning empress regularly visited the St. Petersburg institutes, attended their celebrations and examinations, and distributed prizes to graduates. Sofia must have observed many such visits, beginning with the surprise appearance of the empress shortly after her arrival, and including one by the emperor and empress that occurred in January 1887, a few months before her graduation. The Catherine Institute's veneration of the Romanov dynasty is evident in the ecstatic description of this visit by S. A. Anikieva, a graduate of the institute who worked as a class mistress throughout Sofia's time there. After attending a special prayer service with Sofia's senior class, the imperial couple entered the main hall to receive "loud greetings from the lips and hearts of all." One *institutka* stepped forward to recite an ardently patriotic poem. Anikieva recalled how the girl "was permeated to the depths of her heart with happiness at expressing before the adored tsar everything that overflowed her heart at the sight of His Majesty." After receiving the emperor's thanks and a kiss from the empress, the girl broke down in sobs of joy. The incident illustrates the monarchist ethos that pervaded the Catherine Institute, and that exacerbated Sofia's physical distance from her mother and stepfather with a culture so alien to their constitutionalist principles.[10]

The education offered by the institutes was not as backward as their critics maintained, however. By the late nineteenth century there were only a few differences in curriculum between these elite schools, which emphasized modern languages, and the more accessible and democratic female high schools (*gimnazii*), which offered Latin and Greek.[11] At the Catherine Institute, for example, the curriculum included modern languages, literature, history, geography, natural sciences, physics, and mathematics.[12] By accepting pupils from poor as well as rich families, the institutes also offered educational opportunities that girls from modest means might not have found elsewhere, launching some graduates into independent lives. One graduate of the prestigious Smolny Institute, V. E. Bogdanovskaya, taught chemistry at the St. Petersburg Higher Women's Courses after receiving her doctorate in Europe.[13] Anna Zhukova, a contemporary of Sofia's, was the bright and ambitious daughter of the director of a state gold mine in eastern Siberia, a man of humble origins and little formal education whose civil service rank elevated him into the nobility. After months of pleading, she obtained her father's permission to attend the Institute for Noble Girls in Irkutsk. Overcoming its strict regimen, rote learning, and skimpy food, she

Students at the St. Petersburg School of the Order of St. Catherine, with portraits of the last two emperors and empresses on the wall behind them. (Tsentral'nyi gosudarstvennyi arkhiv kinofotofonodokumentov g. Sankt-Peterburga, D6396)

graduated in 1888 at the top of her class and proceeded from there to medical school in France and St. Petersburg, followed by a career as a psychologist and professor in Soviet Russia.[14]

Rebellious and resentful when she arrived, with little previous experience of any formal educational institution, Sofia initially attracted considerable attention at the institute as the late arrival whose fortune had provoked such a bitter family dispute, and whose shocking handshake with the empress hinted at intimacy with the imperial family. But within months she had adapted to the institution's demands, conformed to its expectations for girls from her class, and integrated herself into its culture. Several of her school notebooks have survived, revealing how Sofia picked up some typical schoolgirl habits. Doodles and sketches suggest less than perfect attention to her teachers. Notes exchanged with friends offer a glimpse into her passions, like going to the theater, concerts, and dances. Others suggest how she, like many other Russian girls, found an imaginative escape from institutional conformity in reading fiction. "Mama has promised to give me all of

Shakespeare," reads one note in her handwriting. "I am now reading *Nest of Gentlefolk* and think about it all the time," another note sighs; "I can't tear myself away from it. . . . And I would desperately like to meet a person like Lavretsky"—the tragic hero of Turgenev's 1859 novel of doomed love. At the same time, Sofia's notebooks indicate that her education at the institute was relatively broad and serious for its time. Her essays and comments on literature are written in French, German, and English as well as Russian. Paragraphs on the works of Gogol, Lermontov, and Turgenev share the pages of one notebook with notes on Shakespeare, *Gulliver's Travels*, German literature, and Greek mythology.[15]

Sofia not only adapted, she excelled in her studies, rising to the top of her class. During 1883–84, her first complete year at the school, she received grades of "10 4/8" out of 12 points for academic work and 11 points out of 12 for behavior. By her fourth year she was receiving "outstanding" grades in all subjects except for math, where her work was "extremely good," and perfect grades in behavior. At her graduation examinations in the spring of 1887, Sofia's teachers awarded her a perfect 12 points in her exams in Russian, German, natural science, and mathematics, and even higher grades of 12+ in all remaining subjects— catechism, French, history, geography, and pedagogy. Sofia's record earned her the rank of fifth in her graduating class and one of the institute's top awards, the gold *"shiffre"*—a badge with the empress's monogram and the institute's insignia. Along with the gold monogram, she and the other award-winners received a photographic portrait of Empress Maria Feodorovna and were invited to the Winter Palace for a ceremony at which the empress herself distributed the prizes. With her perfect record in deportment during her final two years at the institute, it seems likely that this time Sofia kissed rather than shook the empress's hand.[16]

Although this record indicates that Sofia fully accommodated herself to the institute's rules and expectations, that process goes unmentioned in her recollections. When she looked back on her school experience, she emphasized its elitism and hypocrisy. "Children are unusually perceptive and sensitive toward displays on the part of grownups of no matter what kind of bias," she asserted, "whether in the negative or positive sense." Children "demand irreproachably honest treatment . . . , even when we ourselves are being sly . . . ," she continued. "Two [kinds of] truths, two [kinds of] honor are very quickly worked out in our educational institutions: one, the true one for the world of our relations with our comrades, the other for the administration." The moral principles that Sofia claimed to have observed at the institute and that her grandmother represented were the exact opposite of the "HONESTY— indivisible and absolute—that was the cornerstone of the spiritual world and relationships in which mother raised me."[17] Writing about her institute years as an elderly émigré living in the United States, Sofia emphasized her rebellious first months, not her academic success, in order to bring her childhood into conformity with her later defiance of some of the values of the class into which she was born, and the absolutist political system that sustained that class.

Once Sofia entered the institute she was kept almost entirely out of her mother's orbit. Her new stepfather, still a political exile, was prohibited from going to St. Petersburg. Anastasia's own position was painfully difficult. Although Anastasia parted from Ivan periodically to live in the capital in order to see Sofia, mother and daughter were permitted no more than two supervised visits a week.[18] In 1883, shortly before Sofia's second school year began, her mother and stepfather moved to Mashuk, a country estate in the province of Tver, a train ride of several hours from St. Petersburg. They became close friends with the Bakunins, one of the province's most famous noble families, whose members included the anarchist Mikhail. Ivan's brother Mikhail, a physician employed by the local government, married a Bakunin; later, as the two families grew closer, one of Ivan's sons also married into the Bakunins.[19] Through Mikhail Petrunkevich and the Bakunins, who enjoyed a well-earned reputation for progressive social views and political activism in the province, Ivan plunged into politics once again, even though he was not permitted any formal role in local government affairs. Years later, in the late 1890s, Sofia spent part of most summers at Mashuk. She may have even visited there while she was at the institute, judging by the evidence of an undated photo in the Bakunin family album. In a scene reminiscent of a Chekhov story, a young Sofia, looking about sixteen years old, sits outdoors on the grass amid her parents, Ivan's brother and his wife, and her Petrunkevich stepcousins, one of whom strums a guitar.[20]

But such visits must have been rare. Anastasia and Ivan's associations with progressive politics in Tver did little to encourage the Panins to let Sofia spend much time in her mother's radical circle. While a student at the Catherine Institute, Sofia spent most of her Sundays and holidays with her grandmother. The formal routines of a bygone era reigned at the Panin mansion, matching the old-fashioned furniture,

Sofia (*second from left*) with her parents, Anastasia (*sitting, leaning on her elbow*) and Ivan Petrunkevich (*standing, second from right*), and members of the Petrunkevich family, circa 1890. (Bakunin Family Photo Album, located in the Manuscript Division of the Russian State Library, Moscow, f. 218, kart. 1339, ed. 1, l. 16, photo No. 78)

the Gobelin tapestries, and the paintings by European masters. Sofia's cousin Lidia described the Panin mansion as a gloomy, spooky place, pervaded by "a very peculiar smell . . . a mixture of perfumed powder and dusty carpets." The old countess's maid "had only one eye and looked like a witch. The only time I ever dared to speak to her was when I asked her whether great-grandmamma was not afraid to sleep in her bed with its heavy green curtains, which to my mind looked exactly like the bed in which Red Riding Hood discovered the wolf." Mademoiselle Pommier, a French governess whom Lidia described as the "living embodiment of my great-grandmother's ideas," supervised Sofia's studies and acted as her chaperone when the girl was not in school. After Sofia graduated from the institute in 1887, she moved across the narrow river into the Panin mansion. During the next two years she traveled with her grandmother in Europe, and when she turned eighteen in August 1889, she made her debut.[21]

Women of Sofia's social rank generally married young, so her grandmother's principal objective—indeed, the only one in all likelihood—became finding a suitable husband for her. The young Countess Panina

Sofia, circa 1890. (Rossiiskii institut istorii iskusstv, St. Petersburg, Kabinet rukopisei, f. 32, op. 1, ed. khr. 127/3. Photograph taken by Levitsky and Son, St. Petersburg, Imperial photographers.)

was one of the most eligible young women in St. Petersburg in the late 1880s. One family friend recalled, perhaps with some exaggeration, that she was known as the "richest marriageable girl in Russia" at the time.[22] Her distinguished name and title increased her appeal to potential suitors. Now as at the Catherine Institute, Sofia was continually reminded of her own wealth and status. She offered more, however, than an inheritance and social prestige. Sofia at eighteen was cultured and attractive, with light brown hair and a warm, open personality that expressed itself in her face as well as her affectionate letters to Varya (Varvara Petrovna Volkova, née Geiden), a schoolmate and close friend since 1881. She also possessed an energy and zest for life that found outlets in avid reading, love of the outdoors, and sports such as swimming, horseback riding, and tennis. "We must enjoy our young years," she exclaimed in a letter to Varya in late 1889, "and live, live with all the strength of our soul."[23]

After five years cloistered at the Catherine Institute, followed by two years in the company of an elderly grandmother whose views and manners dated from the 1840s, Sofia could not have been well prepared for the sophisticated world she entered in 1889. Well-educated and widely traveled, the aristocrats of *fin de siècle* St. Petersburg resembled the upper classes of other European nations in many ways. Some were individuals of great talent and accomplishment in industry, commerce, and culture; many were connoisseurs and collectors of art, books, and manuscripts. For all their cosmopolitan refinement, however, the love of luxury and willfulness displayed by many revealed the effects of centuries of privilege and serf ownership. In some aristocratic circles appearance mattered more than substance: "external gloss, flawless manners, refined politeness, [and] the ability to present oneself were placed highest of all."[24] Few in number but exercising a disproportionate economic and social dominance in the capital, members of the St. Petersburg elite were famous for their extravagant spending.

The imperial capital glittered with world-class music and art. During the winter season the elite attended the theater, opera, ballet, and fancy dress balls. In addition to exclusive balls given at the Winter Palace by the imperial couple, aristocratic families organized dances and masquerades in their mansions and at fashionable hotels and clubs. Wearing the latest fashions and the family jewels, young ladies danced the waltz and quadrille with cavalry officers in their colorful and splendid uniforms. Special *bals blancs* were held for unmarried girls, who wore white gowns. To prepare her granddaughter for the social season, Countess Panina held dancing classes at her mansion for Sofia, seven other young ladies, and eight young gentlemen.[25]

One of these gentlemen, a junior cavalry officer named Alexander Polovtsov, who was four years Sofia's senior, would become her husband. As the eldest son of a rich and prominent Petersburg family with close ties to the court, Alexander (1867–1944) would not have been attracted to Sofia solely because of her social position or inheritance. His father, also named Alexander (1832–1909), had climbed the bureaucratic ladder to its highest rungs, becoming a member of the Imperial Senate and the State Council, the state secretary to Emperor Alexander III, and a frequent visitor at the imperial court. (Alexander Sr.'s detailed, gossip-filled diaries provide historians with useful insights into court life and high politics in the late nineteenth century.) Sofia's future husband also belonged to one of the wealthiest families in St. Petersburg. His father acquired a fortune when he married Nadezhda Yunina, a woman with an extraordinary background. As a six-month-old infant Nadezhda was found in June 1844 on the grounds of the summer home belonging to the childless millionaire banker Baron A. L. Stieglitz.

Stieglitz, a Jew who converted to Orthodox Christianity, adopted her and gave her the surname Yunina in commemoration of the month in which she was found. Nadezhda was no ordinary foundling: Sofia's future mother-in-law was the illegitimate daughter of Grand-Duke Mikhail, the younger brother of Emperor Nicholas I.[26]

As Stieglitz's only child, Nadezhda brought Alexander Sr. a dowry of one million rubles. After Stieglitz died, she inherited millions more. She also shared her husband's passion for collecting decorative art. (The Polovtsovs' love of the arts led them to persuade Stieglitz to endow a school in his name for fine and applied arts; it opened in 1876 and still exists in St. Petersburg today.) With their enormous collection of European and Asian decorative arts, the Polovtsovs' elegant mansion on fashionable Bolshaya Morskaya Street in central St. Petersburg resembled a museum. There Nadezhda Polovtsova gave some of the most brilliant balls in St. Petersburg. Nadezhda and Alexander's eldest son, and Sofia's future husband, was an urbane young man with a passion for opera, theater, and balls. He also shared his parents' love for decorative arts. As a child and youth Alexander Jr. lived abroad for extended periods with his family in Paris and London, taking holidays at spas such as Biarritz and Carlsbad. He was also wealthy in his own right: when Baron Stieglitz died in 1884, he left his favorite grandson, who was still in his teens, 200,000 rubles, an elegant mansion on one of St. Petersburg's outlying islands, and "Fominki," an estate in Vladimir province of almost 11,000 desiatins (over 29,000 acres).[27]

At the age of twenty-one, after graduating in 1888 from his father's alma mater, St. Petersburg's prestigious Imperial School of Jurisprudence, Alexander Jr. entered an elite cavalry regiment, the Imperial Life Guard. But his heart was never in the military. "To tell the truth," he confessed in his 1934 autobiography, "I occupied myself less with it than with high society life. I loved to dance, and danced everywhere." He cultivated a circle of acquaintances from the Russian and English aristocracy, whose idiosyncrasies and peccadilloes he recounts with evident enjoyment. He boasts of entertaining his guests with the best Gypsy ensembles, and of becoming a regular master of ceremonies at St. Petersburg balls—a position that "in those times was practically a serious occupation." At one of Alexander's own balls the lovesick son of the British ambassador attempted suicide. A quick visit by Alexander Jr. to the St. Petersburg chief of police kept the scandal out of the press.[28]

If Countess Panina intentionally brought Sofia and Alexander together at her dancing classes with hopes of a future marriage, her scheme

Alexander Polovtsov
Jr., circa 1907. (https://
ru.wikipedia.org)

was successful; the couple became engaged in the spring of 1890. As one might expect in an alliance of two wealthy, influential, and proud families, the elder generation played a considerable role in the match. Moreover, the couple was young; at eighteen years old Sofia was still under the guardianship of her grandmother, and Alexander was just four years older. Despite the families' similar social status, Countess Panina's acceptance of Alexander Polovtsov as Sofia's husband is still puzzling. First of all, the Polovtsovs were *nouveaux riches*. They traced their fortune not to land and serfs, the economic base of noble families like the Panins for centuries, but to the banking and entrepreneurial operations of a Jew, albeit a convert to Christianity. Seizing the capitalist opportunities offered in the late nineteenth century, the Polovtsovs speculated in industrial and mining enterprises, with mixed success. They were also *arrivistes*. Alexander Sr. counted members of the imperial family as friends, considered himself the emperor's confidant, and exerted some influence on policy through his work in the State Council. But his stature in the government could not compare to that of Sofia

Panina's illustrious grandfather and her other forebears. Marriage into such a distinguished noble line as the Panins must have held great appeal for the Polovtsovs. It is less clear what Countess Natalia Panina thought to gain from the alliance; perhaps Sofia played a greater role in choosing Alexander than her age and dependence on her grandmother would suggest.

An initial disagreement about marriage terms, and the court gossip it generated, hint at the interplay of ambition and family pride that influenced both sides. Having lost her only son and two of her four daughters to tuberculosis, Countess Panina wished for the Panin line to continue through her son's only child, Sofia. Alexander Sr. records in his diary that she asked his son to agree to become "Count Panin" when he married Sofia in order to prevent the extinction of the family name. He claims that he tried to talk the countess out of this idea. His son's version of the story similarly upholds the Polovtsovs' integrity. "The old lady Countess Panina went to the emperor (without telling me about this)," he explained, "and asked permission for me to be renamed Count Panin. The emperor deigned to consent, but I refused."[29]

A less flattering version of this story circulated in St. Petersburg society. Recognized by his contemporaries as a man of intelligence and administrative ability, Alexander Sr. was nevertheless disliked for his haughtiness and ambition. According to Minister of Finance Sergei Witte, Alexander Sr. had "a weakness for honors and titles" and gladly joined Countess Panina in wishing the Panin name and title to go to his son upon his marriage. But Alexander III refused to let Polovtsov's son bear such a worthy name. According to Witte, the emperor joked that if Polovtsov wished his son to be a count, Alexander Jr. could be called "Polovtsov-Count Petrunkevich"—a name "almost synonymous with the word 'revolutionary.'" Witte, a well-informed and malicious gossip, disliked the Polovtsov family. But friends of Sofia Panina mention similar rumors that the senior Polovtsov pursued the title of Count Panin for his son. If true, they point to both the insecurity of Alexander Sr.'s status as a court insider and the limits of his influence with the emperor.[30]

Sofia's future father-in-law did succeed in arranging what he and his son considered to be another prerequisite to this marriage: Sofia's appointment as a *demoiselle d'honneur* at the imperial court. The prestigious but purely symbolic position of maid of honor was a rite of passage for marriageable young ladies in the highest ranks of society; it entitled them to be invited to balls given by the emperor and empress.[31] Although maids of honor served only until they married, former maids of honor continued to be invited to all the court balls. One can imagine Alexander Jr., who "loved to dance," encouraging his father to help his fiancée obtain access to these most important events of the social season. Sofia's induction as a maid of honor probably resembled that of Nadine Wonlar-Larsky, who described it in her memoirs. The daughter of the minister of justice and the novelist Vladimir Nabokov's aunt, Nadine became a *demoiselle d'honneur* and was presented at court in 1900, ten years after Sofia. The excitement began when an imperial messenger brought her the letter of appointment and the maid of honor's *shiffre*: the empress's monogram in diamonds, "surmounted by a crown with a bow of the pale blue ribbon of the Order of St. Andrew." The most onerous of her duties, Nadine remembered, was wearing the official costume at court—a heavy dress of ruby-red velvet with gold embroidery and an awkward kokoshnik headdress of an old-fashioned Russian folk design.[32]

After a brief engagement Sofia and Alexander married in the afternoon on Sunday, April 22, 1890. All the major St. Petersburg newspapers printed short notices about the wedding, which was attended by a number of grand dukes and duchesses and "many invitees from the highest society of the capital."[33] Some sources claim that Alexander III stood in for Sofia's long-dead father and gave the eighteen-year-old bride away, but the official newspaper notices make no mention of the emperor's presence at the wedding.[34] From the chapel the newlyweds were driven to the Polovtsov mansion, where they received blessings from Alexander's parents and stood in the large second-floor ballroom to receive the congratulations of about two hundred guests. Sofia's mother was probably not among them. In a conversation with Alexander Sr. shortly after the wedding, the Empress Maria Feodorovna praised his daughter-in-law. "We are very happy with this marriage," he replied, but he added, "Only one shadow darkens the picture"—Sofia's mother.[35] Still banned from St. Petersburg, Sofia's parents continued to associate with other "unreliables" in Tver and to participate in local government affairs that Alexander III's government regarded as suspicious at best.

With the marriage, the Polovtsovs not only welcomed Sofia but gained control of her considerable assets, since she was still a minor. One month after the wedding Alexander Sr. visited the elderly countess, at which time the bride's capital was transferred to her new guardians— her husband and father-in-law.[36] Although the Polovtsovs were extremely wealthy themselves, the Panins' riches seem to have made a lasting impression. Years later Alexander Jr. remembered that his first wife "was considered to be and was in fact very rich."[37] Indeed she was. Sofia's own assets in cash, bonds, and other interest-bearing investments amounted to approximately half a million rubles. Her guardians also administered the capital she and her mother had inherited from Victor Panin, which totaled another half a million rubles. Upon her grandmother's death Sofia was due to inherit the rest of the Panin fortune, including properties and estates in St. Petersburg, the Crimea, Moscow, Voronezh, and other provinces.[38]

The marriage began happily, it seems. Writing to her friend Varya three months after the wedding, Sofia sounds giddy with excitement over her new life with "Sasha." The newlyweds spent several weeks in the elite St. Petersburg suburb of Tsarskoe Selo, she recounted, then traveled through Paris to London for their honeymoon. They arrived in the British capital, where Sasha had numerous acquaintances, just in time to catch the last week of the social season. Sofia saw "masses of interesting personalities" in London and enjoyed the whirl of theatrical performances, balls, and a garden party attended by Queen Victoria. "Now we want to see the races, and then—away from London," her letter breathlessly continued; "we want to go around Scotland and the Isle of Wight, [and] if we find a little corner that suits us, we will stay there and go swimming, [but] if not and if it's bad up north, we'll leave for the south to the Mediterranean." After attempting to console her friend for unspecified recent disappointments Varya had experienced, Sofia proclaimed herself to be "so, so happy, that no words can express it, [and] I more than ever wish happiness for others, I would like to teach everyone to value life while it is given us, and there is so, so much love in my heart, that it seems you could never use up even a hundredth part of it."[39]

In October 1891 Sofia and Alexander moved into their own home, a wedding present from his parents, located directly across the street from their own mansion. (In 1897 the house was sold to the mother of Vladimir Nabokov, who was born there. Today, Sofia's former home houses the Nabokov Museum.) One year later, Alexander retired from his regiment. He was bored by military life, he confessed in his autobiography, and feared that if he had stayed in his regiment he would never be useful to his country—or climb the "hierarchical ladder" of promotion.[40] In February 1892, shortly before Alexander entered civilian service at the Ministry of the Interior, he and Sofia traveled to Tambov, where his family had an estate. The purpose of this journey was quite different from their prior visits to Panin and Polovtsov estates around

Russia; this time, Sofia and Alexander were participants in the national relief movement that arose after a catastrophic crop failure struck Tambov and a number of other provinces in central Russia in late 1891. As news of mounting starvation and epidemic disease among the peasantry reached the capital and government relief efforts faltered, landowning nobles joined physicians, teachers, and other Russians from across the social spectrum to distribute aid in the stricken provinces. Alexander's brother-in-law was in charge of government relief efforts in Tambov. Writing decades after the event, Alexander still recalled the harrowing scenes he witnessed. The entire population of one tiny village, for example, lay ill with typhus, and "there was not a single person who could stand on his feet."[41]

Otherwise, the couple was kept busy by the responsibilities and pleasures that accompanied their social status. Writing to Varya from the Panins' Crimean estate of Gaspra in September 1893, for example, Sofia described their travels through the Caucasus and a pleasant journey across the Black Sea from the exotic port of Batumi to Yalta. While Sasha went on to attend to business on his estate in Voronezh, Sofia intended to stay in Gaspra until the end of October. Enjoying the marvelous weather, she played lawn tennis every day, socialized with neighbors, and read new books.[42] The following year, in a letter written to Varya just a few days before her friend's wedding, Sofia still sounded happy and in love with life. "Life is so good, and so few people know how to really love it, therefore so few understand how infinitely much life gives us," she wrote elatedly. "I wish with all my heart that you will always know the richness, the inexhaustibility of life, and all the infinite, limitless love that fills it and constitutes its *raison d'être*. I cannot wish you anything better than this."[43]

For all the *joie de vivre* they express, Sofia's letters to Varya also reveal a growing discontent with society's rules, rituals, and expectations. Women of their social class, she complained in 1893, were too quick to condemn others who strayed from their false notions of propriety, instead of extending a helping hand.[44] By the end of 1895 Sofia, after describing her irritation at the lack of organization at a Christmas charity bazaar, confessed to feeling "alienation" and dissatisfaction as she performed the customary rituals of the elite milieu to which she belonged; "with every year, with every month, I feel more and more strongly how the last threads of even external solidarity are being broken, and how very far I am being taken from this world."[45] Her estrangement seems to have reached a peak when she attended what undoubtedly was the most important social event of the decade: the coronation of Nicholas and Alexandra in Moscow in May 1896.[46] In Sofia's eyes the coronation festivities brought out the worst features of elite society. "If you are sorry that you did not get to Moscow," she told Varya, "please banish that regret, and thank God that this cup passed you by." Although the ceremonies were "magnificent," she was repelled by the surrounding atmosphere in Moscow. "The whole seamy side of the most vulgar Petersburg high society life displayed itself there without restraint and shame: gossip, squabbles, vanity, base servility and boorishness bloomed in all their splendor."[47]

Sofia's intensifying alienation may well have been related to the disintegration of her marriage to the charming and sociable Sasha. By the time she attended the coronation of Nicholas and Alexandra, their marriage had ended. They apparently separated sometime before the end of 1894. Sofia moved out of the couple's mansion and back into her grandmother's, while Alexander left St. Petersburg. Between 1894 and 1897 he carried out assignments from the Ministry of the Interior that sent him to distant regions of the empire—western Siberia, the Caucasus, and Central Asia—and kept him away from the capital for long periods of time. Sometime between 1894 and 1896 Sofia initiated divorce proceedings and resumed using her maiden name. To her credit, Countess Natalia Panina, for all her old-fashioned ways, welcomed her granddaughter back to her home. Although her hopes for continuing the Panin line through this marriage had crashed, she supported Sofia's decision to divorce Alexander. On March 4, 1896, the church granted Sofia a divorce, citing Alexander's adultery (*preliubodeianie*) as the grounds. They had no children. Alexander remarried in 1904, as soon as church law changed to permit remarriage by the guilty party in a divorce, but Sofia never married again—at least, not officially.[48]

It took courage and strength of character for a young woman in her early twenties to file for divorce at this time. Russian law placed married women under the absolute authority of their husbands, whose permission was required before they could obtain a passport, travel, work, or go to school. Formal marital separations were prohibited by law. Women who were estranged from their husbands found themselves still legally dependent upon them, despite some improvements in women's status in the 1890s. With respect to divorce, little had changed in the fifteen years since Ivan Petrunkevich had persuaded his wife to admit adultery so that he could marry Sofia's mother. By the 1890s divorce had become more common, especially on grounds of adultery, but still remained rare and difficult to obtain. Between 1896 and 1900 only slightly more than half of all petitions for divorce for reasons of adultery were granted. The church imposed stiff requirements for evidence of adulterous behavior, compelling some spouses to hire professional "divorce expediters" to stage acts of adultery with paid witnesses. Thus the whole process of divorce, though becoming somewhat easier in the 1890s, continued to cause great expense, distress, scandal, and public shame in Russia, as in Europe and the United States.[49]

While Sofia's growing alienation from the aristocratic social life her husband relished may have played a role, the main reason for her decision to end her marriage reveals just how bold her action was. Although the official reason was Alexander's adultery, Sofia sued Alexander for divorce because of his homosexuality.[50] Her suit reportedly created a noisy and nasty scandal, followed by almost universal silence about the marriage as well as the divorce in the writings of relatives and friends. Neither Sofia nor Alexander mentions their marriage in their memoirs or other autobiographical writings.[51] This silence makes it difficult to determine which was the greater cause of the scandal: Alexander's sexual orientation or Sofia's refusal to tolerate it. But the position of homosexuals in the *fin de siècle* Russian elite suggests that it was Sofia, not Alexander, who violated the conventions of their social circle when she sued for divorce.

Russian law imposed harsh criminal penalties on men who had sex with other men, but in actual practice sexual relations between men were widely tolerated and rarely prosecuted, especially when they involved upper-class men. Same-sex desire and sexual liaisons were particularly common among men of the elite and the officer corps in the 1880s and 1890s. At least seven grand dukes (the emperor's uncles, nephews, or cousins) were homosexual, including probably Alexander III's brother Grand Duke Sergei. Alexander Jr.'s own alma mater, the Imperial School of Jurisprudence, was well-known at the time for its homosexual subculture. One's same-sex relationships and orientation still had to be hidden and could cause personal torment, as they evidently did for the composer Peter Tchaikovsky and perhaps also for Grand Duke Sergei. But as the historian Dan Healey has argued, "society was habituated to the observance of discretion and concealment" and avoided such public exposés as the sensational trial of Oscar Wilde. "When that discretion was breached," Healey continues, "the miscreant used his connections to suppress scandals" before they could be prosecuted.[52] Thus it seems likely that Petersburg high society would have expected Sofia to remain in her marriage and accept her husband's relations with other men as long as he remained discreet. Other wives in her social class probably did. Why did Sofia take a step that brought so much public scandal and personal pain? The answer may lie in her character and upbringing, which may have made it difficult for her to remain in a marriage that rested on what could be interpreted as a lie. Her mother, whose conduct during her own liaison with Ivan Petrunkevich set an example of determination in defiance of public opinion and social convention, had taught her to abhor hypocrisy.

The emotional impact on Sofia of the failure of her marriage is difficult to determine. The only source—her letters to her girlhood friend Varya—are ambiguous and inconsistent. An unusually long letter written a few weeks after the divorce was granted conveys an impression of liberation after a difficult winter. Sofia recounts her annoyance at being confined all winter in Petersburg because of "all kinds of personal matters that demanded my presence, so that I could not absent myself, and it was troubling as well." But that was all behind her now, and "I feel like a free bird that has learned how to value its freedom!" The letter brims with plans for the future: visiting friends over the summer, traveling abroad with her grandmother in the fall, and nurturing the "little seed" she had sown the previous winter—Sunday readings she had organized for factory workers.[53] One year later, however, Sofia sent Varya a letter filled with anguish, although she does not identify the cause. Citing moments in her life, "or more accurately months and years," of extreme duress, Sofia confessed: "I myself do not know how I stayed alive and sane after them; in any case I was very close to suicide and insanity." The letter continues with a cry of complete hopelessness: "everything, absolutely everything, lay around me in ruins, and amidst all this chaos I was absolutely alone."[54] There are really only two times in her early life that were so traumatic as to cause almost suicidal despair: the forced separation from her mother in 1882, and the end of her marriage in 1894 or 1895. It seems likely that the latter event is what gave rise to the pain expressed in her 1897 letter to Varya.

In addition to its impact on her emotional well-being, divorce had powerful implications for Sofia's future. The humiliating scandal it aroused probably brought an end to her participation in the social activities of aristocratic St. Petersburg and effectively closed that world to her. After years of conforming to the scenario written by her grandmother, divorce forced her to reinvent herself at a young age when there were few alternative models available. As the aggrieved party she was not prohibited from remarrying, but the divorce cast a shadow on her reputation that may have affected perceptions of her suitability for remarriage.[55]

Sofia's wealth gave her an enviable measure of autonomy, however. In accordance with Russian law, which guaranteed married women's property rights, the Polovtsovs ceased to be Sofia's guardians on August 23, 1892, when she turned twenty-one and came into full control of her considerable fortune. Thus her situation as a divorcée did not cause her any material hardship. When other women's marriages ended, whether due to divorce, separation, abandonment, or death, they often plunged into great need. Even upper-class women could suffer, as in the case of Sofia's contemporary Ariadna Tyrkova-Williams, who later became her friend and political associate. After Tyrkova-Williams, a well-educated young woman from the provincial nobility, separated from her engineer husband (for reasons she does not explain), she had to earn a living to support herself and her two children. "I had no profession," Tyrkova-Williams recalled. "I felt myself very alone on the new road. . . . There were no beacons by which I could steer my course." The young woman who had enjoyed a life of comfort and a wardrobe full of Parisian frocks now lived primarily on meager earnings from articles written for provincial newspapers under a male pseudonym.[56]

Sofia initially occupied herself with extensive traveling: frequent stays with her parents or her Panin cousins at their country estates were interspersed with autumn months spent in the Crimea and regular trips abroad to Italy and German spa resorts. Writing Varya from Baden-Baden in July 1896, Sofia speculated that if she continued to spend long periods of time abroad, she would become a "bluestocking" because there, where "food for the heart" was lacking, she immersed herself in intellectual pursuits.[57] In fact, that May Sofia had submitted her application to the History and Philology Department of the Higher Women's Courses in St. Petersburg, commonly known as the Bestuzhev Courses and a breeding ground for Russian bluestockings. Competition for the entering class of 1896–97 was unusually stiff. Only women who had received gold or silver medals upon graduating from secondary school were admitted, and out of 550 applications that were submitted, only 150 were accepted—including Sofia's.[58] Thus in the fall of 1896 she embarked boldly on a course that many of her contemporaries regarded with intense disapproval—the pursuit of a formal higher education.

Russia seems an unlikely pioneer in women's higher education, considering its extremely low literacy rate, patriarchal legal system, and socially conservative government. By the early 1870s, however, the first institutions for women began accepting students. They owed their existence in part to determined efforts by early feminists and sympathetic male allies and in part to a change of heart in the government. The authorities decided that allowing women to continue their education in Russia was preferable to letting them study abroad, where they often fell in with socialists. Between 1872 and 1878 higher women's courses opened in four Russian cities, including St. Petersburg, where the Bestuzhev Courses were introduced in 1876. Although their graduates received no formal degree, the higher women's courses were women's colleges in all other respects. Founded by private initiative and supported entirely by tuition and donations, they were also an anomaly in a country where the state funded and ran all institutions of higher education for men. The institutions had two faculties or departments: History/Philology for students in the humanities, and Physics/Mathematics for students in the natural sciences and mathematics. Male professors taught the female students in the same kinds of courses they offered at regular universities; at the Bestuzhev Courses, for example, women students learned history from rising faculty stars at St. Petersburg University such as Nikolai Kareev, Ivan Grevs, and Michael Rostovtseff, who became a lifelong friend and taught ancient history at Oxford and Yale after leaving Russia in 1918.

Many of Sofia's contemporaries regarded the higher women's courses as the incubator of bluestockings, feminists, and socialists, and they condemned higher education for women as unnatural, immoral, or physically harmful. At Anna Zhukova's graduation from the Irkutsk Institute for Noble Girls, for example, the governor's wife denounced the Bestuzhev Courses as leading to "atheism" and "evil thoughts."[59] Elizaveta Diakonova, a young woman from a provincial merchant family who entered the Bestuzhev Courses the year before Sofia, had to overcome her mother's entrenched belief that its women students were little better than prostitutes.[60] For most of the 1880s, the Russian government agreed; in the aftermath of the assassination of Alexander II in 1881, it closed all the institutions for women except the Bestuzhev Courses, which survived under severe restrictions. By the time Sofia applied in 1896, higher education for women had gained momentum again. Over the next decade, all the closed institutions reopened and new ones were established. The numbers of applicants and graduates increased—quite dramatically in the case of the Bestuzhev Courses. Women graduates began to be hired as instructors and even professors.[61]

Graduation from the Catherine Institute with a gold *shiffre* had evidently not satisfied Sofia's intellectual curiosity. Even before applying to the Bestuzhev Courses she set out on a course of self-education, occasionally expressing frustration at having to devote too much time to dealing with petty everyday affairs and trying to satisfy the "stupid and ridiculous demands" of her elders and of "socializing."[62] Sofia devoured not only classics by writers like Stendhal, but works by nonconformist contemporaries such as the bohemian and sexual dissident Vernon Lee (born Violet Paget) and the German socialist August Bebel. In the spring of 1896, when she decided to resume her formal education, she excitedly confessed to Varya that attending the Bestuzhev Courses had long been her dream, though she begged her friend to tell no one that she was enrolling; there will be "masses of unpleasantness for me if anyone from the family or outside finds out"—especially her grandmother, with whom Sofia was living.[63] She may have been inspired by her stepcousin and lifelong friend Alexandra Petrunkevich (1873–1965), who entered the Bestuzhev Courses a year or two before Sofia and graduated with high honors in 1897. A specialist in European history, Alexandra continued her studies in Germany in the early 1900s and in 1908 returned to the Bestuzhev Courses as a member of the faculty.[64]

As it turned out, Sofia spent only a few years at the Bestuzhev Courses and never graduated. She began ambitiously in the fall of 1896 by enrolling in four classes, two each in history and philosophy. Although she continued taking classes during spring of 1897, in September she requested a change in her status from matriculated student to auditor. In her official letter to the director, she explained that she was now involved in "pedagogical activity" whose demands on her time made it difficult for her to fulfill the exam requirements. In late 1895 Sofia had started a project that increasingly competed with the Bestuzhev Courses for her time, the organization of popular Sunday readings for workers. These readings would soon become an integral part of the social work that came to dominate her life. In 1899 Sofia completely withdrew from the higher courses.[65]

Though relatively brief, Sofia's experience as a student had a liberating impact on her social and intellectual development, while also significantly advancing her political education. As a wealthy, titled divorcée, she stood out once again in the alien milieu of the Bestuzhev Courses. Almost all of her fellow students were unmarried, most came from the provinces, and many survived on extremely meager resources.[66] But Sofia dove into this new world with gusto, adapting quickly to the novel role of student and relishing the intellectual stimulation. She came into contact with young women from a wider range of social and economic backgrounds than she had previously known and found that many of them shared her feelings of liberation. Sofia's classmate Elizaveta Diakonova, for example, was exhilarated by the freedom she attained when she entered the Bestuzhev Courses, where she found "so much that is new! An endless panorama of life unfolds before you, inviting you to take part in this uninterrupted movement forward and forward."[67] Emerging from what she had come to regard as the stifling conventions of high society, Sofia entered a world enlivened by debates about the major issues of the day. In arguments about the proper role of women, feminist students advocating liberation clashed with those more interested in fashion and finding a husband. They heard professors lecture about the role of the intelligentsia in society, compare Russian and European law, and analyze the shortcomings of Russian agriculture. At student meetings socialists of different stripes debated with each other about Russia's future; idealists and radicals contended with materialists and pragmatists about the nature and speed of progress.

Sofia also learned firsthand about Russia's increasingly radical student movement. Women students were inspired to action by the same causes that ignited conflicts at this time between students and the administration at male-only institutions of higher education in the capital. In February 1897, on the eve of the anniversary of the abolition of serfdom in 1861, a dispute arose among students at the Bestuzhev Courses about whether to attend lectures on that day. Sofia did not sympathize with radicals who called for a boycott, rejecting as absurd their accusation that support for going to class meant a lack of sympathy for peasant emancipation. "There is a mass of cowardice and one's definite opinion isn't worth a penny," she complained to Varya. "Everyone is so afraid of being thought of as retrograde that they are afraid to say even a single word to contradict the radicals, and it ends up that only the latter speak."[68] This dispute over how to commemorate a historic event was no doubt inflamed by shocking news received by students and faculty at the Bestuzhev Courses at about the same time. Maria Vetrova, a twenty-seven-year-old student who had been arrested at the end of 1896 for revolutionary activity, set herself on fire on February 8 using kerosene from the lamp in her prison cell. Her death inspired a demonstration along St. Petersburg's main avenue that involved several thousand male and female students. Annual demonstrations in Maria Vetrova's memory continued for several years afterward.[69]

Two years later, in 1899, as Sofia began what turned out to be her last term, student radicalism reached a crescendo. On the traditional holiday commemorating the founding of St. Petersburg University, a snowy February day, students in a festive mood suddenly encountered mounted police intent on curtailing their customarily raucous celebrations. This time the police used their whips on the demonstrators, prompting a chorus of outrage at this gross violation of university students' status and civil rights. Outrage turned into protest meetings at higher education institutions across the city, liberal circles voiced their support of the aggrieved students, and in a matter of a few days, the nation's students went on strike.[70] Although Sofia's official letter of withdrawal cited the competing demands of her "pedagogical activity" as her reason for leaving the Bestuzhev Courses, the tense political situation in early 1899 was at least as important a factor. "I will probably quit the courses," she told her confidante Varya. "The fact is that there, as at other higher educational institutions, there are reprisals and utter havoc." Sofia was outraged by the dismissal of "all the best and most engaged of the students," and the two history professors—Grevs and Kareev—she most respected. "In such circumstances" she continued, "it is senseless and unpleasant to remain in the courses. I will send in my withdrawal, although I am terribly sorry to part with the nice life of a student. But what can you do when they defile it!" Sofia also noted how counterproductive the government's repressive actions were. "Almost all the students I know are not being taken back and are going abroad to finish their education. Does our government really want that?"[71] In addition to history and philosophy, the Bestuzhev Courses taught Sofia some basic lessons about the nature of the Russian government.

Although her dream of obtaining a higher education was unrealized, Sofia continued to support the same educational opportunities for other women. She became a life member of the Society for Obtaining Funds for the Higher Women's Courses in St. Petersburg, the voluntary association that raised funds and ran the Bestuzhev Courses. Elected to serve on the society's board from 1899 to 1901, Sofia also helped the institution financially during a time of rapid expansion by providing an interest-free loan that enabled the society to construct a new science and lecture building.[72] Sofia also maintained ties with some of her professors, such as the historians Grevs and Rostovtseff, long after she left.[73] But when she left the "nice life of a student," she also turned away from direct involvement in any organization or cause with overt political implications. Political radicalism, she observed, resulted in "havoc" and repression, threatening the continued existence of valuable institutions such as the Bestuzhev Courses. It was quiet work on behalf of educational and cultural progress, she evidently concluded, that promised more lasting results.

Sofia spent more than a decade in the world of the St. Petersburg aristocracy as an *institutka*, a debutante, and then a society bride. Proving remarkably adaptable and forgiving, she lived in her grandmother's mansion, accompanied the old lady on her travels to European spas, and grew close to the extended Panin family, once her mother's bitter enemies. As she moved from girlhood to young womanhood she also achieved all the indicators of social success her grandmother could have wished—graduation with honors, presentation at the imperial court, and marriage to a wealthy, handsome young officer from an influential family. Once she reached adulthood, however, she found these attainments hollow, and it became increasingly difficult to live according to the values of this elite world. Sofia had entered the Catherine Institute as the powerless object of a personal and political struggle between conservative and progressive forces within her family and the larger society. Even there, while conforming to the institute's traditional norms and flourishing both academically and socially, she began to develop her own moral sense, and to show early signs of an innate spirit of self-determination. When her grandmother's plan for her granddaughter and heir came crashing down, Sofia once again demonstrated the resilience that she had shown upon entering the institute. This time she was no longer the eleven-year-old victim of a struggle between her elders; she had grown into a self-possessed young woman who would have her own say.

Wealthy and independent, the young divorcée turned away from the glitter and opulence of aristocratic society to join a controversial new social group in *fin de siècle* Europe—the "New Women." Raised by parents who believed in the importance of being useful to society, Sofia sought to create a life of purpose and meaning after her marriage ended. For Sofia as for many other young women of her generation, marriage and conventional socializing were no longer the only options. The 1890s offered them unprecedented opportunities for education, employment, and social activism. Economic growth in the late nineteenth century rapidly transformed Russia from an agricultural nation into an industrial power. With modern amenities such as electric streetcars and telephones, its major cities were becoming metropolises filled with thriving industrial, commercial, and cultural enterprises. Newspapers, journals, and book publishing proliferated, while the formation of scientific societies, philanthropic associations, and social clubs expanded Russian civil society. New educational institutions opened, from primary schools to specialized technical institutes and women's colleges like the Bestuzhev Courses. Waves of migrants swelled the population of cities like St. Petersburg, creating a desperate need for more housing, schools, and social services.

Young women seized the opportunities all these changes created. They flooded women's colleges and medical schools with applications; pursued jobs as teachers and telegraph operators; and opened libraries, temperance societies, children's shelters, and Sunday readings for workers. They formed women's organizations to pursue legal and moral reforms and obtain greater rights. Before the eyes of a shocked public, they broke away from physically constrictive social conventions and demonstrated their zest for life by learning to ride a bicycle, as Sofia did under the wary but compliant gaze of her grandmother during the summer they spent together in Baden-Baden.[74] Sofia was still in her twenties when she turned her back on aristocratic society, resumed her education, and took her first steps as a social worker. Disillusioned by both marriage and the government's actions against women's higher education, she found her true calling amid workers and peasant immigrants living in one of the grimmest industrial districts of St. Petersburg—the city she later described as "fated to become the stern master and sovereign of my life."[75]

4

The People's House

Sofia was nineteen years old and recently married when she received a visit from a St. Petersburg schoolteacher twenty years her senior. Tiny, slender Alexandra Peshekhonova was unprepossessing in appearance, with a round face and hair pulled back into a tight little bun. But her confident manner and large, luminous gray eyes made a powerful impression on Sofia. Alexandra came to her with a request: would the countess help her build a free cafeteria for the schoolchildren in her impoverished district? No doubt other strangers had approached the wealthy young aristocrat to ask for donations to various charitable causes, but something about this encounter was different. Many decades later Sofia, in her late seventies and living in the United States, underscored its life-altering significance when she sat down to write about her social work in reminiscences she titled *On the Outskirts of Petersburg* ["Na peterburgskoi okraine"]. "There are minutes in life, seemingly completely insignificant," she began her memoir, "which nonetheless, unbeknownst to us ourselves, predetermine our future. In my life meeting Alexandra Vasilievna Peshekhonova was just exactly such an event."[1]

Alexandra's visit to Sofia in 1891 initiated a collaboration that endured for a quarter of a century. Their partnership combined the schoolteacher's intimate knowledge of the city's poor with the heiress's ample funds and boundless energy. Together they created one of the best-known educational and cultural institutions in St. Petersburg, the Ligovsky People's House, which opened its doors in 1903. With its resemblance to settlement houses and similar institutions for worker enlightenment in Europe and the United States, the people's house helped bring Russia into the mainstream of international progressive philanthropy in the early twentieth century. The spacious red brick structure Sofia built on the city's southern edge also functioned as a self-contained world under her benevolent leadership. There, guided by her older mentor Alexandra and empowered by seemingly unlimited funds, Sofia could implement the credo she gradually formulated to guide her public life. It emphasized the universal power of knowledge and culture—the formal knowledge and high culture of educated Russians, that is, not the survival skills or pastimes of the lower classes—to transform all people regardless of their lowly station. Sofia consistently rejected any political implications of her social activism, insisting that the work her people's house did was above politics. She never envisioned a society that transcended or erased class differences. Instead, she dedicated herself and her fortune to bringing gradual progress to backward Russia by guiding the unschooled working-class inhabitants of the imperial capital in the process of becoming informed, independently thinking men and women.[2]

Alexandra Peshekhonova was an unlikely source of inspiration for Sofia, and the circumstances surrounding that first encounter in 1891 are unknown. The two women were separated not only by age but also social class, financial resources, and life experience. Alexandra, born in St. Petersburg in 1852, came from a family of skilled artisans and traders. Departing from the conventions of their traditional milieu, her parents sent their lively daughter to one of the new secondary schools that began opening in the 1850s and 1860s for girls of all classes, and then to the Alarchin Courses, the first advanced educational institution for women in St. Petersburg, which opened in 1869. There she completed the course of study that qualified her to be a schoolteacher, and in 1882 she was hired as a teacher in the city's primary schools.[3]

Alexandra's school was an urban Russian version of the one-room schoolhouse, introduced in St. Petersburg in 1877 as part of a nationwide effort by municipal governments to provide elementary education to an overwhelmingly illiterate population. One teacher lived at the school and taught all three grades, developing a familiarity with the pupils, their parents, and the conditions in which they lived. Until her death in 1932 Alexandra lived and worked in the same area of the city, an outlying neighborhood south of the center called Ligovka because of its main geographical feature, the fetid Ligovsky Canal (eventually filled in to become Ligovskaya Street), and considered to be one of the city's worst neighborhoods. She never married—female schoolteachers in St. Petersburg, as in many American towns, could not keep their positions if they married—but taught school until her retirement in 1908. She continued to run the library at the Ligovsky People's House until 1923, her modest social origins protecting her from persecution by the revolution that forced Sofia to flee the institution and city she loved.[4]

Today a short car ride takes one from the Moscow Railroad Station in central St. Petersburg along Ligovsky Prospect to Alexandra's neighborhood and the Ligovsky People's House, still operating under the name of the Railroad Workers' Palace of Culture. But a century ago geographical barriers like the Obvodny Canal accentuated the district's social and cultural isolation from the city's glittering imperial center. "The route to here from the center of the city is not short," one newspaper reporter commented in his report on the opening of the people's house in 1903. "One has to go for a long time along muddy, lonely streets, completely unlike those to whose appearance we are accustomed in our capital." The neighborhood's many saloons and crooked wooden houses with their broken windows advertised the poverty and vices of its inhabitants. "On the edge of the horizon," the reporter continued, "tall, eternally smoking factory chimneys pour their smoke into the sky." The district's stables, workshops, taverns, railroad yards, and factories provided employment for an ethnically homogeneous, overwhelmingly lower-class population of artisans, day laborers, and petty traders, most of whom were peasant migrants from the Russian countryside. Sofia called them "the poorest and darkest strata of the urban population," although workers at the new factories in the district, such as the San Galli metal fabrication plant and the Triangle Rubber Works, constituted what she wryly termed the district's "local intellectual aristocracy."[5] In fact, the area's inhabitants were not as backward as Sofia suggests: the literacy rate of the entire population six years or older was sixty percent, and over three-quarters of males and almost two-thirds of the females aged six to twenty were literate in 1900—reflecting the progress Russia was making in elementary education thanks to schools like Alexandra's.[6]

As a Petersburg native and long-time teacher in the neighborhood, Alexandra possessed an intimate knowledge of this population's needs and aspirations. For Sofia, this part of the city was terra incognita, and she needed Alexandra to be her guide. As their collaboration developed so did Sofia's social consciousness, in parallel with the rising working-class radicalism she observed in the capital during the 1890s. "Many arrests have taken place in Petersburg lately, mainly because of the social movement among workers," she reported to her friend Varya in late 1895. "For this reason I have had the opportunity to hear curious things about their development that have very much surprised me. I somehow had not imagined our worker being attracted to Marx!"[7] Six months later, after the first major strike in the capital in twenty-five years ended with some gains by the workers, she expressed wonderment not only at the tens of thousands of strikers, but also at the order and calm with which they presented their demands. "It's practically like Europe!" she exclaimed to Varya.[8]

Alexandra and Sofia had no preconceived plan to guide their work, nor was the project that became the people's house part of an over-arching ideology about transforming the political or social order. Whenever Sofia recounted its origins, she insisted that the people's house grew spontaneously and organically as she and Alexandra worked with the area's children and adults during the 1890s. "Life around us," she claimed, "knocked loudly and insistently at our doors," and they invented ways to respond to the needs they discovered.[9] Their original project, the cafeteria for pupils at Alexandra's primary school that opened in October 1891, became the nucleus around which additional services and facilities grew. With their parents at work all day, the children had no place to spend time after school other than on the streets "in the cold, mud, and darkness of the early Petersburg winter evenings," Sofia recounted. So she and Alexandra decided to keep the cafeteria open after school. When the children's parents and older siblings came to pick them up, they began to ask for "something to read," or "something to listen to or look at," and in late 1895 Sofia and Alexandra began to hold Sunday readings from literature illustrated with magic lantern slides. Regular contact with these adult visitors convinced the two women of the need for a library, a tea room, and finally evening classes for adults, the latter opening in 1900. As the services multiplied and outgrew their crowded rented quarters, Sofia and Alexandra began to dream of a purpose-built structure to house them all and provide the ability to expand still further.[10]

There is nothing particularly original about the children's cafeteria, Sunday readings, or other services that the two women organized in the 1890s, or the people's house they eventually constructed. People's houses, evening courses, and popular recreational facilities for workers first appeared in Russia in the late nineteenth century, many of them established by temperance advocates seeking to lure the masses away from the tavern and other alcohol-soaked leisure activities with tea and alcohol-free entertainment.[11] Similar initiatives were established in European and American cities, beginning with London's famous Toynbee Hall, which opened in 1884—institutions that sought to elevate the minds and morals of the urban poor through what was termed "rational recreation," and to construct a social bridge between educated, affluent society and the working class. Sofia was familiar with these foreign institutions and even visited Toynbee Hall in 1899. Viewed from this perspective, she and Alexandra were part of an international movement for social and cultural reform that stretched from Chicago's Hull House and New York's Henry Street Settlement across the Atlantic to London, Brussels, and Berlin, all the way to St. Petersburg.[12]

But like many founders of philanthropic enterprises, Sofia emphasized the uniqueness of her project rather than its commonalities with other institutions and never cited any Western philanthropic or cultural institution as her model.[13] Notwithstanding the capital's apparently well-behaved strikers in 1896, she believed that Russia's urban lower classes were much more backward than their Western counterparts. Foreign models seemed irrelevant considering the material and cultural deprivations endured by the people with whom she and Alexandra worked.[14] At the same time Sofia drew a distinction between her approach to working with the urban poor and that of fellow educated Russians. Members of the intelligentsia, she argued, for all their dedication to social betterment, were led by their own values of asceticism and self-sacrifice to concentrate their efforts on instruction, and to disdain the equally important need of the lower classes for entertainment and joy. "I believe that the decisive moment and influence in a person's life," Sofia insisted in *On the Outskirts of Petersburg*, "is not work but the leisure time after work. Only in the hours of leisure is there a place for love and joy, for that which turns a robot into a human being and a human being into an individual." Sofia also distanced herself from temperance advocates, who in Russia as elsewhere concerned themselves with how the masses spent their leisure. While deeply concerned about the cultural wasteland that workers in the Ligovka neighborhood inhabited, neither

Sofia nor Alexandra ever named temperance as one of their goals. Instead, she insisted, social reformers must address the poor's "hunger and thirst for joy" and their human need for beauty. Her institution would create a "new symbiosis" of education and entertainment.[15]

Working with Alexandra occupied Sofia during much of 1895 and 1896 and no doubt helped her overcome the pain of her failed marriage. "I am thoroughly occupied with the organization of extracurricular popular readings on the premises of my children's cafeteria," she reported to Varya in February 1896, one month before her divorce was granted, "and I am becoming terribly enamored of this prospect." Not content to participate only by funding the project, she added, "I want to pour my very flesh and blood into the work. Masses of plans are whirling in my head about how these readings could gradually expand." The idealistic young countess exulted in "the possibility of spreading light and warmth around one, even if only in minimal doses! To be the best part of a human heart and . . . ignite in this heart the fire of the highest, most pure ecstasies and aspirations!"[16] In late summer of that year, Sofia spent a merry few weeks with her Panin relatives, the Levashovs and Viazemskys, at the estate of Lotarevo, where her cousin Missy's husband Prince Leonid Viazemsky raised prize-winning racehorses. While enjoying the fresh air of the steppe and amateur theatricals with her cousins, she nonetheless confessed to being eager for the start of winter, when she would return to the city and the projects that engaged her. "I wish," she exclaimed exuberantly, "that every young person of our generation would make it their first priority to sow the same little seed in whatever corner of Russia, and call it to life and light; how infinitely much can be accomplished by such private initiative!"[17]

Lessons she learned as she dealt with suspicious authorities and official constraints tempered some of this enthusiasm. Any expansion of her project, she admitted to Varya, "of course has to be [done] very quietly and modestly, because it is necessary to deal with the unbelievably stupid and contrary Commission; when they all quiet down and forget about our existence, then we will begin to stretch our little wings." The commission was an official body that oversaw all public readings and libraries and maintained a very restricted catalog of approved books. It caused Sofia considerable frustration as she planned the program on history for the Sunday readings in the winter of 1895–96. But by the end of 1896 she could report that she had better relations with the commission's new director, and the readings were going "splendidly."[18]

The year 1899 represents a major milestone in the evolution of Sofia's philanthropy. Withdrawing completely that spring from the Bestuzhev Courses to focus on her social work, in June she gained virtually un-limited financial means to implement the "masses of plans" in her head when her grandmother died at age eighty-nine. During the final years of the ailing countess's life, Sofia had grown closer and more attached to her, traveling with her to the European spas the old lady loved and tending to her during her illnesses. Mourning her death, Sofia also took on heavy duties as her heir. Not yet thirty years old, she became the owner of the equivalent of a large business enterprise, comprised of landed estates in several provinces, urban properties, bonds and other investments, and the Panins' extensive art collection. Although a busi-ness office managed the properties and other assets, Sofia confessed to being overwhelmed by "the mass of obligations and the enormous re-sponsibility that have landed on me." Would she be able to handle them, she wondered, and was she worthy of such a fortune? "Will I be able to return in full even those five talents that I have received," she asked Varya, "when I would like so passionately to give back a hundredfold for all that I possess!"[19] Despite such self-doubts, Sofia moved quickly to direct her inheritance to the project she and Alexandra had dreamed about for almost a decade—the construction of a building to house the expanding services they were providing to the residents of Ligovka. In 1900 she used her inheritance to purchase several properties on adja-cent streets in the neighborhood where the two women had been work-ing for almost a decade. After the ramshackle buildings on these sites were demolished, she employed an architect and embarked on the usu-ally difficult process of obtaining government permission to open an educational and cultural institution for workers.[20]

There is a certain fictional quality to this story of the heiress who devotes her fortune to the inhabitants of a slum. A striking parallel, in fact, exists between Sofia and the heroine of a once renowned, now mostly forgotten Victorian novel, Walter Besant's 1882 bestseller *All Sorts and Conditions of Men: An Impossible Story*. The novel's central char-acter is Angela Messenger, a twenty-year-old heiress and England's richest woman. Angela disguises herself as a seamstress and lives in London's East End among the workers whose grinding labor produced her wealth. Observing their cultural impoverishment, Angela pledges her inheritance to the creation of a "Palace of Delight" for workers. Fic-tion turned into reality in 1887 when Besant, with the financial help of a brewery magnate, built one of Victorian London's most famous cultural institutions, the grand People's Palace on Mile End Road.[21] Perhaps the novel, which was translated into Russian under a more titillating title, *The Wealthy Heiress's Secret*, helped to inspire Sofia. When she visited London in 1899, she must have heard about the People's Palace, with its grand art galleries, lecture series, and offerings of "rational" entertainment; perhaps she visited it as well. Unlike Angela she did not disguise herself as a working woman when she entered the Ligovka neighborhood. But at least one of Sofia's contemporaries remarked on the parallel between her and Besant's heroine, and on the similarity between Sofia's people's house and Angela's dream of a "crystal palace" for London workers. Like the novel's heroine, Sofia saw art and beauty as one antidote to urban poverty and ignorance, and she also believed that the poor deserved joy and pleasure no less than the rich.[22]

To realize her dream, Sofia had to overcome significantly greater obstacles than any English heiress, fictional or real, thanks to the Russian government's censorship policies and the legal strictures it placed on all forms of public initiative. Trade unions and political parties were prohibited in Russia until 1906. Charitable societies and institutions were legal but could not exist without prior government authorization, which could take years to obtain. It took the founders of a people's house in Kiev, for example, fifteen years to plan, obtain approval for, and build their institution.[23] Tsarist authorities were particularly suspicious of philanthropic projects that involved urban workers, with their potential for promoting strikes or other unrest, or that might be a front for socialist organizations. As Sofia herself learned while running her Sunday readings for workers, organizers of all forms of mass education or entertainment were required to obtain official permission, and to use only books and plays that were on the government's approved list.

Yet it took only months instead of years for the Petersburg municipal government and the city commandant to grant Sofia's petition for permission to build a people's house on her newly acquired property.[24] The explanation for the ease with which Sofia obtained approval for the people's house may lie in her status and connections. Although the state security police began collecting information about Sofia in 1902, there is no evidence that they considered her or her project a threat to public order or political orthodoxy. Surveillance reports in Sofia's dossier briefly note her contacts with individuals whose correspondence the police monitored, but the dossier surprisingly omits her mother's reputation for political unreliability and her stepfather's decades-long record of opposition to the government. Instead, the police noted her connections to two high-ranking individuals with close ties to the court: Princess Evgenia Oldenburgskaya, who was related to the imperial family, and Prince Viazemsky, the director of the imperial family's landholdings and a member of the State Council, who was married to Sofia's cousin Missy. The police identified both as Sofia's collaborators in the project to build a people's house, although other sources do not mention any direct involvement by either of them in the project.[25]

Nor does Sofia's own account of the founding of the Ligovsky People's House make reference to any highly placed supporters. In fact, she barely mentions herself. Instead, she represents the institution as the result of a joint effort with Alexandra in which the schoolteacher, not the heiress, took the lead. It is no exaggeration to say that Sofia— rich, young, and attractive—idolized the diminutive Alexandra. "In my entire long life," she recalled decades later, "I have never since met a person who so harmoniously combined the best human qualities of mind, will, enthusiasm, practicality and administrative ability, self-possession and capacity for work."[26] Such deep admiration of Alexandra suggests that as Sofia became an adult, she turned to the older woman not only as a mentor, but also for the fulfillment of her need for someone to love and admire. An artfully posed studio photograph, probably taken in 1913, depicts the relationship of the two women at least as eloquently as Sofia's words, while underscoring the inversion of social status that defined their respective roles. A fond smile playing on her lips, Sofia gazes with total concentration at Alexandra's smaller figure, while the latter turns from Sofia to look steadily, even sternly into the camera. Although it was Sofia who supplied the funds that built the people's house, in the photo her hands are empty; it is Alexandra who holds some kind of text, suggesting that she, not her younger associate, was the author of their joint project.

Similarities between Alexandra and Sofia's mother, who were almost the same age, provide additional insight into Sofia's attachment. Both possessed some of the qualities that Sofia admired in members of that generation: their honesty and idealism, for example, and their passion for social betterment. Alexandra may also have offered to Sofia a kind of substitute for maternal guidance, since Anastasia continued to center her life on her husband and his rising political career. In 1903 Ivan and Anastasia traveled to Switzerland to participate in founding the Union of Liberation, Russia's first liberal political association. During the revolution that erupted two years later, Ivan stood at the center of political strife—addressing meetings, conferring with government ministers,

Sofia and Alexandra Peshekhonova, circa 1913. (Tsentral'nyi gosudarstvennyi arkhiv
kinofotofonodokumentov g. Sankt-Peterburga, G7538)

and leading the transformation of the Union of Liberation from an
underground, illegal circle into Russia's most important nonsocialist
political movement, the Constitutional Democratic or Kadet Party,
founded in 1905. As the Kadet Party's first chairman, Ivan came to be
recognized as the father of Russian liberalism.

Ariadna Tyrkova-Williams, the only female member of the Kadet
Party's central committee before 1917, observed Sofia's parents many
times at party meetings held at their elegant Petersburg apartment. Her
acerbic recollections of their relationship suggest that it may have been
difficult for Sofia to gain much of her mother's attention at this time.
Members of the party central committee sat around the Petrunkeviches'
huge dining table, set with crystal vases and laden with cakes, wines,
and other expensive treats, Tyrkova-Williams recalled. Tall, stately, and
still beautiful in her fifties, Anastasia treated her guests with gracious
hospitality. But she herself never sat at the table. She took her place
against the wall, behind Ivan's chair, and remained quiet until someone dared to object to Ivan's opinions. Then she leapt into the debate,

exclaiming at the dissident's temerity and hotly defending her husband's position. Still as impetuous and passionate as in her youth, she "took everything ardently to heart, and could at any moment unexpectedly blaze up and say a lot of unnecessary things." But all it took was for Ivan to look over his spectacles at her "with his hard, dark eyes," and she immediately fell silent. Anastasia regarded her husband as a hero, Tyrkova-Williams observed. "She not only surrounded his everyday life with small attentions, carefully thought out comforts . . . but what was much more important, she created a cult to him, raised him on a pedestal, thanks to which this average person seemed to many to be much taller than his actual height." Tyrkova-Williams considered Anastasia the more talented of the two, but she was so completely wrapped up in her husband that she never developed her abilities.[27]

Yet Tyrkova-Williams seems wrong to limit Anastasia's importance for the Kadet Party to the care and adulation she lavished on its founder. As Victor Panin's coheir with Sofia, she inherited a sizable portion of his estate when Countess Natalia Panina died in 1899. It seems quite likely that this inheritance enabled Anastasia to become one of the sources of financial support for the liberal cause, beginning with the illegal newspaper *Liberation* that Ivan cofounded in 1900 and culminating in the Kadet Party. Thus the old countess's fears that the Panin fortune would end up funding anti-government organizations may well have been realized twenty years after she had warned Emperor Alexander III of her daughter-in-law's political unreliability.[28]

Despite Anastasia's preoccupation with her husband, there is no evidence of any estrangement between mother and daughter. On the contrary, Anastasia approved of Sofia's social work and rejoiced in the friendship between her daughter and Alexandra. When the Ligovsky People's House celebrated its tenth anniversary in 1913, Anastasia wrote Alexandra a loving letter of congratulation. After praising the institution's contributions to the liberal movement led by her husband, she thanked Alexandra for introducing "this great good work" into her daughter's life. "I can only thank God," she continued, "for the happy coincidence of your paths that made you the guiding spirit of her life." Having defied aristocratic conventions herself, Anastasia could have had few regrets when her daughter left high society to work in St. Petersburg's slums. Her letter indicates joy, and perhaps also relief, that Sofia, guided by another member of her idealistic generation, had found a worthy purpose for her life—one that Anastasia interpreted as contributing to Ivan's cause of reforming the Russian political system.[29]

The enormous credit that both Sofia and her mother gave to Alexandra Peshekhonova for the creation of the Ligovsky People's House cannot obscure the fact that the institution simply would not have existed without Sofia's inheritance and her willingness to spend it unstintingly. It was Sofia who purchased the land for the institution and she who engaged the services of architect Yuly Benois, a member of a dynasty of prominent St. Petersburg architects and artists that included his cousin Alexander, the renowned designer for Diaghilev's *Ballets Russes*. Sofia had used his services to renovate the house she had purchased around 1901 on aristocratic Sergievskaya Street, where she moved from the Panin mansion several years later.[30] Working with Sofia and Alexandra, Benois designed an ensemble of two spacious, three-story red brick buildings for the large lot she had purchased at the corner of Tambovskaya and Prilukskaya Streets one block from Ligovskaya Street. In addition to purchasing the land, Sofia paid the entire construction cost of approximately 400,000 rubles, or about 200,000 US dollars by the exchange rate of that time (and approximately $6 million today).[31] Designed at a time when exuberant Russian historicism and Art Nouveau were the dominant trends, the architecture of the two buildings of the people's house combined sober, utilitarian functionality and minimal ornamentation with balanced, harmonious proportions. The most striking element of the main building is its tall windows, especially the enormous arched window on the second floor above a graceful wrought iron entryway. Unlike Hull House, which adopted a cosy domestic style, or Toynbee Hall, with its nostalgic resemblance to an English vicarage, there is no mistaking the Ligovsky People's House for a real home. Benois's design also rejected the grandeur of Besant's People's Palace in London, with its soaring dome over an ornate reading room. The institutional design of the new building more resembled a railroad station, while its red brick construction echoed the many factories that dotted the city's industrial landscape.

Despite its austerity and relative lack of architectural originality, Sofia's edifice amazed contemporaries. Much of the reason lay in the stark contrast between its imposing ensemble and the surrounding neighborhood of tenements and workshops, which dramatized the incongruity of building such a fine structure to serve the poor. One reporter remarked how "the buildings of the People's House appear like some kind of wondrous castle out of a fairy tale, a cathedral of light, a crystal palace, with its gigantic windows that take up almost the entire wall." The institution not only projected order, harmony, and rationality,

The Ligovsky People's House, circa 1903. (Rossiiskii institut istorii iskusstv, St. Petersburg, Kabinet rukopisei, f. 32, op. 1, ed. khr. 117/3)

but also reminded its contemporaries of a utopian social vision. Progressive Russians associated the vision of a "crystal palace," first evoked by the one constructed for the 1851 Great Exhibition in London, with utopia ever since Nikolai Chernyshevsky's radical novel *What Is to Be Done* (1863) popularized the image during the era of reforms and nascent radical movements in the 1860s. It also attracted admiration for its modern amenities, including electricity and the latest heating, ventilation, and fire prevention systems. In its design, industrial construction materials, spaciousness, and up-to-date technology the building symbolized Sofia's goal of bringing the residents of a Petersburg working-class slum out of darkness and backwardness into light and modernity.

The new institution was dedicated before a joyful crowd on Easter Sunday, April 7, 1903, "amidst the sounds of Easter bells," Sofia recalled fondly ten years later.[32] It contained a theater that could seat more than eight hundred people, cafeterias and tea rooms for several hundred children and adults, two libraries, spaces for classrooms and recreational activities, a savings bank, and an office providing legal aid.

One year later an astronomical observatory opened on the roof, giving the city its first public telescope. By housing activities for both children and adults, the main building provided working-class families with a refuge from their overcrowded apartments. This was not a settlement house with residential space where upper- or middle-class young men and women lived; the entire space of the building was devoted to the use of the working-class visitors.[33] The interior of the main building contrasted with its austere exterior, serving to convey Sofia's aim of using beauty to promote intellectual and moral education. The spacious foyer, broad staircases, and second-floor hall were painted in shades of pink or blue, with ornate bronze light fixtures. The theater's crystal chandeliers and art nouveau decoration above the stage added aesthetic touches. Sofia and her coworkers used these interior spaces to develop visitors' pride in their own Russian cultural and intellectual heritage while at the same time increasing their knowledge of the wider world. Russian and European paintings, portraits of Russian writers, and marble sculptures Sofia purchased in Italy adorned the walls and corridors. Rotating exhibits of pictures and artifacts presented information about special topics such as the Arctic, the oceans, and countries around the world. Sofia's decision to display Russia's and Europe's cultural heritage side by side conveyed her message that despite its political or economic backwardness, Russia by virtue of its high culture had earned its place as part of the West.[34]

The people's house offered an array of activities to relieve the cultural poverty and joyless existence of adults and children from the surrounding neighborhood. In addition to the original cafeteria and a library for children, the institution provided day care, an after-school program, and special entertainments for its youngest visitors. There were classes for adolescents who had finished primary school but were too young to begin work or an apprenticeship. The girls in the "Handicraft Classes" received lessons in sewing, Russian, arithmetic, drawing, and "*mirovedenie*"—knowledge of the wider world, in order to stimulate their "interest in life around them, to teach them to relate thoughtfully to the phenomena of life, to develop and support habits of rational reading, [and] send them into life with at least some consciousness of personal responsibility and a feeling of duty." The boys who attended the "Instructional Workshop" were trained to become "knowledgeable and intelligent" factory workers. The curriculum included drafting, drawing, and geometry as well as history, geography, and "*mirovedenie*"; in the third year, boys learned physics and mechanics while also receiving instruction from master craftsmen. In keeping with Sofia's philosophy about the importance of art and culture, the boys were taken on excursions and organized their own literary and musical presentations.[35] With social and economic mobility still limited in prerevolutionary Russia, the classes did not pretend to prepare children to ascend out of the working class. Sofia and her coworkers envisioned an economic future for these children that combined the probability that they would earn their livelihood in gender-segregated manual labor—the sewing trades for women, artisanal or factory work for the men—with the aim of preparing them for material security. But the classes had higher expectations for the children's moral future; although Sofia did not employ the term "citizenship," she still expected girls as well as boys to become independent, thinking adults capable of assuming their responsibilities as contributing members of society, even within the confines of Russia's still authoritarian political system.

While the people's house provided children of the district with cultural enrichment and a chance to see beyond the borders of their slum environs, its primary focus was on their parents and older siblings. As Sofia had hoped, adult visitors came to the Ligovsky People's House primarily for relaxation and entertainment. Open every day, the cafeteria and tearoom received tens of thousands of visits a year. On Sundays and holidays, one admiring reporter recounted, the tearoom filled with workers and their families, who came "to 'drink tea with the family,' take a rest from their cramped, stuffy corners, look at the pictures, read a newspaper."[36] The Sunday and holiday readings filled the theater with an average of several hundred attendees. Although most featured readings from Russian and foreign literature, topics also included geography, historical events, scientific subjects such as the undersea world and "how people sail through the air," and very rarely, Christian religion.[37]

Young working adults were the main constituency for the institution's evening courses. Held on weeknights and Sundays, the courses offered a general education program with a separate division for illiterate women workers. While attrition was high, those who managed to stay viewed the courses with gratitude. V. Anisimov, a worker who was one of the first to attend the courses when they opened in 1900, recalled in 1913 how the courses united teachers and students as "older and younger comrades . . . [into] a single family."[38] For Anisimov and other literate visitors, the library offered another opportunity to widen their horizons or escape their dreary daily lives through reading. Under the

Tearoom at the Ligovsky People's House. (Rossiiskii institut istorii iskusstv, St. Petersburg, Kabinet rukopisei, f. 32, op. 1, ed. khr. 117/9)

guidance of librarian Alexandra Peshekhonova, books were chosen carefully, with the aim of elevating readers' tastes. Like other Russian and Western social reformers, Alexandra sought to divert working-class readers away from popular melodramas like *The Bandit Churkin* toward "good" literature. Despite patrons' requests, she refused to stock contemporary bestsellers like Anastasia Verbitskaya's racy *The Keys to Happiness* or other new fiction she considered cynical or vulgar. In other respects, however, the library attempted to satisfy its clients' interests. Advanced readers took advantage of its collection of science, history, and works of Russian and world literature both classic and modern. During the revolutionary years of 1905–6 librarians scrambled to meet the explosion of demand for works on political and social questions, although they found that interest quickly receded. In the post-revolutionary period the library answered a growing number of requests from a minority of "serious" readers for works of psychology and philosophy.[39]

Adult evening class at the Ligovsky People's House. (Rossiiskii institut istorii iskusstv, St. Petersburg, Kabinet rukopisei, f. 32, op. 1, ed. khr. 117/7)

Sofia also tried to develop visitors' artistic sensibilities. She regarded art as a means to elevate them and "catch dark and blind human souls in nets of beauty," as she told an audience in 1912.[40] She and her friend Lidia Yakovleva tried holding summer art exhibits but found that attendance was low and the artwork confused the few who attended.[41] The experience with music was more gratifying. Visitors formed their own choir and balalaika orchestra and performed operas and concerts of European and Russian classical works.[42] Sofia was especially proud of the theater she established, which was under the direction of a prominent figure in theater history whose career continued into the Soviet era, Pavel Pavlovich Gaideburov (1877–1960). The theater staged classic works by Alexander Pushkin, Alexander Ostrovsky, and Nikolai Gogol, whose *The Inspector General* was performed every year to large and enthusiastic audiences. Gaideburov also introduced new plays by Anton Chekhov, Maxim Gorky, and Leo Tolstoy. Sophocles and Shakespeare, Byron and Molière, Shaw and Ibsen were performed on the stage of the people's house as well. Sofia worked with Gaideburov to select plays that not only followed the censor's dictates—tsarist law required theaters like the one at the people's house to adhere to a limited list of permitted plays—but also met their own artistic and moral standards. In keeping with the institution's mission of enlightenment, they rejected the melodramas and farces that other popular theaters presented and chose plays with literary and artistic merit, clarity and universality in their characters' psychology, and no "pessimistic world view."[43]

While the theater attracted both critical praise and an appreciative working-class audience, the most popular entertainment proved to be movies—to the dismay of the administration. In the 1907–8 season, for example, when the people's house began showing films, the average attendance at the monthly shows exceeded even the attendance at the popular Sunday readings.[44] Like other members of Russia's educated elite, Sofia and her coworkers believed that the only art and literature worth transmitting came from European and Russian high culture—a single, unifying culture whose superiority and transformative power they never questioned. Sofia's taste in art tended to look back to Russia's Golden Age of realism, not to the vibrant modernist culture that was exploding in early twentieth-century Russia. The works of such symbolist poets and writers as Alexander Blok and Fyodor Sologub, the self-named "bard of death"; futurist artists like Konstantin Malevich; and avant-garde composers such as Igor Stravinsky found little place at the Ligovsky People's House. Perhaps Sofia considered modernist works too complex for the unschooled visitors, whom she described as "benighted and blind souls" needing the guidance of the educated. Or perhaps she simply disliked Russia's modernist cultural trends herself; growing up amid the Panins' extensive collection of European art, and educated at the conventional Catherine Institute, Sofia appears to have had fairly traditional artistic tastes.

So to Sofia and her coworkers, the transmission of knowledge and culture was a one-way street; but they believed that their clients shared their values and yearned for their kind of enlightenment. The popularity of the Ligovsky People's House indicates that to a considerable extent they were right. Visitors flocked in large numbers to its presentations of "good" literature, theater, and (to a lesser extent) art, seizing the opportunities for self-improvement. Out of the evening courses for adults arose what Sofia regarded as one of her greatest successes—a "literary circle" that formed the kernel of the institution's own working-class intelligentsia.[45] Sofia and Alexandra's values were mirrored in the circle, whose founders cited concern over the absence of "rational, healthy entertainment" for workers as their motive. During the summer of 1908, for example, members staged six Sunday public readings before a "full house," with recitations of poems and stories by canonical writers such as Pushkin, Nikolai Nekrasov, and Mikhail Lermontov, musical pieces for piano and mandolin, and on some evenings, dances that lasted until midnight. A more formal literary evening in September included presentations on Tolstoy and Ivan Turgenev. The circle produced an anthology of members' poems and essays under the evocative title *Awakening Thought*; it also organized excursions and educational tours.[46]

Operating the Ligovsky People's House was expensive. Most of the lectures, readings, and classes and all of the children's activities were free. Adult visitors paid small fees to attend the plays, movies, and other entertainments, or to visit the astronomical observatory. Every year the institution ran huge deficits of thousands of rubles. The institution received no funds from local government or the state; Sofia not only paid the entire cost of constructing the new building, she provided most of the operating funds and covered the deficits. She was a regular and visible presence at the people's house and chaired its executive council, which met at least monthly.[47] Charitable institutions in Russia usually had some kind of governing board and a cohort of honorary members, but Sofia seems not to have invited anyone from her extensive circle of family and friends to serve as directors, patrons, or honorary members, or even to make donations. Its viability during her lifetime depended solely on her continued commitment and largesse, and an undated document suggests that she sought to ensure the institution's self-sufficiency after her death by bequeathing an endowment for it to the St. Petersburg municipal government.[48] Sofia was so closely identified with her institution that contemporaries often called it "Countess Sofia Panina's People's House." After being subjected to the will of others as a child and young woman, from her mother and grandmother to those who set the rules of aristocratic society, Sofia intended to retain control over her creation.

At the same time, operations at the people's house relied on a devoted corps of coworkers who ran its various departments with a considerable degree of independence. Roughly two-thirds of them were women, including many of the paid staff and virtually all the volunteers. Many had worked with Sofia for years.[49] At the heart of the institution was a trio of unmarried schoolteachers who had worked with Sofia since the 1890s—Alexandra, Elizaveta Popova (known as "Auntie Liza"), and

Nadezhda Yalozo. To some of the coworkers the institution became a surrogate family; the three schoolteachers, for example, lived together in an apartment nearby from at least 1908 until first Auntie Liza, then Alexandra died in the early 1930s.[50] Relations between Sofia and her coworkers were warm and affectionate. "I am glad," one woman volunteer wrote "dear, precious Sofia Vladimirovna" in 1913, "for these ten years with you, endlessly grateful for that happiness that you gave me and for the existence of the House, and the opportunity to work there. . . . I warmly embrace you, my dear, [and] wish from my heart that the work so dear to all of us will develop and grow stronger." Another volunteer was Liudmila Grammatchikova, sister of the eminent jurist Anatoly Koni. Her emotional letters to Sofia, written after the revolution, further demonstrate that for some longtime female volunteers, unmarried and lonely, the people's house gave purpose to their lives, and its founder inspired both admiration and devotion.[51]

On a warm and sunny April afternoon in 1913, the diverse social constituencies of the people's house assembled in its theater to celebrate its tenth anniversary. Coworkers and visitors alike, including the workers who belonged to the literary circle, had been planning and preparing for the event for months. The festivities began when Sofia entered the theater to fervent applause. The curtain rose and a chorus sang a "Jubilee Cantata" composed by one of the members of the workers' literary circle. It hailed the institution for opening a road to "bright golden goals," and acknowledged the "noble hand"—Sofia's—that had created it:

> Greetings to you, People's House! . . .
> From the surrounding forges we, labor's children,
> Forgotten in eternal struggle,
> Assembled here for your bright holiday,
> And put together a song to you:
> Hail, hail, People's House!
> You were born in the fight with darkness,
> And bestowed by a noble hand. . . .
> You generate strength and faith
> With your true light.

The audience demanded an encore, and stood while the cantata was performed a second time. Next, a children's chorus sang their own "cantata." With all of the coworkers on stage, Sofia, Pavel Gaideburov,

The Ligovsky People's House, tenth anniversary celebration, April 7, 1913. (Tsentral'nyi gosudarstvennyi arkhiv kinofotofonodokumentov g. Sankt-Peterburga, E5291)

and others then gave speeches about the institution's ten-year history. One speaker was Alexei Mashirov-Samobytnik (1884–1943), one of the leaders of the literary circle who gained some renown as a proletarian poet after the Bolshevik Revolution and died of starvation during the blockade of Leningrad. Alexei—his nom de plume, "Samobytnik," means "the original" or the "self-made one"—read a poem he had composed for the occasion, which compared the Ligovsky People's House to a "bright" ship that brought joy to the "forgotten" inhabitants of "gloomy, wild" shores.[52] Sofia was then presented with a huge, velvet-covered album entitled "The Book of Deep Gratitude," as an "emblem of the unity that reigns within the walls" of her people's house. It contains scores of letters, drawings, watercolors, poems, and similar tributes to Sofia and her institution from coworkers and working-class visitors past and present. Ardent and intensely personal expressions of love and gratitude alternate with reverent formality in the poems and letters addressed to Sofia.[53] A photograph taken of the anniversary celebration illustrates the vision of social harmony that united Sofia, her coworkers, and visitors on that day. Scores of men, women, and children, posing under portraits of Russia's literary giants, fill the entire stage of the theater. It is not easy to differentiate the working-class visitors, many dressed in their Sunday best, from the modestly attired teachers and other staff. Dressed in a plain dark suit, Sofia stands near the center amid coworkers, visitors, and children holding handicrafts. To her left is Alexandra, appropriately sitting directly under the portrait of Pushkin, Russia's most revered writer. For at least one day the social, economic, and political differences that fractured Russian society were forgotten in a celebration of faith in progress achieved through education and cultural uplift.

Sofia had traveled a great distance to arrive on the stage of the people's house for this festive tenth anniversary. Every day that she left her home in the capital's gilded center to travel over the wide, polluted Obvodny Canal into the grimy, industrial Ligovka neighborhood she crossed social and economic as well as geographical boundaries. Her social work there differed markedly from the conventional charitable work with which ladies of her class usually occupied their time, such as local Red Cross chapters or the provincial committees of national charities that enjoyed the patronage of members of the imperial family. The people's house was not an occasional pastime, but the core of Sofia's public life and the major object of her benevolence before World War I. It brought her into daily contact with people from across the social spectrum and enabled her to observe at close range the deprivation, ignorance, and discontent of the urban lower classes. What motives impelled Sofia to dedicate herself so passionately to this work?

Anglo-American settlement houses had deep roots in their founders' own religious convictions and longing for meaningful spirituality. In her 1892 lecture "The Subjective Necessity for Social Settlements," for example, Jane Addams traced the motives behind the settlement movement to the search by young people for a way to live Christian values every day.[54] Russian history offers numerous examples of women who, inspired by the teachings of Orthodox Christianity on the centrality of charity and compassion, founded religious communities dedicated to feeding, healing, or teaching the poor.[55] But religion is strikingly absent as a motive behind Sofia's social work. Though an Orthodox Christian, Sofia never referred to faith as an influence on her public life, and her people's house paid scant attention to religion other than to celebrate Christmas and Easter with magic lantern shows and children's parties. In design the building was wholly secular, with no chapel or other

space devoted to its visitors' spiritual needs. Sofia seems to have paid
little attention to whether visitors or coworkers were leading Christian lives. It is suggestive of her attitude toward religion that she invited
Father Grigory Petrov, a city parish priest well known for his progressive views, to give a speech at the opening of the people's house in 1903
on the topic of the importance of education for the masses; a few years
later he was defrocked because of his radical views.

Nor did Sofia seek social reconciliation by personally experiencing
the privations of the poor and sharing their lives. Such motives, along
with a desire to preach socialism, had impelled thousands of young
Russians in the 1870s to "go to the people" by donning bark shoes and
peasant tunics, moving to remote villages, and working alongside the
poor as teachers, medics, or even migrant agricultural laborers. Similar
feelings of social responsibility had combined with curiosity and voy-
eurism to inspire other young people, not only in Russia but also in
Europe and America, to venture into urban working-class districts disguised as artisans or seamstresses.[56] In the Anglo-American settlement
house movement, young men and women from the upper classes left
Oxford or Bryn Mawr to move into slums in order to live with the poor
and build communities that transcended class divisions. But the settlement house model never took root in Russia. No one—not the coworkers, and not the working-class visitors—lived at the Ligovsky People's
House. Unlike Addams, who made Hull House her home and regularly
visited its neighbors to help nurse the sick or care for newborns, there is
no evidence that Sofia ventured into the crowded rooms that her visitors
called home. Although she spent a great deal of time at the institution
on the city's outskirts, Sofia continued to reside in its elite center—first
in the Panin mansion, then in her new home in the fashionable Liteiny
district. Showing surprisingly little interest in learning about the physical conditions in which the poor lived, she focused instead on their interior lives, conducting surveys, for example, of the audiences at the
institution's plays and lectures in order to understand visitors' cultural
and intellectual desires and aspirations.

Guilt about inherited privilege strongly influenced the ethos of service to society embraced by the Russian intelligentsia, many of whom
came from the nobility. It informed Tolstoy's literary depictions of the
repentant nobleman, so effectively represented in Levin's character in
Anna Karenina, along with Tolstoy's own conversion to Christian anar-
chism. It is a particularly common motif in the lives of female social
activists in Russia as well as in the West, from the early Russian feminist

Anna Filosofova to the fictional heiress Angela Messenger. Was Sofia similarly impelled to dedicate herself and her fortune to the poor out of remorse over her inherited wealth and status? Did she feel the need to expiate a sense of responsibility for poverty and exploitation? Sofia's grandfathers had been two of Russia's greatest serf owners, and her inheritance was founded on the labor of the peasants and workers they exploited. But the stereotype of the repentant heiress does not fit Sofia. She did not renounce her wealth or give it away, a doctrine preached by Tolstoy and practiced by many of his disciples, such as Muriel Lester, the English heiress, Christian radical, and settlement house founder.[57] Sofia enjoyed traveling abroad, vacationing at the country estates of friends and relatives, and experiencing the many other advantages that came with her wealth and status.

At the same time Sofia felt that her wealth and position were not earned but instead were merely accidents of birth. They imposed a responsibility, even a duty, to serve others and give back to society. These sentiments in turn motivated her to commit herself to the limits of her time and energy. Writing to her friend Varya in the spring of 1898, for example, Sofia declared herself to be exhausted after an extremely busy but "terribly interesting" winter. But she claimed to have no right to complain. "Life and people spoil me," she explained, "and I only want terribly much to give back out of [my] surplus [izbitok] those 'five talents' that fell to my lot."[58] Those feelings intensified when she inherited the Panin fortune in 1899. A month after her grandmother's death Sofia confessed to Varya that she worried a great deal about her ability to be a good steward of her fortune. "In the full sense of the word I feel like the camel before the eye of the needle, but I know that I will be able to live with peace in my heart only if I am able to transform myself from a camel into a thread."[59]

Additional insight into the motives behind Sofia's commitment to social service may be gained by examining the emotional circumstances under which she began her collaboration with Alexandra Peshekhonova in 1891. Sofia spent her teen years and twenties in an emotional desert. Her mother was physically distant and absorbed in the life and political causes of her husband. Although the large Panin and Maltsov families endowed her with numerous cousins, augmented by stepsiblings and more cousins when her mother married into the Petrunkevich clan, Sofia grew up largely alone. An occasional school vacation spent with her elderly grandmother and stern French governess in the musty formality of the Panin mansion provided Sofia with her principal respite from the drafty corridors of the Catherine Institute. Her brief marriage to the cultured, charming, but deceptive Polovtsov ended in scandal. Even though her life was filled with intellectual pursuits, relatives and friends, and her growing social work with Alexandra, Sofia sometimes characterized it as deeply solitary. The isolation of every individual is an "absolute fact" of human existence, she maintained in an unusually pessimistic letter in 1897, and no amount of friendship or love was capable of "throwing a little bridge" across the abyss that separated every individual from others.[60]

When Alexandra entered her life, nineteen-year-old Sofia found an escape from her isolation. As their collaboration developed, she gained a mentor and friend in the older woman and transformed herself from the society bride whose marriage had collapsed into an increasingly well-known and respected social reformer. Her new identity was an amalgam of the charisma of a gracious, enlightened noblewoman and the Russian intelligentsia's devotion to the common good. The self-contained world Sofia built at the Ligovsky People's House represented the personal and financial independence she gained in adulthood. It was also an affective community from which she derived considerable emotional gratification. Deprived of the opportunity to create a family of her own, she gained the gratitude, admiration, and affection of both volunteers and visitors. The institution was, she told her friend and co-worker Lidia, a "magic kingdom" whose "miracle-working powers" always put her in a good mood, gave purpose to her life, and made her feel useful to society.[61] In a Russia that was still highly patriarchal, the people's house was a female-dominated realm coruled by Alexandra, a kindly, older spinster schoolteacher just like many of the volunteers, and Sofia, whom her closest collaborators likened to a gracious fairy princess with seemingly unlimited powers to make wishes come true.[62]

Finally, the Ligovsky People's House provided Sofia with the means to help build a progressive future for her country, one based on her ideas about the power of culture and knowledge to turn the benighted poor into enlightened citizens. What she did not anticipate was the stiff challenge to her philosophy of gradual social betterment that arose amid the political turmoil of the early twentieth century. As radicalism on the left and right mounted in the years before 1914, punctuated by violent revolution in 1905–6, it took considerable will and optimism for Sofia to keep walking the tightrope of moderation. No matter how she sought to define herself and her work as nonpartisan, politics intruded into almost every aspect of her public life in the years before World War I.

5

The "Red Countess"

The audience that crowded into the theater of the Ligovsky People's House on May 9, 1906, was excited, though not by the prospect of another entertaining performance of Gogol's *The Inspector General*. They came to hear representatives of newly legalized political parties speak on the subject of the first popularly elected parliament in Russian history, the State Duma, which had opened just two weeks earlier. Impassioned debate filled the theater. Members of the liberal Kadet Party, which had won the largest number of seats, tried to persuade the working-class audience why it was necessary to support the infant legislature, despite voting laws that largely disenfranchised them and the constraints Nicholas II had imposed on its powers. Speakers from socialist parties, who had boycotted the March elections to the Duma, denounced the government's promised civil rights and constitutional concessions as a sham. One of most intransigent opponents of the new order was the Bolshevik leader Vladimir I. Lenin. Posing as a worker named Karpov in order to evade arrest, he mounted the stage and exhorted the audience to beware of the bourgeois liberals' false promises. Years later this occasion, which was the first time Lenin addressed a mass audience in Russia, won the Ligovsky People's House a small but honored role in the Soviet Union's ubiquitous commemorations of

Lenin's life, including the plaque on the building, a 1936 painting, and a 1968 poster.[1]

By the time of the May 9 meeting the inhabitants of St. Petersburg had experienced almost a year and a half of political upheaval. Angered by repeated losses in the war against Japan, Russians first organized protest meetings in the fall 1904. Discontent with the government's conduct of the war turned into revolution on January 9, 1905, the day that came to be known as Bloody Sunday. On this day, tsarist troops fired on working-class men, women, and children marching peacefully toward the Winter Palace to present a petition begging Nicholas II to relieve their sufferings and grant them justice. The shocking violence against peaceful petitioners provoked outrage and waves of sympathy strikes in the capital and across the empire. In the months that followed, the tsarist government was rocked by the disastrous naval defeat at Tsushima in May, assassinations of high-ranking officials, mutinies in the army and navy, and rebellions by the empire's national minorities. It finally capitulated in October 1905, in the midst of a nation-wide general strike. The Manifesto of October 17, 1905, reluctantly signed by Nicholas II, promised civil liberties, representative government, and limited male suffrage. The tsar's concessions split the revolution: while liberal parties grudgingly committed themselves to taking advantage of the imperfect democratic reforms, socialists called for militant action to push for radical political and economic change. From the final months of 1905 well into 1906, revolution continued to grip the empire, often becoming violent, with peasant revolts, pogroms against Jews, and a week-long armed uprising in Moscow. In countryside and city alike, Russians used the unprecedented freedom to express their grievances and hopes not only through demonstrations and strikes, but also through newly created political associations and meetings like the one at the Ligovsky People's House.

It seems unlikely that Sofia approved of the extremist rhetoric from the left that filled the theater on the night of May 9. Although she often let outside groups use the people's house for their meetings, this event conflicted with the philosophy on which she based her public life. Reflecting many years later about the goals of her institution, Sofia explained how she and her collaborators "strove precisely to 'enlighten,' to take people who were helplessly wandering in the darkness and put them on their feet." It would be deeply dishonest, she continued, to attempt to impose any kind of political doctrine on people who lacked sufficient knowledge and understanding to make rational choices.

Political propaganda, whether from the left or right, conflicted with "our views on the dignity of the individual and on the obligatory honesty of any kind of 'enlightenment.' To abuse the ignorance and intellectual helplessness of the weakest, when you become their 'teacher,' we considered to be as impermissible as to use physical force to abuse a child."[2] The May 9 meeting teetered on the boundary separating what Sofia regarded as honest, beneficial educational work from the exploitation of ignorance that political propaganda seemed to represent.

Sofia consistently defined herself and her people's house as outside politics. Before 1917, she asserted in *On the Outskirts of Petersburg*, "I had never belonged to any political party and my interests were concentrated on questions of education and general culture, which alone, I was deeply convinced, could provide a solid foundation for a free political order." As this credo reveals, however, her claim seems disingenuous. Since the 1890s her experience running popular Sunday readings, lectures, and evening courses had taught her that such initiatives for workers inevitably acquired a political coloration in the eyes of the government, which regarded them with even greater suspicion as labor unrest and the socialist movement grew after 1900. Sofia herself acknowledges in the words quoted above that the goal of her efforts was, in the end, political: to build a "solid foundation for a free political order."[3]

Sofia's attempts to maintain her self-definition as standing above politics while simultaneously engaging in politically charged social causes encountered a similar challenge in 1900, when she took on a leading role in Russia's anti-prostitution association, the Society for the Protection of Women. In tsarist Russia, where prostitution was illegal but tolerated and regulated by the police, discussions of it not only "impinged on questions relating to labor, sexuality, urbanization, public health, and the status of women," the historian Laurie Bernstein points out, but readily led to criticism of structural inequality and injustice.[4] In short, Sofia's choice of social causes—educating restless urban workers and protecting women from sexual exploitation—implicitly if not explicitly addressed Russia's social, political, economic, and gender inequities. Some contemporaries even called her the "Red Countess."

But is this sobriquet apt? By suggesting that she sympathized with socialism, it fails to convey the complexity of her motives and objectives as well as her principled rejection of radicalism on the left or right. It also minimizes the challenges she faced when trying to maintain her nonpartisanship. Adopting a public position of political neutrality required careful navigation around hostile government authorities and partisan groups that, if they could not co-opt her, would denounce her as an enemy—and endanger the causes to which she was dedicated. Sofia's effort to hold onto a reputation as having no political affiliation was arguably as difficult as taking an openly political position. It also was destined to fail. Two years of revolution in 1905-6, followed by major political reforms, transformed the nature and impact of social work like Sofia's.

The prolonged and intense unrest that erupted in St. Petersburg in 1905 was the first serious test of the Ligovsky People's House, which had opened just two years earlier on a foundation of nonpartisanship and cross-class cooperation. Looking back on those "stormy days," the authors of the institution's 1908 report on its first five years boasted that "without taking upon itself any leading or directing role," the Ligovsky People's House opened its doors to political meetings where debates about "all kinds of social, political, economic and labor union questions" took place. At the same time the report echoed its founder's credo by expressing satisfaction with how the people's house managed to adhere to its exclusively "cultural-educational" goals and to remain "non-party" throughout the revolution.[5]

The distinction was undoubtedly less clear to the government than it was to Sofia and her coworkers since the people's house often served as a site for protest and radical speech during the revolutionary years of 1905-6. At a meeting held by the Kadet Party on February 8, 1906, the tsarist police reported, orators "pronounced extremely antigovernment speeches." One month later at a meeting of printers—among the most educated and politically active members of the proletariat—its chairwoman, a copyeditor for the Kadet newspaper *Rech'*, called upon those assembled to stand in memory of the slain revolutionary hero Lieutenant Schmidt. The action immediately prompted the police to close the meeting. They also disbanded the meeting on May 9 that featured Lenin, since instead of keeping to the original topic of the new national parliament, the event "deviated from the designated program and concluded with the proclamation of a resolution of a revolutionary character." Just two weeks later a meeting of bootmakers had to be warned twice by the police observer not to stray from the topic of their approved agenda, a discussion of their economic needs. In the end the officer closed this meeting, too, when its chairman denounced him with the words, "You see, comrades, how they restrict our freedom," and the crowd cried in response, "Down with the police!"[6] By allowing labor and political groups to use its spacious halls for meetings, the people's house compromised its "non-party" neutrality during the 1905 Revolution, at least in the eyes of the police. It seems unlikely that Sofia was unaware of the political meetings held at her people's house, and likely that she gave at least an implicit blessing to them.

In the calmer years after the revolution the Ligovsky People's House continued to concentrate on its principal mission of bringing enlightenment to its neighbors and advocating self-improvement as the path to progress. But the post-1905 parliamentary and constitutional experiment in Russia changed the context in which that work proceeded. Sofia's institution responded to the introduction of a national parliament, the promise of civil rights, and unprecedented opportunities for legal political organizations by offering ever more opportunities for its visitors to raise their political awareness and educate themselves for citizenship. The institution held special events to mark historical milestones in Russia's progress toward civil freedoms and constitutional, representative government. In early 1911, for example, four lectures and other events for children and adults "triumphantly" celebrated the fiftieth anniversary of the abolition of serfdom.[7] Commemorations of the fiftieth anniversary of the Great Reforms continued in 1914 with lectures on the reforms of the judicial system and local government, including one on zemstvo local government given by Sofia herself.[8] Visitors to the people's house could find answers to questions about their rights at its legal aid office, which in the words of the 1908–9 report was "always swamped with work."[9] Further indications of Sofia's implicit support of ideas and causes that challenged the tsarist status quo may be found in the public lectures regularly offered at the Ligovsky People's House. Attended by as many as a hundred visitors, the lecture series mixed scientific and literary subjects with contemporary issues that carried clearly political messages in the years after 1905. Among lectures given on bacteria, cholera, and the solar system, for example, were ones on "Illness, Mortality and Accidents Among Workers," labor unions, illegitimate children, and "On Freedom."[10]

Russian law required institutions like the Ligovsky People's House to obtain advance permission from the city commandant's office for every lecture. The commandant sent police observers to ensure that lecturers kept to their approved topics and did not cross the bounds of political or moral acceptability. Proposed lectures on topics that were considered too dangerous were forbidden, and if, in the opinion of the police observer, a lecturer deviated from the approved topic, the lecture was stopped. Despite the institution's protestations of "complete

Magic lantern show, the Ligovsky People's House Theater. The uniformed man in the third row is probably the police representative. (Rossiiskii institut istorii iskusstv, St. Petersburg, Kabinet rukopisei, f. 32, op. 1, ed. khr. 117/5)

nonpartisanship [*bespartiinost'*]" in its lectures, the topics it selected often crossed those boundaries and brought the institution into repeated conflict with the authorities. The report for 1907–8, for example, complained bitterly about repeated disruptions caused by the government's "refusal to permit any lectures whatsoever on social questions," which "demoralized" the organizers, lecturers, and audience.[11] The difficulty of predicting what the police would deem to be impermissible demonstrated the ambiguity of just what "political" meant in post-1905 Russia. In 1910–11, for example, the city commandant's office prohibited lectures on "What is Justice?" and "The Condition of Women from Ancient Times" but allowed one on the history of property and another on the development of the family.[12] The police also approved a lecture in March 1914 titled "Woman and the State," which addressed women's suffrage and the position of women in the economy, higher education, and local government.[13] In September 1913 the people's house planned a series on economic topics, beginning with a lecture on "Labor and Cooperation." The city commandant granted permission for that lecture and others on "American Multi-millionaires," "Trade," and "Money," but rejected "General and Historical Definitions of Capital" as "inappropriate" for a working-class district.[14]

Clearly the authorities were not persuaded by assurances from the administration of the people's house about the nonpolitical nature of its work. Their caution is hardly surprising: with their focus on science, labor, economics, and political questions, the lectures encouraged attendees to think critically about contemporary issues. In a sense Sofia and her institution were trapped in the dilemmas inherent in Russian liberalism when they insisted on ideological neutrality in a context in which the government considered virtually any civic or political activity to be partisan and potentially subversive. By educating the lower classes to become thoughtful, informed citizens, the people's house challenged the absolutist foundations of the Russian state.

Moreover, unlike the Sunday readings, which were most popular with working women and children, the lectures tended to attract an audience composed primarily of young working men—just the population attracted to socialism.[15] In fact, Sofia's people's house was well-known among socialists in the capital. The non-party socialist Alexander Kerensky, who became prime minister in 1917, began his legal and political career there in 1904, when he asked Sofia to allow him and a Social Democratic colleague to open a legal aid office. She consented, provided they did not use it to conduct political propaganda—a promise the future prime minister had little intention of keeping. Kerensky worked at the office for two years, through the 1905 Revolution.[16] According to a Soviet-era account, the Ligovsky People's House was used by the Bolshevik faction of the Social Democratic Party for legal and illegal work. Lenin attended political meetings there at least twice before the one on May 9, 1906.[17]

The people's house also provided ample opportunities to discuss politics at its adult evening courses and meetings of the literary circle. A number of the students in the adult courses had socialist ties. One was the poet-metalworker Mashirov-Samobytnik, who played such a prominent role in organizing the institution's tenth anniversary celebrations in 1913. When another worker, Mikhail Efremov, began attending the evening courses in 1911, other students introduced him to the "revolutionary struggle of the working class." At the beginning of 1914, he claimed in his 1932 autobiography, the close-knit group of worker-students at the people's house decided to create an "active party cell" of "committed Bolshevik activists." According to E. A. Evdokimova, another Bolshevik who worked in the institution's library, an underground revolutionary cell at the people's house conducted propaganda work and hid weapons there.[18] One of the teachers of the adult evening classes, who identified himself as a member of the right-wing Union of the Russian People, complained to the police after he was fired from the people's house that the administration consistently expelled any staff member who did not sympathize with revolutionary ideas—a claim perhaps informed more by his irritation at being fired than actual fact.[19]

The truth of these recollections by visitors to Sofia people's house, and the nature and extent of the socialist and revolutionary activity that they claimed took place there, are difficult to determine. Writing as Communist Party members after the October 1917 Revolution, these memoirists had good reasons to emphasize their revolutionary work and their Bolshevik credentials. They may have sought to justify their prerevolutionary involvement with such bourgeois projects by equating the kind of self-education that went on at people's houses with organizing and radicalizing the proletariat. A case in point is the worker-poet Mashirov-Samobytnik, who claims he already was a Bolshevik activist when he enrolled in the evening courses in 1908–9. In a 1922 compilation of reminiscences about wartime revolutionary activity in Petrograd, he recounts how he won the trust of the "sentimental individuals" who headed the people's house by displaying his literary talents at the evening classes, all the while advancing his socialist agenda. Yet Mashirov-Samobytnik also developed a deep attachment to the institution; in his autobiography written during the 1920s, he credited the Ligovsky People's House with developing his love of literature and nurturing his literary talents. Threatened by arrest for the socialist activity he pursued outside the people's house, he even lived there in hiding for a time.[20]

Sofia and her collaborators appear to have been either unconcerned about how some of the more radical visitors might use the people's house, or willing to regard their activities as consonant with the institution's mission of furthering civic education. Milestones in the history of the Ligovsky People's House became occasions for public restatements of a philosophy that reflected Russian liberals' hopes to build bridges with the left. The celebration of the tenth anniversary of the adult evening classes in 1910, for example, optimistically stressed how this event renewed participants' sense of working together and being part of one family, despite the conflicts and disunity that divided Russian society. As a little "cell" of that larger society, the people's house "had to confront and struggle with the same social phenomena," the institution's report for that year admitted, obliquely making reference to the 1905–6 Revolution. Yet hope remained strong that the feelings of "sincere warmth and spiritual uplift" that had infused the anniversary celebration "will help us go farther on our designated path, uniting us in the consciousness that a new, better life can be won and built only *by united humankind*."[21] In her speech at the 1913 jubilee, Sofia reinforced the message of unity when she expounded on her vision of the people's house as a community that transcended politics and class. She thanked the working-class visitors for bringing their "thirst for enlightenment, trust, and all good feelings" to the people's house. They were not the objects of charity, she reminded them, but "our coworkers in one common enterprise of building a new, better life." She used the occasion to speak indirectly but firmly against imported radical ideologies, such as Marxism, in which some of her audience placed their hopes. "That better, harmonious life," she instructed her listeners, "is not in foreign lands, as some of our visitors think, and that truth, which is hidden from the people, is not beyond distant seas." People must look for that "hidden truth" within the borders of their own consciousness and will. They must "extend a hand to each other and walk toward the designated goal in harmonious unity," she insisted.[22]

Although the people's house consumed the largest share of Sofia's philanthropic energy and resources before World War I, she also devoted considerable attention to improving the condition of women. Beginning in the 1890s the Russian women's movement gained momentum as debates about women's roles entered public discourse, new organizations for women's rights were created, and the words *feminizm* and *feministka* entered the Russian language. By the early twentieth century a number of feminist organizations advocated for equal rights, including suffrage. Sofia's sensitivity to the oppression of women may have had its roots in her own childhood, when she herself became the helpless object of contending parties. Several programs at the people's house were designed to educate and empower women and girls, demonstrating that she regarded the "woman question" as well as the "worker question" to be integral to her agenda for social progress. But Sofia avoided affiliating herself with radical feminist positions on women's status and rights, and she stood aloof from the political movement for women's suffrage until after the tsarist monarchy fell in

February 1917. Instead she focused on the fight against prostitution, a cause that attracted support from women and men across social and political lines.

The cause of redeeming fallen women had long been a popular one with philanthropic ladies from Russia's upper classes, who had funded shelters for penitent prostitutes for more than fifty years. But by the early twentieth century the struggle to eradicate, outlaw, and prevent prostitution extended well beyond the realm of elite charity to become a broad-based social movement that crossed national borders and attracted supporters with diverse backgrounds, political convictions, and objectives. On the one hand, the anti-prostitution cause gained force from a full-fledged panic that arose in the late nineteenth century out of sensational journalistic claims that European and American women were being tricked or abducted into brothels at home and abroad. The "white slave trade" became an international *cause célèbre* that galvanized crusaders across Europe and the United States and inspired meetings like the congress held in London in June 1899, where Russia was represented by a delegation that included both government representatives and female activists.[23]

At the same time many Russian anti-prostitution activists sought the causes of prostitution not in trafficking but in the social, economic, and political structures that oppressed women. Ever since the abolition of serfdom in 1861, a growing stream of vulnerable peasant girls left their villages for the city in search of work. The jobs they found in service or industry were often so poorly paid that they supplemented their earnings with prostitution. The state also came in for its share of the blame. As in other nations of continental Europe prostitution was tolerated in Russia, where the police licensed brothels, registered prostitutes, and subjected prostitutes to humiliating medical examinations in an often fruitless effort to prevent the spread of venereal disease. The state's complicity in vice enraged many Russian reformers, who pushed for abolition of the system of regulation and an end to official toleration. One of the most outspoken was Tolstoy, whose sensational final novel, *Resurrection*, published in 1899, recounts the fall of a young peasant maidservant, seduced and abandoned by her employer's nephew. She ends up working in a regulated brothel. "Thus Maslova entered into a life of habitual sin against every commandment, human and divine," Tolstoy thundered, "a life which is led by hundreds and thousands of women, not only with the consent but under the patronage of a government anxious to promote the welfare of its citizens, a life which ends for nine women out of ten in disease, premature decrepitude, and death."[24]

One result of the multiple currents that fed the Russian anti-prostitution movement at the turn of the century was the creation of the Russian Society for the Protection of Women in early 1900, an organization closely aligned with the tsarist government and enjoying the patronage of the Princesses Elena Saksen-Altenburgskaya and Evgenia Oldenburgskaya, both related to the imperial family. It is somewhat surprising to find Sofia among the high-ranking bureaucrats, jurists, and titled aristocrats who were the founders of this society. She generally avoided participating in any of the capital's other prestigious female charitable organizations with royal connections, such as the Imperial Women's Patriotic Society and the Russian Red Cross. Since she makes no mention of her association with the society in her memoir or surviving correspondence, the reasons for her embrace of the anti-prostitution cause in 1900 are left to speculation. Perhaps her work with Alexandra Peshekhonova in the 1890s acquainted her with the hard lives of working women and the risks they faced. The neighborhood around the Ligovsky People's House, with its numerous saloons and ready clientele of horsecab-drivers and laborers, was one of the capital's red-light districts.[25] Sofia served on the board of directors of the Society for the Protection of Women until World War I, established and directed its Prevention Department, and turned over a rear wing of her mansion on the Fontanka for the society to use as its main office from 1901 to 1909.[26]

The Prevention Department ran a hostel for transient women in St. Petersburg. The hostel opened in June 1900 in a building on Ligovskaya Street not far from the site of the future people's house. While modest charges for food and lodging covered some expenses, the rent for the space was paid equally by Sofia and Princess Saksen-Altenburgskaya. It provided young women with temporary housing as an alternative to living in overcrowded slum apartments or flophouses, "in the society of drunks, habitual beggars, vagrants, prostitutes and other depraved members of the population of the capital, whose company has a corrupting influence," in the lurid words of one of the society's early reports.[27] In 1908 the hostel moved up Ligovskaya Street and across the Obvodny Canal to a larger space much closer to the Nikolaevsky train station, a major point of arrival for migrants from central Russia. It now offered two kinds of accommodation: four dormitories with a total of thirty beds for transient working-class women, and a section of more private rooms for thirty-eight educated women, who generally stayed for longer periods. The overwhelming majority of the women who used it were young and unmarried, and approximately three-quarters of them were peasants seeking work in the capital.[28]

After a decade of experience in providing aid to prostitutes and women at risk, Sofia and the other leaders of the society were ready to bring discussion of the scourge of prostitution to the national stage by organizing a national congress on the problem. At planning meetings the society's leaders differed over whether the congress should limit itself to the narrow topic of prostitution or tackle broader social questions related to its causes—poverty, alcoholism, child neglect, ill-paid wage labor, and the legal inequalities suffered by women. Sofia argued in favor of the broadest possible agenda, and the majority supported her.[29] They may not have fully anticipated what the consequences of this decision would be, or realized how politically explosive the issue of prostitution had become. In post-1905 Russia a cause once associated with charity and social control had been transformed into a lightning rod for feminist and socialist critiques of the political, social, and economic order.

The First (and, as it turned out, only) All-Russian Congress on the Struggle Against the Trade in Women and Its Causes opened in St. Petersburg on April 21, 1910, and ran for three days from mid-morning to almost midnight. The participants came from across the political and social spectrum; high-ranking civil servants, physicians, and legal specialists mingled with aristocrats, charity activists, and, at the last minute, five workers representing labor unions. A sizable minority of the women attending the 1910 congress belonged to major feminist organizations.[30] Although the attendees shared a moral revulsion against prostitution, the cause proved incapable of transcending the political differences that divided Russians. Radical feminists and socialists such as Alexandra Kollontai lambasted the congress even before it opened for its restrictive invitation list and the heavy presence of princesses and bureaucrats; one socialist commentator mocked the "splendidly attired, satisfied ladies" among the attendees.[31] Debates about the causes of prostitution quickly turned into fierce arguments about social inequality and political repression. The congress's tiny but feisty worker delegation seized every opportunity to press their position that the solution to prostitution was not philanthropy but radical economic and political change. While they frequently clashed with congress leaders, on other occasions the worker representatives joined forces with them in objecting to interference by police observers, who issued rebukes and warnings whenever the discussion overstepped the bounds of the government-approved program and touched upon labor reform or civil rights.[32]

Ordinarily avoiding the public spotlight, Sofia took an unusually prominent role at the congress. In addition to presiding over the Second Section, which dealt with various schemes to prevent prostitution, she presented a paper, joined in discussions, and reported on her section's resolutions to the congress's general assembly. The sessions over which she presided generally proved to be less stormy than those in the other two sections, but even in the Second Section the vociferous worker delegation made clear its disdain for charitable schemes and piecemeal approaches. Thus the atmosphere was already charged when, on the congress's second day, Sofia stepped up to speak about "Taking Care of Young Women Who Come to the City for Work." Like most women of the time she had little experience with speaking in public and could be quite nervous before an audience. In an undated letter to her friend Lidia Yakovleva, she is harshly self-critical of how she delivered another speech. "For some reason I was terribly embarrassed, muffed the whole thing, and was impossibly boring, fortunately at least I was brief . . . Never in my life, it seems, was I so talentless!"[33] The published text of her presentation at the congress on prostitution bears unmistakable traces of the emotion with which she approached her subject and the passion with which she delivered her speech. The topic she chose, on how to help women avoid prostitution and construct self-sufficient lives, provides insight into Sofia's views on social responsibility, class relations, and the characteristics of the poor.

In her speech Sofia argued for the need, indeed the obligation, for women like her to extend a compassionate, "friendly hand" to their less fortunate sisters—particularly to the young, illiterate, and helpless peasant woman, driven from her village by poverty or family pressure, who comes to the "big, strange, and terrifying city" in search of work. "Who will hear her voice . . . amidst the roar of many thousands of inhabitants?" Sofia asked. "How will she win her place in this terrible struggle for existence, where the one who will notice her first is, of course, the one who somehow or other wants to extract his own advantage from her helplessness, inexperience, and youth?" This is a critical moment, Sofia warned her listeners, which demands the attention, sympathy, and assistance of women like themselves. "We, women of the city, are obligated to it for so much . . . for all the joys and riches of spiritual and cultural life, we *must* come to the aid of our younger, unfortunate sister, we must shelter her, concern ourselves with the well-being of her material and spiritual life." The modern city, in Sofia's formulation, wore two faces: the source of enlightenment and cultural uplift for educated women like her, but a dangerous trap for their naïve, ignorant sisters from the countryside.

Sofia expressed particular alarm about the absence of help for women at the critical moment when they first arrived in the city. Russians could find a good model for such assistance, she told her audience, in the German *Bahnhofsmission* founded in 1894 (and still in operation today). The German organization posted volunteers at urban train stations to meet young women from the countryside "day and night" and helped them find safe lodgings. Sofia called upon her listeners' national pride as well as their concern for the fate of their peasant sisters. "Before such a picture of the outstanding results attained by the indomitable energy of the women of Western Europe," she lamented, "our poor homeland looks dead and lifeless! And most important—it is dark!" Russian reformers confronted greater challenges than their Western counterparts, she admitted. It is harder to reach the "darkened mind and suspicious, fearful heart" of Russian peasant girls, but the need to aid society's "weakest, least experienced, and most defenseless members" is that much greater. The work would be difficult, requiring patience and love toward women who may be suspicious, even hostile. "But is Russia really poorer than other countries, its neighbors, when it comes to patience and heroism? Of course not. And the work *must* be and will be done." Sofia ended her passionate appeal to the patriotism and compassion of her audience with two pragmatic proposals for the capital: the organization of "railroad missions" to meet and assist new arrivals, and the creation of a central employment bureau for women.[34]

Sofia's speech raised predictable objections from the politically and socially divided audience. Critics mocked her faith in the ability of what they termed charity to prevent social ills. The speaker's proposals, one delegate protested, are so insignificant that they cannot save a single peasant girl from prostitution. Legal reform is needed, argued another, not agents at railroad stations or shelters. Still another listener criticized Sofia's lack of attention to the need to build the initiatives she proposed on a Christian foundation. We already have enough women, retorted another member of the audience, who think social ills can be eradicated by prayer. One worker delegate claimed that only local governments, not private individuals, can properly protect working women. Eager to use the congress as a platform for political action, he called upon the audience to adopt a resolution calling for democracy and complete freedom for labor unions. His call for a vote on that resolution was ignored, and a majority of those in attendance approved Sofia's practical proposals. Three years later, the Society for the Protection of Women began posting teams of volunteers at three train stations in St. Petersburg from dawn to late at night to assist young women arriving in search of work. Sofia's "railroad missions," scorned by socialists at the 1910 congress, were continued by the Communist Party's Women's Department in the early Soviet era.[35]

For all of its heartfelt expressions of compassion and concern, Sofia's speech is condescending, its proposed actions modest. She makes no attempt to identify the causes of the ignorance, helplessness, and suspicions of the peasant women she seeks to help. Patriarchal social customs, legal inequalities, economic exploitation, and other structural factors go unmentioned. Her characterization of young women at risk is consistent with her views of the people who came to her people's house, whose ignorance made them susceptible to corrupting influences: ultimately they could be made capable of taking initiative and improving themselves if their well-intentioned social betters showed the way and provided opportunities. By exhorting educated, urban women to help peasant women conquer their ignorance and fear, and establish independent lives, Sofia's speech at the 1910 congress argued for an ethos of sisterhood that crossed class lines. But Sofia did not believe that the timid, defenseless women she sought to help were ready for political equality.

Women's suffrage, like prostitution, was a major issue in the Russian feminist movement as well as in Europe and the United States in the early twentieth century. Before 1905, when there was no Russian national legislature and only a small minority of men with property could vote for representatives to rural and municipal councils, both women and men were disenfranchised and without rights. The introduction of the Duma in 1906 and a suffrage law that gave the majority of men the vote threw the disenfranchisement of women, regardless of their economic status, into sharp relief and moved the issue of women's suffrage to the forefront of the Russian feminist movement. The political inequality of Russian women was magnified by a little-known but extraordinary concession made by Nicholas II to the nationalist revolutions that swept the borderlands of his empire in 1905–6. Seeking to keep the duchy of Russian Finland in the empire, the tsar signed a decree in July 1906 that granted universal suffrage to his male and female Finnish subjects.[36]

Sofia's feminism is difficult to define. Her first association with the Russian women's movement dates to the mid-1890s, when in addition to enrolling in the higher women's courses, she joined the oldest and largest national feminist organization, the Russian Women's Mutual Philanthropic Society. The society, she reported to her friend Varya, was growing rapidly, with all "intelligent" women seeking to join. Although she believed its work would have a "great future," her account of the general membership meeting she attended betrays an element of skepticism about how ready Russian women were to collaborate successfully. With two hundred fifty women in attendance, she told Varya, "you cannot imagine what a Babel it was! It is clear how little accustomed our women have become to the discipline and order [needed in] large meetings: it would only take one to begin talking, and immediately about fifty people would begin to yell, shush each other, and applaud."[37] The women's organizations to which Sofia committed significant time, resources, and energy—the association that raised funds for the higher women's courses in St. Petersburg and the Society for the Protection of Women—though connected to the advancement of women, fit more comfortably within the realm of philanthropy. Up to the 1917 Revolution she avoided taking a public position on women's suffrage and never affiliated herself with any of the radical feminist organizations that emerged during and after the revolutionary events of 1905, such as the League for Women's Equal Rights.[38]

Sofia's social work brought her into regular contact with a wide range of female activists, from Princess Saksen-Altenburgskaya to Ariadna Tyrkova-Williams and Anna Miliukova, both leaders of the women's rights movement and members of the Kadet Party. She read with sympathy and approval such contemporary works on women's rights as *Women in the Past, Present and Future*, by the German socialist August Bebel, and *Memoirs of a Socialist*, by the German feminist Lily Braun.[39] Sofia was also friends with the colorful feminist and radical vegetarian Natalia Nordman-Severova, the second wife of Russia's preeminent realist painter Ilya Repin. Natalia's views about women's emancipation apparently were more militant than Sofia's: in a letter she wrote to Sofia during the 1910 congress on prostitution, Natalia gently chastised her friend for not "thundering against men" in her presentation. But Natalia's husband approved of the way Sofia approached the woman question. Women like her, Repin wrote in the album presented to her at the tenth-anniversary celebration of the people's house, disprove the "obsolete juridical nonsense that a woman is not capable of

Sofia with the artist Ilya Repin and her friend Lidia Yakovleva, circa 1909. (private collection)

occupying the highest responsible positions, that she must be subordinated to a man." Yet, he continued, she is not a "destroyer" like suffragists in England, but "a *creative* personality."[40]

In some respects Sofia's brand of social activism owed almost as much to family traditions as it did to modern feminism. Driven by a combination of compassion and condescension, and keeping aloof from overt political causes, she followed an ethos of social responsibility rooted in the paternalism—or maternalism—of noble landowners toward their peasants. Her great-grandmother and namesake, Countess Sofia Vladimirovna Panina née Orlova, was renowned for her charity and her "indefatigable concern" for the well-being of her serfs.[41] Sofia's grandfather Victor was a comparatively benign overlord for his day, providing his serfs with educational opportunities and serving both their economic interests and his own through initiatives to promote their prosperity. When Victor's widow died in 1899, her young granddaughter Sofia inherited not only the Panin estates, but also the Panin seigneurial tradition.

Marfino, May 2011. (photograph by the author)

Marfino, the magnificent estate located forty kilometers north of Moscow, was Sofia's favorite, where she often spent part of her summer. There her father and baby sister were buried. There, often joined by friends and her parents (Sofia jointly owned Marfino with Anastasia), she enjoyed the respite from her busy public life offered by Marfino's pastoral tranquility. Amid the "quiet and abundance of rural life" and the beauties of nature she found a chance to read and catch up on correspondence.[42] Sofia followed the example of her grandfather and great-grandmother in caring for the material and intellectual well-being of Marfino's peasants. In addition to supporting educational enterprises in and around the estate, such as the village school founded by her grandfather and the local library, she also supported the local cooperative and the poor relief council, where she served as the honorary chairwoman.[43]

Gaspra, another Panin estate that Sofia co-inherited with her mother, was located on the spectacular southern coast of the Crimean peninsula.[44] The mansion had been built in the 1830s for Prince Alexander N.

Golitsyn, one of the most influential of the ministers of Alexander I, who named it Alexandria after the emperor. Viktor Panin bought it in the 1860s, at the time when the Crimea, home to countless generations of Muslim farmers, began to change into a fashionable vacation destination, Russia's own Riviera with a semi-tropical climate and Mediterranean landscape. In the 1890s, when Sofia began regularly visiting Gaspra in the late summer and fall, she threw herself into various improvement projects: expanding the estate with additional land purchases, renovating the dilapidated Gothic-style castle, and planting new orchards and vineyards. As at Marfino, she also contributed to improving the health and education of the local inhabitants. She helped fund the local hospital, including paying the salary of a woman obstetrician, and together with a neighbor supported a small people's house that opened in 1910 on land she donated, which had a reading room, tea room, and small theater.[45]

At Marfino and Gaspra, Sofia's contributions to the welfare of local inhabitants did not differ significantly from the efforts of other enlightened landowners of her day. But at Veidelevka, the largest estate Sofia inherited from her grandmother, her philanthropy took on a more modern character. Sofia rarely visited this remote estate, a vast ranch on the steppes of the rich agricultural province of Voronezh that raised purebred cattle, sheep, and horses. In addition to establishing the district's first hospital and a people's house there, Sofia supported the efforts of her estate manager, V. I. Volkov, to create a small nature preserve of virgin steppe in 1908. Three years later, she was approached by members of the St. Petersburg Imperial Society of Natural Science Researchers, who had been looking for a place to establish a biological research station for the study of steppe ecology. Sofia readily agreed to support such a station, for which she donated both land and funds to expand the preserve and construct the facilities. The grateful society named the station in her honor and elected her to honorary membership. Members of the society, along with women students from St. Petersburg, continued to conduct research there well into the war years, but in the turmoil of Russia's Civil War, the station was burned to the ground in 1919.[46]

Sofia's great-grandmother and grandfather would no doubt have been shocked and dismayed, however, by another use she found for the Panin properties she inherited: as a refuge for political dissidents. Gaspra is the best known of her estates for just this reason. In mid-1901 an elderly and already ailing Leo Tolstoy fell gravely ill. When his

Countess S. V. Panina Steppe Biological Research Station, main building, circa 1916. (V. S. Il'in, "Istoriia vozniknoveniia, organizatsiia i deiatel'nost' Stepnoi biologicheskoi stantsii imeni gr. S. V. Paninoi," *Trudy Petrogradskogo obshchestva estestvoispitatelei,* vol. XLVI [1916], otd. Botaniki [No. 1], 13)

doctors insisted that a change of climate was crucial for his recovery, Sofia offered Gaspra to the writer and his family for as long as needed. Tolstoy, his wife, and various other members of his family lived for ten months on the estate in 1901–2, his recuperation regularly interrupted by visits from admirers, including fellow writers Anton Chekhov and Maxim Gorky. Sofia's generous hospitality was simultaneously a political statement. By providing Tolstoy with a place to convalesce, she openly associated her name with the most famous Russian dissident of the day at a critical moment in his public career. Tolstoy was not only a renowned writer and moral philosopher, but also a relentless critic of the Russian state and Orthodox Church, which had excommunicated him just a few months before Sofia's invitation.

Russia's preacher of simplicity found the comfort and luxury of Sofia's mansion unlike anything he had ever experienced. "The beauty here is extraordinary," he wrote a friend shortly after arriving, "and I would be completely content but for my conscience."[47] Another letter to his brother rhapsodically described the elegant fountains, wide lawns, and exotic gardens that surrounded the mansion, where roses bloomed in abundance and the vineyard produced the most delicious grapes. The mansion's two terraces offered spectacular views of the mountains above and the sea below, and when Tolstoy grew stronger, he often

Gaspra, circa 1902. (private collection)

rode on horseback down the paths that led from Gaspra's heights to the
shore. As for the house, all of its furnishings and amenities were "first-
class." "So much for the simplicity in which I wanted to live," he ruefully
commented.[48]

    Although Sofia did not share Tolstoy's convictions about the sim-
ple life and the need to renounce wealth, she revered the man for his
literary masterpieces, his personal contributions to improving popular
welfare, and his courageous defense of social justice. Writing to Varya
in early 1896, for example, she praised the author for his "excellent" article against corporal punishment.[49] The famous opponent of church
and state occupied a prominent place in the activities of the Ligovsky
People's House. His works consistently ranked as the library's most
popular books. The institution marked the day of his burial in November 1910 with readings and discussions of his literary legacy and significance for adults and children.[50] Three years later, Sofia organized an
evening at the people's house devoted to Tolstoy, at which she herself
gave a lecture; the topics she chose included his school for peasants, his
work to promote literacy, his participation in famine relief, and his
work for the Moscow city census in 1889, which took him into some of
that city's worst slums and had an important influence on the evolution

of his political and social doctrines.[51] At the people's house as well as at Gaspra, Sofia paid little attention to political risk when honoring a man she admired and extending assistance to him at a time of need.

Gaspra also played a significant role in the history of the Kadet Party. As co-owner of the estate, Anastasia spent long periods of time there with her husband and relocated permanently to Gaspra in 1915 after Ivan retired from leadership of the party. The mansion frequently hosted informal political gatherings of Kadet leaders and liberal activists. One study of women in prerevolutionary St. Petersburg goes so far as to claim that Sofia turned Gaspra into "a real conspiratorial apartment for legal, semilegal and even completely illegal social organizations. Plans for the future reconstruction of Russia were laid at Gaspra. Deputies of the State Duma, Kadet Party activists, workers, zemstvo teachers and physicians, nurses—here they all found a refuge, support, and often generous material assistance from Countess Panina."[52] Considering the lack of evidence that Sofia directly supported the Kadets before 1917, the "Countess Panina" described in this account perhaps better fits her mother Anastasia. Sofia appears to have had no objection, however, when Anastasia and Ivan turned Gaspra into the liberal party's occasional southern headquarters.

Political dissidents of a different kind found shelter at the estate of Veidelevka, according to the memoirs of peasant activist Ivan Stoliarov. Born in 1882 to a family of impoverished potters, Stoliarov joined what he called the struggle for "justice and truth" while a student at an agricultural school. He was arrested and sent to his native province of Voronezh to live under police surveillance. There he met Alexander Bakunin, the close friend and neighbor of Sofia's mother and stepfather in the province of Tver. After Bakunin asked Sofia about possible employment for Stoliarov on her estate, she hired the young peasant revolutionary as a surveyor. There he joined other "politically unreliable" employees, who included the director of the local hospital founded by Sofia—a member of the Socialist Revolutionary Party, and the estate manager—an agronomist whom Sofia had taken on after he had been expelled from Tver as a "red." With the manager's tacit approval Stoliarov began conducting revolutionary propaganda among local peasants, urging them to join the national Peasants' Union organized in 1905. Sofia came to Stoliarov's aid a second time after he was arrested for political agitation and briefly imprisoned. She and Bakunin arranged for him to escape police surveillance in Voronezh and take a train to St. Petersburg. When he arrived in the capital, he recalled, he found her waiting on the station platform. She seated him in her carriage and took him to an "illegal apartment." It would be dangerous to stay long in St. Petersburg, Sofia warned him, so she came again for him the next morning, put him on a train to Finland, and gave him letters of recommendation to friends in Helsinki. With Sofia's financial assistance Stoliarov made his way to France, where he eventually earned a university degree in agricultural sciences.[53]

Stoliarov's recollections of Veidelevka as a haven for radicals are supported by police records. A secret police report on Sofia in 1916 identifies a physician's assistant who worked on her Voronezh estate, Andrei Shcherbachenko, as a local peasant leader whom the police kept under surveillance because of his "political unreliability." The man was thought to distribute illegal literature to peasants, "but very cautiously." Employing their usual method of guilt by association, the police supported their suspicions of Shcherbachenko by citing the "close relations and correspondence" he maintained with unnamed individuals who were "politically compromised." "Countess Panina," the report continues, "evidently protects Shcherbachenko. Thus his own brother and two of his sisters are being educated in secondary schools with Panina's funds."[54]

Yet the gendarmes do not appear to have kept Sofia herself under observation, or to have considered her or the causes she supported politically suspect. Overall, the normally hypersensitive tsarist police took a remarkably benign approach toward the "Red Countess." The 1916 police report states that "for eleven years of [its] existence, the activity of the departments of the 'People's House' of Countess Panina has not aroused doubts in [her] political reliability." After listing the roles Sofia played in other social organizations, such as the Society for the Protection of Women, and enumerating the St. Petersburg properties she owned, the report characterizes Sofia as "siding with" the liberal Kadet Party in her political views, although it specifies that she is "by no means to the left of it."[55]

Others were not so sure about her political reliability. Sofia's Panin relatives regarded the ways she spent the family fortune as "eccentric," she once told a young relative. Prince Viazemsky, her cousin's husband, warned her that she needed to keep a careful eye on the people's house, and not let her coworkers or visitors betray her trust and use it as a breeding ground for revolutionary propaganda.[56] Many of the working men and women who came to the Ligovsky People's House certainly perceived the political significance of her project. On the occasion of its tenth anniversary, for example, three women visitors wrote in Sofia's "Book of Deep Gratitude" to praise the people's house as a "broadly democratic" institution that upheld the values of "equality, fraternity, and liberty of the individual."[57] A letter Sofia received in 1913 from a former schoolmate at the Catherine Institute combined congratulations on the institution's tenth anniversary with an acknowledgment of the risks taken by the countess who worked in the slums of St. Petersburg. The schoolmate wrote that when she returned to the capital after a long absence, she heard some people praise Sofia's social work, while others accused her of being a "revolutionary." Russia, she told Sofia approvingly, needs more revolutionaries like her![58]

Such conflicting perceptions of Sofia demonstrate her skillful pursuit of a course of social action that received praise from progressives and gratitude from its beneficiaries, while never provoking the authorities to stop her work or her Panin relatives to sequester her inheritance, as they had three decades earlier in the case of her mother. Her repeated assertions of the nonpartisan character of her social work, while undoubtedly sincere, were also politically expedient. Perhaps one reason for her success lies in her extensive family connections within the close-knit world of the Russian elite and her choice of high-ranking allies such as Viazemsky and Princess Saksen-Altenburgskaya, whom Sofia shrewdly used to deflect suspicion aroused by her unconventional philanthropic causes. Such connections probably explain why her 1901 petition to establish the people's house received government approval in a matter of months, instead of years, and why the "Red Countess" was able to keep it open during the turmoil of 1905–6.

Another reason for Sofia's success in charting a middle course amid political extremes may be found in her personal qualities. Her energy, warmth, and sincerity exerted their magic on people she met from across the social spectrum. Visitors to the people's house found her approachable and genuinely interested in their lives. Writing after Sofia's death in 1956, Alexei Kapralov, a former student in the evening classes who became a professor of agronomy in Europe, published a tribute to her in a Paris émigré newspaper. A frequent visitor to the people's house in the years before World War I, Kapralov regularly met Sofia at the tea table, in the auditorium, and at the library. "Every time," he recalled, she "produced an unforgettable impression on me: sometimes it became simply incomprehensible how she, so distant by birth, education and life from the popular working masses, managed to approach them so simply and closely." She was "a true popular democrat," he

Sofia, circa 1913. (Tsentral'nyi
gosudarstvennyi arkhiv kinofotofonodokumentov g. Sankt-
Peterburga, G7534)

claimed, and remained one to the end of her life. At the same time, he
continued, her moral strength "ennobled everyone who came in contact with her."[59] Members of the Russian intelligentsia admired her
commitment to social service and progress through education, which
fit squarely within its progressive ethos. Sofia even dressed like an *intel-
ligentka*: in formal photographs such as one taken around 1913, she is
dressed modestly and conservatively, eschewing the latest ladies' fashions and jewelry and looking more like a teacher than a countess.

Yet no matter how much she mingled with the workers, teachers,
and volunteers at the people's house, Sofia could never completely
transform herself from an aristocrat into a "popular democrat." Nor is
it clear that she wished to do so. Unlike Tolstoy, who renounced his
right to be called "count," Sofia used her title all her life. Many visitors
and coworkers could not envision her in any other role than the noble
and generous benefactress. Even Alexandra Peshekhonova perceived
the gulf between them. In a remarkably frank yet tender letter she

managed to send to Sofia in Geneva in 1923, Alexandra responded to what appears to have been an outpouring of anguished self-criticism in a letter, now lost, from Sofia. How could she ever have reproached Sofia, Alexandra wrote, when she loved and respected her so much? "Would it have been appropriate," Alexandra continued, "for unworthy me to instruct or reproach someone who was liberating herself continuously and unrestrainedly from her shortcomings," and developing "before our eyes?" No effort by Sofia to erase the social distance between coworkers and herself could have succeeded, Alexandra implies. "During the first years of our acquaintance, you stood so far from all of us: you were the sorceress who appeared amongst us for the realization of our daring dreams. . . . And later we knew you almost exclusively as the head of the House, who continually took care that things were as warm and bright as possible for everyone." The rest of Sofia's life, Alexandra noted, was "behind seventy little locks."[60]

Refusing to rebuke her "immeasurably dear and deeply beloved" Sofia for any aloofness, Alexandra seems to have recognized how those around the young countess, by idealizing and revering her, played their own part in keeping Sofia "so far from all of us." While coworkers called her by her name and patronymic, "Sofia Vladimirovna," the respectful form of address used across social classes, others, especially working-class men and women, often referred to her as "Your Excellency" [*Vashe Siiatel'stvo*]. Within the walls of the people's house centuries-old habits of social deference coexisted uneasily with its more egalitarian ethos. Russians continued to be legally defined by their social estate—peasant, merchant, noble—for decades after the abolition of serfdom in 1861. To be sure, advances in education and economic modernization were eroding the once rigid class structure, creating the kinds of new social identities and opportunities for cross-class interactions found at places such as the Ligovsky People's House. Its visitors, primarily peasant in origin, had left their villages to find a living in urban occupations; they flocked to the people's house to learn urban ways. Yet because many of them were children or grandchildren of serfs, they understandably reverted to customs of deference when interacting with a countess.

The social origins of Sofia's friends and coworkers were significantly more diverse, reflecting the capital's social and economic complexity. Some, like Alexandra, were the educated offspring of skilled urban craftsmen, while others, such as Liudmila Grammatchikova and theater director Pavel Gaideburov, came from the families of journalists, actors, or members of similar professions. Collectively they belonged to the

lower ranks of the capital's intelligentsia, a mixed middle stratum of
teachers, artists, professionals, and social activists. None of Sofia's coworkers was a social peer. While perhaps less awed than the working-
class visitors by her august lineage and wealth, they hardly would pre-
sume to consider her their equal, no matter how much she might have
wished to be treated as one. It was people around her, not Sofia, who
created the image of her as "our little sun" or the "good fairy" found in
so many of their letters and testimonials.[61] When added to her youthful
energy, warm demeanor, and personal charm, Sofia's status as a countess contributed to her charisma.

The philosophy that guided Sofia's public life derived from values
and traditions of both the social class she was born into and the class
she adopted. Drawing on the aristocratic traditions of her Panin forebears, she believed in taking care of those who depended on her. She
was committed to being a good steward of her inherited wealth. At the
same time she shared the intelligentsia's faith in the necessity of knowledge and culture in order to create the basis for a "free political order."
Her opinion of the common people was widely shared by educated
Russians of her day. She did not idealize the poor as morally superior
to the upper classes, as did Tolstoy. On the contrary, she approached
the working-class men and women of Petersburg from a position of
educational and cultural superiority, sometimes characterizing them as
childlike in their ignorance. Believing that they shared the needs common to all human beings—the need for knowledge, hope, beauty, and
joy as much as for food and shelter—Sofia sought to raise them to her
level, not to lower herself to theirs or minimize the social and economic
differences that separated them. Her idealism was rooted in her faith in
the power of culture and education to transform individuals, and not in
the possibility of creating a new and better world by righting the injus-
tices of the old one.

Sofia's belief in the feasibility of cross-class understanding and collaboration echoes themes found often in the history of Russian liberalism. At the very beginning of the movement in the late 1870s, as radicals
waged a campaign of terrorism against the state, Ivan Petrunkevich,
liberalism's founder and Sofia's stepfather, initiated unsuccessful attempts to convince them to cooperate with his more moderate opposition movement. Again during the 1917 Revolution and the Civil War
that followed, she and her fellow Kadet Party leaders struggled and
failed to create similar coalitions with socialists and find a common
set of revolutionary goals. But in the prewar years when the Ligovsky

People's House flourished, reformers such as Sofia found a common language with at least a segment of the working class, the language of cultural enlightenment and self-improvement. Rather than seeking to change the system, Sofia aimed to prepare Russia's masses, one man and woman at a time, for their future responsibilities in a democratic polity. With the political reforms wrested from the autocracy by the revolution of 1905 that future seemed to be on the horizon, until war engulfed Russia along with the rest of Europe in the summer of 1914.

6

Sofia Goes to War

The fateful month of July 1914 began in St. Petersburg with a storm of labor unrest that raged for almost two weeks. A violent confrontation between police and workers on July 3 at the Putilov Armament Works grew into city-wide protests against police brutality and government repression. Thousands of laborers from the city's outlying factory precincts went on strike, erecting barricades, overturning trams, and fighting with mounted Cossack soldiers. Although the city center remained calm, the worst labor demonstrations since the 1905 Revolution embarrassed the imperial government, which was hosting a visit by the French president. The mood in the capital changed abruptly, however, after July 19 (August 1). That evening the German ambassador delivered his country's declaration of war to the Russian foreign minister. The next day, patriotic crowds replaced enraged workers in the squares and streets of the capital. According to Alexander Kerensky, "the revolutionary strikers of the evening before marched in their thousands to the Allied embassies," joining "huge crowds from all walks of life" who "cheered their sovereign and sang 'God Save the Tsar.'" Although Kerensky was a man highly disposed to hyperbole, numerous contemporaries also remember how the capital's streets changed overnight when the news of war broke.[1]

The war originated as yet another flare-up of nationalist tensions in the Balkans—the third since 1908—with the assassination in late June of the Austrian Archduke Franz Ferdinand in Sarajevo by a Serbian nationalist. Over the course of the following month the European powers became entangled in the diplomatic crisis provoked by the assassination. When Serbia did not agree to all of the draconian conditions of its ultimatum, Austria-Hungary declared war. Seeking to support its Slavic sister and maintain its prestige as a Great Power, Russia began the process of mobilization. Germany followed suit the next day and then escalated the crisis with its declaration of war against Russia on July 19 and against France two days later. Within a few days France and Great Britain had joined Russia and Serbia against the Central Powers in the first all-European war since the defeat of Napoleon one hundred years before.

On Sunday, July 20 (August 2), Emperor Nicholas II, Empress Alexandra, and their children stepped onto the balcony of the Winter Palace. The vast open square below was filled with tens of thousands of loyal Russians, many on their knees, others waving their hats, all singing the national anthem.[2] Among the throngs in Palace Square was an unlikely patriot—the feminist journalist Tyrkova-Williams. The recollections of that day by a woman who had been an outspoken liberal opponent of the autocracy since the 1905 Revolution convey the spirit of intense patriotism and national unity that seized the capital's educated classes in the war's first weeks. "The danger that unexpectedly arose before Russia sharply changed the mood of the rebellious intelligentsia," she claimed. This was visible on Palace Square that day, where "many had tears in their eyes. It seemed that Russia—renewed, unanimous, and brightened—rushed to the walls of the Winter Palace, around which the Empire rose up and became stronger. It was an amazing sight." Similar patriotic demonstrations took place across the empire. The complex operation of mobilizing almost 4 million men into the army during the first weeks of the war went surprisingly smoothly. But a discerning observer would have noticed the somber mood and occasional antiwar protests that accompanied the military call-up in many places, and might have wondered whether the lower classes shared educated society's wholehearted dedication to the war effort.[3]

Sofia was not present to witness the stirring display of patriotism on Palace Square. As usual, she was spending the summer at her Marfino estate. Like Tyrkova-Williams and most Russians—indeed, like most Europeans—she was caught by surprise by the outbreak of war. Three weeks after it began, as the Germans occupied Brussels and clashed with the Russian army in East Prussia, she sat down to write a letter to Lidia Yakovleva, her friend and coworker at the people's house. Far from the patriotic tumult of the capital, surrounded by Marfino's bucolic summer scenery, Sofia reacted to the news of war with mixed sentiments of shock and excitement. The outbreak of war had "overturned" everything, she wrote. "It seems that everyone and everything have been displaced, have begun to live in a new way, and one has to adapt everything to this dislocation." A sense of apprehension about the war's inevitable horrors did not dampen her eagerness to be part of the war effort. "I would like to fill the entire letter with exclamation marks," she continued, "because my entire heart is filled with them. These are exclamations of horror and ecstasy and astonishment—but in general, despite all the horror, how terribly interesting it is to live, and *how* instructive!" Sofia longed to get into the "whirlpool" of public life in the capital, she told her friend, where "I would like to apply myself to work as intensively as possible." She was already thinking about how the Ligovsky People's House could help; at the very least, it should take a leading role in aid to soldiers' families, "and in this area the work that lies ahead is enormous." To judge by this letter, which lacks any expression of the devotion to the Romanov dynasty that had so moved Tyrkova-Williams on Palace Square, it was Sofia's passion to serve those in need, not God and Tsar, that moved her in the late summer of 1914.[4]

The Great War, modern history's first total war, not only mobilized millions of men into mass armies but also depended on the efforts of countless civilians, especially women, to support the military effort and bear the burdens of war on the home front as well as the frontlines. It imposed exceptional economic and social demands on civilian populations and by necessity pulled women into unfamiliar roles. Russia faced especially formidable challenges both at the front and behind the lines. The empire confronted three opponents—Germany, Austria-Hungary, and its longtime rival Turkey, which joined the Central Powers in October 1914—across a front that extended for hundreds of miles from the Baltic Sea to the Black Sea and all the way to the mountains of the Caucasus. Little troop support could be expected from its principal allies, France and Great Britain, fighting far to the west. The scale of Russian mobilization was enormous: more than 18 million men served in the Russian army during the course of the war, 5 million of whom were drafted in its first five months. Roughly 2 million soldiers were killed and millions more were taken prisoner, wounded, or permanently disabled.[5] On the Western Front the conflict quickly settled into a war of attrition in the trenches of Belgium and France. On the Eastern Front, however, a vast swath of Russia's western borderlands fell to German occupation in the Great Retreat of 1915 and created a massive refugee crisis.

Recurring mobilizations left huge holes in Russia's labor force. As war depleted villages of able-bodied men, women performed most of the agricultural labor. In large-scale manufacturing, the proportion of women workers rose from 30 percent to nearly 40 percent, and in St. Petersburg, the center of Russia's metalworking and engineering industries and the site of numerous armament factories, the number of women working in industry doubled.[6] As in other European cities, the capital's residents had to get used to the sight of women driving trams and performing other often dangerous jobs from which they were traditionally barred. By 1917, for example, women had replaced men as the janitors, doorkeepers, and furnace stokers at Sofia's people's house.[7] As the war dragged on, women's auxiliary army corps were created in Britain, Austria, and Germany, where thousands of young women in uniform replaced soldiers in clerical and service jobs. In Russia, where individual women had joined the regular army since the beginning of the war, the army permitted the formation of all-female battalions in 1917, partly in response to demands by young female patriots, partly to shame male soldiers increasingly prone to desert. A few of the women's battalions even saw combat.[8]

Women also stepped forward to provide assistance to the millions of soldiers and civilians whom the war plunged into acute need. After a few short weeks of crash training, thousands of women donned the white headdresses of Red Cross nurses and traveled to military hospitals at the front and in the rear. Well-to-do women in Russia as elsewhere in Europe converted their mansions into infirmaries for wounded soldiers, opened workshops and canteens for soldiers' families, and raised funds for orphans and refugees. In a dramatic gesture of patriotic support for her countrymen in arms, Tyrkova-Williams raised funds to equip forty-eight freight cars with food, field kitchens, horses, hospital equipment, and medicines for the front in December 1914. Accompanied by her husband, son, and daughter, who had recently become a nurse, she then traveled with the train from the capital to the front, where she spent the entire first winter of the war.[9]

The war profoundly changed Sofia as well. In July 1914 she was an energetic woman in her early forties, a successful and respected philanthropist. While her name was a familiar one among Petersburg's liberal intelligentsia and members of city government, she seldom ventured outside of her particular causes—cultural enlightenment, adult education, the prevention of prostitution—into a broader public arena. Sofia's August 1914 letter to Lidia suggests that unlike Tyrkova-Williams, she first responded to the outbreak of war with thoughts of the needs of its female victims on the home front, not those of soldiers. She imagined that her contribution to the war effort would take place within the familiar walls of the Ligovsky People's House, in collaboration with longtime friends and coworkers there and in service to the working-class population she knew well. But the war's growing demands soon drew her out of the Ligovka neighborhood into city-wide relief work and municipal affairs. Gradually but inexorably Sofia left the comfortable role of benevolent progressive philanthropist for the responsibilities and high visibility of a civic leader in the empire's capital in wartime.

When Sofia returned to the city in the late summer of 1914, it already bore all the signs of a country fully committed to war. The "fever" of general mobilization had seized the city, she remembered years later. During July and August alone approximately one hundred thirty-eight thousand of its adult male residents were drafted.[10] The war even transformed the name of the capital. In mid-August, as the first Russian troops met the German Army in the forests and swamps of the Eastern Front, Nicholas II issued a decree changing St. Petersburg's German-sounding name to a more patriotic, Russian one—Petrograd. The Ligovsky People's House was one of numerous buildings that were converted to war-related uses. It became one of the city's mobilization centers, where reservists called up for active duty bid farewell to their families. Sofia also turned its entire second floor, with its spacious theater, into an infirmary for wounded soldiers. The cafeteria began providing thousands of free meals to soldiers' families. Although the theater was closed, volunteers and paid staff managed to keep the libraries, children's activities, instructional workshops, and even some of the adult courses running. Sofia's commitment to war relief is also reflected in the scale of the funds she supplied to operate the people's house. In addition to funding the remaining prewar activities and employees until the end of 1917, she provided almost all of the financial support for the infirmary and the expanded cafeteria. She also paid to have the entire interior repainted, new toilets installed, and the heating repaired.[11]

In addition to beds for the wounded, free cabbage soup for the hungry, and day care for the children of the growing number of mothers entering the workforce, the Ligovsky People's House provided Petrograd's home front with badly needed volunteers, necessary to staff a new state assistance program of unprecedented scale and significance. Military mobilization deprived families all across the empire of their main breadwinners. According to an important new law of 1912, the wives and families of soldiers called to active duty were entitled to receive monthly allowances (*paiki*) from the state, but the law had never before been implemented. A system to locate, register, and assist those entitled to assistance had to be devised quickly. While the funds came from the state treasury, the law entrusted the distribution of aid to local governments, which were expected to determine their own procedures and recruit their own personnel to carry out the task.

It is difficult to overstate the significance of the 1912 law. First, it may fairly be said that the system of wartime allowances that the law initiated in late summer of 1914 eventually contributed to driving the imperial government into fiscal crisis.[12] Second, by mobilizing thousands of civilian volunteers for its implementation, the system brought educated, upper- and middle-class Russians into close contact with the families of rank-and-file soldiers in their homes and at registration offices. These encounters acquainted the well-to-do with the burdens the war placed on the poor, opening a window through which the wealthy could witness the popular mood. Moreover, for the first time in the history of social welfare in Russia a category of people received a legally fixed entitlement to government assistance that was unrelated to the extent or nature of their need. In addition, as historians have pointed out with respect to similar allowance systems in Austria and Britain, women entered into an unprecedented financial relationship with government, which took on the responsibilities of a "surrogate husband." Finally, the outbreak of war revealed the political implications of the 1912 law. According to its terms, the *soldatki* (soldiers' wives) who were its beneficiaries were not needy recipients of charity, but citizens—or at least the wives and mothers of citizens—with a right to state support. The countless difficulties of implementing such a vast and complex system, the delays in disbursement, and the inevitably growing gap between the payments and the rising cost of living eventually incited discontent against both the war and the state among female recipients of this entitlement. By planting the seeds of political consciousness among *soldatki*, the law "laid down a 'time bomb' that would explode in 1917," in the vivid words of the historian Liudmila Bulgakova.[13]

When mobilization began in July and August 1914, the Petrograd city government had a system already in place to implement the 1912 law: a network of twenty district "guardianships for the poor" (*popechitel'stva o bednykh*). The guardianships were first developed in Moscow in 1894 to provide a decentralized system to deliver effective assistance to the urban poor by using district visitors to investigate needy cases. Although charity experts applauded the Moscow experiment and dozens of other towns adopted it, the St. Petersburg city government did not introduce guardianships until after the 1905 Revolution. Unlike Moscow, with its civic spirit and history of grassroots initiative, civil society in the capital was stunted, in the eyes of contemporaries, by a conservative city government and a population dependent on service in the imperial bureaucracy.[14] Most of the city's guardianships for the poor "dragged out a miserable existence" before the war, recollected Prince Vladimir Obolensky, a liberal leader active in war relief in the capital and friend of Sofia's. They attracted mostly "retired officials and bored ladies," he claimed, who distributed meager handouts to widows and orphans.[15] The war radically altered not only the tasks entrusted to the guardianships, but the underlying principle of their operations: the aid they now distributed was not charity, but the state's monetary recognition of the sacrifices made by those who sent their husbands and sons to war.

The short history of the 13th Guardianship, which opened in 1908 and served the district that included Sofia's people's house, illustrates the ways the war pushed the capital's torpid residents into civic action. In peacetime the guardianship supported two cafeterias and a small home for elderly indigent women. In addition it distributed modest monthly or one-time grants, helped poor schoolchildren with school fees and shoes, and passed out gifts of food and clothing at Christmas and Easter.[16] With the outbreak of the war the 13th Guardianship was suddenly put in charge of thousands of families of active-duty soldiers and mobilized reservists. Accustomed to distributing kopecks, shoes, and Easter cakes to a handful of poor clients, it now bore responsibility for the legal, fair, and accurate disbursement of hundreds of thousands of rubles from the state. In addition, guardianships were expected to provide supplementary assistance to families in particular need, using their own and municipal funds.

The area of the city served by the 13th Guardianship posed additional challenges. The Alexander Nevsky district covered an enormous territory, larger than that of any other guardianship. It extended to the southwest in an expanding triangle from the Nikolaev Railroad Station at the city's center for several miles to the city's edge. Since public transportation barely extended into the district, volunteers and clients had to rely mainly on their feet to reach each other. The district's wartime population, which exceeded one hundred sixty thousand, was overwhelmingly working-class and one of the city's poorest. That economic profile produced an extremely lopsided ratio of those needing aid to those distributing it. Very few residents of Alexander Nevsky district had either the means or the leisure time to volunteer with the 13th Guardianship. On July 19 and 28, when the first two mobilizations called up about nine thousand men from the district, many of the guardianship's officers and regular volunteers were away on summer vacation. Those members still in the city, joined by about forty new volunteer and paid investigators, worked from seven in the morning to midnight to locate and register draftees' families.[17]

Sofia's people's house was one of the few community institutions in the district, and its experienced staff of teachers, librarians, and other coworkers knew the local population well. Yet for reasons that the reports of neither organization divulge, the people's house and the 13th Guardianship kept their distance from each other before the war. An unnamed representative of the Ligovsky People's House had a seat on the guardianship's investigating committee, and Alexandra Peshekhonova sat on its cafeteria committee, but otherwise the two organizations were not connected. In the first frantic weeks of mobilization no one from the Ligovsky People's House appears to have joined the 13th Guardianship to assist in the massive effort of organizing and distributing state allowances to soldiers' families.[18]

That relationship changed radically once Sofia returned from Marfino to the capital in mid-August and turned her energies to war relief. Meeting on August 30, the governing council reorganized the 13th Guardianship to incorporate a large number of new volunteers, many from the people's house, with Sofia at their head. Eight new commissions were created, the most important of which, the new "Investigative Commission," bore responsibility for locating, registering, and keeping track of the soldiers' wives and families entitled to assistance. Its cochairs were Sofia's cousin Nadezhda Zurova and the director of

Payment of state assistance to soldiers' families at the 3rd Guardianship, Petrograd 1916. (Tsentral'nyi gosudarstvennyi arkhiv kinofotofonodokumentov g. Sankt-Peterburga, D3385)

the people's house theater, Pavel Gaideburov, who had managed to get home after being stranded in Switzerland at the beginning of the war. They supervised fifty-six investigators, many of them affiliated with the people's house. In addition to determining eligibility for state allowances, the investigators, some of whom managed more than a hundred families each, recommended their clients for supplemental aid in money or kind. After another four thousand five hundred men from the district were called up on November 15, the Investigative Commission had several thousand families under its care.[19]

Most of the other commissions created on August 30 were also led by coworkers from Sofia's people's house. Her beloved mentor Alexandra, for example, headed the commission in charge of the 13th Guardianship's children's services. Sofia herself joined the Work Commission, whose knitting and sewing workshops gave temporary work to *soldatki*, and also served on the employment and finance committees. On September 3 the council of the 13th Guardianship established a central bureau to coordinate all of its war-related relief activities. At the bureau's first meeting two days later Sofia was elected chairwoman, thus placing her at the head of all war-related assistance conducted by the 13th Guardianship. The reorganization was completed on September 8, when the general assembly of the entire guardianship voted to enlarge the governing council by sixteen new members, including Sofia and six of her closest associates from the people's house, and also unanimously elected her to be an honorary member. The guardianship's general assembly also selected Sofia as its candidate for elections to a new city-wide Council for the Relief of Soldiers' Families, made up of elected representatives from all the guardianships.[20]

The meeting on September 8 solidified the partnership between two long-estranged organizations, the Ligovsky People's House and the 13th Guardianship, brought together by necessity due to the war. It also marked a turning point in Sofia's public life. At the people's house Sofia was used to being in charge and to working with people she knew well. By joining the guardianship she entered a new social orbit, and although she quickly rose to positions of leadership, she also gave up a certain measure of control. The partnership united her efforts and those of her coworkers at the people's house not only with a rival charitable organization, but also with the city government, which oversaw the operation of the system of family allowances, and with the central government, which funded them. For the first time, Sofia placed herself before the public as a candidate for an elective office when she successfully ran as her guardianship's representative for a seat on the city-wide guardianship council. As a result of her decision to work with the 13th Guardianship Sofia moved into the center of war relief operations in the Russian capital.

The transformation of the 13th Guardianship from a stale charity office before the war into a bustling hub of social services exemplifies the ways that the early years of World War I energized Russians. The number of volunteers in all twenty of Petrograd's guardianships increased six-fold in the first two months of the war.[21] All across the empire, men and especially women joined municipal guardianships, formed refugee relief societies, and staffed hospitals and canteens for soldiers. Initially Russians appeared to be united across class lines in a common cause, from the empress and grand duchesses who nursed the wounded in the palace at Tsarskoe Selo to the schoolgirls who registered soldiers' families.[22] Organizations like the 13th Guardianship gave women in particular the vehicle they needed to contribute meaningfully to the war effort while staying within the familiar, feminine realm of social

service. Sofia greeted the outpouring of voluntary activism with elation. "How much has happened in public life . . .!" she exclaimed in
June 1915 in another letter to Lidia, who also volunteered for the 13th
Guardianship. "All around there reigns unusual animation and fever-
ish activity, and this gladdens my heart." The members of the city
guardianships, most of whom worked without pay, performed "a kind
of voluntary military service," she reflected many years later. "Not
without reason," she wrote with pride, "we considered ourselves to be
also sitting in the trenches, continuously, during the course of all three
years of the war."[23] In 1915 A. K. Yakovleva, the founder and editor of a
new magazine, *Women and War*, used words similar to Sofia's to describe women's service: the war, she claimed, moved women into the
"front lines of life" and turned "everyone into fighters."[24] Both comments
testify to women's sense of a vital interdependence between military
and domestic needs, and their conviction that by serving on the home
front they too were taking part in the nation's great struggle.

Sofia's involvement in war relief soon extended beyond the boundaries of the district encompassing the people's house and the 13th
Guardianship to take on city-wide, then national dimensions. In 1915
she founded the Central Information Bureau of Petrograd Guardianships to coordinate all twenty of the city's guardianships, and was
elected its chairwoman. In August of that year, as waves of refugees
from German-occupied territory poured into the capital, she joined the
Petrograd City Committee for Assistance to Refugees and began attending its weekly meetings.[25] In May 1916 she was elected to the governing
council of Russia's national association for charity and public welfare.[26]
War relief connected Sofia to the two national federations of local governments, the All-Russian Union of Towns and the All-Russian Union
of Zemstvos, created at the beginning of the war to take charge of medical aid to soldiers. War relief also connected her to these federations'
liberal leaders. One of these was Obolensky, a member of the Kadet
Party's Central Committee, who led the Petrograd branch of the Union
of Towns. Obolensky came to know Sofia in 1915 through the committee
for aid to refugees, which he chaired, as well as through his involvement
with the city's 19th City Guardianship, and they remained lifelong
friends.

Obolensky's recollections of Sofia, written in the late 1920s or 1930s,
offer insights into the reputation she enjoyed among municipal leaders
and liberal politicians. "This remarkable Russian woman" was no
typical high society philanthropist, content simply to make monetary

donations, he insisted. "She took the most active part in the organizations she created," injecting her "inexhaustible energy and initiative"
into them. She worked "like a man," introducing precision, order, and
accountability into every endeavor she joined. In addition to her organizational talents, her ability to find and attract the right people guaranteed
that "every project she undertook succeeded in her hands." Working
"like a man" with experienced local government leaders like Obolensky,
Sofia gained respect and visibility among the capital's male-dominated
liberal political elite.[27]

   The challenges faced by Sofia, Obolensky, and other leaders of relief
in the capital escalated dramatically in the war's second year after a
series of devastating military reversals. A powerful German assault
on the Third Army in April 1915 triggered what came to be known as
the Great Retreat, during which up to a million soldiers were killed or
wounded, another million were taken prisoner, and a huge swath of
territory fell under German occupation. Wave after wave of recruits,
many of them with barely any military training, departed for the front,
where the staggeringly high casualty rates quickly depleted their
ranks. Acute shortages of artillery shells became evident in late 1914,
followed by deficits in rifles and ammunition in 1915. The retreat and
shortages naturally weakened morale. In the words of the historian
Allan K. Wildman, the "Russian Army was held together by the slen-
derest of threads in the fall of 1915," afflicted by mass desertions and
insubordination.[28]

   Petrograd's inhabitants had a front-row seat to observe both the
collapse of army morale and the imperial government's increasing in-
ability to prosecute the war. The state of the army on the frontlines
could be sensed from the mood of the tens of thousands of soldiers who
recuperated in the city's hospitals or waited in its garrisons to be sent to
the front. Letters that families received from their husbands and sons
complained of fatigue, meager rations, and poor leadership at the front;
many questioned the whole point of the war. The monarchy's growing
dysfunction deepened the pessimism and discontent. Scandals in the
highest ranks of government and conflict between the tsar and the State
Duma filled newspapers and fed the capital's rumor mill. After being
removed from his position in June 1915, Minister of War Vladimir Su-
khomlinov went on trial for treason in March 1916. Nicholas II, who
took over as Commander-in-Chief in mid-1915 against the advice of
most of his cabinet, now spent most of his time eight hundred kilometers
from Petrograd at General Headquarters in Mogilev, leaving the

empress and a sorry collection of her inept or corrupt ministerial cronies to represent the monarchy in the capital. Persistent if false rumors that Alexandra was conducting a sexual relationship with the monk Grigory Rasputin and supporting her native Germany against Russia fatally undermined Russians' loyalty to the Romanov dynasty. Both soldiers and civilians increasingly blamed treason at the top for the military failures.[29]

The advances and retreats along the front during 1915 brought new demands for military equipment, medical services, and relief. With their trust in the government shaken, Russians redoubled their commitment to the voluntary associations and quasi-government organizations that had channeled civilian aid to the war effort since late summer of 1914. In those first months of the war Sofia never imagined that these public organizations would have to assume responsibility for procuring not only bandages but also basic military supplies. In December 1914, for example, she attended a meeting of a committee created to raise money for war-related needs. A proposal to collect boots for soldiers provoked a heated discussion. Petrograd's mayor Count Ivan Ivanovich Tolstoy, who chaired the meeting, recorded in his diary how Sofia "absolutely opposed" the idea, "considering it shameful in the eyes of all of Europe, including our enemies, for the military and for the government itself" to rely on voluntary organizations to supply such military essentials as soldiers' boots.[30] By 1916, however, the Union of Zemstvos and the Union of Towns, now united under the name Zemgor, were delivering not only boots but even bullets to Russian soldiers at the front—a graphic demonstration of the central government's ineffectiveness.

Sofia still found grounds for hope when she reflected on the transformative effects of war relief at a meeting of the League for Women's Equal Rights in February of 1916. The "flames of war," she told her audience, had ignited even the "indifferent hearts" of the capital's residents and finally created an active citizenry in a city whose inhabitants were notoriously apathetic toward municipal affairs. It had taken a world war to raise Petrograd to this new level of civic consciousness and make it more like other large European cities, where "every city-dweller, recognizing that he is also a citizen, considers it his elementary duty to participate in local self-government and local public life." The outpouring of patriotism and dedication to aiding victims of the war had created a rare and welcome spirit of unity. "All of our separate gardens turned into one common field," she rejoiced, and "we all felt ourselves part of one common organism, whose life and well-being depended on how each of us would do that small but crucial work to which we were appointed." Sofia also took note in her speech of the momentous democratic implications of the 1912 law on state allowances to soldiers' families, and the voluntarism it relied upon for its implementation. The war, in her view, had transformed the aid provided by the city's district guardianships for the poor from routine charity into a "matter of justice, law, and the social order." The guardianships now attracted "democratic and educated forces, who have nothing in common with the usual, old 'do-gooding.'"[31] War relief, in short, had upended old definitions of poverty and charity, turning Russians from passive subjects into active citizens.

Sofia's reference to "democratic and educated forces" in this speech hinted at the increasing disillusionment of public activists, who were losing confidence in the tsarist government and becoming "democratic" in both composition and mood. Tens of thousands of civilian volunteers and paid employees from all classes of society were now providing essential services at the Zemgor's medical facilities, refugee evacuation centers, canteens, and supply depots, efforts that were beginning to pay off in a better-equipped, better-supplied army in 1916. The vocabulary Sofia employed in her speech—words like "justice," "law," and "citizen," along with references to the ways voluntary organizations contributed to "the highest state interest"—had acquired unmistakable political implications by early 1916. Her words would not have been lost on her audience from the League for Women's Equal Rights, which continued to lobby the government for women's suffrage and civil rights during the war.

Yet Sofia's speech is as notable for what she does not say as for what she does. Although she was addressing Russia's largest feminist association, she made no mention of women's special contributions to the war, let alone the subject of suffrage and equal rights. She used a democratic vocabulary but stayed silent about the need for political change. Instead, she focused on the rebirth of charity, hailing the transformation of the Petrograd municipal guardianships as volunteer aid organizations. It is entirely possible that the Russian censors deleted from the printed version of her speech any explicit references she may have made to the need for women's suffrage or other reforms.[32] Alternatively, Sofia may have chosen to continue to identify herself publicly as working within the feminine sphere of social service, not the masculine arena of political combat. The speech also suggests her continued attachment to the ideal of national unity that had animated her prewar work at the

Ligovsky People's house—an ideal that rejected class divisions and political partisanship.

Two months later Sofia tried to make a similar argument about the liberating and unifying effects of war when she spoke at a meeting organized by one of the guardianships. The social services now provided by the guardianships, she assured her audience, bore no resemblance to the conventional charity they had dispensed during the prewar period. The war, "like a storm," had ripped away the "swaddling bands" that had previously restrained social initiatives. War—mankind's "terrible, depressing, and sinister gray companion," in Sofia's words—must and will be replaced by the "living organism" created by "our concerted efforts," she predicted hopefully. Once again, in public she tried to voice optimism about the future.[33]

But Sofia's celebration of national unity in her upbeat speeches in February and April 1916 was at best wishful thinking and at worst a denial of the darkening mood and simmering conflicts within both the capital's educated class and its working classes in early 1916. It seems likely that by this time Sofia privately shared the liberal elite's growing disillusionment with the war and the country's leadership. Like virtually everyone else she paid attention to the rumors that saturated wartime Petrograd. Visiting the ailing Mayor Tolstoy in late 1915, she regaled him with the latest news about the possible resignation of the commander of the Northern Army and his likely replacement; she also gossiped about the influence of Rasputin. In early 1916, she told Tolstoy about a visit she had received from Prime Minister Boris Stürmer, a crony of Rasputin's whom the liberal elite detested. Like many other Russians with German-sounding last names who sought to dodge the widespread hatred and suspicion toward anything German, Stürmer came to Sofia to seek her consent to change his name to Panin, his mother's maiden name. (After consulting with relatives, she refused.) Mayor Tolstoy also recorded her horrified reaction to the city council election of February 1916, which resulted in the defeat of progressive candidates and the victory of conservatives. The outcome caused her such extreme distress, according to Tolstoy, that she considered resigning from the Bureau of Guardianships.[34] Her dismay is understandable. The relief committees to which she belonged depended upon the city council's support. The election, which was conducted under prewar laws that gave the right to vote to only a small percentage of the urban population with the necessary property qualifications, dramatized the glaring discrepancy between Russia's extremely narrow franchise and

the de facto democratization generated by the contributions and sacrifices millions were making to the war effort. By demonstrating the persistent right-wing orientation of the narrow Petrograd electorate, the
election of February 1916 must have seemed a discouraging setback to
the civic progress Sofia publicly celebrated at the meeting of the League
for Women's Equal Rights that same month.

The return of conservatives to the city council occurred amidst a
visible deterioration of economic and social conditions in the capital. For
the first year or so of the war, Petrograd appeared to cope reasonably
well with its burdens. The city's voluntary organizations and municipal
authorities provided soldiers' families and other needy groups with
necessary aid and kept city services in operation. The Petrograd population appeared to accept the war with passive resignation, and there
was as yet little organized anti-war propaganda or agitation. The socialist parties were weakened by prewar arrests, wartime mobilization, and
internal disagreements over whether to support or oppose the war. A
number of the most stridently anti-war socialist leaders were abroad,
including the Bolsheviks' Lenin. But the military catastrophes of spring
and summer 1915 undermined both the material and psychological
well-being of the capital's residents. While the horrifying costs in lives,
territory, and national pride shocked and dismayed Russians all across
the empire, the Great Retreat exerted an especially powerful impact on
the citizens of Petrograd. The defeat of the Russian Northern Army and
Germany's conquest of Russian Poland appeared to leave the capital
wide open to the enemy's advance. Rumors about possible German occupation and the evacuation of the government led to an outburst of
panic in the late summer of 1915. The army's constant need for soldiers
resulted in repeated mobilizations. (There were nineteen national call-
ups from July 1914 to March 1917.) They drained the city's labor force
of male workers, adding thousands more *soldatki* and their children to
the government relief rolls. By the end of 1915 Petrograd, which already
had more than two million inhabitants at the beginning of the war,
had actually grown by more than three hundred thousand souls. This
growth was fed by increasing numbers of soldiers garrisoned in the
capital, along with the flood of refugees from the war zones and the
arrival of tens of thousands of wounded at the city's military hospitals.[35]

From 1915 to 1916 the prices of fuel, housing, foodstuffs, and other
consumer goods rose alarmingly. The impact of galloping inflation and
shortages could be seen on the city's streets, in the long lines of people
waiting to buy essentials. With the disruption of deliveries of coal to the

Free canteen for the poor, 14th Guardianship, Petrograd, February 1916. (Tsentral'nyi
gosudarstvennyi arkhiv kinofotofonodokumentov g. Sankt-Peterburga, E2625)

city, institutions like the Ligovsky People's House switched to wood to
fuel their furnaces.[36] City services began to buckle under the pressure:
passengers filled tram cars to overflowing, hospital beds grew scarce,
and the municipal government plunged deep into debt. While well-to-
do citizens continued to enjoy French farces at the capital's theaters and
Russian melodramas at its cinema houses, hungry soldiers' families
sought warmth and free tea and bread in crowded charity canteens. In
November and December 1916 the city received only 14–15 percent of
the grain shipments it needed. By 1916 Petrograd's home front, with
its proximity to northern battle zones, numerous garrisons, and military industries—and a population swollen by the continuing influx of
refugees—came to feel like the frontlines.[37]

   After two years of war relief work, Sofia felt the strain of her own
mounting administrative responsibilities amid the intensification of
popular suffering. The excitement and optimism she had once expressed
about Petrograd's thriving civil society had vanished. In a letter to Lidia

in August 1916 from Marfino, where she had finally escaped from the city for a month's vacation, Sofia sounded exhausted. She had sunk into a "terrible" mood in Petrograd, she explained, and "decided it was time to go on strike." "Now it has already been a week that I have been here and I am reveling in everything that surrounds me, and I sleep endlessly," she wrote her friend, "and I am terribly lazy." She dreaded the inevitable return to Petrograd in early September: "I desperately do not want to begin the endless winter."[38] Her apprehensions were realized as soon as she arrived back in the city. In a brief letter written in September 1916, Sofia apologized to another friend, the feminist journalist Liubov Gurevich, for not yet meeting with her. "I have been choked with meetings," she explained, "from the first days after my return."[39] In addition to her city-wide responsibilities, she continued to allocate a few days each month to personally distributing allowances to soldiers' families in the Alexander Nevsky district in order to maintain a direct connection with those in need.[40]

By playfully characterizing her retreat to Marfino as "going on strike," Sofia may have intended to suggest a measure of sympathy, even solidarity, with the capital's exhausted workers. She was certainly aware that the great majority of Petrograd's inhabitants could not escape the war's shortages and anxieties by taking a month-long vacation in the countryside. With twenty years of social service among the working class, she had reason to believe that she understood their sufferings and their hopes. She had nurtured the intellectual development and independence of working men and women since the 1890s in evening classes, lectures, and Sunday readings. Two years of wartime relief work in the guardianships had brought her face to face with the exceptional burdens the war imposed on the city's poor. In spite of inflation and shortages, she kept the doors of the people's house open for them. The theater, now occupied by wounded soldiers, had to discontinue its popular performances of Gogol, Shakespeare, and Ibsen, but the cafeteria and tearoom continued to offer inexpensive food, warmth, and a gathering place. Working women and soldiers' wives could find a respite from hardship and anxiety at the extremely popular Sunday literary readings. Intellectually ambitious workers could still borrow books, take classes, and gaze at the stars from the rooftop observatory on overcast Petrograd's rare clear nights.

But Sofia did not seem to have understood that the rudiments of political consciousness instilled by her people's house before 1914 would become manifest as the war progressed and taught its own lessons about power and citizenship. By adapting the institution to uses that supported the war effort, she also turned it into a site for expressing discontent and staging subversive actions. When the people's house became an assembly station for mobilized reservists in July 1914, for example, one working-class agitator remembered how it offered "favorable ground" for anti-war and anti-government propaganda. "Wives thronged there with their kids," the Bolshevik T. K. Kondratiev recounted in 1922. "The wives cried, and that was just what we needed to ignite this crowd. . . . We told the crying wives, look, they are taking your husbands, and perhaps they will get killed in the war, the children will become hungry and cold, but you should always keep in mind our [socialist] organization, which . . . will come to your aid." He and his comrades distributed a few hundred self-produced pamphlets denouncing the tsar and the war to the crowd of new soldiers and their wives, to what effect he does not say. The lectures that Sofia continued to sponsor provided another forum for anti-war passions. Mashirov-Samobytnik, the socialist metalworker and proletarian poet who had led the workers' prewar literary circle and helped organize the tenth anniversary jubilee, boasted of one incident in which he disrupted a history professor's chauvinistic lecture on the war. He ended his speech, Mashirov-Samobytnik claims, with the cry, "Long live the [Socialist] International!" This produced an uproar, he recalled proudly, as sympathetic workers applauded and outraged staff of the people's house shouted "Bolshevik!" and "hooligan!"[41]

One might expect the war and its impact on social and political conditions in the capital to challenge Sofia's attitudes toward the poor, and cause her to rethink her views on the need for cultural uplift and gradual reform as prerequisites to citizenship. But working with soldiers' wives appears to have done little to change her core belief that Russia's lower classes had a long distance to travel before they were ready for political responsibility. In her speech to the League for Women's Equal Rights in early 1916, for example, she described efforts by the city guardianships to help their female clients find employment. They encountered great difficulties, she claimed, because of laboring women's "depressing ignorance and complete lack of preparedness . . . for any kind of skilled work whatever, or for individual, autonomous initiative."[42] These women, she believed, were held back by their lack of education, not class oppression, and needed training, not slogans. Her condescending and derogatory characterization of poor working women in 1916 had changed little if at all from the ways she described them in her presentation to the congress on prostitution in 1910: ignorant, naïve, vulnerable, and in need of benevolent guidance from well-intentioned, educated women like herself. Both then and in 1916 she characterized the work of aiding poor women as a difficult but necessary burden, one that better-off women owed "their younger, unfortunate sister." Although Sofia had changed much about herself in order to respond to the war's demands, her fundamental judgment about the needs and capabilities of Russia's lower classes remained largely unaffected.

The years 1914–16 had indeed fulfilled the expectations Sofia expressed to Lidia at the outbreak of war: "despite all the horror," it was a "terribly interesting" time to live, and extremely "instructive." Pulled into ever more responsible and visible roles, Sofia tested and proved her administrative skills, developing her heretofore suppressed potential for leadership. World War I created ways for women like Sofia to express their patriotism and to define themselves as members of a national community. The home front came to be seen as a natural extension of the battlefront, and women felt empowered by their service. As the war redefined gender roles and opened unprecedented opportunities for civic involvement, it bolstered women's claims to citizenship. Like many other reform-minded activists, Sofia hoped that the war would also advance Russia's gradual evolution toward democracy.

But as the war dragged on into its third year with no victory on the horizon, the elation that characterized Russians' early response gave way to a dogged commitment to the increasingly harder work of meeting the needs of the millions it affected: tending the wounded, supplying the army, registering and assisting soldiers' families, and feeding refugees. The appalling slaughter on the battlefield shocked even the most die-hard patriots. The relentless demand for still more young recruits depleted homes, farms, and factories. The efforts made by Sofia and countless others proved incapable of stopping Russia's slide into defeat and chaos by the winter of 1916–17. Although the army was better supplied in early 1917 than at any other time during the war, morale was disintegrating, and soldiers began to refuse orders. It became difficult to maintain faith in the war's power to unite the nation or advance democracy, or to believe that the war served any purpose at all.

All of the combatant nations struggled on the home front against shortages and inflation, which deepened the pervasive discontent with the war and sparked sporadic unrest. But the malaise that affected Petrograd by the winter of 1916–17 was especially profound. Battered by rumors of scandal, the antics of inept ministers, and a collapse of

morale in the civil bureaucracy that paralleled the army's loss of resolve, the tsarist government descended into paralysis. In one of the
most sensational moments during the final months of the Romanov
monarchy Paul Miliukov, leader of the Kadet Party, delivered a speech
in the Duma on November 1, 1916, that electrified his audience and the
public at large. Reciting the long list of government failures, Miliukov
directly addressed Prime Minister Stürmer with his famous question:
"Is this stupidity or is it treason?" He and other Duma leaders demanded
a government of ministers answerable not to the tsar but to the people;
only a broad expansion of civil and political rights, they believed, could
reverse the country's military fortunes.[43] The following month a group
of monarchist conspirators assassinated Rasputin, but the death of the
imperial couple's infamous favorite did nothing to alleviate the pessimism and alarm that pervaded Petrograd society.

Pushed by the war's demands from of the outskirts of Petrograd into
the center of municipal affairs, Sofia stood poised in early 1917 to take
even greater advantage of the opportunities that the war opened to
women. After almost three years of mounting hardship, Petrograd's
working women and soldiers' wives were also ready to act on the lessons in political awareness that they learned at recruitment stations, in
bread lines, and within the walls of well-meaning cultural institutions
like the Ligovsky People's House.

7

Revolution in Petrograd

Sofia finally relinquished her self-identity as a nonpartisan social worker and entered the political arena when the monarchy and tsarist government fell at the end of February 1917. As in the lives of countless others, the war proved to be the impetus for this decisive turning point in her life. War-related relief work drew her increasingly closer to the liberal opposition as she collaborated with its leaders, such as Vladimir Obolensky, and affiliated organizations, such as the Union of Towns. As she discovered her previously untapped leadership potential in citywide roles, Russia's liberal leaders also noted her talents and ability to "work like a man," in Obolensky's words. In the wake of the February Revolution, they elevated Sofia to unprecedented political prominence. In rapid order she accepted both elected and appointed positions in three major political bodies that were playing decisive roles in the unfolding revolution: the Petrograd City Council, the Central Committee of the Kadet Party, and the cabinet of the Provisional Government, where as an assistant minister she became its only female member.

Sofia's experience in 1917 stands out as a striking exception in the annals of the Russian Revolution. It is generally presumed though seldom explicitly noted in the historiography that men led and dominated the revolutions of 1917. The leadership of parties across the political spectrum was overwhelming male. Russia led Europe in the introduction of universal female suffrage in 1917, the culmination of a decades-long feminist movement. But when the newly enfranchised women and men of Russia voted in mid-November for delegates to a new national Constituent Assembly, there were few women on the party lists of candidates.[1]

Sofia's unusual prominence in 1917 won her international attention as the first woman in history to hold a ministerial position. Described as "the First Woman Minister of State," she was even listed with such women as Joan of Arc, Queen Victoria, and Susan B. Anthony in *Famous Women of the World*, a little pamphlet produced in the United States around 1920 and distributed to American mothers with bottles of pepsin syrup for children.[2]

By agreeing to take these high-level governmental and party positions, Sofia transformed herself from a philanthropist into a political actor on the national stage and entered the vortex of Russia's crisis in 1917. At Kadet party conferences and meetings of the Provisional Government's cabinet she observed at close range liberal politicians' struggle to control the accelerating pace of the revolution. In the volatile political atmosphere of the Petrograd City Council she heard Bolsheviks advocate a course that she believed would bring her country into a state of anarchy and ruin. In the streets the workers she thought she knew from her years at the people's house rejected the leadership of well-intentioned moderates like herself and voiced anti-war, pro-socialist slogans inflected by class hatred. Sofia's involvement in the revolution tested her endurance, courage, and most cherished beliefs—the possibility of harmony between classes, the natural leadership of the educated and cultured, and Russia's destiny as a peaceful, enlightened, European nation.

The year 1917 began in Petrograd in an atmosphere of impending crisis, intensified by widespread rumors about government paralysis, treason, and conspiracies. Economic disaster, signaled by a spike in prices and extreme shortages of food and fuel, loomed over the city. The especially cold winter compounded the misery. In January Petrograd's workers voiced their discontent in demonstrations commemorating "Bloody Sunday," the day in 1905 when the tsar's troops had fired on peaceful marchers and ignited Russia's first revolution. On February 21 the socialist Nikolai Sukhanov, whose detailed diary of 1917 is an often-cited eyewitness account for that year's events in Petrograd, recorded a conversation he heard between two typists in his office, who were chatting about food shortages, quarrels in bread lines, ware-house break-ins, and "unrest among the women." "D'you know," he recalls one of the young women saying, "if you ask me, it's the begin-ning of the revolution!"[3] The typist's prediction materialized two days later. Eyewitnesses and historians agree that the first Russian Revolu-tion of 1917 began on February 23, the socialist holiday of International Women's Day (March 8, according to the Western calendar), when "thousands of housewives and women workers . . . poured into the streets, enraged over the need to stand in line for hours in freezing cold in order to purchase bread."[4] Between ninety thousand and one hundred thousand workers, men and women, went on strike that day, making it the most serious episode of labor unrest since July 1914.

The number of strikers doubled the next day, fed by men from metal-working factories and armaments plants and women from the city's textile mills. Columns of people bundled up against the bitter cold and shouting "Down with the war!" and "Down with the tsar!" marched across the frozen Neva River from the factory districts into the city cen-ter. Students, tram and horse-cab drivers, artisans and servants, profes-sionals and office workers joined the strikers in the days that followed. Demonstrators defied orders to disperse. Mounted police, Cossack regi-ments, and soldiers from Petrograd's garrisons began to waver when commanded to put down the unrest. The "Great Mutiny" of 1917 that would destroy the discipline, morale, and fighting effectiveness of the Russian army had begun.[5]

As civil and military authority in the capital disintegrated and pro-tests reached a crescendo, Sofia took her first steps onto the political stage. Soldiers from the city's garrisons, having ignored previous orders to quell the demonstrations, openly joined the revolt on February 27. Crowds of workers and soldiers thronged the major avenues of Nevsky and Liteiny Prospects. The soldiers, one unsympathetic upper-class eyewitness recounted, "were disheveled, in unbuttoned greatcoats with their hats on the backs of their heads…. They ran back and forth from one corner to the other and did not look military at all." He remem-bers seeing Sofia, whose home on Sergievskaya Street was just a few steps from Liteiny Prospect, moving between her house and the "mob" of soldiers and workers who swarmed along the broad avenue. She ig-nored the tearful pleas of her elderly servant not to go out onto the street, assuring him that the crowd would not harm her. Communicating by telephone, she kept the city council informed of the situation around her house and the mood of the soldiers.[6]

A short distance away stunned members of Russia's parliament, the Duma, milled inside the Tauride Palace, uncertain about what to do next. After observing the soldiers wandering aimlessly along nearby Liteiny Prospect for some time, Sofia rushed into the palace and began to berate the politicians. "They are waiting for orders," Sofia reproached them. "They are expecting the members of the Duma. Go to them. Take them in your hands. Look," she continued, "this is a flock that has gone astray"—a metaphor consistent with her long-held opinions about the lower classes' sheep-like gullibility and need for leadership.[7] Later that day, on February 27, Duma leaders formed a temporary committee to take control while socialists created a rival center of power, the Petrograd Soviet of Workers' and Soldiers' Deputies. The revolt reached its climax on March 2, when Nicholas II was persuaded to abdicate on behalf of himself and his hemophiliac son in favor of his brother Michael. Michael refused the throne, however, ending the Romanovs' three-hundred-year rule. The Kadet leader Miliukov announced the creation of the Provisional Government, and although he and others originally hoped to create a constitutional monarchy, virtually overnight Russia became the world's largest republic.

The February Revolution met with an ecstatic response in the capital. "The first night of the revolution was like Easter," one contemporary recalled. "One had the sense of a miracle close by, next to you, around you."[8] The minority that may have mourned the fall of the Romanov dynasty was largely silent; it certainly did not include Sofia, whose surviving writings lack any expression of regret over the fall of Nicholas II and Alexandra or attachment to the institution of monarchy, despite the Panin family's long tradition of loyal imperial service.[9] Crowds tore down flags and monuments bearing the imperial double-headed eagle and sang the "Marseillaise" in place of "God Save the Tsar." A strong sense of unity and renewed patriotism bound the demonstrators from all classes who filled the streets of the capital during those exhilarating "February Days." Many believed that the fall of the corrupt, incompetent tsarist government had removed the main obstacle to military success. Russia, now free and democratic, seemed bound to prevail against the autocratic Central Powers with its allies, the other great European democracies and, as of April, the United States.

Contemporaries hailed the February Revolution as bloodless (which it certainly was, compared to later events in the capital), but it nevertheless claimed as many as two thousand victims.[10] Troops and police loyal to the old regime initially fought against strikers, demonstrators, and mutinous soldiers before retreating or going over to the side of the revolution. Once military authority collapsed, thousands of armed, unruly soldiers wandered Petrograd's dark streets. The February Revolution's violent undercurrent immediately struck Sofia very close to home. On the evening of March 2, the same day as Nicholas's abdication and the creation of the Provisional Government, her cousin Dmitry Viazemsky was riding in the front seat of an automobile carrying the Provisional Government's new minister of war, who was driving around the city in an effort to persuade rebellious soldiers to return to their barracks. Suddenly a volley of shots exploded from behind the car, and a bullet struck Dmitry.[11] He died the next day, the first of many sacrifices Sofia and her family would make to the revolution.

Sofia's first official role resulted from an internal revolt within the Petrograd City Council in early March, when progressive deputies deposed the conservative mayor, who had succeeded Sofia's friend Ivan Tolstoy, and elected a moderate liberal, Yuri N. Glebov. At the council meeting on March 8 Glebov introduced a resolution to bring women into the council's executive committees. Approving the mayor's proposal, the council invited several women who had been longtime leaders in charity, education, and public health in the capital to join the standing committees that dealt with those matters. Only a year before, Sofia had worried about the municipal government's commitment to supporting war relief when the narrow electorate returned reactionaries to power on the council. She must have been pleased, then, by the ouster of conservatives in March 1917 and the new leadership's apparent commitment to serving the needs of the city's poorest. Although the council co-opted only a small number of women into committees that fell safely within the feminine sphere, their tentative step acknowledged the political significance of women's contributions to the war effort and affirmed women's rights by choosing prominent feminists and women with strong Kadet ties, including Tyrkova-Williams and Anna Miliukova as well as Sofia, as its first female members.[12]

Sofia and the other first female deputies on the Petrograd City Council were harbingers of the political equality that supporters of women's rights had been seeking for two decades. Russia's leading feminists were well aware of the tepid support for political equality within the Kadet Party, which controlled the Provisional Government, and the considerable resistance their cause still faced in 1917. To force the issue, the League for Women's Equal Rights—the feminist organization that Sofia had addressed in 1916—organized a massive and unprecedented demonstration. On March 19, a surprisingly mild late winter day, an estimated forty thousand women accompanied by brass bands playing revolutionary anthems marched down Nevsky Prospect to the Tauride Palace. Led by an open automobile carrying both feminist leaders and the former terrorist Vera Figner, the marchers waved banners demanding rights for women. Initially the country's new political leaders in the liberal Provisional Government and the socialist Soviet advised the women that their demands were "premature" at this time of revolution. But they finally conceded to the crowd outside the palace that any law introducing universal suffrage would include women's right to vote. Doubting the dependability of such promises, leaders of the women's rights movement sought an audience with the new prime minister, Prince G. E. Lvov. Two days after the march Sofia joined Figner and feminists from the center and the left to meet with Lvov, who assured them of the new government's commitment to women's suffrage. Shortly thereafter the Provisional Government introduced a series of laws establishing equal rights, culminating in a law of July 20, 1917, that made Russia the first European nation to grant full voting rights to women in national elections.[13]

In addition to her new duties as a city council deputy, Sofia assumed greater responsibilities as pressures on the system of relief to soldiers' families intensified. When food rationing was introduced in Petrograd in March, the guardianships were entrusted with its implementation. "We had to set up meetings with bakers, the owners of eating-houses, [and] draymen," Sofia recalled, in order to create an infrastructure for administering the new rationing system. The guardianships also had to devise ways to feed the refugees who poured into Petrograd and Chinese migrant workers brought from Manchuria to work on the railroads.[14] Sofia's 13th Guardianship struggled to keep providing state and supplementary assistance to soldiers' families, and even managed to expand its services, constructing a winter playground for children in December 1916 and a new soup kitchen the following February. But the burden on its dwindling staff of volunteers was tremendous. In May 1917 alone they distributed almost a quarter of a million rubles in state aid to 24,500 clients, more than any other guardianship in the city.[15] In the conditions of rapid inflation, the monthly allowances for soldiers' families could barely satisfy the most basic necessities, and the government's fiscal crisis meant that payments were often late. All of the guardianships struggled to stretch their shrinking resources to meet the needs of increasingly desperate wives and mothers, though the needs in the vast working-class district served by the Ligovsky People's House and the 13th Guardianship were especially acute.

The climate of suspicion about the motives and objectives of the bourgeoisie added to the challenge. The political rhetoric surrounding the February Revolution had finally brought to light the full political implications of the system of state assistance, and turned access to soup kitchens and monthly allowances into questions about political rights and economic justice. Petrograd's soldiers' wives soon joined the countless other groups holding demonstrations and making demands during 1917. More than six hundred women from the district served by Obolensky's 19th Guardianship, for example, met to call for increased benefits and equal treatment for common-law wives. They elected ten representatives to take their demands to the Provisional Government. Their meeting set off a chain reaction in other guardianships. Four hundred soldiers' wives met in a factory cafeteria in the district of the 20th Guardianship, elected a chairwoman, and voted to take control of the preparation and distribution of food. Representatives of other guardianships reported that soldiers' wives were issuing similar demands: a direct role in the distribution of aid, allowances for common-law wives, even the complete elimination of the guardianships, so that the aid could be distributed by recipients themselves.[16]

Another sign of the mobilization of working women came on April 9, a few weeks after the women's rights demonstration and the visit by Sofia and other feminists to the prime minister, when a considerably larger protest march took place in Petrograd. More than one hundred thousand women, carrying banners and flags, marched through the center of the city to the Provisional Government's headquarters. They demanded increases in their state allowances, equality for women, and a constituent assembly to determine Russia's future government. As the banners they carried made clear, these women based their claims to full citizenship rights on their relationship to soldiers, and used both traditional and revolutionary terms to describe their husbands and sons in arms—"defenders of the motherland" and "defenders of freedom and popular peace." Socialists seized the opportunity this march presented to draw working women away from the liberal promises of "bourgeois feminism" and to fan the flames of their resentment. Stepping forward to support the marchers' demands that Sunday was the Bolshevik feminist Alexandra Kollontai. Like a number of other Bolshevik leaders, Kollontai had spent most of the war in Europe and America, returning to Russia only after the fall of the monarchy, when she became one of the few female members of the Petrograd Soviet. Sharing Lenin's opposition to what Bolsheviks called the "imperialist war," Kollontai abetted the anti-war sentiments of the female demonstrators who bore its burdens on the home front.[17]

Sofia's continued involvement with the guardianships brought her into direct contact with the radicalization of Petrograd's working women. The day after the mass march in April the central guardianship bureau appointed Sofia and two other women to act as liaisons between the guardianships and the Petrograd Soviet. The bureau also decided to include one representative for every thousand *soldatki* to serve as an unpaid voting member. Paid positions for these representatives would be opened on the bureau's various commissions.[18] One of Sofia's colleagues on the guardianship bureau applauded the efforts of soldiers' wives to organize and to work in cooperation, she hoped, with the guardianships. But for Obolensky the reversal of the conventional relationship between donor and recipient was too much: he quit his position in the Union of Towns when refugees accused him of pocketing their aid and demanded to take charge of its distribution themselves.[19]

Years later Sofia mused on how war, hardship, and revolutionary rhetoric had transformed the working-class wives and mothers who had first filed into the people's house in 1914 to register for state assistance. They were "helpless creatures" back then, like "blind moles emerging for the first time from their burrows." But by the spring of 1917 that helplessness had disappeared. Soldiers' wives started holding "mass meetings on the street around the people's house," Sofia recalled, "amid the piles of dirty melting snow, accusing us of stealing their allowances, and of building the people's house itself on money stolen from the people." Reflecting on the events of 1917 decades after the revolution, Sofia blamed the transformation of "blind moles" into angry protestors on their ignorance: such moments "are inevitable in times of great popular upheavals. Ignorance is always suspicious and wants to know 'where is the truth that is being hidden from the people.'"[20] In this as in her other reminiscences about the revolution, Sofia proved either unable or unwilling to probe more deeply in order to understand the underlying causes of the popular anger and resentment that exploded in 1917.

Petrograd was not the only city that experienced the growing militancy of women in 1917. The war, which continued to slaughter husbands and fathers at the front and siphon off the lion's share of food, fuel, and other essentials, imposed heavy losses and hardships on

women in the other combatant nations as well. Conditions in Berlin
bore a close resemblance to those in Petrograd, especially during the
bitterly cold "turnip winter" of 1916–17. Ragged and half-starved women,
angry after standing in endless lines for detested yellow turnips, cabbage,
and ersatz foods, demanded larger rations and a more just distribution
of food and essentials. The Berlin authorities, like Sofia and her associates in the Petrograd guardianships, promised to bring worker representatives into the city's food distribution system. Nevertheless, in the late
spring and summer of 1917 Berlin echoed Petrograd with often violent
demonstrations, riots in marketplaces and food lines, and processions
of protesters demanding bread and justice.[21] While government authorities in both Petrograd and Berlin may have deplored the women's
tactics, they generally sympathized with their desperation. In June the
Provisional Government agreed to extend state allowances to common-
law wives, for example. But in Petrograd the fury of exhausted women
tapped deep springs of hostility and suspicion toward the rich, which
revolutionaries such as Kollontai abetted with increasingly uncompro-
mising and radical demands.

After entering the Petrograd City Council and the movement for
women's rights in March 1917, Sofia finally declared her political affiliation by joining the Kadet Party. The reason she gives in the memoir
she wrote thirty years later is straightforward. "Many of those around
me considered me a socialist" because of her years of work with the
city's laboring poor, the woman some called the "Red Countess" explained. Therefore "I considered it necessary, at the moment when the
political struggle intensified, to establish my position with complete
precision and dissociate myself from the socialist madness that had
seized the country." She chose the Kadets because it was the only party
that "openly battled with advancing bolshevism." Sofia considered this
a life-altering decision: "my entire future fate," she claimed, "was determined by this moment."[22]

In retrospect Sofia may have considered that taking a stand against
socialism was her primary reason for choosing the Kadets, but there
were other factors that made this an obvious choice, including her parents' long association with the party and the close ties with prominent
Kadets she developed through her war relief work. The Kadet Party
was the natural ideological choice as well. As the name indicates, the
Constitutional Democratic Party, or Kadets, believed that Russia's absolute monarchy should be replaced by a constitution based on representative, democratic government. Such political restructuring was an

essential step in Russia's advancement along the path toward becoming an enlightened European nation equal to Great Britain or France. Committed to the rule of law, the party had fought since its founding in 1905 to replace Russia's arbitrary, corrupt bureaucracy with a government that upheld civil liberties and protected the rights of all. Sofia shared not only these core principles but also the ambivalence of many of its members toward the rough and tumble of partisan politics. As the historian William Rosenberg has written, the Kadets were more of a "loose association" of sincere liberals than a "tightly knit, monolithic" political organization. Many Kadets shared Sofia's preference for *"nadpartiinost'"* or nonpartisanship, seeking to work with all parties and like-minded people toward a government that guaranteed civil and political rights to all citizens.

With her strong commitment to social unity, Sofia also shared the Kadets' rejection of class-based interests in favor of a *"vseklassovyi"* ("all-class") orientation. Although its socialist opponents labeled it "bourgeois," there were few true capitalists in the party. The party differentiated itself from other parties, its program proclaimed, "in that it struggles for all citizens, and not for one particular social class."[23] While supporting better conditions for labor, progressive taxation, land reform and similar changes, Kadets generally believed in the necessity of protecting the rights of all over promoting the interests of one socioeconomic group over another. The party's all-class and above-party principles were linked to its commitment to Russia's integrity and greatness as a nation. Kadets saw themselves as true patriots, and during the war and the 1917 Revolution they steadfastly supported Russia's fulfillment of its military obligations to the Allies. Their continued support for the war and insistence on the primacy of national interest over class prevented Sofia along with many of her fellow Kadets from appreciating the depth of popular class-based resentment toward the rich and the rising wave of anti-war anger that affected the battlefront and the home front in 1917.

Almost as soon as she officially joined the Kadets, Sofia vaulted into the party leadership. Meeting on April 10, 1917, the party's central committee decided to increase its size by coopting new members; Sofia was elected by secret ballot as one of them. Her membership on the central committee was reaffirmed on May 12, the last day of the party's Eighth Congress, when an expanded committee of sixty-six members was elected.[24] Along with lawyers, physicians, and long-time civic and local government activists, the committee included such eminent scholars as the scientist Vladimir Vernadsky, the Oriental studies specialist Sergei Oldenburg, and the historian Miliukov, the party's leader. Others were titled members of old aristocratic families. Prince Obolensky, Prince Dmitry Shakhovskoy, and the twin Princes Pavel and Peter Dolgorukov belonged to the party not because it defended their class interests but because they shared its principles—constitutionalism, political and cultural progress, and national greatness. In the party's overwhelmingly male leadership, Sofia and Ariadna Tyrkova-Williams were the only women. Unlike Tyrkova-Williams Sofia was a newcomer, but she already knew many on the central committee. One third of its members were from Petrograd, after all. She had worked with party veterans in war relief. Her friendship with another party leader, the physician Andrei Ivanovich Shingarev, dated to the first years of the twentieth century, when they established a hospital together near her Voronezh estate. The party's central committee even brought her face-to-face with a chapter of her past she had tried to erase. Vladimir Nabokov, another member of the party's inner circle and the future novelist's father, lived with his family in the mansion that had once belonged to newlyweds Sofia and Alexander Polovtsov. Sofia may have attended some of the party meetings that were occasionally held at the Nabokovs' during 1917.

From February until October the Kadets managed to hold onto ministerial positions in a succession of cabinets, first in alliance with moderate parties to the right, and then in coalition with the major non-Bolshevik socialist parties. Sofia received her initial ministerial position in the wake of the governmental crisis that erupted in mid-April. It was the first of several confrontations between the country's dual authorities—the Kadet-dominated Provisional Government and the socialist Petrograd Soviet—over Russia's objectives in the war and the revolution. The two-week crisis resulted in the resignation of Miliukov, who as the minister of foreign affairs won the distrust of the left for what they interpreted as his imperialist war aims. After difficult negotiations, the party and the Soviet cobbled together the first coalition cabinet in early May, which placed socialist representatives of the Soviet in ministerial positions alongside Kadets. Another result of the negotiations was the creation of a Ministry of State Welfare to give Kadets additional representation in the cabinet and to balance the socialist-led Ministry of Labor. Prince Shakhovskoy was appointed minister of welfare. A longtime zemstvo activist, Shakhovskoy had helped Sofia's stepfather create the illegal Union of Liberation in 1902, participated in founding the

Kadet Party in 1905, and assumed a leading role in the first, short-lived national parliament in 1906. He was also one of the few Kadet leaders who remained in Russia after the Bolshevik Revolution, a decision the elderly prince paid for with his life when he was executed in 1939 during the Stalinist terror. At a meeting on May 24, 1917, two weeks after her formal election to the Kadet Central Committee, the Provisional Government cabinet appointed Sofia to be Shakhovskoy's assistant minister.[25]

How did Sofia, a political novice, become one of only two women on the Kadet Central Committee and the only woman in the Provisional Government? One factor may have been her familial relationship to Ivan Petrunkevich, the party's founder; by appointing his stepdaughter to such visible positions, the Kadet leadership may have meant to honor the now elderly Ivan and his loyal wife. Or the party may have wished to advertise its commitment to women's equality by naming a female minister, although there were other women with equally valid claims to such an honor. A brief look at two other prominent Kadet women, Tyrkova-Williams and Olga Nechaeva, may also help explain why Sofia was chosen. That she was appointed instead of these women demonstrates both the possibilities and limits of women's political participation and influence in Russia, the result of gender expectations that persisted despite challenges from the feminist movement and women's enormous contributions to the war effort.

Outspoken, independent, and beautiful, Tyrkova-Williams (1869–1962) had supported herself and her children as a journalist since divorcing her husband around the same time Sofia left Alexander Polovtsov. An ardent feminist, she wrote voluminously about women's rights. She was no less devoted to the cause of Russian democracy. Before 1914 she proved her commitment to political change by demonstrating against the tsarist government and smuggling copies of illegal liberal publications into the country. These acts resulted in two arrests, a short prison stay, and flight abroad to escape a longer term. As soon as she returned to Russia in late 1905 she joined the Kadets, becoming the only woman on its central committee from 1906 until Sofia joined her in 1917. Party wits called her "the only man in the Kadet Party" because of her decisiveness. At the Eighth Congress in May 1917, she received more votes than Sofia in the election to the central committee, no doubt in recognition of her party service and sacrifices. But she disguised neither her staunch support of right-wing party positions nor her hostility toward Miliukov. These positions, along with her outspoken feminism and the perception of her masculine forcefulness, may have undermined her eligibility for a government position in the eyes of the party's leaders.[26]

A generation older than Sofia, Olga Nechaeva (1850–1926) had a similar record of service to charitable and educational causes in St. Petersburg, especially assistance to young women workers and students in the higher women's courses. If Tyrkova-Williams was the "only man" in the party, Olga Nechaeva seemed to personify femininity. Obolensky remembered her as the "sweetest, kindest" woman, with "large, luminous blue eyes," "who preserved her youthful ardor and a kind of sweet naïveté in relation to people and events." At the same time he attributed the success of the Kadet party committee in Petersburg to her many years of leadership and organizational talents.[27] Obolensky omitted mention of another, less traditionally feminine aspect of her public life. During the war Nechaeva headed the Russian Army's Commission on Women's Labor Service and chaired the Women's Military Congress in early August 1917, which brought together women involved in war relief with women serving in military and quasi-military units.[28]

All three women, then, had long and distinguished records in the feminine realm of social service. In sharp contrast to Sofia's aloofness from politics before the war, Nechaeva and Tyrkova-Williams had devoted years to the Kadet Party. But while they embraced the Kadets' ideals and goals, Sofia truly personified them. When party leaders placed the avowedly apolitical Sofia in the cabinet, they expressed their enduring commitment to nonpartisanship, or *nadpartiinost'*. The philanthropic countess with her years of service to the laboring poor also displayed the Kadets' dedication to the primacy of the well-being of the whole nation over what they considered to be narrow class interests. At the same time, Sofia brought experience, practical skills, and knowledge to the new Ministry of State Welfare, the creation of which had been a goal of Russian charity activists for many years. Sergei Gogel, one of the leaders of the national charity association that had elected Sofia to its board the previous year, hailed the new ministry. Saying almost nothing about the minister of welfare, Shakhovskoy, Gogel praised Sofia as a national leader in charity and social welfare. This first appointment of a woman to a government post was greeted with universal approval, he claimed; everyone hailed this appointment of "*the right man [sic] on the right place*," he wrote effusively.[29] Sofia herself never explains why she accepted the position in the Provisional Government. She may have agreed with Gogel that serving in the new Ministry of

State Welfare was a logical extension of her long career in social service, since its tasks included aiding the masses of dispossessed refugees, crippled veterans, helpless orphans, and grieving widows that the war continued to produce. New to the Kadet Party, she may not have fully appreciated the rivalries and animosities that undermined its effective leadership of the Provisional Government.

Sofia carried out a variety of functions during her stint as assistant minister of welfare but stayed outside of both the public spotlight and the inner circle of her party and government. She attended a number of cabinet meetings in Shakhovskoy's place during late May and June.[30] But important policy decisions tended to be made outside cabinet meetings, which quickly took on a dull and formalistic routine. Her fluency in English and French (as well as German) seems occasionally to have provided her entrée into meetings with some of the numerous American, British, and French officials who trekked to Petrograd after February to observe the revolution with their own eyes and assess the political and military capabilities of their faltering ally. When President Woodrow Wilson's Root Mission arrived for talks with the Provisional Government in June, for example, Sofia met with one of its members, the American evangelist and YMCA leader John Mott, to discuss prospects for the establishment of a YWCA in Russia.[31]

Her principal responsibility in the new ministry involved determining the fate of the hundreds of schools, orphanages, and other charitable institutions that had been supported wholly or in part by the tsarist government and members of the now deposed imperial family. Among the institutions slated for reform were the institutes for noble girls, including her alma mater, the Catherine Institute, and its old rival Smolny. Sofia toured some of the institutes in June 1917. Several had been turned into military hospitals, she discovered, while others were closed, the girls gone for the summer. But a few still housed a small number of former pupils without homes or families. "Panic and confusion reigned everywhere in these institutions," she recalled in a poignant handwritten memoir, "for in the eyes of even the most moderate revolution[aries], they appeared to be a survival and anachronism in contemporary life, nests and bulwarks of the 'old regime.'" Her mission led her to make two visits to Smolny, where its elderly retired headmistress, Princess Golitsyna, still lived with one of the former inspectresses and a few stranded pupils. When Sofia arrived the women were fearful, "seeing in me a representative of the terrible and hated revolution," although their attitude softened when they learned that their official visitor was a countess and former *institutka* herself.[32]

The February Revolution had left its mark upon Smolny, Sofia discovered. One section had already been taken over by a military unit.
Additional dramatic evidence of the revolution's impact was revealed
in one of the large and empty classrooms, where four huge portraits of
the two last emperors and empresses had been torn off the wall and
thrown face down on the floor. Visiting one of the dormitories, Sofia
could not help but notice a photograph of Minister of War Kerensky
pinned over one girl's bed, evidence of the heroic status he enjoyed in
the early summer of 1917, when the advance on the Austrian front he
was leading still promised success. Although the imperial portraits had
been taken down, traces of Smolny's august past still lingered, including
the perfectly preserved apartment of Emperor Alexander I's mistress,
which still retained "all the charm of its pure empire style" despite the
passage of a hundred years. "The power of the past was so strong here,"
Sofia reminisced, "that for a long time I could not tear myself away
from the fascination of the 'dust of the centuries' that, on that June day,
was completely bathed in the dark green light of the sun shining into it
through the thick masses of surrounding lime trees." At the same time,
uncertainty and fear pervaded the old building. Scattered groups of
frightened girls huddled in the huge classrooms, "representatives of
this once proud and pampered Institute . . . [and] of something gone
and doomed, living fragments of history, so young and helpless before
the approaching hurricane that was fated soon to scatter them across
the entire face of the Russian land."[33]

Written in emigration and tinged with nostalgia for a lost world, Sofia's account captures how the revolutionary future and the discarded
past were still closely intertwined during 1917. Representing herself as
an intermediary, she travels in the liminal space between the imperial
past, where the old headmistress weeps silently amid discarded portraits of deposed rulers, and a future full of hope, where girls naïvely
transform radical lawyers like Kerensky into revolutionary heroes.
With the benefit of hindsight, she knew that along with the Smolny Institute, the lives of its young pupils were "doomed." Indeed, Smolny's
days as a symbol of the prerevolutionary past were numbered. Sofia's
ministry fought to hold onto the spacious building, hoping to turn it
into a model institution for preschool education, but the Petrograd Soviet of Workers' and Soldiers' Deputies wanted it for its headquarters.
When another government crisis erupted in early July, a few weeks after
Sofia's visit, Minister Shakhovskoy reluctantly joined the other Kadet
ministers in resigning from the Provisional Government. His successor
gave in to the Soviet's demands, and Sofia had to return to Smolny to

inform Princess Golitsyna that her beautiful building now belonged to representatives of Petrograd's workers and soldiers. This sad errand accomplished, Sofia also resigned from her ministerial position.[34]

While Sofia was carrying out her official responsibilities in Petrograd in the spring and summer of 1917, the revolution spread from the city to the countryside, from striking factory workers and mutinous soldiers to the millions of peasants who made up the great majority of the population. The February Revolution's rhetoric of equality and freedom, coupled with the Provisional Government's tentative efforts toward land reform, reignited peasants' deeply held grievances against the nobility and their belief that land belonged only to those who labored on it. As police authority in the countryside collapsed, peasants resorted to time-honored practices of disobedience to claim what they believed was rightly theirs. Sofia herself felt the effects as early as May 1917. Among the boxes of personal papers she donated to Columbia University is a folder entitled "events at one of S. V. Panina's estates, 1917," which reveals that the wave of peasant unrest reached her beloved Marfino early that summer. The "events" took the form of direct actions that defied the principle of private property: inhabitants of several villages around Marfino started pasturing their livestock on Sofia's meadows and cutting hay and wood on her land, allegedly without her estate manager's permission.[35] Sofia may have experienced the confrontation between her manager and local peasants firsthand, since her resignation from the ministry in mid-July left her free to resume her habit of spending the summer in Marfino. Whether she was present during the peasant disturbances of 1917 or not, the outbreak of discontent at Marfino must have come as a shock. Sofia was known as a relatively progressive landowner who fostered local economic development and education. But in 1917 it did not matter how benevolent she or her Panin ancestors had been.

Nor was the dispute necessarily directed at her. The resentment Marfino peasants expressed had deep roots in their long experience of serfdom. Three years of war, which drained their villages of young men and turned their children into orphans, exacerbated their feelings of grievance and oppression. The collapse of tsarism in February undermined habits of deference as well as the structures of authority that had maintained order in the countryside. For its part, the Provisional Government abetted peasants' perennial land hunger by first raising the issue of land reform and establishing local reform committees, then deferring its resolution. All these events set in motion a chain of peasant actions against nobles who in peacetime had been their neighbors and employers, and in many cases their benefactors as well. Sullen resentment turned into open disputes like the one that erupted at Marfino, as peasants all across rural Russia demanded land that summer and fall. Demands exploded into threats, harassment, and violence. Peasants occupied fields, meadows, and forests belonging to non-peasant owners, looted manor houses and barns, and chased noble families off their estates. Some torched the elegant manor houses that had graced the rural landscape for a century or more, tore up their gardens, and stole or smashed their furnishings. Books were used for cigarette paper, and grand pianos were chopped up for firewood.

At least for the time being, the Marfino peasants pursued their claims peacefully, by submitting their request to rent Sofia's meadows and cut wood in her forest to the district government and the newly established land committee, with what outcome the documents do not say. In a number of other instances, however, rural violence escalated into murder. In August family tragedy struck Sofia for the second time in six months. Insurgent peasants drove her cousin Boris Viazemsky, Dmitry's older brother, and his wife Lili off the family estate of Lotarevo in the Tambov steppe. Imprisoned briefly in the village school, the couple was liberated by other more sympathetic peasants, only to have Boris beaten to death at the railroad station by a band of soldiers who were passing through. Over the next few weeks peasants looted and destroyed all the buildings on the property, including the model stables and barns for Lotarevo's prize-winning horses and cattle. Sofia had always been close with Missy, her older first cousin and the mother of the murdered brothers, and their father Leonid, who helped her found the Ligovsky People's House. Before the war she sometimes visited Lotarevo during the summer. The murder of a second Viazemsky son must have seemed to her both tragic and senseless. On August 27 she met the train in Moscow that carried Boris's body and his widow from Lotarevo and then accompanied them to Petrograd for the funeral liturgy and burial.[36]

Thus by the end of the summer extremism and violence had begun to change the once relatively bloodless revolution. The holiday atmosphere of liberation and promise in early March had given way to anger over the war and apprehension over the future. The violent deaths of the two Viazemsky brothers, along with the defiant actions taken by peasants at Marfino, brought Sofia face-to-face with the disintegration of law and order occurring across the empire. Russia's major summer offensive against the Austrians had turned into a rout, with countless soldiers deserting the front to head for home. In Petrograd the Bolshevik party had already staged one abortive attempt to seize power during the "July Days," precipitating another crisis that brought down the first coalition. When a second coalition government was formed in late July, the erstwhile hero Kerensky became prime minister, although his original popularity in the army and the working class was already in decline. Only five Kadets served in a new cabinet that was now dominated by socialists. One of the Kadets was the scholar Sergei Oldenburg, who was named minister of education. Sofia accepted her second government position as his assistant minister.[37] Her appointment demonstrates once again the respect she enjoyed within the liberal political elite in the capital. She may also have been named to the education ministry in order to strengthen its credentials, for neither Oldenburg nor the scientist Vernadsky, the second assistant minister, could match her reputation or experience in matters of popular education. Finally, in making this appointment just a few weeks after issuing the law on women's suffrage, the Provisional Government may have also been trying to present an appearance of including women in the political process.

It is more difficult to explain why Sofia accepted the appointment, and why she remained in the cabinet for the rest of the Provisional Government's short life. Unlike Oldenburg, who resigned after serving only two months, she continued to serve as assistant minister under his replacement up to and even after the Bolshevik seizure of power.[38] She left very little record in general of her experience in the government, barely mentioning her ministerial service in her one published memoir about 1917. A feeling of patriotic duty may have motivated Sofia to enter a government whose future seemed doubtful in August. At a time when liberal principles and hopes were under attack, she may also have acted out of loyalty to the Kadet Party and its democratic ideals. Perhaps she believed, or at least hoped, that in the Ministry of Education she might find the opportunity to implement her long-cherished ideas about the transformative and civilizing power of education. At the ministry she headed a special conference on adult and external (vneshkol'noe) education, where she pushed for government funding to expand facilities such as people's houses and libraries that would bring literacy and culture to the masses.[39] A cryptic entry in her colleague Vernadsky's diary even suggests that she planned to donate Marfino to the ministry.[40]

But it was in the Petrograd City Council, not the Provisional Government, where Sofia played the most dramatic role in her political career up to the Bolshevik Revolution in late October. On August 20, 1917, more than half a million Petrograd residents—forty percent of the electorate—defied hunger and despair to vote for a new council. These were the first elections held in accordance with the new law on universal suffrage. According to Isai Milchik, a council deputy from the Socialist Revolutionary (or SR) Party, all the major political parties took the municipal elections extremely seriously. The Petrograd elections defined the ongoing political struggle in the nation's capital and foreshadowed the outcome of the elections scheduled the following month for a national constituent assembly, whose task would be to decide the country's political future.[41] The municipal election results reflected the capital's increasingly radical political mood and the Bolsheviks' growing influence. Out of two hundred deputies elected on August 20, seventy-five belonged to the SRs, Russia's largest socialist party. The Bolsheviks came in second with sixty-five seats. The Mensheviks, the more moderate Marxist party, held onto only eight seats, a clear indication of their dwindling popularity. The elections signaled the Kadets' decline as well. In June, when elections for an interim city council had been held, the liberals had won significantly more seats than the Bolsheviks, and almost as many seats as the SRs. But in August only forty-two Kadet deputies were elected to the new council, one of whom was Sofia.[42]

The newly elected Petrograd Council included many of Russia's political luminaries. Sofia joined the Kadets Nabokov, Shingarev, Obolensky, and Miliukov, along with Miliukov's wife Anna, Tyrkova-Williams, and Nechaeva. The SR Party leaders Victor Chernov, Prime Minister Kerensky, and Maria Spiridonova—a well-known terrorist of the prewar era—were also elected, although the latter two seldom attended. The Bolsheviks, who assiduously studied the history of past revolutions, regarded the Petrograd Council as analogous to the revolutionary Paris Commune of 1871. Their deputies, led by the future Soviet Commissar of Enlightenment Anatoly Lunacharsky, quickly became the Kadets' most determined opponents in the council.[43]

From the day the new council opened on September 1 political combat, not the city's escalating needs, dominated its sessions. The Bolshevik delegation stridently called for an end to the war, the elimination of the Provisional Government, and the transfer of power to the soviets of workers, soldiers, and peasants. Pushed inexorably to the right and alarmed by growing chaos in the army and the country, Kadet deputies called in vain for the restoration of order. Although the SRs held the plurality of seats, they and other moderate socialists lost influence as they vacillated between the right and the left. The so-called Kornilov Affair, which occurred just before the new council opened, heightened the political tension. This unsuccessful military coup against the Petrograd Soviet compromised Prime Minister Kerensky and strengthened popular distrust of the Provisional Government. The incident also gave the Bolsheviks ample evidence for their repeated warnings about counterrevolution and the two-faced Kerensky, whom they accused of aspiring to the role of military dictator, as played by Napoleon Bonaparte when he betrayed the French Revolution. At the new council's first session Lunacharsky demanded that the Kadets, the "party of counterrevolution," be excluded from all leadership and executive positions.[44] The warring deputies did share one belief—that the democratically elected council represented the voice of the people. But they differed sharply on what that popular voice was saying in the fall of 1917.

Lengthy speeches and party declarations made meetings interminable. Deputies argued over politicized issues that had little to do with the city's urgent needs, such as whether soldiers at the front who refused orders to advance should face the death penalty.[45] Most of the deputies had neither experience nor genuine interest in municipal governance anyway. Deputies proposed resolutions and statements to demonstrate their revolutionary ardor; arguments over the wording lasted for hours. The new mayor, a white-bearded socialist named G. I. Shreider, was little better. Scathingly described by Obolensky as "an extremely dull-witted, talentless and narrow doctrinaire," he pronounced "contentless, pathetic speeches, invariably underscoring his socialist credentials and suspicion toward us, 'representatives of the bourgeoisie.'"[46]

While council deputies harangued each other the city fell into a catastrophic state. Shortages of fuel severely affected its electricity and water supply. Prices continued to climb, while ration norms for bread, sugar, oil, and other regulated foodstuffs were repeatedly cut. Freight cars with food shipments stood on railroad sidings until the contents rotted because labor shortages in the city left no one to unload them. Soap almost completely disappeared. No one collected refuse or repaired buildings. As one contemporary observer wrote, "the population is drowning in dirt and garbage, and is being eaten up by insects." Cases of infectious and nutritional diseases like typhus, scurvy, and dysentery soared, but in city hospitals, which lacked medical personnel and even the most basic medicines, patients walked around dirty and barefoot. The municipal government was buried in debt, its workers on strike.[47]

Unlike many deputies, Sofia appears to have taken day-to-day municipal affairs seriously, despite the obvious reality of mounting chaos and dysfunction. The transcripts of council sessions show her participating in discussions about setting up children's clubs (September 11) and buying books for new city libraries (October 20).[48] She served on the committee on municipal people's houses, chaired by Bolshevik faction leader Lunacharsky, along with several of her longtime coworkers from the Ligovsky People's House.[49] It was almost business as usual at the Ministry of Education as well. On October 24, the day before the Bolsheviks toppled the Provisional Government, Sofia met with Minister Salazkin, Assistant Minister Vernadsky, and other assistant ministers to continue discussion of a major initiative for adult education, her particular sphere of interest. The plan was ambitious and very expensive, they agreed, but also extremely important for Russia's future.[50]

While the Ministry of Education may have been able to continue functioning on the eve of the Bolshevik coup, the politically polarized Petrograd City Council sank into paralysis. Ordinary questions of municipal life were simply "blown away," in the words of socialist deputy Milchik, "by the whirlwind of revolution."[51] Meeting on October 24, deputies could talk of little else besides the rumors of the Bolsheviks' impending armed insurrection against the Provisional Government. Over the protests of Bolshevik deputies, the council denounced "all violent armed actions" and called upon the city's inhabitants to "unite around the council, as its authorized representative organ." A "Committee of Public Safety" was formed, provoking yet another declaration, this one from the Bolshevik delegation, which denounced the council.[52]

On the eventful night of October 25, the council opened at 8 p.m. with a dramatic announcement from Mayor Shreider. Armed workers and soldiers had surrounded the Winter Palace where the Provisional Government was meeting. They had sent an ultimatum to the besieged ministers: surrender by 9 p.m., or Bolshevik sailors on the navy cruiser *Aurora*, anchored in the river across from the palace, would open fire. "In the name of humanity," Shreider exclaimed, the council should do all in its power to prevent the fall of the Provisional Government and the Russian Republic. After wasting time in arguments about what was actually going on, and what the council should do about it, the deputies were informed that the government ministers had received a second warning. The *Aurora*'s assault on the Winter Palace was minutes away. Finally accepting the mayor's call to take action against the insurrection, the council created three delegations. One group of three deputies would go to the Winter Palace, the second to the Petrograd Soviet in Smolny, and the third would attempt to board the *Aurora* and persuade the sailors not to fire on the ministers.[53]

Out of nine delegates selected by the council that night to resist the Bolshevik coup, Sofia was one of two Kadets and the only woman. Perhaps she was one of the few members of the council willing to volunteer for such a dangerous assignment. Perhaps council members believed that with her long record of social service to the Petrograd working class, Sofia's voice would be persuasive with the rebels. Whatever the reasons behind her selection, it was her strong sense of duty and commitment to the rule of law, along with a significant measure of fearlessness, that once again impelled Sofia to join what must have seemed a mission most unlikely to succeed.

When viewed a century later, the events that followed combined drama with elements of comedy, but in the eyes of the participants the crisis was deadly serious. Sofia, the SR Milchik, and the socialist assistant mayor N. A. Artemiev set off by automobile up Nevsky Prospect toward the river and the cruiser *Aurora*. The trio did not get far. At the Kazan Cathedral, less than five minutes from the council building, an armed patrol from the Bolshevik-led Military Revolutionary Committee forced them to turn back. Upon their return, the council began to debate a proposal to march en masse to the Winter Palace. If the ministers of the Provisional Government in refusing to surrender were ready to die, many delegates argued that night, then the council should go to die with them. As anxiety and excitement mounted, Sofia was moved to speak out. According to Obolensky, she did not utter any "pathetic words," which would have been "organically impossible" for her. But she did declare herself ready to march with other deputies and stand before the guns aimed at the Winter Palace. Milchik claims she challenged the Bolsheviks "to shoot at the Provisional Government through [our] heads."[54]

After more debate and over the objections of the few remaining Bolshevik deputies, the majority voted to march to the palace to provide moral support to the ministers—and if necessary, to die there. As deputies began preparing to leave, new voices warned against taking on the role of martyr. The council's delegation to the Winter Palace, which had been stopped by armed revolutionaries at Palace Square, reported that the streets were dark and dangerous. Electricity was sporadic, and shooting could be heard. Since telephone communication with the ministers in the palace had been cut, no one even knew whether they were still alive. Returning at this time from his unsuccessful talks with Leon Trotsky, the chairman of the Petrograd Soviet, Mayor Shreider advised the deputies that resistance was futile.

Undaunted, Sofia and the other deputies put on their coats, picked up bags of bread and sausage for the besieged ministers, and formed a procession. At 1:30 a.m. three hundred men and women in rows of eight began marching in silence up Nevsky Prospect toward the Winter Palace. The streetlights were out, and the weather was foul, rainy, and foggy. Amid the sounds of their own footsteps, the marchers heard occasional shots ring out as Bolsheviks took control of the city. But after only a few minutes armed sailors halted the procession at the corner of the Catherine (now Griboedov) Canal. Deputies at the front tried to argue with the sailors to let the people's elected representatives pass, but they met with sullen silence, then irritation and hostility. The procession began to fall apart, Milchik recalled, as nervous sailors fingered their rifles and deputies grew aware of their powerlessness and the "absurdity" of their position. Breaking into scattered groups, the discouraged marchers silently returned to the city hall. A hungry few, Milchik claims, furtively ate the bread and sausage intended for the embattled ministers. The remaining deputies voted to form a "Committee to Save the Fatherland and the Revolution," then finally adjourned at 3 a.m.[55] Meanwhile the Military Revolutionary Committee infiltrated the Winter Palace, defeated the cadets and women soldiers guarding the Provisional Government, and placed the ministers under arrest. Lenin proclaimed that the masses had overthrown their capitalist oppressors, and Russia was now a socialist republic.

Sofia never mentions the momentous night of October 25–26 and the leading role she played in any of her surviving memoirs about the year 1917. Her silence is striking but understandable, since the council's actions that night demonstrated so dramatically the impotence of the Bolsheviks' opponents. Perhaps she shared the view expressed by her friend Obolensky. In retrospect, he wrote in his memoir, he regarded the council's decision to march to the Winter Palace as "ridiculous," and the entire episode made him feel uncomfortable and ashamed of participating in "such a banal farce" during that tragic night.[56] Other eyewitnesses agreed. The pro-Bolshevik American journalist John Reed came upon the procession's encounter with Red sailors on the corner of Nevsky and the Catherine Canal as he dashed around Petrograd that night with other American journalists. His description in *Ten Days that*

Shook the World of the hapless marchers—"men in frock coats, well-dressed women, officers, all sorts and conditions of people," melodramatically proclaiming their readiness to die—set the tone for subsequent accounts that mock or dismiss the incident.[57] But the civic spirit and courage Sofia displayed in the face of armed bands of workers and soldiers in the dangerous streets that night contrasts with the behavior of others who quickly admitted defeat.

Sofia's stand against Bolshevism demonstrates how far she had traveled since World War I interrupted her peaceful summer at Marfino. In the war's early months she defined her role and responsibilities clearly and unambiguously: women served their country by serving the needy on the home front. Few could have predicted how relief work would politicize both donors and clients, drawing both sides into conflicts barely discernible in the initial outburst of patriotism in 1914. Sofia's progressive reputation and administrative talents, along with her wealth and social prestige, elevated her to positions of city-wide authority and led her from what she called the "whirlpool" of social activism in 1914 into the whirlwind of politics in 1917. She was right when she wrote that her decision to join the Kadet Party determined "my entire future fate." Membership on the party's central committee placed her squarely and unambiguously on one side in the intensifying revolutionary struggle. It confirmed her eligibility for positions in the Provisional Government and the Petrograd City Council, where she came face-to-face with her party's socialist adversaries. When the Bolsheviks triumphed, Sofia's political allegiance and position made her a highly visible target for arrest and persecution as the revolution's enemy.

But Sofia also magnified the transformation of her public identity by erecting an artificial boundary between political activism and her pre-1917 public activity and ignoring the numerous ways that social welfare reinforces class differences in rights and access to power. The hardships and disillusionment the war produced as it dragged on aggravated the differences between women who distributed aid and women who received it. As she began to recognize in early 1916, and as women's demonstrations in March and April 1917 would confirm, the war produced new concepts of citizenship—not only among her fellow volunteers from educated society, but also among working-class women and soldiers' wives and mothers. The February Revolution made all women into citizens and gave them unprecedented opportunities to engage directly in political action. Its rhetoric of liberation and equality empowered them to express their demands, while its introduction of formal political rights enabled them to enter government.

At the same time Sofia's experiences in 1917 reveal how limited women's political rights still were. Despite her pedigree as the step-daughter of the Kadets' revered founder and the widespread respect she enjoyed, she exerted little if any influence over party or government policies. It is difficult to resist viewing her appointments as assistant minister of welfare and education as tokenism. Her tenure in the short-lived Provisional Government was too brief to make this "First Woman Minister of State" anything more than a symbol of what women might achieve in the future.

What impelled a woman who had avoided the public spotlight her entire life to accept highly visible roles in some of Russia's major political institutions in the midst of a revolution? Sofia was no pawn in a game played by men; she consciously chose the positions she occupied in 1917. In part she seems to have been motivated by the same sense of patriotic duty that her wartime service had cultivated. She also defined a specific role for herself in the political realm as an intermediary, not a partisan politician. This was a role that grew naturally out of her belief that Russia's "dark," uneducated working men and women were a "flock that had gone astray," in need of guidance and leadership. On the snowy streets of Petrograd during the February uprising she moved between leaderless soldiers and bewildered political leaders. As the guardianships' liaison with the socialist Soviet, she tried to reconcile the demands of soldiers' wives with the constraints of the city's exhausted resources. Her self-definition as a mediator comes out especially vividly in her account of visiting Smolny Institute in the summer of 1917, at the moment of its transformation from a bastion of privilege into a communist headquarters. Finally, it was Sofia whom the Petrograd Council chose for its unsuccessful mission to negotiate with sailors on the *Aurora*. Although her government fell that night, Sofia would not allow herself to be dismissed so easily, or her political career to end so ignobly. No longer an intermediary between the forces of moderation and extremism, she now reinvented herself as one of the leaders of the anti-Bolshevik resistance.

8

Sofia Goes Underground

On November 28, 1917, one month after the coup that overthrew the Provisional Government, Sofia was awakened before dawn by one of her servants knocking loudly at the bedroom door. A Bolshevik commissar, he informed his mistress, had just arrived with a convoy of soldiers to search the house and arrest its owner. The sound of heavy footsteps and the rattling of weapons confirmed the presence of the uninvited guests. Their appearance occurred on a day Sofia and her fellow Kadets had eagerly anticipated for months. Delegates to the Constituent Assembly, chosen in mid-November in Russia's first elections based on universal suffrage, were due to meet in the Tauride Palace for its official opening. Opponents of the Bolsheviks expected this body to take over leadership of the struggle they had been waging since the October coup. But by the time the assembly was scheduled to open at 2 p.m., Sofia was sitting under guard in Smolny, the headquarters of the Petrograd Soviet, awaiting interrogation. Two weeks after her arrest, charged with sabotage and theft of government funds, she faced her accusers in the Bolsheviks' first trial of their many political enemies.[1]

Sofia's arrest and trial occurred during a period of great uncertainty and contradiction in the capital. The hastily constructed Soviet government erratically but doggedly extended its control over communications, transportation, government, and financial institutions. Most public services ceased to operate, leaving no one to run the trams or remove the carcasses of dead horses that lay in the streets. Armed bands of undisciplined, often drunk soldiers, sailors, and workers looking for "enemies of the revolution" made parts of the city extremely dangerous.[2] At the same time, the Bolsheviks' rival political parties, including the Kadets, managed to function despite harassment, even conducting public election campaigns for the Constituent Assembly in early and mid-November. Anti-Bolshevik newspapers protested the arbitrary actions of Lenin, Trotsky, and the other commissars who claimed to be Russia's new government, while dissension raged within the Bolshevik Party. The city erupted in violence on October 29 when officers and military school cadets launched an ill-advised rebellion against the new regime, resulting in more than two hundred casualties. In the words of the historian Alexander Rabinowitch, "Petrograd was a battle zone, gripped by anxiety, fear, and fierce antagonism."[3] In the actual battle zones of the Eastern Front the Russian Army, though depleted by waves of desertions, still faced its German, Austrian, and Ottoman opponents even as active hostilities largely ceased, while both the Allies and the Central Powers struggled to understand what Bolshevik rhetoric about revolutionary war actually meant. It was a time, Sofia later remembered, when "chaos reigned in life and unexpected things happened that would have been quite impossible later on. Real terror had not yet begun" in late 1917, she continued, "and not only we, but the bolshevists themselves did not yet believe in the stability of their power."[4]

The indeterminate and volatile atmosphere presented the Bolsheviks' political opponents in the capital with a paradoxical freedom of choice. The circumstances permitted a range of different responses: flight or resigned acquiescence, open confrontation or clandestine resistance. To be sure, according to the Leninist version of Marxist identity politics, class affiliation determined whether one stood with the new rulers or against them, and therefore how one would be treated by the new regime. Sofia met all the qualifications of a class enemy. As she sardonically recalled, "I had on my conscience more sins than necessary to justify my [arrest]: I was—oh horror!—an aristocrat, a countess, [and] I was very rich." Moreover, since the spring she had been a member of the one political party "that remained in the field to fight against socialism and its extremes, thus becoming particularly odious to the bolshevists," she claimed, because of its resolute defense of democracy.[5]

But Sofia's fate was determined in late 1917 not merely by her class or Kadet affiliation, but even more by her actions. From the night of October 25–26 until her arrest one month later, she participated in several major organizations in the capital that attempted to resist the Bolshevik takeover. Her commitment to their oppositionist political activities represented the final step in a personal transformation from social worker to political figure that had begun in August 1914, when she had hastened from Marfino to Petrograd to serve the war effort. Then and throughout the war years, she tied her public life to the fate of her country, first as Russia faced the threat of German aggression and now as it confronted what she considered certain ruin if it remained under Bolshevik rule. This time, coming to the defense of her country brought great personal risk. The prison in the Peter and Paul Fortress was quickly filling with other Bolshevik opponents, and street violence was escalating against those who looked like members of the hated bourgeoisie. Ignoring her own safety, Sofia became one of the few women to play a part in the life-and-death political struggle that began in Petrograd in late 1917.

In the two decades that followed the revolution, numerous Kadets living in emigration penned memoirs that seek to analyze the entire course of the revolution and to understand the causes of the Provisional Government's defeat and the Bolsheviks' victory.[6] By contrast, Sofia's surviving autobiographical writings pay little attention to events before the October Revolution, concentrating instead on her own experiences during November and December, especially her arrest, imprisonment, and trial. Unlike her telling of the history of the Ligovsky People's House in *On the Outskirts of Petersburg*, in which she underplays her contributions to the institution's creation and operation, her recollections about late 1917 emphasize her leading role in the anti-Bolshevik opposition, at times to the point of grandiosity. In a speech in English she delivered to an audience in Los Angeles in 1939, for example, shortly after immigrating to the United States, Sofia emphatically claimed that "after the fall of the Provisional Government I had practically—this time clandestinely, certainly—been the soul of the strike of all the governmental service in Petrograd and had joined all possible conspirative [*sic*] organizations aiming at the overthrow of the bolshevist regime, which I considered to be the ruin of my country."[7]

Sofia did not seek the deeper causes of what she termed the "nightmare and anarchy of Bolshevik rule."[8] Her writings reflect little understanding of why the positions and slogans of the radical left resonated with an exhausted, anxious, resentful population still holding onto promises of peace, freedom, land, and justice, however hollow those promises may have seemed to her. In Sofia's eyes the Bolshevik Revolution was an attack against civilization itself, one that produced nothing but dirt, disorder, and moral degeneration. But if her accounts yield few insights into the causes of the Bolsheviks' success, they shed light on the immediate consequences of their seizure of power and the responses of their political enemies. They also help to redress an imbalance in historical and eyewitness accounts of 1917, which are usually told from a male-centered perspective.

In the immediate aftermath of the Bolshevik coup a number of organizations in Petrograd openly opposed Lenin and his hastily improvised government. The Bolsheviks' arbitrary and contradictory actions alienated not just their liberal and right-wing opponents but also other socialists. One center of resistance was the "Committee for the Salvation of the Fatherland and the Revolution," created in the early hours of October 26 by council leaders. Its first act was a proclamation calling upon all citizens to unite around it and oppose the illegal seizure of power. Along with fellow Kadet deputies Nabokov and Obolensky, Sofia joined the committee to represent the city council's Kadet faction. Consequently she spent a great deal of time during those post-October days at the city hall on Nevsky Prospect. The building resembled an ant-hill, Nabokov recalled; initially everyone who opposed the Bolsheviks gravitated there. Socialists and union leaders held non-stop meetings. Secondary school students arrived to volunteer for guard duty or staff first-aid stations and canteens. Signs at the entrance announced the latest news and the numbers of casualties in clashes with the Bolsheviks. Rumors swirled through the building about Prime Minister Kerensky's imminent arrival in the capital at the head of troops loyal to the Provisional Government. On the streets outside crowds protested against the new regime from early morning until well past midnight.[9] Meeting twice a day from late October into early November, the city council issued anti-Bolshevik proclamations and formed investigative commissions. Sofia was elected to head one such commission, charged with verifying reports that Bolshevik followers had raped the women soldiers guarding the Provisional Government during the attack on the Winter Palace on October 25–26. The reports, her commission determined, were false, though the women had been roughed up and insulted.[10]

The Bolsheviks' opponents, Kadets and non-Bolshevik socialists alike, believed that Lenin's new government was both illegitimate and

ephemeral, and that the country's political future must be determined
only by the lawfully elected Constituent Assembly. Nevertheless, it
proved impossible for liberals and socialists to unify their efforts or
even find a common language of opposition.[11] Along with her fellow
Kadets Sofia dutifully attended the daily meetings of the Committee for
the Salvation of the Fatherland and the Revolution, initially hoping that
it would be able to undertake some kind of effective action. But as the
committee's only nonsocialists Sofia, Nabokov, and Obolensky felt
awkward and isolated. While the Socialist Revolutionaries and Mensheviks called each other "comrade," Obolensky remembered, they
pointedly addressed the Kadets as "mister," "citizen," or "committee
member so-and-so." The socialists distrusted the Kadets and kept them
at arm's length; the Kadets in turn suspected them of trying to use the
committee to supplant the legitimate Provisional Government.[12]

Since the Bolsheviks themselves were uncertain of their hold on
power, they moved relatively cautiously against some of their adversaries. The Council of People's Commissars, which Lenin chaired, did
not outlaw the Committee for the Salvation of the Fatherland and the
Revolution until November 10. Another center of resistance was the
Petrograd City Council, which issued a principled but meaningless
joint Kadet-SR resolution that rejected Bolshevik power. The council
continued to meet even after a Soviet decree on November 16 dissolved
it. Four days later, however, as a deputy was addressing the council
about public works, thirty armed sailors and workers burst into the
chamber and declared that if the council did not immediately disband,
they would begin shooting. Deputies regrouped elsewhere a half hour
later and defiantly scheduled another meeting for November 22, but it
never took place.[13]

Repressions against the Kadet Party began immediately after the
Bolshevik coup, leaving the party leaderless and imperiled. Kadet
ministers in the last Provisional Government languished in the Peter
and Paul Fortress, in the same dank cells where Russia's tsarist rulers
had incarcerated revolutionaries since the early 1870s. Other party
leaders, including Miliukov, evaded arrest by fleeing the capital for
Moscow. Armed detachments of Red Guards seized the party's headquarters and burned copies of its daily newspaper. The Soviet regime
stepped up its offensive against the Kadets when the results of the Constituent Assembly elections conducted on November 12–14 revealed
that more than a quarter of the Petrograd electorate had voted for the
liberals. Armed sailors ransacked the apartments of party leaders and

its Petrograd political club. Tyrkova-Williams published a broadsheet called "The Struggle" that compared Lenin and Trotsky to Rasputin and the detested tsarist minister Stürmer. To avoid arrest, she slept at different friends' apartments.[14] Nabokov and other members of the Constituent Assembly's electoral commission were seized on November 23. They spent several uncomfortable days in a filthy and crowded makeshift prison in the basement of Smolny, where Sofia visited them shortly before her own arrest.[15]

Heretofore a secondary figure in the Kadet party leadership, Sofia stepped forward to help fill the vacuum left by the repressions. Because of her positions as assistant minister, deputy to the city council, and member of the Committee for the Salvation of the Fatherland and the Revolution, she uniquely linked the Kadets to other major opposition groups in the capital as well as to those Provisional Government institutions that continued to function after the coup. One indication of the depth of her commitment is her willingness to allow various clandestine political bodies to meet at her home on Sergievskaya Street. The October Revolution thereby erased the boundary Sofia had long maintained between her private and public lives, between the elegant tranquility of her domestic space, adorned with the Panins' paintings and tapestries, and the contentious public arena of revolutionary politics.[16]

While Sofia's own accounts say little at all about the effectiveness of the "conspirative organizations" to which she belonged, her colleague Nabokov, writing less than a year after the events, has left scathing descriptions. The morning meetings of the Kadet Central Committee were taken up with aimless conversations and "so-called 'information,' half of which, if not more, consisted of various unverified rumors and fantastic stories," he recalled. Then the Committee for the Salvation of the Fatherland and the Revolution met for "long, exhausting, completely fruitless debates, ending with the passage of some draft appeal or completely useless resolution." Nabokov concludes: "the 15–20 people who met recognized all too clearly, without any question, their complete powerlessness, isolation, [and] the absence of organizations on which they could rely."[17]

Sofia may well have shared his opinion; perhaps that is why her writings about this period provide few details about her membership in these political bodies, which lacked concrete information and spent more time in debate and mutual recriminations than in action. None of the committees possessed any real resources with which to combat a determined cadre of radical socialists, backed by thousands of armed

workers and soldiers. As the Bolsheviks intensified their repression of
political dissent in November, such opposition groups increasingly met
in secret. While in retrospect their impotence may seem obvious, it
nevertheless required courage even to meet and determination to carry
on the anxious search for feasible means of resistance. Looking back on
those days, Obolensky expressed amazement at his fellow Kadets'
"fearlessness," which he could explain only by the fact that "we simply
could not imagine the danger that threatened each of us."[18]

Sofia found a more powerful means to resist the Bolshevik takeover
in her government position than in her membership on either the party
central committee or the city council. The central government apparatus
initially survived the Bolshevik coup intact, despite the flight of the
prime minister from the capital and the arrest of the other ministers on
October 25. The new Soviet authorities, facing myriad other challenges,
did not turn their attention to the ministries and their employees for
some time. Although they generally stayed away from ministry offices,
the Provisional Government's assistant ministers remained at liberty,
and civil servants continued to report to work. The assistant ministers
began meeting daily in late October at the initiative of Assistant Minister of Justice A. A. Demianov, first at his apartment and then at Sofia's.
Minister of Food Supply S. N. Prokopovich, the only minister not arrested on October 26, became the chair of the council and de facto prime
minister when he returned to Petrograd from Moscow. Four socialist
ministers from the last cabinet, imprisoned only briefly after October
25, soon joined them, bringing the council to a total of two dozen or
so, with Sofia its only female member. Meeting from late October to
November 16, the so-called "Little Council" considered itself Russia's
legitimate government, authorized to make decisions, allocate money,
and issue orders in the name of the entire Provisional Government.[19]

In certain ways this underground Provisional Government differed
little from the other conflict-ridden opposition groups meeting continuously in the first weeks after the October coup. Belonging to different
political parties, its members disagreed fundamentally on how best to
combat the Bolsheviks. The majority insisted on meeting in secret, while
a minority wanted to announce the government's existence and work
openly with other anti-Bolshevik groups and army leaders. Some favored giving the Committee for the Salvation of the Fatherland and the
Revolution money to publish anti-Bolshevik pamphlets for distribution
in the army; others, including Sofia, questioned the legality of using state
funds for political purposes. In another dispute, this one over payment

of salaries to civil servants, Prokopovich threatened to resign. Both Demianov and Nabokov later dismissed the members of this would-be legitimate government with contempt. Demianov remembered them as well-intentioned people who were completely lacking in resolution and a sense of reality. Nabokov came away depressed from the one meeting he attended at Sofia's urging, dismayed by the excruciatingly longwinded speeches he heard, filled with empty rhetoric and delivered by panicky former representatives of state power.[20] Disgusted by what he regarded as the group's passivity, Alexei Nikitin, a Menshevik socialist and former minister of the interior, resigned on November 12; Demianov and other members of the minority followed him.[21] The underground Provisional Government, Demianov bitterly concluded in his recollections, "vegetated" during its month-long existence, and accomplished absolutely nothing.[22]

Sofia evidently shared some of their discouragement. On November 14 she visited an ailing Vernadsky, the fellow Kadet leader who had served as the other assistant minister of education and also belonged to the Little Council. The previous day's meeting, she told him, was "tragic." She was astounded by the weak and confused behavior of the council's members, especially Prokopovich. According to Vernadsky, she told them that she—the only female member—felt like one of the few real men in the entire group.[23] Her comments to Vernadsky, recorded in his diary the evening of her visit, suggest that Sofia saw herself as having assumed a male role in the struggle against Bolshevism while male colleagues failed to display manly courage and conviction. The remark serves as additional evidence of the self-reinvention that had begun earlier in 1917, when Sofia accepted positions in male-dominated political bodies and became "the first woman minister."

Such negative judgments about the underground Provisional Government seem overly harsh, considering the leadership it provided for some of the stiffest resistance the Bolsheviks encountered in the capital in their first weeks in power—a boycott and strike conducted by its civil service employees. The action originated in an order issued by Kadet ministers Alexander Konovalov and Nikolai Kishkin, besieged in the Winter Palace on the night of the coup, who instructed government agencies to keep funds and records out of Bolshevik hands. Regarding it as their duty to carry out Konovalov and Kishkin's order, assistant ministers instructed their subordinates not to hand over the keys to ministry cash boxes and files, but instead to transfer ministry funds to foreign banks in the name of the legitimate government to be established by the Constituent Assembly.[24] They also approved a strike by government workers in all nonessential ministries. Sources differ about who was responsible for the idea of a government strike. According to Demianov, the initiative came from the civil servants themselves, who sent a delegation to the underground government to gain its approval. Obolensky attributes the initiative to the Committee for the Salvation of the Fatherland and Revolution, however, and some historians of the Kadet Party along with Sofia herself have suggested it was she who proposed a strike by government workers at one of that committee's first meetings.[25] Regardless of who initiated it, the underground Provisional Government monitored, encouraged, and funded the strikers throughout its short existence.[26]

The resistance by civil servants in the government's ministries initially hindered Bolshevik efforts to take over government authority after their coup. But on November 13 representatives of the revolutionary government succeeded in taking control of the State Bank. At the Little Council's meeting the following day, the assistant minister of finance announced that with the bank in Bolshevik hands, the government would no longer be able to take any actions that required state funds, nor would it be able to pay civil servants their salaries on the next payday, November 20, a promise it had made to the strikers. The civil servants' boycott and strike seemed to be coming to an inevitable end. An unwavering supporter of the strike, Sofia made one final effort to thwart the inevitable Bolshevik takeover of her own ministry. With the last minister of education, Dr. Sergei Salazkin, under arrest since the night of the Bolshevik takeover, she considered herself responsible for the ministry's employees and funds. On November 15 she sent a note to V. K. Diakov, a ministry official, ordering him to give all funds on hand "immediately" to two other ministry employees she named and go with them to deposit the funds for safekeeping in a place the two would designate. The investigation that followed revealed that the amount removed was almost 93,000 rubles in cash and securities. Despite the rampant inflation of 1917 that was still a substantial sum, equivalent to over $45,000 according to the prewar exchange rate and over one million dollars today.[27]

It was the principle, however, and not the amount that mattered most when a Bolshevik named Isaac Rogalsky arrived at the Ministry of Education with orders to assume control on behalf of the Soviet Commissariat of Education. The ministry employees who had carried out Sofia's instructions showed him her order of November 15. A greatly irritated Rogalsky filed an accusation against Sofia with the Investigative Commission of the All-Russian Soviet, a new agency created to investigate counterrevolutionary activity. In a report dated November 26 the Investigative Commission ruled that she had indeed removed "the People's money" from the former ministry. By doing so she had committed "criminal sabotage" against the revolutionary government and had "thrown into disorder the government apparatus in general and the People's Commissariat of Education in particular." The Investigative Commission ordered Sofia's arrest and trial.[28]

Unaware of the imminent threat to her freedom, Sofia opened her home for a very important meeting of the Kadet Central Committee on the evening of November 27, the day before the scheduled convocation of the Constituent Assembly. Kadet leaders anticipated the opening of the assembly with great hope, wanting to believe that it would finally turn the tide in the battle against Bolshevism and mark the first step in the construction of a new, legitimate political order. Under a banner headline proclaiming "Hail to the Constituent Assembly," the lead article in the November 28 issue of the Kadets' principal newspaper employed its loftiest rhetoric to remind readers of the years of heroic sacrifice that had brought Russia to the day when the "long-held dream" of democracy would be realized. The somber news and anxious editorials that filled the issue's other columns painted a dark backdrop, however, to the "triumphant holiday" hailed on page one. Members of the electoral commission for the Constituent Assembly were still under arrest. Soldiers posted at the Winter Palace to guard it were looting its wine cellars. The newspaper itself barely managed to publish in the face of raids and confiscations. Other announcements in its November 28 issue convey the eerie semblance of normalcy that hovered over parts of Petrograd as winter set in. Residents could still see the operetta "Kukolka" at the Palace Theater on Mikhailovsky Square, for example; or they could make plans to attend a forthcoming concert of the State Philharmonic Orchestra of Petrograd under the baton of Sergei Kusevitsky, who renamed himself Serge Koussevitzky after emigrating in 1920 and became the revered conductor of the Boston Symphony Orchestra.[29]

Thus emotions ran high among the Kadets who met at Sofia's home on the eve of the opening of the assembly. Some were colleagues who had been elected to the assembly from Moscow and other parts of the empire, and had managed to find transportation to the capital amidst the chaos that was gradually taking over the country. Expecting the Bolsheviks to try to block the assembly from meeting, there were legitimate concerns for the delegates' personal safety. Another topic of discussion at Sofia's was how to join forces with other anti-Bolshevik groups on November 28 in mass demonstrations in support of the assembly and against Soviet power. Despite a month of experience with the methods employed by their Bolshevik opponents and the city's evident slide into lawlessness, Kadet leaders clung to their liberal faith in the rule of law, the electoral process, and the fundamental sanity of their fellow Russians. As William Rosenberg has observed, the establishment of the Bolshevik regime "simply pressed most party members closer to their basic system of values." Or as Sofia ruefully remarked years later, "from the bottom of the well all the stars look brighter."[30]

Sofia steadfastly maintained her political principles in the face of her disheartening experience with the ineffectual opposition during the four weeks following the Bolshevik takeover. Chosen by the party in early October for its candidate list, she even ran for a seat in the Constituent Assembly for the Petrograd electoral district. Despite her well-known name, she was not elected. The reasons lie in both the system of voting and the election's disappointing outcome for the Kadets. Voters chose a party list, not individual candidates, and the number of votes cast in each electoral district for each party's list determined the number of seats it won. Since parties ranked their candidates, those candidates with higher positions on the party lists were more likely to win, especially, as in the case of the Kadets, when the vote for the list was smaller than the party hoped. Despite the turmoil in the city, almost eighty percent of eligible voters participated in the elections for the Constituent Assembly in Petrograd. With slightly more than twenty-five percent of voters choosing their list, the Kadets finished second after the Bolsheviks, who received forty-five percent of the total vote. Listed in seventh position, Sofia was not ranked high enough on the Kadets' list to win a seat.[31]

In light of the circumstances of the elections, however, the chances of victory for even a well-known female candidate running in her home district were very slim. Although female turnout was very high, women comprised only a tiny percentage of the candidates. Tyrkova-Williams was defeated despite her high position on the Kadet party list in two provinces, including her native Novgorod. She was already skeptical about the salvation other Kadets looked for in the Constituent Assembly when she cast her vote in Petrograd on November 25. "The Russian people had to select their representatives amid the crackle of rifle and machine gun fire," she claimed. "Amid the whirlwind of anarchy and civil war illiterate men and women, unaccustomed to political thinking, had to make sense of complicated [political] programs which they had heard about for the first time only a few months before."[32] It was surely too much to expect a newly enfranchised electorate to elevate women to political office. As it turned out, only ten of the total of 767 elected deputies were women, all of whom were members of the Bolshevik or Socialist Revolutionary party.[33]

Unlike Tyrkova-Williams, Sofia still hoped for a democratic resurgence despite a month during which the Bolsheviks gave every indication of their unwillingness to share power, even with other socialist parties. After the party meeting broke up around 1 a.m., she recalled, by "some strange irony of fate" she fell asleep

> with a feeling of a kind of calm and safety. The Constituent Assembly opening on the following day completed some kind of stage, [it] had to end as it were the dominion of unrestrained arbitrariness, and take upon itself the whole responsibility for further struggle, which up to that time we, the fragments of the Provisional Government and local self-government institutions, had been conducting. And on that last night I already felt myself under the protection of this returning consciousness of law. We were then still very far from a true understanding of Bolshevism and for this understanding we subsequently had to pay with our blood.[34]

Those hopes ended abruptly with the arrival of the Bolshevik arrest party before dawn on November 28.

As Sofia narrates them, that morning's events clearly demonstrated what she regarded as the Bolshevik usurpers' total lack of legitimacy. Her account is inflected by the condescending class and ethnic prejudice that were widespread in privileged Russian society but are still jarring to hear in the voice of a progressive social reformer. In Sofia's description the leader of the search party, a man who introduced himself as Gordon, was an inept and unprincipled opportunist. Describing him as "a little clean-shaven Jew in civilian clothes," she presumed that he also "was without doubt an old and experienced worker in the former [tsarist] security police." When she demanded that he show her the arrest order, "he had trouble finding [it] among the handful of other orders of an analogous nature." The "ingratiatingly insolent" Gordon then rummaged around in her desk for more than an hour and a half by the dim light of several candles, since the electricity was not working. Sentries guarded the rest of the house, although from the adjoining room Sofia heard "the resonant snoring of one of the soldiers who had made himself comfortable there on the divan." As she later acknowledged, she was not treated badly. "When I now compare this search to other, later Bolshevik 'invasions' into private apartments, I must acknowledge the entire propriety of the way actions were conducted then from the external, visible side," she conceded. They did not yell at her or rob her, "they did not put a revolver to my forehead. . . . They tried to prove that they knew how to conduct themselves 'as in the best society.' . . . They even offered to let me drink a cup of tea before taking me away." By nine in the morning Sofia was in Gordon's car, rushing toward Smolny. The sun had risen by now, and the day was clear though very cold. Gordon was gleeful over her arrest, Sofia recounted with disdain. "Oh, oh, oh," he crowed, "how amazed my descendants will be when they read that I, Gordon, searched and arrested Countess Panina, the first woman in Russia, such a famous philanthropist, the woman-minister."[35]

Although it is not possible to determine who exactly Comrade Gordon was without his first name, as a Jew and a Bolshevik he fit a common profile. Legal and economic discrimination, along with alienation from the traditional Jewish life of the *shetl*, had driven a disproportionate number of young Jews into the socialist movement since the 1870s. It was common for contemporaries to comment explicitly on the Jewishness of political actors during the revolution, according to the historian Oleg Budnitskii, and Sofia is no exception here. Her characterization of Gordon echoes a view prevalent among some of the Bolsheviks' opponents and the Russian population at large that Jews dominated the Bolshevik movement and the Soviet regime, especially its organs of political repression.[36] Nor is it possible to confirm Sofia's assertion that he formerly worked for the tsarist secret police. Regardless of whether her allegations about his past were true, her characterization of him is consistent with her unshakable belief in the Bolsheviks' moral bankruptcy. In contrast to the principled stand she and her fellow Kadets were taking in defense of democracy, their opponents employed agents like Gordon who served any master, tsarist or Soviet. While mocking Gordon for his ineptitude and crude efforts to mimic the civilized manners of his social betters, she also took offense at his "insolent" behavior and the liberties taken by his sleepy armed guard. Yet she concludes her account on an ironically self-glorifying note by recollecting how he acknowledged her superior position as the "first woman of Russia."

Sofia was not the only Kadet leader arrested that morning. Two prominent Kadets had spent the night at her home: her longtime friend Dr. Shingarev, a minister in the first and second provisional governments and the leader of the Kadet faction in the city council, who lived at the opposite end of the dangerous city; and Fedor Kokoshkin, the former state controller, who had traveled with his wife from Moscow for the opening of the assembly. Not expecting this windfall, Gordon left them under guard at her home but proceeded with her to Smolny for instructions from the Petrograd Soviet.[37] Sofia devotes considerable attention to these two men in her autobiographical accounts of the events of November–December 1917. To her they personified the kind of selfless advocacy for the public good that motivated the best leaders of the Kadet Party and exemplified the tragic fate of such heroes under Bolshevism.

When Sofia finally arrived under guard at the headquarters of the Petrograd Soviet in Smolny, she was shocked. The elegant building had changed drastically since her visit in June, and its condition, in her mind, symbolized the catastrophe that had befallen Russia. Machine guns now guarded its elegant neoclassical entrance. Loitering groups of shabby, dirty, and insolent soldiers had replaced the frightened headmistress and timid pupils of the previous summer. The Petrograd Soviet, she charged, had turned the building into "the foulest pigsty"—"as dirty, foul-smelling, worn-down, and bespattered with grime as all the other buildings that had been seized by 'revolutionary democracy.'" In fact, the term "pigsty" was not really fair, she added, since animals, unlike people, possess "the saving instinct of self-preservation" and lack the creativity "that people apply, alas, not only to good, but also to evil." The staircases, corridors, and classrooms of the institute, which "had sparkled," she claimed, "with irreproachable cleanliness just a few months ago, now all wore the traces of this 'creativity'"—the indescribable filth of the revolution.[38] To Sofia, the condition of Smolny demonstrated the inevitably disastrous outcome when the class order is upturned and the natural leadership of the educated is rejected. Filled with anger and contempt, her account expresses a deeply visceral response to the October Revolution and its makers, who sank below the level of animals in their offenses against order, cleanliness, and civilization. Though heavily influenced by knowledge of the revolution's tragic impact upon the lives of her friends and country in the future, Sofia's description of Smolny reveals the toll the events of 1917 were taking on her prewar faith in human progress.

Sofia was brought into a spacious former classroom whose windows looked out on the Neva River. At that early hour there were only two other people in the room, she later reminisced: "a guard, who was peacefully dozing with his rifle in his hands in a chair by the entrance," and a cleaning woman with her skirt tucked up, who was attempting to wash the floor. Comrade Gordon "scampered away" to pick up orders to arrest Shingarev and Kokoshkin. Making herself comfortable in an ancient leather armchair, Sofia remembered feeling "strange" and "alone with my thoughts in the middle of the magnificent frame of the past, on the boundary of the unknown future." Questions filled her head: "What had served as the grounds for my arrest? What were they charging me with? What questions will they ask? And I did not find answers to them," she continued. "There was a great deal of anti-Bolshevik guilt on my part, for since the coup I unceasingly had done all that I could to overthrow them, but what guilt exactly they had established, I did not know." If she was frightened, her account of that morning contains no hint of it. Instead, her musings convey pride in her arrest as a sign that the Bolsheviks recognized her implacable rejection of their rule. The arrival of Shingarev, Kokoshkin, and his wife soon ended her solitude. An hour later, the little group welcomed Prince Pavel Dolgorukov and another Kadet party member, who had been arrested outside Sofia's house when they arrived for a meeting there that day. "And so," Sofia remembered, "our society was complete and we cheerfully and not without interest spent that entire day in Smolny, observing the life seething around us."[39]

As the room filled up with additional detainees, Sofia and her fellow Kadets set about establishing a kind of cozy domestic order, an act of defiance against captors who had turned Smolny into a "pigsty." Friends brought pillows, blankets, books, and food. Shingarev helped Sofia make tea. Accentuating the impotence of the Bolsheviks' socialist opponents, Sofia's account of that morning includes a visit by leaders of the moderate wing of the Socialist Revolutionary Party, alarmed at learning that fellow delegates to the Constituent Assembly had been arrested. "They apologized in confusion," Sofia contemptuously recalled, "grew indignant, promised to 'clear up the misunderstanding' and . . . vanished." To drive home the contrast, she makes a point of the kindness Shingarev showed toward a new detainee who was dragged in and rudely pushed to their end of the room: a skinny, pitiful individual in a torn military greatcoat, arrested for posting some announcements the Bolsheviks considered counterrevolutionary. When the doctor gave him some food, he learned that the "criminal" was illiterate and did not understand the text of what he was posting.[40]

The captive Kadets disagreed over who among them was more at risk, and in Sofia's telling, vied with each other over who was the most selfless. Kokoshkin and Shingarev were apparently convinced that their immunity as assembly delegates would soon earn them their freedom and believed that her fate would be the most serious.[41] The men chivalrously decided not to leave without her and to demand her liberation together with theirs. Rejecting their concern, Sofia claimed to be more worried about her fellow detainees, and for good reason. Although Dolgorukov remained characteristically cheerful, Shingarev and Kokoshkin were seriously ill. Suffering from tuberculosis, Kokoshkin spent the whole day and evening huddled in his overcoat next to his wife without moving or speaking. Shingarev, physically ill and also grieving over the recent death of his wife, paced restlessly. The Bolsheviks had not known about the Kadet meeting at her home when they arrived to arrest her the next morning. Had Kokoshkin and Shingarev not spent the night there, they might have evaded capture, as did other prominent Kadets who assembled in Petrograd that day for the Constituent Assembly. The emotional tone of Sofia's recollections is colored by feelings of guilt that she had indirectly led to her friends' incarceration.[42]

The steady influx of other prisoners into the former classroom reflected the tense situation and dramatic events occurring outside Smolny's walls that day. Citizens of the capital who opened their copies of the Soviet government's newspaper *Izvestiia* on the morning of November 28 found it filled with alarming stories of counterrevolutionary plots in which the Kadets starred with Cossack generals as the principal villains. Supporters of the Constituent Assembly marched in a large procession to the Tauride Palace that afternoon, singing the "Marseillaise" while Bolshevik supporters jeered and attempted to drown them out with the socialist anthem, the "Internationale." Since only a fraction of the delegates to the assembly had managed to reach the capital for the opening, they met only briefly, and the official opening was rescheduled to January 5.[43]

At Smolny the unplanned arrests of Shingarev, Kokoshkin, and Dolgorukov initially created a greater problem for the Soviet authorities than Sofia's case. As delegates to the Constituent Assembly, Shingarev and Kokoshkin were supposed to be immune from any harassment. There were no grounds, the men protested, for their detention. They denied knowledge of Sofia's alleged sabotage and theft and of Kadet party ties to the Cossack generals whom the Soviet authorities feared were organizing opposition in the east and south.[44] The Council of People's Commissars solved the dilemma for the captors of the three Kadets by creating grounds for their arrest *ex post facto* that night when they approved a decree proposed by Lenin, which outlawed the Kadet Party and declared its leaders enemies of the people. The decree ordered the party's leaders to be arrested immediately and tried by revolutionary tribunals. Dolgorukov, Kokoshkin, and Shingarev were promptly transported from Smolny to the prison in the Peter and Paul Fortress.[45]

It was close to midnight when Sofia was called in for interrogation. She readily admitted that she had signed the order to remove 93,000 rubles from the Ministry of Education, but she refused to say where she had ordered the money to be sent. Her interrogators warned that unless she restored the funds, she would be sent to prison. Sofia was not intimidated by the threat; according to the protocol of her interrogation, she defiantly declared that "I consider it my obligation to give a report about the whole activity and about the money only to the Constituent Assembly, as the single legitimate [government] authority. I refuse to make any explanations to commissars or the Investigative Commission."[46] Perhaps Sofia would have been freed had she revealed the whereabouts of the funds, but her defiance challenged Soviet power. The commission ordered her to remain under arrest and committed her for trial before the newly created Petrograd Revolutionary Tribunal. Finally, at the end of an extremely long day, she was escorted by two soldiers to the city's Women's Solitary Prison, part of a massive prison complex of dark red brick known as "The Crosses."[47]

The three weeks Sofia spent in prison and on trial at the end of 1917 were a brief but intense period that she remembered with a complex mixture of emotions for the rest of her life. On the one hand, she took ironic pride in the arrest. "So you see," she told her audience in Los Angeles in 1939, "I could have no moral objection in my personal case when the door of the prison closed behind me. Yes, I was their enemy. Had I the necessary power, I would certainly have put in jail and would have never released those who, at that moment, had the upper hand and the power to put *me* in jail." After the extreme tension of the past month of underground oppositional activity, she also felt a certain sense of relief; prison brought "the relaxation of lawful rest after months and months of strained activities." Ignoring the risks incurred by the civil servants who had carried out her "theft" at the ministry, she claimed to be relieved finally to know "that I was accused of a deed in which I had no accomplices and that I should have to answer for myself alone."[48] In addition, Sofia had a number of encounters at the Women's Solitary Prison that she interpreted as a vindication of her lifelong commitment to serving Petrograd's working men and women, and as expressions of their gratitude. While claiming to recognize that the new rulers had good reason to detain such an implacable enemy as herself, she seized upon any and all evidence that the masses rejected her arrest and, by extension, the legitimacy of the Bolsheviks' revolution.

As she had at Smolny that morning, Sofia took note of the untidiness caused by revolution when she arrived at the prison's seedy office, where cigarette butts and empty or half-drunk glasses of tea littered the overheated and dimly lit room. But the welcome she found at the prison was gratifying, the first indication of popular dismay at her arrest. The old clerk in charge of registration was dozing, and her arrival well past midnight woke him up. Without raising his eyes, he pulled his thick record book toward him, took up his pen, and asked the new prisoner for her name and occupation. "Countess," came the unexpected reply, "and Assistant Minister of Education." The clerk's eyes widened in amazement, and he stood up. The prison matron also expressed shock. "Oh my God, oh my God, what will happen next!" Sofia remembered her exclaiming. When asked why she was upset, the matron protested, "But surely we know about the People's House!"[49]

Sofia's subsequent interactions with fellow prisoners enabled her to persuade herself that she was still tied to her lower-class sisters by bonds of mutual gratitude. The wing in which she was incarcerated held mostly women accused of ordinary crimes such as theft; she was one of only a few political prisoners. While political prisoners were allowed only thirty minutes a day of solitary exercise in the walled prison yard, some of the regular inmates moved freely around the prison, cleaning cells and distributing meals to the prisoners, and so soon came into contact with the new arrival. On her first morning in prison a fellow inmate peered into Sofia's cell and asked, "Is that you, Sofia Vladimirovna?" "Who are you?" Sofia inquired in turn. "Why I'm Nyusha, Nyusha Evseeva, don't you remember me? I often visited your People's House, I looked at the pictures and listened to the music. But how could you remember all of us! I remember you well. My Lord God, what are they doing putting you in here, the monsters?" Other women prisoners, many of whom knew Sofia's philanthropic reputation, gave her cell a thorough cleaning, polished her brass prison washbasin and pitcher until they shone, and scrubbed the common bathing facility before she went for her weekly bath. They brought her extra pieces of bread, and were offended when she refused them. "No sisters or friends," she later mused, "could have been more attentive and solicitous than these dear young women, who had stumbled somehow into life's snares."[50] By restoring a semblance of the cleanliness and class hierarchy overturned by revolution, prison also returned some of Sofia's faith in the intrinsic goodness and common sense of her social inferiors, temporarily led astray by Bolshevik rhetoric of class hatred.

Sofia noticed that her fellow inmates suffered from excruciating boredom: "the prison silence was broken only by the prisoners' completely animal-like yawns." They languished in their cells, sleeping or passing the time in idle, repetitive pastimes like combing their hair. The solution, she concluded, lay in teaching the illiterate prisoners how to read, as the people's house had tried to do with female workers before the revolution. The prison's Bolshevik commissar refused permission, however, out of suspicion, she surmised, that she would conduct counterrevolutionary propaganda among the women.[51] No doubt bored herself, Sofia returned to a project that had long been underway, a manual on people's houses. The project had originated in 1913, when the celebration of the tenth anniversary of the Ligovsky People's House attracted requests from across the country for guidance on establishing similar institutions. With funding from Sofia, experts were recruited and the first national survey of people's houses was conducted.[52] Sofia used some of her time in prison to write a brief introduction, which reads more like an obituary than a celebration of the movement to which she had dedicated twenty years. The people's house had been developed for the conditions of prerevolutionary Russia, and "now, of course, loses its significance" after the Bolshevik takeover. The information gathered so painstakingly had only "historical interest," she noted sadly. This introduction, one of Sofia's few surviving contemporary writings, suggests that in the last months of 1917 the pessimism that so colored later memoirs already competed with Sofia's hopes for a restoration of order and legality.[53]

Although the authorities initially did not allow Sofia to have visitors in prison, she could pass the long hours and ease her loneliness by reading the letters that poured in. News of her arrest and imprisonment raised an outcry in Petrograd. Working-class inhabitants of the Alexander Nevsky district organized a protest meeting and sent a petition to the Council of People's Commissars with hundreds of signatures that demanded the release of "our friend," the "creator of our well-being."[54] Educational, professional, and women's associations and workers' groups deluged the press and the prisoner with messages of outrage and solidarity.[55] Writing in the non-party socialist newspaper *New Life* on December 6, Maxim Gorky, the world-famous proletarian writer, denounced the arrest. "Hundreds of proletarians learned how to think and feel in her 'People's House,'" he thundered. "The entire life of this enlightened individual was dedicated to cultural activity among workers. And now she sits in prison."[56] Others similarly praised Sofia for her contributions to popular education and cultural development, her selflessness, and her defense of freedom and justice in tsarist times. In a letter portraying Sofia as a political martyr, parents and teachers at a Petrograd high school were typical in characterizing her as combining both masculine and feminine virtues; her "civil courage" and "fidelity to duty," on the one hand, were matched by her "enormous reserve of love."[57] Even to those who may have sympathized with the socialist revolution, the incarceration of such a familiar public figure, known not for her politics but for her good works, seemed to be a terrible mistake, an offense against revolutionary justice.

In spite of the many migrations and losses of her later years, Sofia managed to hold onto a precious packet of these letters and newspaper clippings until the end of her life. They came from strangers and friends, illustrious figures and ordinary people, organizations she belonged to and many more that she did not. In the memoir she wrote thirty years later, Sofia looked back on this moment as an affirmation of her life's work. Like a poet, she mused, she had awakened "good feelings" with her "many-stringed lyre," the Ligovsky People's House: "I personally was only one of the strings of this instrument, but in those days of great upheavals I was given the good fortune of convincing myself that over the years we had truly awakened in people's hearts those 'good feelings' in the name of which we approached them. This good fortune was rare and little deserved." Sofia cited one of the letters she had received to illustrate this point. "My father was a serf," wrote its author, a woman she did not know personally. "I work as a clerk. Accept my deep regards from a daughter of the people to whose emancipation you have devoted your life." The writer ended by wishing Sofia would someday have the "joy of seeing the fruits of your labors—a truly free Russian people, capable of creating conditions whereby the best people of the country are its leaders, and not prisoners, as they are now."

Sofia chose to interpret such expressions of support from across the social spectrum as evidence that Russians could be united by values they held in common—and that they rejected the Bolsheviks' doctrines of class hatred. She also believed they affirmed the position she had taken against the October coup. "Of course," she asserted, "the greater part of the feelings expressed to me then related not so much to me personally, as to the symbol that I represented at that time"—a symbol of resistance to the Bolsheviks' hijacking of the revolution. However biased her interpretation of popular sentiment toward the revolution may have been, the memory of the protests against her arrest became a source of pride and comfort to Sofia during her long years of emigration.[58]

The angry popular reaction appears to have given the authorities second thoughts. On December 5 she was summoned to the Petrograd Soviet, where one of the members of the Investigative Commission, a sailor named Alexeevsky, offered her a deal: they would release her from prison if she paid bail in the amount of 180,000 rubles. Sofia refused, accusing the commission of trying to extort from her twice the amount she had ordered removed from the ministry.[59] She was ordered back to prison, but the Soviet had no automobile available. So she and the prison matron returned to The Crosses by tram. On the way, Sofia later remembered, they joked about how easy it would be for her to go in an entirely different direction; but "in those times 'another direction' did not enter my calculations," and besides, she added wryly, she knew that an especially delicious dish would be served for dinner at the prison that day—the ubiquitous Russian potato and vegetable salad, *vinagret*.[60] Her decision to return dutifully to her cell repeats a pattern established during her day-long detention in Smolny, awaiting interrogation. Poorly guarded, she and her fellow detainees could easily have walked out of the building and gone into hiding. Their refusal to do so, like Sofia's return to prison after refusing the Soviets' offer of ransom, reflected liberals' principled yet self-defeating loyalty to their conceptions of justice and legality, to which they clung despite their equally unshakable belief in the revolutionary government's illegitimacy .

Sofia's month of intense and dangerous political activity in the anti-Bolshevik movement yielded meager results. The government boycott and strike quickly fizzled once the Soviet authorities took control of the State Bank. The various groups to which she belonged, including her own party, vacillated and argued over how to oppose the usurpers.

They proved powerless in any case against a foe that rejected their notions of legality and asserted power by means of radical slogans and unruly, embittered workers and soldiers carrying rifles. The outcome of the elections to the Constituent Assembly, with victories for socialist candidates and resounding defeats for the Kadets, showed the population's impatience with voices of moderation.

Arrest ironically brought liberation for Sofia. After months of intense political activity she finally could return to more familiar and compatible roles: benefactress, beloved progressive reformer, and a symbol of the selflessness of the Russian woman. Angry and disgusted over the fate of her country, now in the hands of uncouth soldiers and impertinent outsiders like Comrade Gordon, Sofia wanted to believe that her experiences as a prisoner affirmed her faith in the inherent goodness and reason of the Russian people. Inside the Women's Solitary Prison, respectful and solicitous fellow inmates restored order and cleanliness. Outside, voices rose in mass protest against her imprisonment in one of the largest demonstrations against Soviet power to occur in the weeks after the October Revolution. Imprisonment deprived Sofia of her liberty but turned her into a unique and powerful public symbol of anti-Bolshevik resistance. Her trial on December 10 also enabled her once again to place herself above class and politics as the bearer of light and civilization, the representative of a once vital, now doomed alternative to class war and dictatorship.

9

Enemy of the People

Two weeks after her arrest, charged with sabotage and the theft of government funds, Sofia faced her accusers. Hers would be the first case tried by the Petrograd Soviet's new revolutionary tribunal, and the Bolsheviks' first trial of a political enemy. The tribunal had only been created a day or two before her arrest, following a Bolshevik decree on November 24 that called on local soviets to establish revolutionary tribunals and investigative commissions "for the struggle against counter-revolutionary forces . . . and profiteering, speculation, sabotage and other misdeeds" of the bourgeoisie.[1] The confrontation between "Citizeness Panina" and the Petrograd Revolutionary Tribunal on December 10 took center stage as an important symbolic event in the battle between the Bolsheviks and their liberal opponents in those first uncertain weeks of Soviet power. The trial became a spectacle in which Bolshevik principles of class struggle and retribution clashed with the liberal intelligentsia's belief in progress, individual self-sacrifice, and the nobility of Russian womanhood. As both sides improvised in the weeks following the Bolshevik coup, events such as Sofia's trial first affirmed and then cast doubt on the faith held by both sides that the Russian people stood with them.[2]

The choice of Sofia as the Bolsheviks' first defendant was in some respects both unlikely and problematic. The prison cells of the Peter and
Paul Fortress and The Crosses were full of other political enemies, all
suitable candidates for a trial that would showcase the Bolsheviks' new
apparatus of revolutionary justice. Her participation in anti-Bolshevik
organizations and the civil servants' strike was neither unique nor particularly threatening to Soviet power. Male senior government officials
had also encouraged the boycott and participated in resistance actions,
and male Kadet leaders possessed much greater potential to lead an
effective opposition. As a woman and a philanthropist, Sofia seems to
be entirely unsuited to the role of an enemy of the people, as many of
the protests against her arrest pointed out. Even as late as December 5 it
appears that the Soviet authorities had not yet decided what to do with
their defiant prisoner. On that day the Kadets' party newspaper reported that the newly established Petrograd Revolutionary Tribunal
would hear its first case in a trial against not Sofia but the notorious
right-wing politician Vladimir Purishkevich. It is difficult to imagine a
defendant more unlike Sofia than Purishkevich, a coconspirator in the
murder of Rasputin a year earlier who led a failed military plot to restore the monarchy after the October Revolution.[3]

Other considerations may have persuaded the Bolsheviks to try
Sofia first. The case may have seemed straightforward and the outcome
certain: Sofia's accusers had clear evidence of her "theft" in the form of
her signed order to remove government funds and her own admission
of the act. Perhaps the Bolsheviks were also reacting to the outpouring
of protest. Under arrest, Sofia was an innocent female victim of ruthless
commissars, while an open trial would demonstrate her criminal actions
and justify her imprisonment to the public. A trial would also help to
validate the November 28 decree outlawing the Kadet Party, which had
evoked strong opposition from non-Bolshevik socialists. Sofia's refusal
to cooperate or compromise probably strengthened the Soviet's resolve.
The decision to put her on trial instead of Purishkevich may have been
provoked by her refusal of the Soviet's offer of release in exchange for
cash. A successful trial with such a well-known defendant would also
direct public attention to the new tribunals and the principles of revolutionary justice they represented. Finally, Sofia symbolized everything
the October Revolution opposed: titled aristocracy, inherited wealth,
noblesse oblige philanthropy, and bourgeois liberalism. A public trial of
a rich countess on charges of stealing "the people's money" must have

seemed a valuable propaganda opportunity to a new regime that characterized itself as the defender of the oppressed and the enemy of exploiters of all kinds.

Sofia's trial attracted considerable public attention. In the capital and beyond, the Russian press of various political affiliations reported on it, as did foreign newspapers such as the *New York Times*. The famous American socialist correspondents John Reed and Louise Bryant attended the trial and wrote their own, often inaccurate accounts of the proceedings. Given the polarized political atmosphere surrounding the trial, it is not surprising that all of these sources, including the unpublished transcript, are contradictory, biased to varying degrees, and sometimes erroneous. It is possible, however, to reconstruct the courtroom drama on December 10 with reasonable accuracy by using the trial transcript, the longer and more detailed newspaper reports, and the narrative that Sofia's designated defender, Yakov Gurevich, wrote and published immediately after the trial.[4]

The location chosen for the trial symbolized its revolutionary significance. It was held in a beautiful *style moderne* palace on the embankment of the Neva River across from the Winter Palace. It had belonged to Grand Duke Nikolai Nikolaevich, the emperor's cousin and Russia's first commander-in-chief in the war. Overcoming resistance from the grand duke's loyal servants, the Petrograd Soviet had commandeered the palace for the Revolutionary Tribunal a short time earlier.[5] Although the public was admitted by special ticket only, the palace's small concert hall was filled to overflowing long before the trial was scheduled to begin at noon. More people crowded outside around the entrance. The spectators fell into two distinct groups. A small, predominantly male contingent of workers and soldiers was outnumbered by Sofia's friends and supporters, both men and women—coworkers from her people's house and other artists, educators, and public activists, characterized as "predominantly intelligentsia of the 1860s type" by one newspaper. Also present were Isaac Rogalsky, Sofia's original accuser; Peter Stuchka, chairman of the Investigative Commission and the Soviet Commissar of Justice; and Menshevik socialist G. M. Kramarov, a member of the Executive Committee of the All-Russian Soviet, who intended to speak in Sofia's defense.[6]

The trial was scheduled to begin at noon, but the defendant was late because the automobile carrying her and her convoy of Red Guards broke down twice on the way from the prison. By the time the members of the tribunal filed into the hall at 1 p.m., the spectators were barely

Petrograd Revolutionary Tribunal at Sofia's trial. Ivan Zhukov, the chairman of the tribunal, is in the center. (Courtesy of Occidental College Special Collections and College Archives and the Beatty Family, Papers of Bessie Beatty)

able to contain their excitement and impatience. The revolutionary tribunal consisted of two soldiers and five workers from different Petrograd factories. Six were members of the Bolshevik Party, including the chairman, a joiner named Ivan Zhukov. Like both Sofia and Isaac Rogalsky, he had been a member of the Petrograd City Council. Their clothing blurred the distinction between the bourgeoisie and the proletariat so evident in the audience; although the two soldiers on the tribunal wore their uniforms, the proletarian judges donned starched white collars, ties, and dark suits, in an effort, perhaps, to boost the court's credibility in the eyes of a hostile public. The men took their places behind a raised, red-draped table, sitting on exquisite upholstered chairs of Karelian birch formerly belonging to the grand duke. According to one observer, the hall was illuminated by two "garish red glass lamps with green shades" because electricity in the palace had gone out.[7]

The decree on tribunals provided no definitions or guidelines for procedures, forcing its chairman, Zhukov, to invent his own system of revolutionary justice. As he admitted in a brief memoir written ten years later, the tribunal was organized in haste and had to contend with the hostility and hatred of the "bourgeoisie." Lacking "the slightest experience in judicial matters," he found his position as chairman very difficult. No one gave him any directives or guidance, forcing him to conduct the trial "in the complete absence of procedural rules only as [my] revolutionary conscience dictated."[8] The proceedings of this first trial thus combined conventional courtroom procedures with some

"The Intelligentsia before the Court of the 'Tribunal,'" reporter's sketch of Sofia with an armed escort, December 10, 1917. (Drawing by Foma R. Railian, published in F. R. Railian, "Intelligentsiia pered sudom 'Tribunala' [Vpechatleniia i nabroski v zale suda]," *Novaia petrogradskaia gazeta*, December 12, 1917, 1. Courtesy of the Russian Public Library, St. Petersburg, Newspaper Division)

imaginative judicial innovations. Chairman Zhukov opened the trial with a brief speech in which he cited the revolutionary tribunals created in France "sixty-nine years ago" as the model for Russian revolutionary justice. (Zhukov's shaky knowledge of French history caused him to confuse the revolution of 1848, which had no revolutionary tribunals, with 1789.) Like its French model, he warned, the Russian tribunal "will severely judge all those who go against the will of the people, who obstruct it on its path." Those who are "innocent before the will of the revolutionary people," however, will find the tribunal "the most reliable defender." Although Zhukov never mentioned the guillotine, his evocation of the French Revolution must have sent shivers through Sofia's supporters in the audience. He then ordered the defendant brought into the hall.[9]

Escorted by two guards carrying rifles, Sofia then entered the courtroom. With her "pleasant, round, well-bred face," black tailored suit, and close-fitting hat, the defendant reminded one of the trial's foreign observers of an American social worker, not a threatening enemy of the people.[10] The audience, which had defiantly remained seated when the tribunal entered, rose from their seats with shouts of greeting and lengthy applause. Thus the anti-Bolshevik sentiment prevailing in the courtroom was evident from the beginning. "Citizeness Panina," Zhukov asked, "do you admit to being guilty of taking and hiding 93,000 rubles from the Ministry of Education that did not belong to you?" "Guilty?" she replied, "no, I do not declare myself guilty." Zhukov read aloud the Investigative Commission's report with its charge of criminal sabotage against Sofia, and presented documents (but no witnesses) as evidence, including Sofia's original November 15 order to officials in her ministry. He then sought a prosecutor from among the spectators: rising from his seat, Zhukov announced to the courtroom, "the prosecution has the floor. Is there someone [to act as prosecutor]?" No one volunteered.[11]

Continuing to improvise the tribunal's procedures, Zhukov allowed Gurevich to speak first for the defendant. Gurevich was a long-time friend of Sofia's and the brother of her feminist friend Liubov. Her choice of this well-known educator to serve as her defense counsel at the tribunal reinforced her identity as a social reformer rather than a politician. Gurevich himself emphasized this point by beginning his speech with a reminder to the judges that he was not a lawyer, but an ordinary citizen like themselves. He argued that the court could not possibly convict Sofia: not according to law, because at present, "in the heat of the political struggle," there were no universally recognized laws in Russia; and not according to their conscience, for her services to the Russian people were too well-known and significant. "You can only try her," Gurevich insisted, "as [her] political opponents, but then this would not be a court, but a continuation of civil war." It was not Sofia, he implied, but concepts of legality, justice, and morality that were on trial. He concluded by reminding the judges that the eyes of the world were upon them. "You must not, before the entire world, repay good with evil and love with violence. Don't commit violence in the name of the Russian people to their shame before the entire world."[12]

When Gurevich finished, spectators burst into applause. "A kind of ecstasy of unanimity seized the hall," reported one newspaper, and many in the courtroom wept. An old man with a huge beard, who had spent years in political exile and now worked at Sofia's people's house, fell into hysterics. Sobbing, wailing, and wringing his hands, he cried out, "I can't, I can't, I don't have the strength to survive this. Why, oh

Sofia in the courtroom, with Gurevich (bearded) speaking in her defense. (Courtesy of Occidental College Special Collections and College Archives and the Beatty Family, Papers of Bessie Beatty)

why do they do this, I can't, I'm dying." Still sobbing and repeating, "why, oh why," he was carried out of the courtroom.[13]

Managing with difficulty to restore order to the hall, Zhukov gave the floor to a man from the audience who identified himself as N. I. Ivanov, a factory worker by occupation and a Socialist Revolutionary by political affiliation. To the amazement of the tribunal, the audience, and the defendant herself, Ivanov spoke passionately in Sofia's defense. Like Gurevich, he turned the trial into a test of the revolution's moral principles. The countess, Ivanov reminded the court, had worked for the masses through the dark years of tsarist repression. Undeterred by the "people's sweat and smoke," she had personally taught classes for them, "lighting in the working masses the holy fire of knowledge." Emphasizing her maternal dedication and love for the common people, Ivanov described how workers found "light and joy" at her people's house and their children found more affection there than in their own families. Such a woman was not the Russian people's enemy, he declared, but its best friend. "Don't shame yourselves, the revolution, the Russian people," he begged, "with a conviction." Ivanov concluded with a dramatic personal gesture: "I myself was an illiterate, benighted [*temnym*] person," he confessed. At Sofia's people's house he had learned how to read and write, and had come "to know the light." He then turned to the defendant, made a deep bow, and said, "I thank you."[14]

Ivanov's speech landed like an exploding bomb on the hall. Even her most ardent supporters could not have hoped for a more eloquent vindication of her life's work than this tribute from a member of the proletariat. Sofia, who claimed not to know Ivanov personally, was profoundly moved by his words and the sincerity with which he spoke. It is possible, of course, that Ivanov's speech was not spontaneous but arranged in advance by her supporters. One journalist wrote that the worker's speech left the "impression of a staged defense, concocted behind the scenes by his party," though which party that would be, he does not say. But everyone in the hall seems to have been taken by surprise, including the tribunal and Commissar of Justice Stuchka.[15]

Zhukov quickly improvised a new approach. First, he asked Sofia if she would agree to return the money taken by her within two days. She refused. The tribunal's next step was to bypass Kramarov, the member of the All-Russian Soviet who had been promised an opportunity to speak in Sofia's defense, and to give the floor to another worker, identified only as Naumov. Naumov spoke heatedly for Sofia's conviction. Playing on the dual meaning of the word "nobility," he demanded the sacrifice of the individual, however noble and virtuous, for the cause of the revolution. For all the countess's good deeds, she still represented the class that had exploited and oppressed the Russian masses. "If there are those who saw the light in Sofia's little window, millions never saw that light. . . . It would be a crime to forget this." Sofia's real crime lay in her participation "along with all the representatives of her class" in organized opposition to the people's revolution. Urging his comrades on the tribunal not to be swayed by Sofia's record of social service, Naumov called upon them to punish anyone who sought to obstruct working people's "right to happiness." "In the name of the millions of oppressed, I call upon you to act. If in our path there stands a noble individual, we are very sorry, but so much the worse for her." Naumov's speech, with its threatening implications, was interrupted several times by hostile shouts from the audience.[16]

Zhukov then gave the floor to Rogalsky, the Commissariat of Education's representative, "for factual observations." Unlike Naumov, who at least allowed that Sofia may have done a few good deeds, Rogalsky accused her of embezzlement and impugned her motives. Attacking the defendant herself rather than her class, he attempted to turn her reputation for selfless charity against her. Sofia's actions caused real suffering, he charged, for the funds she took were unpaid wages owed to ministry workers and their families who had been called to military service. (In fact, Sofia herself referred to the funds as uncollected wages in her own 1948 memoir.[17]) Grouping Sofia with male oppressors from the bourgeoisie, Rogalsky dramatically pointed to the hungry, sick, impoverished people who came to her ministry every day to beg for help but received nothing "because some gentlemen [sic] allow themselves to take other people's money for safekeeping." And if the minister, assistant ministers, and other high officials were worried about the safety of government funds, why did they allocate money for holiday bonuses for themselves, he demanded? Greed and self-interest, not state interests or the common good, motivated Sofia's acts of sabotage in Rogalsky's searing indictment. If she were to be acquitted, he concluded, the entire working world would protest.[18]

Zhukov gave the final word to the defendant. Sofia insisted that she, as the only top official of the Ministry of Education still at liberty after the October coup, had a duty to move its funds to a safe place. Appealing to the soldiers on the court and in the hall, she played a variation on Rogalsky's theme, inverting both gender and class in her defense. "I think that soldiers will understand me best of all," she told the court. "Soldiers who know the role of the sentry know that no one can take a sentry from his post except the one that placed him there. I was that sentry at the ministry. The people placed me there, and I can give a report [and] return the money only to the people, only to its legal representative—the Constituent Assembly. That I will do." At this point Sofia almost lost the composure she had maintained throughout the proceedings. In a voice breaking with emotion, she thanked Ivanov for his words in her defense, from which she obtained "all that I could have wished to receive" in return for her work on behalf of the people. A "tumultuous and lengthy ovation" followed her remarks.[19]

Spectators and participants alike remained agitated after the tribunal filed out to confer on a verdict. Some of Sofia's supporters surrounded her surprise defender Ivanov to shake his hand and thank him. Kramarov, the socialist who belonged to the All-Russian Soviet, loudly protested Zhukov's refusal to let him speak in Sofia's defense. Sofia's accuser Rogalsky demanded to give the tribunal additional documents and fumed when he was refused. Gurevich filed two protests, one against Rogalsky and a second against the court for reversing the customary order of judicial proceedings by putting the prosecution *after* the defense. Former Minister of Education Oldenburg marched up to Rogalsky and exclaimed, "You know perfectly well that you are lying!" Nor did the courtroom quiet down when the tribunal returned less than an hour later. Kramarov rose to demand the floor; Zhukov in great annoyance told him to sit down, and when the Menshevik continued to speak, he ordered the guards to remove him. As Kramarov was being dragged from the courtroom, he shouted, "This will be a blot on your conscience!" Amidst all the tumult, Sofia waited in apparent calm to learn the verdict, gazing at the mass of "dear, friendly faces" in the courtroom, many of whom she was seeing for the last time.[20]

When a degree of order finally fell on the courtroom, Zhukov read the tribunal's unexpected and contradictory judgment. The tribunal found "Citizeness Panina" guilty of "opposition to the people's authority," and therefore she would remain in prison until she handed the money she had taken over to the new regime's Commissariat of Education. At the same time, "taking into consideration the past of the accused," the tribunal limited her actual punishment to "public censure." The unusual verdict caused another storm in the courtroom; even the transcript of the trial tersely admits that an "indescribable tumult" filled the hall. While some in the audience laughed, others whistled in approval. Sofia's supporters applauded, waved their hats and handkerchiefs, and shouted "hurrah!" As spectators threw themselves toward her, armed guards hurriedly conducted the defendant out of the hall to be returned to her prison cell.[21]

With its unexpected twists and odd, contradictory verdict, Sofia's trial mirrored the confusion and uncertainty of the early days of the revolution, and therefore lent itself to competing interpretations. As Gurevich stated in his defense, in late 1917 no one could really say what the law *was* at this time. Kadets struggled to uphold prerevolutionary principles of legality, while the Bolsheviks were engaged in inventing a new system of law and justice. No one could know for certain the relative strengths of the opposing sides and the final outcome of the struggle between them. Participants and observers saw in Sofia's trial a reflection of their hopes and fears for the revolution. The Bolsheviks' opponents, on the one hand, were jubilant over the trial's outcome, which they interpreted as a personal victory for Sofia, a vindication of the intelligentsia's ethos of social service, and an exposé of the Bolsheviks' unpopularity. Even *People's Will*, the newspaper of the Socialist Revolutionary Party, praised Sofia's "outstanding" conduct during the trial.

The victory she claimed, the editorial added, was affirmed by the entire Russian people and socialists all over the world.[22] Others singled out the speech by the worker Ivanov as the trial's turning point. "We experience a feeling of joy," an editorial in a liberal newspaper declared triumphantly, "because once again we find faith in the ignorant [*temnuiu*] crowd that for a time had lost its reason."[23]

The trial encouraged Sofia's fellow Kadets to believe that the Russian masses would soon see through the Bolsheviks' empty promises. Their interpretation of the trial revealed the party's considerable capacity for self-delusion after the October Revolution. By focusing on it as a moral triumph for Sofia, they gravely underestimated the strength of their opponents. As late as December 1917 the Kadets' faith in the power of law encouraged them to believe that it would be possible to fight the Bolsheviks with legal arguments and methods. Moreover, although the defendant attracted sympathy and support, she did so less as a representative of the Kadet Party than as an embodiment of virtues often ascribed to Russian women. Maintaining an attitude of aloofness from class and political conflict, Sofia appeared as a woman with a deep sense of public duty who had devoted her life and fortune to serving others. Instead of indicting the Kadet Party and the Provisional Government, then, the Bolsheviks unwittingly put feminine virtue on trial.[24]

Unlike the pro-liberal Russian press, the mainstream Western press tended to represent the trial as an absurd spectacle in which virtue was assailed by evil. Though pointedly titled "Farcical Trial of Countess Panin," the *New York Times* article by Harold Williams, Tyrkova-Williams's husband, gives a largely accurate summary of the proceedings. But Williams emphasizes the absurdity of the trial by contrasting Sofia, a "woman of great energy, practical ability and public spirit," to her judge Zhukov, "an ignorant toiler." "It is an odd world," his article ironically concludes.[25] Readers of the *Times* of London on January 31, 1918, would have found an even more opinionated account by a certain Princess Dolgoroukoff, a recent arrival from Russia who claimed to have attended the trial. She similarly accentuates the defendant's virtues: "Her life, since her earliest youth, has been one of continuous toil and self-devotion, endowing hospitals, schools, and libraries on her estates, and, generally speaking, she looked upon her great wealth as a trust to be used for the alleviation of the lot of those less favoured than herself." Her accusers are depicted as a gallery of villains: Zhukov, "a factory hand with a mean, petty face"; Rogalsky, "an evil-visaged individual, who might have sat for a portrait of Judas Iscariot"; and another unnamed accuser, probably Naumov, who "rushed across the room . . . and whirling his right arm round and round with such violence that it seemed as if it must be wrenched from its socket [he] proceeded to arraign the countess in violent and incoherent terms until he was forced to stop from sheer exhaustion."[26]

On the other side, Russia's new rulers originally regarded the trial as an opportunity to display their innovative concepts of justice and to invent new instruments of authority. As Zhukov acknowledged, there was no prepared script or procedure for Sofia's trial. Instead, its organizers expected revolutionary justice to emerge out of the spontaneous interaction of the court and the public. But spontaneity and improvisation produced some unwelcome surprises for the prosecution. The workers and soldiers who sat on the tribunal were inexperienced and insufficiently coached. The trial's organizers surely regretted allowing Sofia's supporters into the courtroom, for the tribunal from the beginning confronted a vociferously hostile audience. Instead of a voluntary accuser "from the people," the audience produced a genuine member of the proletariat who spoke in Sofia's defense. Sofia also turned out to be a poor choice for the revolutionary tribunal's first trial. Maintaining her self-control throughout the proceedings, she defied Zhukov's attempts both to intimidate her and to reach a compromise. It proved difficult to make her crimes against the revolution appear serious enough to outweigh her record of social service. For its next session, the Petrograd tribunal put its original choice of defendant on trial, the infamous monarchist conspirator Purishkevich.[27]

Thus it is hardly surprising that no one in the Bolshevik party or Soviet government declared the events of December 10 to be a triumph. The central party newspaper, *Pravda*, did not report the trial at all. The government's newspaper *Izvestiia* published a highly selective account that characterized the event as an exposé of the counterrevolutionary sentiments held by the former assistant minister and her supporters from the bourgeoisie.[28] The party leadership also attempted to use Sofia's "crime" to its advantage before a Western audience. British citizens could buy for seven pence a pamphlet titled "The Bolshevik Revolution: Its Rise and Meaning," written by the future Soviet foreign minister Maxim Litvinov and translated into English by his British wife. "Because Countess Panin, Minister of Public Relief [*sic*] in the last Kerensky Government, refused to deliver the funds of her department to her Bolshevik successor," Litvinov explained, "she was put into prison and kept there until the money was restored to the State." Omitting any mention of her trial, Litvinov used Sofia to demonstrate the resistance the Bolsheviks had to overcome, and to dispute allegations that they used violent means to do so. Litvinov also sought to appeal to the law-abiding British by implying that the Soviets were the Kerensky government's legitimate successor.[29]

If Bolsheviks at home tended to ignore or minimize the trial, their sympathizers from the United States hailed it as a resounding victory for the revolution, an assessment they supported by distorting what actually occurred. Writing for the American communist magazine *The Liberator*, John Reed deplored the bourgeois audience's hostility and disrespect toward the court. He emphasized the sharp contrast between the "smooth speech" of Sofia's defender Gurevich, whom he errone-ously called "one of the cleverest lawyers of Petrograd," and the worker Naumov's heartfelt support of the prosecution. In her memoir *Six Red Months in Russia*, Louise Bryant completely misrepresented the trial's outcome, reporting that Sofia "decided at once to relinquish the funds." Both Reed and Bryant (whose knowledge of Russian was poor to non-existent) emphasized the fierce-sounding revolutionary tribunal's hu-manity and restraint. Instead of sentencing her to the guillotine, Reed mendaciously wrote, the tribunal freed the defendant and allowed her "to return to her palace!" Bryant asserted that "in almost any other country in such tense times they would have killed Panina, especially since she was one of the chief sabotagers against the new regime." She concluded with her own indictment: "With her experience she could have been of great assistance, but she did everything possible to wreck the proletarian government."[30]

Other American observers also hailed the tribunal, though with greater accuracy and less hostility toward the defendant. Bessie Beatty, correspondent for the *San Francisco Bulletin*, believed that the tribunal's mild verdict demonstrated the revolution's humanity: "It was a far cry from this exhibition of revolutionary justice to the guillotine, almost as far as it was from that system of organized injustice of the Tsars that kept the endless procession of men and women marching toward exile and death." She optimistically and, as it turned out, erroneously pre-dicted that there would be no Red terror in revolutionary Russia. The socialist labor organizer Albert Rhys Williams, who wrote for the *New York Post*, was impressed by the judges' solemnity (something that un-sympathetic observers found quite comical) and regarded the revolu-tionary tribunal as the embodiment of "sublime innocence and un-dimmed hope." At least in the eyes of their foreign supporters, the

Bolsheviks' first attempts at innovative revolutionary justice were a success.[31]

As for Sofia herself, one theme predominates in her later accounts of the trial: her belief that it ended, as she told her Los Angeles audience in 1939, "with my complete triumph." Like her Kadet colleagues, Sofia chose to represent the events at her trial as a defeat of the Bolsheviks' clumsy and malicious attempts to stir up class enmity and a victory for the liberal intelligentsia's progressive principles. Although in hindsight Sofia became more aware of its amusing moments, describing it in Los Angeles as a "semi-tragic, semi-comic situation," she always narrated it as an exposé of the illegitimacy of Bolshevik claims of popular support. The most important moment for her, as for her supporters, was the speech by the unknown worker Ivanov. With his most common of Russian surnames, he seemed to symbolize the common sense of all the Ivanovs in the Russian masses. Sofia interpreted his intercession on her behalf, along with the kindness of her uneducated fellow prisoners, as the vindication of her faith in the Russian people and lifelong commitment to their cultural and educational elevation.[32]

On the afternoon of December 10, however, when the doors to the Women's Solitary Prison closed behind her again, Sofia struggled to maintain her composure and optimistic outlook. She felt "trapped in a hole without possibility of escape" when she returned to her cell, she later confessed to her American audience. As long as she refused to hand over almost 100,000 rubles to her sworn enemies, she faced an uncertain and potentially dangerous future. "I mentally began to prepare myself," she wrote in 1948, "for a long term in prison." Although the conditions of her imprisonment improved slightly—she now could meet her visitors in the prison reception room instead of behind two barred gates—it became increasingly difficult for her to maintain faith in her principles and hope for Russia's future. She and her fellow inmates could hear random shooting and yelling by drunken crowds on the streets outside the high walls of the prison yard where they took their daily exercise. Inside, the prison authorities were increasingly nervous, a condition "that involuntarily passed to us," the inmates, she remembered.[33]

While Sofia's later recollections of her trial and imprisonment tend to be upbeat, one surviving letter she wrote in prison offers a deeper look into the psychological impact of these experiences and the Bolshevik coup. Composed when she learned that the theater at the Ligovsky People's House was about to reopen after a long wartime hiatus, this somber letter is addressed not to her coworkers, but to her institution's visitors, the working men and women whom the Bolsheviks claimed to represent and champion. It reveals her awareness of how the violence of many years of war had penetrated the home front, replacing mutual trust with class warfare, and her unequivocal condemnation of the Soviet regime for stifling Russia's newly won freedom. "My dear friends," it begins, "I send you my warmest, most heartfelt greetings!" How long she had waited for the joyous day, she told them, when she would once again throw open the theater doors and "ignite fire in our hall and joy in your eyes." She had believed that this day would take place in a country at peace, where freedom reigned—"for an enlightened, just, and generous person can grow and develop, and a conscious and courageous citizen can be raised, only where there is freedom." But that future, she wrote, had turned out to be very different; instead of peace and harmony, "war and hatred were transferred from the front deep into the country, and freedom, having shed its light on us for one brief moment, has once again abandoned Russia." The country was now subject to the power of "new despots and a new tyranny." "And as for me," her letter lamented, "I am not with you and not among you, but in prison."[34]

For all its expressions of affection, Sofia's letter also admonishes Petrograd's radicalized workers, reminding them of the higher principles that her institution represented. The Ligovsky People's House had absolutely no party affiliation, she reminded the visitors, and all who came there enjoyed "the freedom to preach their own beliefs, their own convictions." Its mission was founded on principles that she insisted were inherently apolitical: knowledge as the necessary condition for independence and strength, honesty toward oneself and others, and love and absolute fairness toward one another. "It is on these three foundations that a free and strong, good and generous person is formed, and that is precisely how I wanted to see all of you, visitors and pupils of the People's House," she wrote, "since I am firmly convinced that only a person who is guided by his mind and his conscience can be a real citizen, useful to both his fatherland and all humanity." There is no other route, the letter asserts, from "slavery" to citizenship. Sofia ended her letter with an analogy that tried to diminish her individual importance while simultaneously elevating the symbolic significance of her imprisonment. If you think of me, she wrote, remember what Peter the Great said before facing the Swedes in 1709 at the Battle of Poltava, when he proclaimed "that life was not precious to him, as long as Russia lived in glory and prosperity." All of us must live by these words, she concluded; "it is not important that I have been deprived of my freedom, what is important is that freedom itself is dying in the Russian land! Let that not happen!" Her patriotic appeal to the working men and women of the Ligovsky People's House barely masked her despair that the fight for freedom in Russia had already been lost.[35]

If Sofia felt little concern about her own lack of freedom, outside The Crosses her friends in Petrograd were deeply worried. They threw themselves into raising 93,000 rubles to ransom her out of prison, and on December 19 handed that sum over to the Petrograd Soviet to be transferred to the Commissariat of Education.[36] Soon thereafter Sofia received an unexpected late evening visit from the matron, who told her she was wanted in the prison office with her suitcase. When she arrived, the Bolshevik commandant announced to her that she was free and handed her a copy of the order for her release. Sofia met this news with mixed emotions, for the unexpected liberation upset her plans. Concerned about her fellow prisoners' boredom, she had obtained the consent of the prison authorities to give a magic lantern presentation to the prisoners on Christmas. The necessary apparatus and slides had already been delivered to the prison office from the Ligovsky People's House. As she prepared to leave The Crosses on the evening of December 19, the Bolshevik commandant asked her, "But what about the reading on Christmas that was promised to the prisoners?" "Yes, what about the reading?," sadly echoed the elderly prison clerk and the matron. If they wished, Sofia replied, she would happily return on Christmas day and put on the presentation. The commandant, menacing in his Bolshevik leather jacket with a revolver jammed into his belt, gratefully took Sofia's hand and gallantly kissed it.[37]

Sofia kept her promise. On Christmas Day she and her cousin clambered through the snowdrifts that blocked Petrograd's uncleared streets, making their way across the perilous city and the frozen river to the massive prison. The recreation hall was jammed with eager spectators; in the first row, under special guard, sat female murderers in handcuffs, while lesser criminals took their places in the back rows. In between slides of Palestine and European paintings of the Nativity, Sofia read the Christmas story from the Bible to her audience. When she finished, the fierce-looking prison commandant asked her to give the presentation again the following day for those who could not be seated in the overcrowded hall. Sofia gladly complied. Perhaps she still clung to some shred of faith in the Petrograd populace, or the possibility of a return to public order, for it took considerable courage to travel all the way across the dangerous city. When she describes this epilogue to her imprisonment more than three decades later, Sofia says nothing about the danger or apprehension she may have felt. Instead she chooses to interpret this incident as an affirmation of the possibility of dialogue and cooperation across the class divide. "So, for a brief moment," she mused, "a link was established between two edges of the city," and "a bridge of mutual understanding" connected people of different classes, education, cultural levels, and political views. "For me," she concluded, "those days have forever remained the emblem of open possibilities."[38]

Whatever lingering hopes for "open possibilities" and faith in the Russian masses Sofia may still have held in December—and her letter from prison indicates they were dwindling—were shattered shortly after the New Year in a sequence of terrible events. The first shock came when she was released from prison, which had insulated her from the deteriorating conditions in the city. Sofia was appalled by the changes she found. "The general political atmosphere in Petrograd had significantly worsened and grown tense during this month," she recalled, "more and more saturated with hate and anarchy. During that time the city experienced a series of lootings of wine cellars, when people drowned after choking in the wine that they poured out around themselves and lapped up from puddles on the sidewalks, lying on their stomachs in the mud."[39]

As winter set in the desperate economic situation that had contributed to the Bolsheviks' success grew even worse: supplies of food and fuel dwindled, the electricity functioned for a few hours a day, city trams did not run, and many factories came to a standstill, deprived of supplies, fuel, and funds for wages. All of these conditions produced random violence, accelerated the breakdown of law and order, and intensified the human degradation that so horrified Sofia.

Sometime much later, perhaps during the 1920s, Sofia described her last weeks in Petrograd at an occasion honoring her fellow Kadets Shingarev and Kokoshkin, who had been arrested with her on November 28. Unlike her other accounts about late 1917, including the melancholy letter she wrote to visitors of the people's house from prison, this document is pervaded by undisguised anger and revulsion. It reveals Sofia's much darker outlook after prison, and the reasons behind her decision to leave Petrograd less than two months after her trial ended in "triumph." The sequence of events began as soon as Sofia was released from prison, when she turned to the needs of Kadet leaders who were still incarcerated. She was particularly alarmed at the physical and mental deterioration of Kokoshkin and Shingarev, whom she visited in the Peter and Paul Fortress.[40] Although she had ignored the threats to her own safety when she was a prisoner, Sofia was gravely worried about the lack of security at the fortress. "The prisoners in PP Fortress [*sic*] lived constantly under the threat of violence and murder from those parts of the garrison stationed at the Fortress," she recounted, and only the dedication of the prisoners' guards, influenced by their contact with "those noble people," prevented their lynching. Together with Kokoshkin's and Shingarev's relatives, Sofia sought to get the men transferred out of the prison and into a hospital as soon as possible.[41]

The situation of imprisoned opponents of the Bolsheviks grew more dangerous as the day approached for the opening of the Constituent Assembly, rescheduled from November 28 to January 5. Final election results had revealed the new regime's tenuous popularity, for less than one quarter of voters in the whole nation supported Bolshevik candidates, and over half of the elected delegates belonged to the Socialist Revolutionary Party or their allies. Would Lenin's party allow the assembly to meet, when it would be dominated by their socialist enemies? "We lived in a furiously boiling and tightly sealed cauldron," Sofia later recalled about those days, "awaiting an explosion any second."[42]

The explosion finally occurred on January 5, the assembly's opening day. As a large procession of the assembly's supporters marched toward the Tauride Palace, they encountered bullets instead of the jeers and renditions of the "Internationale" with which Bolshevik supporters had assailed them on November 28. Most of the clashes occurred in Sofia's own neighborhood. A crowd of one thousand demonstrators marching down Sergievskaya Street refused to obey an order to halt and turn around, issued by a detachment of Red Guards. After a few warning shots, the Red Guards aimed their rifles directly at the marchers and fired. Despite the turmoil and bloodshed on the streets outside, the assembly began its first session with the election of the leader of the Socialist Revolutionary Party as its chairman and proceeded to debate the issues of land and peace, despite the hoots and boos of soldiers in the gallery. After many hours of bitter argument the Bolshevik delegates walked out, followed soon after by the Left SRs. Around 5 a.m. on January 6 the first session was adjourned, and the remaining exhausted deputies finally departed. Later that day Lenin's government locked the doors to the Tauride Palace and dissolved the assembly for good, shattering the Kadets' hopes that the assembly, as Russia's legitimate authority, would lead the country to political renewal.[43]

For Sofia there was at least one bright spot in the gloom that followed the dispersal of the Constituent Assembly: Kokoshkin's and Shingarev's supporters received word that the two ailing Kadets would be moved out of prison. "However terrible it seems now, when we look back," she recalled, "we regarded the permission finally received to transfer K. and Sh. to the hospital as a deliverance and salvation." On the frigid afternoon of January 6 a procession of four sleighs moved from the fortress across the river and down Liteiny Prospect to Mariinsky Hospital, whose stately neoclassical façade of Corinthian columns must have seemed a beacon of calm and security. The first sleigh carried an armed convoy, including, Sofia remembered, an unknown individual in a grey sheepskin hat. The next carried Shingarev and his sister, with Kokoshkin and his wife in the third; a fourth sleigh with armed guards closed the procession. That night, after the prisoners had been made comfortable in their hospital beds, Kokoshkin's wife returned to Sofia's house, relieved and satisfied at last that her husband and Shingarev had finally found a safe refuge in one of the city's best hospitals. That illusion was shattered early the next morning, when Sofia received a terrible phone call from the hospital.

> Sh. and K. had been murdered at night by sailors who had burst in on them. As it later became clear, that very individual in the gray sheepskin hat who had conducted the prisoners on the morning of that day from the fortress to the hospital had been the leader of this gang, which without doubt had been organized in advance. They had waited and watched for the departure of relatives from the hospital, after which they immediately and without obstacle entered the very wards where the patients lay, and shot them. K. was killed on the spot, Sh. lived and suffered in agony for several hours, seriously worried about his numerous and still young children, and turning to the people around him with one question only—"why?" . . .

How many Russians since then, Sofia lamented, have asked in vain that same "hopeless, answerless question." Less than a month after her own trial before the Petrograd Revolutionary Tribunal, a very different and horrifying kind of revolutionary justice had been exacted on her fellow Kadets.[44]

This tragedy marked yet another turning point for Sofia in the long year of 1917. Rushing to the hospital, she found the victims' bodies "barely covered under torn sheets," lying in a hospital mortuary overflowing with the victims of the shootings on January 5. Their deaths brought her face-to-face with a Russian people very different from the workers and their families who before the war came to her people's house seeking education and culture. Ignoring the possibility that other visitors may have been searching for their own loved ones among the bodies, Sofia reacted to the scene she witnessed in the morgue with revulsion.

> For two days we stood guard continually in this crypt, protecting our murdered ones and their relatives with a living chain of our bodies from the savage curiosity of the insane crowd, greedy for any spectacle, which passed in an uninterrupted line, shoving and hurrying somewhere through this impossibly crowded, cold chamber. I have never seen a crowd more repulsive than that one. And when we went out onto the street, we landed in an atmosphere of such intense malice that if anyone, following Dante, wanted to depict one of the circles of hell being suffocated by its own malice, he would have had to describe Petrograd at that time. It is necessary to live through such days in order to know that the spiritual atmosphere can at times be transformed into something materially tangible, thick and poisonous.

Sofia's recollections of the terrible events of early January 1918 end with a final indictment of Bolshevik justice, a reminder of the high ideals her murdered friends represented, and a deeply pessimistic vision of her country's future:

> They say that in high-ranking Communist circles this crime was not anticipated, not desired. The murderers were ordered to be arrested. The gray sheepskin hat turned out to be a certain Basov, who was let go after being detained for a while, and the investigation of the murders did not go any further. Now [in the 1920s] these events and these graves seem endlessly far away. But it will not be soon, not soon, when people who have lost

their senses in their malice understand that the paradise on
earth they sought for can be created not by bayonets and machine
guns, but by that same burning, self-sacrificing heart and clear,
selfless reason and service whose beating and life were stopped
on that night and on many other terrible nights.[45]

The funeral of the murdered Kadets a few days later provided an occasion for a mass demonstration by middle- and upper-class Petrograd
against the new rulers. Several thousand mourners defied rumors of
violent reprisals to accompany the bodies of Kokoshkin and Shingarev
up Nevsky Prospect to St. Alexander Nevsky Monastery for burial.[46]
Once Sofia saw her friends properly interred in the monastery's Nikol-
skoe cemetery, she did not stay in the city much longer. By January 24
she was in Moscow. Writing to her friend Liubov Gurevich, the sister of
her defense counsel at the trial, Sofia offers no explanation of the circumstances of her departure except to characterize it as sudden and
rushed. Perhaps she finally became concerned about her own safety,
for the rest of her letter is devoted to anxious questions about a woman
she and Gurevich both knew, whose behavior and alleged Bolshevik
connections aroused Sofia's suspicions. Although this letter explains
neither her own connection to the woman nor the circumstances that
caused her such anxiety, it suggests how the intensifying revolution
was beginning to affect the composure and fearlessness she had displayed at her trial.[47]

For countless people in Petrograd and the wider world, the October
Revolution inspired joy and hope at what seemed to be the dawning of
a new era in human history. Many shared the belief of the Americans
who observed the trial of Citizeness Panina that Russia's revolution
would finally bring freedom and justice to the exploited working masses
who, as Marxist doctrine taught, had long been denied the wealth their
labor created. The Petrograd Revolutionary Tribunal was hailed as a
shining example of that promise: a semi-educated joiner, Ivan Zhukov,
along with other workers and soldiers now sat in judgment of thieving
countesses like Sofia and assassins like Purishkevich.

But for Sofia the October Revolution brought grief, disillusionment, and loss. The Bolsheviks' victory turned Comrade Gordon's "first
woman of Russia" into a refugee and, eventually, an impoverished exile,
like many thousands of other Russians. But Sofia lost much more than
her luxurious home on Sergievskaya Street, her dear friends and coworkers, and her life's work when she fled Petrograd in January 1918.

Her seemingly triumphant trial in December 1917 had briefly turned her into a feminine symbol of liberalism's courageous, principled opposition. But the murders of Shingarev and Kokoshkin in January showed her and other Kadets the kind of enemy they faced; moreover, Sofia felt personally responsible since she believed that her actions had led to their imprisonment and death. Under the Bolsheviks, her beloved city fell into a condition she likened to "involuntary incarceration in an insane asylum."[48] While Sofia's public accounts of her imprisonment and trial interpret them as a vindication of her work and principles, more private documents reveal that the events of late 1917 and early 1918 undermined her faith in the humanity of her fellow Russians. The working-class men and women of Petrograd, whom she thought she knew and understood after years of philanthropic work among them, turned into repulsive crowds that lapped up wine from puddles and stared brazenly at the corpses of her murdered friends. Rejecting the tutelage of liberals like herself, they embraced doctrines of class hatred and vengeance. Yet Sofia did not give up the struggle she began on the night of October 25. As Russia sank into a savage civil war, she rededicated herself to her party, her liberal principles, and a free Russia.

10

Fighting the Bolsheviks

When Sofia left Petrograd in January 1918, the Bolsheviks' ability to hold onto power seemed far from certain. It took more than two years of brutal civil war for the Bolsheviks, renamed the Communist Party in 1918, to complete their revolution and establish control over most, though not all, of the former Russian Empire. The fledgling Soviet Republic faced a staggering number of enemies, internal and external, including not only the Kadets and the anti-Communist socialist parties, but also right-wing groups seeking to undo the February as well as the October Revolution and to restore the tsarist order. The inexperienced Red Army faced White armies in the north, south, and Siberia led by some of the former Imperial Army's most effective generals. During most of 1918 Germany occupied large areas of Ukraine, Poland, and Russia. The Communists also fought for control over vast swaths of the former empire against separatist movements, which took advantage of the general chaos to form national republics. Last but far from least, Great Britain, France, Japan, and the United States helped to prolong World War I on the Eastern Front by intervening in Russia's bloody civil conflict in support of the anti-Communist Whites. As the historian Peter Holquist has noted, what is called the "Russian Civil War" was actually "a series of overlapping civil wars and national conflicts," in which all sides redirected the practices of coercion, repression, and surveillance used during World War I against foreign combatants toward those now identified as internal enemies.[1]

While other members of her class fled Russia by the thousands, Sofia took her place at the center of these political and military conflicts. From the Kadet party underground in Moscow to the headquarters of the White Volunteer Army in southern Russia, she participated in many of the most important anti-Communist movements. The literature on this period includes histories of the many political groups that challenged the Soviet state and accounts of the efforts by Western powers to support the anti-Communist cause. Those stories are told almost exclusively from the perspective of men. Sofia stands out, as she did in 1917, as one of very few women to take a visible role in the anti-Communist movement during the Civil War, and her story helps us to understand the nature and implications of Russia's highly gendered politics during this prolonged period of national crisis.[2] Looking at her experiences also yields a deeper understanding of this war from the perspective of the losing side. Sofia's story reinforces how volatile and contingent the conflict was for those who lived it and highlights the moral dilemmas as well as personal dangers that confronted the White armies' political supporters. Her experience of war especially underscores the liberals' high hopes for aid and support from Russia's wartime Western allies and their profound disillusionment when the Allies abandoned the anti-Communist cause.

As Russia descended into violence and moral anarchy in 1918, Sofia made two radical and morally ambiguous choices. First, she immersed herself in the anti-Communist struggle. On the fringes of the Kadet leadership for most of 1917, she entered the inner circle of the now persecuted and fractured party, where its leaders struggled to formulate a unified strategy and tactics. In making this first choice, Sofia, like her fellow liberals, confronted the agonizing dilemma of principle versus expediency. Incidents she had witnessed such as Lenin's effortless dissolution of the Constituent Assembly and the murders of Kokoshkin and Shingarev demonstrated that it would take war, not peaceful protests or legal means, to overthrow the usurpers. But could violent means restore Russia as a unified nation founded on the principles that the Kadets held dear—democracy, the rule of law, and human decency? The White armies that were their natural allies were tainted by leaders who were reactionary monarchists, Cossack separatists, or bold-faced opportunists. Would alliance with them betray those principles and destroy their hopes for national renewal?

Sofia's second choice in 1918, though linked to the political role she adopted, was personal. The tragedy that was the Civil War became more bearable for her when she became the inseparable companion of Nikolai Ivanovich Astrov (1868–1934), one of the Kadet Party's most important leaders. She shared his political principles, joined the same underground groups, and attended the same meetings. The partnership was more than political: Sofia and Nikolai lived in a "civil marriage" (*grazhdanskii brak*), so called because it was unsanctioned by the church. From the Civil War to Nikolai's death in Prague in 1934, Sofia dedicated herself to the protection of his health, well-being, and reputation. What made her choice morally ambiguous was the fact that when she fled Moscow with Nikolai in August 1918, he left a wife behind.

Sofia left virtually no account of her Civil War experiences, effectively erasing this period from her autobiographical record. Only a few of her letters have survived, offering glimpses into her interpretation of events. Nikolai, on the other hand, was something of a graphomaniac, maintaining a steady correspondence during the Civil War and writing several reminiscences of his experiences. Former political associates of the couple shared Nikolai's compulsion to write about their experience during the revolution and Civil War, creating a large émigré literature that seeks to understand who lost Russia to the Communists, and why. These sources, while not sufficient to fully satisfy Sofia's biographer, make it possible to reconstruct and understand this most challenging and tragic chapter of her life.

For Sofia the Civil War began in Moscow, where she joined other members of the Kadet Central Committee who met cautiously but regularly in various private apartments. While some party leaders adopted disguises or avoided their homes, she seems to have lived in Moscow quite openly with her longtime friends Emilia Nikolaevna and Alexei Ilich Bakunin (nephew of the anarchist Mikhail), physicians who operated a well-known private clinic in the center of the city.[3] The party took advantage of her relative obscurity in Moscow by posting her outside on the sidewalk if a designated meeting place became unsafe and entrusting her with leading members to another, more secure location.[4]

Sheltered by the Bakunins, Sofia was fortunate to find a measure of comfort and protection as living conditions in Moscow worsened. By the time she arrived in January 1918, the fuel shortage had reached crisis proportions and residents engaged in an increasingly desperate search for food. The rapid change of governments in 1917 had produced a bewildering array of currencies in circulation—tsarist, Provisional Government, and Soviet—and ration coupons came to be preferred over money. Increasingly people bartered for what they needed. At giant black markets like Sukharevka, the formerly well-to-do displayed their jewelry, ball gowns, and silver in hopes of exchanging them for potatoes or flour at exorbitant rates.[5] Finding something to eat posed particular difficulties for people such as Sofia and Nikolai, who belonged to the group known as "former people," a new social category created by the Communists for members of the nobility and other class enemies. The Soviet class-based rationing system relegated former people to the lowest category, entitled to a bare minimum for subsistence. The new authorities unleashed a barrage of additional edicts against the old regime's "blood-sucking exploiters," seizing their estates, homes, and other assets, and depriving them of political rights.[6]

Sofia lost virtually all of her landed property, liquid assets, and possessions in this campaign of expropriation. A fellow émigré who knew her in Geneva and Prague recounts a romantic story, purportedly told to him by Sofia herself, about the fate of one part of the Panin fortune. Traveling south by train sometime during the Civil War, his story goes, Sofia carried a small, shabby suitcase filled with diamonds, jewelry, and gold—a treasure she intended to give to the White Army. Along the way the train stopped at a station so that passengers too ill with typhus to proceed could be taken off. When Sofia recognized an acquaintance among the helpless victims, she stopped to assist him. Amidst the bustle she forgot the suitcase for a moment; when she turned to pick it up, it had disappeared. There was no time to look for it—the train was leaving. "Thus Panina appeared in the south with empty hands," he concludes his story, and then "ended up a penniless émigré. One must be fair to her, she evidently never mourned her lost riches."[7]

A dramatic and poignant tale—but did it really happen? Though still living in Czechoslovakia, the writer published his tendentious, pro-Soviet memoirs in the USSR in 1966, where censorship and stereotypes of White Russians may have encouraged him to embellish or even concoct this story. Nikolai, who was Sofia's constant companion on her journeys across Russia during the war, mentions no such incident in his detailed memoirs. The tale has its plausible elements; attempts to smuggle valuables are common in the stories of former people fleeing Soviet power.[8] True or not, his story highlights the reputation Sofia enjoyed among her contemporaries for dedication to the anti-Communist cause, responsiveness to the needs of friends, and indifference to the loss of her wealth.

What *is* true is that Sofia lost everything she possessed during the Civil War. The fate of Marfino followed a typical scenario for the homes and estates of former people. After seizing the estate in 1918, Soviet authorities converted its Gothic mansion into a refuge for homeless and orphaned children. Sofia visited her beloved Marfino at least once during the summer of 1918, where she saw her dear friend Alexandra Peshekhonova for what became the last time. When she visited, Marfino was already under the control of a Bolshevik commissar, who like the leather-jacketed commandant of her Petrograd prison treated her with great courtesy. But by late 1921 Marfino was in a sorry state, according to news Anastasia Petrunkevich received from a friend who had spent the summer there. The mansion had been "completely gutted [opustoshen]," and its library, paintings, and other furnishings had been taken away. The children's colony now bore the name of Commissar of Enlightenment Anatoly Lunacharsky, Sofia's former Bolshevik adversary in the Petrograd City Council, who frequently visited the eponymous refuge with his wife. But his patronage, an outraged Anastasia reported, had not prevented the colony from turning into a "dirty, disgusting den of vice" under the commissar's very nose. Such horrors were taking place not just at Marfino but everywhere in Soviet Russia, she claimed, and demonstrated the harmful effects of Soviet rule on Russian youth.[9]

The process of appropriating Sofia's Petrograd home took longer and encountered some resistance. After her departure for Moscow the majority of her servants scattered, most back to their native villages. Only two remained, Lena and Fedor—whether out of loyalty or necessity it is impossible to say. They were soon joined by Ivan Petrovich Karkhlin, Sofia's property and office manager, and his family. These former employees succeeded in protecting her house and its contents until Easter 1919, when agents of the Cheka (the Soviet secret police) finally arrived and arrested Lena and Karkhlin. Two days later the Cheka returned with trucks to begin removing the valuables; what those valuables were Karkhlin does not say, but they probably included the silver and pieces from the Panin art collection. All in all, the Cheka conducted seven searches of Sofia's home. Released after a brief imprisonment,

Karkhlin continued living at the house with his family, the two former servants, and two families of strangers whom the authorities moved in, until the Karkhlins fled to Latvia in 1921. "And so, Your Excellency," the loyal manager reported to Sofia from Riga with more than a hint of pride, "we managed to save and preserve in the house all of your furniture, all of the musical instruments, almost all the carpets, your entire library, all the dishes in the sideboard, and all the copper kitchen utensils." Everything would be there for her, Karkhlin assured her, when the Soviet regime was finally overthrown—an event "which we awaited and now continue to await, in complete certainty that it will happen sooner or later."[10]

While some disaffected citizens like Karkhlin merely waited for the Soviet regime to fall, the Kadets who gathered in Moscow in the spring and summer of 1918 took enormous personal risks to try to overthrow it. One of the most active was Nikolai Astrov, who belonged to several underground coalition groups in Moscow: the "Nine," which included representatives of civic organizations and industry; its successor, the "Right Center," which brought Kadets together with former tsarist ministers and conservative nationalists; and the "Union of Regeneration," a left-leaning coalition formed in April 1918.[11] All these organizations debated the same urgent questions. Was Germany still Russia's enemy, or should the anti-Communist resistance now seek German assistance to defeat the Bolsheviks? Would alliance with the White military forces forming in the south and Siberia save the revolution or betray its promise of a democratic Russia? Should the elected Constituent Assembly still be considered the legitimate political authority in Russia? Or was a dictatorship by a military strongman the best hope for defeating the Soviet regime?

These agonizing questions fractured not only the various anti-Communist coalitions but also the Kadet leadership itself. The one issue that more than any other threatened to destroy the party in 1918 was Germany. Despite America's entry into the war in 1917 Germany was still a powerful foe who had taken advantage of the chaos after the October Revolution to advance deep into the former Russian empire. Its ability to continue fighting only increased after the Communist government signed the Treaty of Brest-Litovsk with Germany in March 1918, which brought an end to Russia's war with Germany. Steadfast in their commitment to Russian national honor, Sofia and Nikolai, along with most Kadets, were appalled by this betrayal of France and Britain, whose battered armies were still fighting on the Western Front. They

watched in horror as the March 1918 treaty also accelerated the disintegration of their great multinational empire and allowed the German
Army to occupy virtually all of Ukraine, Poland, and the Baltic lands.

And yet, others asked, might Germany be just the savior they were
looking for? Believing that the Allies would neither win the war nor
help the anti-Communist forces, some members of the Right Center
turned to Germany as an ally against Lenin. Even more alarming to
Moscow Kadets were reports from Rostov in southern Russia, where
Miliukov had fled, that the party leader now advocated an alliance between Germany and the anti-Communist movement as the best means
to end the Soviet nightmare. In the wake of the Brest-Litovsk Treaty,
which freed Germany to concentrate all its might on the Western Front,
Miliukov believed that it, not the Allies, would win the Great War. He
and his supporters were further inclined to pin their hopes on Germany
after they observed how quickly the efficient Germans restored order in
the Russian territories they occupied.[12]

The issue of Miliukov's "German orientation" came to a head at a
critical meeting of the Kadet Central Committee on May 14–17 at the
party's Moscow club, where participants debated Russia's and the
Kadets' future in a state of heightened emotion. With Miliukov absent,
they denounced their leader's "Germanophilia"; the Central Powers,
they agreed, remained Russia's enemy, and collaboration with them
would destroy the country's honor and independence. Committed to
the unity of multinational Russia, the Moscow Kadets were similarly
shocked by reports that Miliukov supported Ukrainian Hetman General Pavel Skoropadsky, whom they considered a German puppet, and
that several Kiev Kadets had entered Skoropadsky's government. The
conference ended on a buoyant note of party unity, with participants
convinced they had acted "according to conscience and honor" by
pledging their loyalty to the Allies and rejecting Miliukov's pro-German
and pro-separatist sympathies.[13]

It is not known whether Sofia attended the May Kadet conference,
but she supported the resolutions adopted there, especially the rejection of the German orientation. Writing to party veteran Maxim Vinaver
the following month, she condemned Miliukov's position as a "great
and irreversible mistake" that was "inexpressibly painful" and damag-
ing to both the party and the country. Western support for the anti-
Communist cause was fragile, she pointed out. Miliukov's position
undermined the prospects of aid for their cause from abroad by arousing

"great confusion" among the Allies, who were still at war with Germany, "for they rightly say that for Europe the Kadets and Miliukov are one and the same thing." "It is necessary to set them right," she insisted, and "declare that the entire North and East do not go with Miliukov." Sofia also expressed an unwavering commitment to the integrity of the former Russian empire and condemned those Kadets who supported national separatism. The party faced additional challenges in Moscow, she reported to Vinaver, where twelve leaders remained in prison. Yet her letter ends on an upbeat note. Their cause was attracting "very good and respected names," she assured him, and the growing anti-Communist movement in the Volga region "raises some hopes."[14]

Such hopes notwithstanding, the state of the Kadet Party in Moscow had become perilous by the time Sofia wrote Vinaver in June. On May 18, the day following the party conference, Soviet police agents raided party offices, seized party membership lists, set up ambushes at members' apartments, including Nikolai's, and arrested dozens of party faithful. Nikolai escaped arrest by going underground. Shaving off his short beard and exchanging his customary soft brimmed hat for a gray peaked cap, he spent his days in clandestine meetings with Kadets and other opponents of the Communists who still enjoyed their freedom, while at night he moved from one friend's apartment to another.[15] Sofia, still able to move freely around Moscow, joined Dmitry Shipov, the founder in 1905 of the moderate Octobrist party and Nikolai's longtime friend, to act as Nikolai's trusted intermediary with the party and the outside world. She also began to serve as his political confidante and adviser, helping him compose political letters and memoranda, a role she continued to play for the rest of his life.[16] Aligning herself with Nikolai's left-leaning wing of the Kadet Party, she followed him into a new alliance called the "National Center" and became its only female member. Committed to the liberals' core values, in mid-1918 the National Center became "a surrogate for the Kadets' own party apparatus," in Rosenberg's words, now scattered and decimated by Soviet repression.[17]

While Sofia's involvement in the National Center at this time seems to have been limited, even titular membership in the organization carried great risk. The new group's ambitious goals included forging a broad anti-German and anti-Communist alliance that would raise recruits and funds for the White armies forming in the south and Siberia. Nikolai met with such well-known opponents of the Soviet regime as Bruce

Lockhart, the British agent in Moscow who funneled British pounds and French francs to the opposition.[18] The National Center supported efforts to organize uprisings in Petrograd and Moscow, and they began planning for the government that would succeed the Soviet regime when it fell—as they believed it surely must. Nikolai's friend Shipov became the National Center's chairman and treasurer. He paid a high price for his dedication to the cause: arrested in 1919, he died in a Cheka prison in 1920.

Who was the man to whom Sofia dedicated her life in 1918? Although she and Nikolai belonged to the same generation (Sofia, forty-seven years old in 1918, was three years younger than he), the couple differed considerably in background, life experience, and temperament. Unlike the more cosmopolitan Sofia, Nikolai was someone whose entire personal, professional, and political life revolved around Moscow, his "first and last love," in her words.[19] Also striking is the social distance between Sofia, the wealthy daughter of two aristocratic dynasties, and Nikolai, whose father was the son of a rural priest. Yet the Astrov family illustrates the fluidity of Russia's class structure and the opportunities for upward mobility in the nineteenth century. Overcoming poverty and hardship, Nikolai's father, Ivan Nikolaevich, left his village in Tambov to attend a seminary and then entered medicine. He married up: Nikolai's mother was a general's daughter. Their son Nikolai rose so high in the judicial and civil bureaucracy that he attained the rank that automatically conferred nobility in the Russian civil service system.

Like Sofia, Nikolai lost a parent early when his mother died of tuberculosis before he reached the age of six. Nevertheless his lengthy reminiscences describe an idyllic childhood. Nikolai grew up with three brothers in a warm, loving household, whose activities were bounded by his close-knit neighborhood, enlivened by visits with numerous relatives and family friends, and regulated by pious fidelity to Russian customs and the Orthodox religion. Though not particularly well off, the Astrov family aspired to higher social status and combined their commitment to education with a strong work ethic. The boys had French governesses and private tutors, and they attended an elite secondary school. Although Ivan Nikolaevich was the family patriarch, the moral center of the household was Yulia Mikhailovna, the boys' beloved stepmother, a dedicated volunteer in various Moscow charitable organizations. Both parents raised the Astrov boys to commit themselves to public service.[20]

After completing his law studies at Moscow University, Nikolai became a member of the city's professional intelligentsia and governing elite. In addition to serving as a justice of the peace, he was elected to Moscow's famously progressive city council and its liberal provincial zemstvo. The 1905 Revolution propelled him into national politics when he was elected to the Central Committee of the Kadet Party, which he joined as soon as it was founded. Nikolai's public service career continued to expand in the years after 1905, when he served on the editorial board of the liberal newspaper *Russian News* (*Russkiia vedomosti*) and the governing board of the progressive Shaniavsky Moscow City University. In short, Nikolai exemplified the career path of a liberal professional of late imperial Russia: a legal education followed by a distinguished public service career in positions that supported Moscow's progressive civil society. The Great War raised his profile even higher. In 1914 Nikolai helped to found the All-Russian Union of Towns and became its director in 1917. Indeed, that organization's success in mobilizing Russia for total war may be attributed at least in part to his administrative talents and many years of executive experience. After the monarchy fell, the Moscow City Council honored his years of service by electing Nikolai to be Moscow's mayor, a post he held briefly from late March until the end of June. Invited twice by Kerensky to join the Provisional Government (he refused), he ran successfully on the Kadet party list for a seat in the ill-fated Constituent Assembly.[21]

Nikolai's career before and during the war connected his life to Sofia's in several ways. One of the Kadet Party's original members, he was a friend and political protégé of her stepfather, Ivan Petrunkevich, who may have introduced him to Sofia. The relief organizations Sofia worked with in Petrograd during the war were affiliated with the Union of Towns, which Nikolai directed. Once Sofia was elected to the Kadet Central Committee in May 1917, the two would have encountered each other at party meetings. In fact, Nikolai was one of the Kadet leaders who attended the fateful party conference at Sofia's home on the night of November 27, barely escaping arrest the following morning. Despite these intersections, Sofia and Nikolai do not seem to have been closely acquainted before 1918.

The couple differed not only in background but also in personality, temperament, and the impression they made on contemporaries. Sofia's warmth and charm won her numerous friends and admirers. The Kadet leader Shingarev, for example, first met Sofia in 1903 when he worked with her in his role as provincial physician to build a hospital on her

Voronezh estate. He was "captivated," he recalled in his prison diary in late 1917, by her "modesty, simplicity, business-like manner, and a kind of aloofness from private life. I wore everyone out with my lavish praise of Panina."[22] Nikolai, on the other hand, made enemies as well as friends, no doubt due at least in part to his long career in partisan politics at the municipal and national level. His leftward political leanings and conciliatory attitude toward moderate socialists during the revolution and Civil War inspired distrust in some of his fellow Kadets. To one right-wing party member who worked briefly with Nikolai in the Moscow anti-Communist underground in 1918, Nikolai was one of those "incorrigible" leftist Kadets: "extremely sweet, entirely like taffy," he scathingly recalled; "but behind this sweetness a large dose of ambition and cunning lay hidden." Tyrkova-Williams, who gravitated toward the right during the Civil War, described him in similar terms as "sweet, crafty and indecisive," and labeled him the Kadets' own "little Hamlet [*Gamletik*]."[23]

Other party colleagues discerned the complex personality that lay behind the public servant and politician. Vladimir Obolensky, who had known Nikolai since 1905, liked the "youthful-looking Muscovite" with his sincere manner, "melodious voice," and "thoughtful eyes," expressing intelligence and kindness. He also admired Nikolai for his deep sense of moral duty, the loyalty he showed to friends, and his devotion to public service. In fact, Obolensky believed that public service dominated Nikolai's life to such a degree that he was "completely unable to live a private life and have private interests"; his personal life "merged with his public life . . . and his public work considerably determined his personal relations with people." At the same time, Obolensky recalled, this dedicated public servant was a highly emotional man with strong passions, whose relationship to the world around him "was either loving or hostile." "Such people are rarely happy," Obolensky reflected sympathetically, "experiencing every loss and disillusionment tragically." Everything that Nikolai loved most, according to his friend—his three brothers, his native city, his political party, and his homeland—was lost during the Civil War. Tyrkova-Williams's acerbic characterization of him as a "little Hamlet" is echoed with more kindness by Obolensky. For the unfortunate Nikolai, "the ordeals that fate sent to people of our generation caused him more suffering than many others." Reacting to life "in an exaggeratedly tragic way," he agonized over past mistakes and was plagued by guilt.[24]

Nikolai Ivano-
vich Astrov, 1924,
Geneva. (private
collection)

In Sofia's eyes Nikolai was no "little Hamlet," but rather a tragic
hero who remained true to his noble principles. She respected the dedicated public activist who shared her faith in incremental progress and
her sense of moral duty. She admired the courage he displayed during
the revolution and Civil War, when he ignored personal danger to
carry out his party and patriotic responsibilities. But she also deeply
loved, and perhaps pitied, the sensitive and sentimental man with the
tragic air, who wrote poetry, painted watercolors, and was, in the
words of a Moscow City Council colleague, "a tender and dreamy soul,
fragile as a flower."[25] Barely a month after his death in 1934, she drafted
a letter to a mutual friend in which she described "knowing and loving"
a man whose personality remained consistent throughout his life. "You

"To Nikolai Ivanovich," undated poem in Sofia's handwriting. (private collection)

must either accept or reject him in his entirety," she wrote. She was grateful for not only the "happiness" but also the "honor" of being his "collaborator (*sotrudnitsei*) and friend," if only during the "final, tragic and most difficult period of his life."[26] Abandoned in the valise Sofia left after her death is the draft of an unfinished poem in her handwriting, entitled "To Nikolai Ivanovich." The poem's two complete stanzas hint at how his inner sadness evoked her loving sympathy:

Evening light,
Evening bells,
And a quiet soul—
Oh it is you my love,
My evening glow.
You are gentle, tender, like the sunset,
Sad, like the evening bells,
And in the quiet of your soul
I hear an eternal moan.

Nikolai repaid Sofia's devotion with his own kind of love, a combination of admiration and gratitude. Calling her "my faithful friend and companion," Nikolai deeply valued their partnership. His friend Obolensky's observation that he was "completely unable to live a private life and have private interests" suggests that for the somewhat self-absorbed Nikolai, the affection he felt for Sofia was linked to the political cause they shared, as well as to his dependence on her for moral support during the war and in the long years of exile that followed.[27]

By late August Moscow had become far too dangerous for Sofia and especially Nikolai. Full-scale civil war finally erupted that summer. The threat to Soviet power intensified when the Germans threatened to declare war against Soviet Russia after their ambassador was assassinated in Moscow in July. At the end of August Lenin was shot and badly wounded while visiting a Moscow factory on the same day that the head of the Cheka in Petrograd was assassinated. In response to these growing threats to its existence, the Soviet government redoubled its searches and arrests of real and imagined opponents, and the days when Nikolai could move safely around the city, even in disguise, were clearly numbered.[28]

As most of the Kadet leaders prepared to leave Moscow, the conspirators made some important political decisions. After long and passionate debate in a small, secret apartment on a tiny side street, a coalition of Kadet and anti-Communist socialists, the "Union of Regeneration," settled on a plan for a new supreme authority for Russia: a five-man "Directory," which would constitute a parallel civilian government associated with the White military leadership in the south and east. Nikolai accepted the Union's invitation to represent it on the Directory despite reservations about the feasibility of its grand political schemes, and he began making plans to leave Moscow. He would first travel to Kiev, crossing both Soviet Russia and German-occupied Ukraine. There he would meet with Miliukov, who had gone to Kiev in late May to discuss possibilities of collaboration with German authorities. Then Nikolai planned to travel south in order to make contact with General Mikhail Alexeev, the leader of the White forces in southern Russia. Finally, he was directed to head east for Ufa, where remnants of the Constituent Assembly had gathered, to participate in the formal creation of the Directory.[29]

There was no doubt about whether Sofia would accompany Nikolai on all these travels. While he decided on his next political steps, she made the arrangements for their dangerous journey. "Without her," he admits, "I do not know how I would have managed to get out of Moscow, which suddenly had become hostile and turned its savage face toward me."[30] Against the advice of the protective Sofia, Nikolai paid a farewell visit to each of his beloved brothers, not suspecting that it would be the last time he would ever see them. Hurrying through the streets from one final meeting to another, he was shocked and dismayed at the rage and hostility he observed in his fellow Muscovites, like the group of agitated young men carrying rifles, their eyes bloodshot, who presented "an ugly, terrifying sight." He did not stop at his own apartment or see his wife.[31] His home had already been searched at least twice—turned upside down, he recalled, and his wife placed under house arrest. Later hospitalized on doctors' orders, Ekaterina Vasilievna Astrova suffered a nervous breakdown, "from which she did not recover for a long time."[32] This is the only time Nikolai mentions his wife in any of his memoirs, and other sources that would cast light on their relationship are lacking. Once he left Russia Nikolai seems to have largely erased his marriage to her; in an identity document issued to him in February 1920, for example, he described himself as a bachelor. Ekaterina Vasilievna's subsequent fate is unknown, although it seems probable that she somehow survived the revolution, since Nikolai's marriage to her was later cited by at least one mutual friend as the reason why he and Sofia never officially married.[33]

Their departure from Moscow was full of drama. Early in the morning of August 23, Sofia knocked on the door of Nikolai's room in his last hiding place, an apartment in the city center. "Are you ready?" she asked. "We need to get going." Drawing back the curtains, he "froze": directly outside his window was the enormous Cathedral of Christ the Savior "in all of its magnificence." The cathedral was as much a patriotic as a religious monument, for it was built in the nineteenth century to commemorate Russia's victory over Napoleon. United in unspoken consciousness of the significance of this monument and this moment, Sofia and Nikolai both knelt and bowed to the ground in a gesture of veneration and farewell. "It was farewell *forever*," Nikolai later wrote. Sofia, the more practical half of the couple, cut the moment short: "Well, it's time, time to go! This is completely impossible. Let's go!"[34]

Carrying bundles and baskets, Sofia and Nikolai hurried on foot to the railroad station. There they received their fictitious identity documents and tickets, clambered aboard the packed train, and somehow found seats in a third-class car. Finally the train began to move, carrying Sofia and Nikolai southwest toward Kiev, their first destination the small railroad town of Unecha in the former Jewish Pale of Settlement, near the border between Soviet Russia and German-occupied territory. Their journey featured several of the common dangers and adventures experienced by travelers during the Civil War. Fear of being recognized and arrested as class enemies made Nikolai nervous and suspicious of bystanders. Their fellow passengers, timid and quiet during most of the trip, voiced their own apprehensions as the train neared Unecha. Would they be searched? Would the train be shot at? Sofia, by contrast, maintained the sangfroid she had displayed in Bolshevik Petrograd and Moscow, listening to the passengers' agitated conversation calmly and attentively, Nikolai recalled, as though it were a "curious story that had no connection at all to us."[35]

The couple's brief stay in the impoverished shtetl of Unecha brought more anxious moments, which Sofia handled with her usual aplomb. Left at the station to sit at an unoccupied table while Nikolai searched for lodgings, she discovered that local Cheka officers considered this to be *their* table, for when they returned, they forced her to move and tossed her belongings on the floor—but did not recognize the fugitive countess. The couple spent the night in a tumble-down hut on the edge of town, where Sofia slept on the table and a cholera victim languished in the next room. Traveling to the town of Surazh by freight car the next morning, the couple met their contact, who provided them with a tarantass—an old-fashioned carriage with no springs—and her "rather wayward" brother as their driver for the border crossing. As they approached the Soviet-German border their tarantass joined a long line of other carts and carriages, all traveling in the same direction and all, it turned out, smuggling both refugees and contraband. The tarantass and its passengers survived the search by soldiers at the Soviet border unscathed, although one guard longingly examined Nikolai's galoshes before their owner pointed out that they would not fit. At the Ukrainian border they encountered German soldiers—cleaner and more disciplined than the Soviet guards—who commanded them to turn back. A bribe changed hands, however, and as night fell the tarantass was allowed to circumvent the border post and pass through the pitch-dark forest into occupied Ukraine. Obtaining passes and tickets from local German military authorities, Sofia and Nikolai arrived in Kiev without further incident, three days after leaving Moscow.[36]

Miliukov and the other Kiev Kadets greeted their arrival with joy, astonished by the couple's success in escaping from Moscow and surviving a perilous journey. Sofia and Nikolai joined Miliukov as guests in a spacious apartment in the city's verdant upper-class district of Lypky. "Everything was good and cozy" in their shared lodgings, where Miliukov entertained them in the evening by playing his violin.[37] But their days were dominated by political disagreement. Convinced of the rightness of their pro-Allies position and hoping to preserve party unity, Sofia and Nikolai tried in vain to convince Miliukov to drop his "Germanophilia." To their dismay, Miliukov continued to believe in Germany's ultimate victory. Mutual respect and a common hatred of Bolshevism still united them, and in Kiev Sofia and Nikolai helped Miliukov draft a proclamation to world powers calling for international sanctions against the Soviet regime. But Sofia and Nikolai's tendency to believe that theirs was the only morally correct position, while drawing them together, also made them politically ineffectual and even more vulnerable to disillusionment.[38]

The couple was similarly appalled by the behavior of Kievans in the German-occupied city, who were caught up in a frenzy of speculation that drowned "all civic feelings, conscience, duty and even concern for tomorrow," in Nikolai's bitter description. His words exemplify the revulsion that sometimes characterized the couple's reactions to the human frailties, vices, and cruelties they witnessed during the Civil War. "In general," Sofia wrote Miliukov succinctly in October 1919, Russians who lived away from the front were "repulsive." The source of their moralistic condemnation of people experiencing all the traumas of civil war lies in the high-minded mentality characteristic of the intelligentsia of their generation, which placed service to the common good and moral integrity high above self-interest. It also stemmed from their refusal to accept that brutality and tragedy had become normal, a view expressed in a short obituary Sofia wrote in London in 1920 to honor a Crimean physician who had died of typhus. "Death in our day has turned into that 'everyday phenomenon' which the living hasten to pass by without slowing their pace even for a second," she lamented, "and which does not attract their indifferent attention." Her essay reflects not only the air of moral superiority she at times assumed during the war, but also her effort to resist indifference and preserve the dignity of the individual in the face of mass suffering.[39]

With little to show besides party disagreements after two weeks in Kiev, Sofia and Nikolai set off for the Panin estate of Gaspra in German-occupied Crimea, where they arrived on September 17. Sofia was reunited with her mother and stepfather, who had lived there since 1915, and the Kadet leader Vladimir Nabokov and his family, who had found a refuge in Gaspra after fleeing Petrograd in late 1917. While young Vladimir, the future novelist, composed poems and chased butterflies and women through the magnificent Crimean spring and summer, the elder Nabokov wrote a bitter memoir analyzing why the Provisional Government failed.[40] Sofia arrived from Kiev in her usual excellent health, but Nikolai, whose health was delicate at the best of times, fell victim to the Spanish influenza pandemic and lay ill for almost two weeks. Finally he was well enough to participate in a meeting with other Kadet Central Committee members at Gaspra on October 2.[41]

It was reassuring for Nikolai and Sofia to be back among party colleagues who shared their pro-Western position and supported cautious cooperation with the anti-Communist forces in southern Russia and Siberia. Although the Germans still occupied the Crimea in October 1918, their evident preparations to withdraw signaled to those gathered at Gaspra that the Great War was ending. Surely the victorious Allies would finally come to the aid of the Volunteer Army, now led by General Anton Denikin after the death of General Alexeev in September. The imminent end of the war and the peace conference that would follow presented the liberals meeting at Gaspra with threats as well as opportunities. As staunch defenders of Russian national unity against both Communists and national separatists, the Kadets must lead any effort, Nikolai maintained, to ensure "that the idea of a united and independent Russia is accepted and realized at the Peace Conference."[42] Rejecting the original plan to travel to Ufa, where hopes to establish a Directory had collapsed, Sofia and Nikolai prepared to leave for Ekaterinodar in southeastern Russia, capital of the Kuban Cossacks and Denikin's headquarters. If Sofia felt reluctant to leave her mother, now in her late sixties, and the even older, ailing Petrunkevich, she did not let it deter her. At Gaspra, according to Nikolai, she "decided to dedicate her strengths to the same struggle and work to which I had given myself."[43] Leaving her elderly parents looks like yet another decision by Sofia to put public ahead of private duty. At the same time, it demonstrates how much she was now invested in Nikolai's political cause and personal welfare.

As the couple traveled to Ekaterinodar in October 1918, they crossed landscapes scarred by recent military action, over half-destroyed bridges and through railroad stations overflowing with refugees. The town itself was a "military camp," Nikolai recalled, filled with officers and gendarmes wearing uniforms from the old regime. Funeral processions through Ekaterinodar's streets reminded the new arrivals that the front was nearby. Although the armistice on November 11 halted the Great War on the Western Front, full-scale civil war now dominated life in southern Russia.[44]

Arriving on the eve of another major Kadet conference, Sofia and Nikolai reunited with party members from other towns, including Miliukov from Kiev. To their dismay, the conference revealed the transitory nature of the party unity they had enjoyed at Gaspra, and the ways that the goal of winning the Civil War distorted the party's democratic principles. While some party colleagues saw restoration of the monarchy or military dictatorship as the means to victory, Nikolai and Sofia insisted that White forces could win only if they attracted broad popular support by committing to fundamental political and social reforms. They feared—correctly, as it turned out—that the Volunteer Army's reactionary orientation would isolate and destroy it, concerns that Miliukov dismissed as indicative of their "confusion." A compromise resolution proposed by Nikolai won majority support at the Ekaterinodar conference. Skirting the issue of whether to restore the monarchy, his resolution committed the party to complete support for the White forces despite the Whites' anti-democratic orientation.[45]

The conference over, Nikolai and Sofia threw themselves into Ekaterinodar's intense political life. General Denikin invited Nikolai to join his civilian cabinet, the Special Council, with responsibility for planning policies on land, labor, nationalities, and other issues for the democratic government that would take control, it was hoped, after the White victory. While his official position probably afforded Nikolai and Sofia a measure of financial support and access to scarce commodities, it also diminished their faith in the White movement. Nikolai felt isolated on the council and considered most of its members to be nonentities at best. Denikin's choice of General Abram Dragomirov as its chair was especially unfortunate; the general was not only a monarchist reactionary and anti-Semite, but also "a regular hysteric who at times lost his self-possession over trifles."[46] Representing the Kadet Central Committee, Nikolai and Sofia also resumed their involvement with the more congenial National Center, which began meeting in Ekaterinodar in December 1918. Sofia was elected to the center's board—which managed its membership, set meetings and agendas, and conducted correspondence—and also to its "Propaganda Commission."[47]

Sofia's activities in Ekaterinodar reproduced her experience in 1917 in at least one significant way: she was the sole woman to participate regularly in the National Center or any other political organization there. It undoubtedly required considerable determination and self-confidence to survive in a political milieu that had always been male-dominated but now existed within the hyper-masculine environment of a military headquarters. A growing friendship with General Denikin and his young wife, Ksenia, lessened her isolation. Sofia and Nikolai frequently visited the Denikins and their baby, Marina, at their modest home. Observing the general in a family setting strengthened their loyalty to him and faith in his leadership. Nikolai and the general became especially close despite their differences in outlook and experience, each respecting the other for his integrity and patriotism. The personal relationship forged with the Denikins in Ekaterinodar continued in emigration for the remainder of their lives.[48]

Ekaterinodar's skewed political spectrum was dominated by right-wing monarchists seeking to turn the clock back to before February 1917. Nikolai found himself on the left, regarded not only by military leaders but also by some fellow Kadets as too pro-Western, excessively reformist, and soft on socialism. Sofia shared Nikolai's positions on all the major political questions but stayed in the background. On rare occasions when she spoke at meetings of the National Center or Kadets, she urged a united stand on such basic questions as universal suffrage, land reform, and the future of the Constituent Assembly.[49] Recalling how Miliukov's German orientation had threatened to split the Kadets in 1918, she privately criticized the party leader to his face, telling him that "in spite of you" Russia could never go back to what it was.[50]

Another recurring topic of debate and speculation at meetings of the National Center was distant Europe, finally at peace but suffering post-war nationalist and socialist upheavals of its own. What were the attitudes of politicians and the public in the West toward the "Russian question," Sofia and her comrades wondered, and the chances of getting aid now that the Great War was over? When would Western leaders finally recognize that providing anti-Communist forces with enough resources to defeat Soviet power was not only right, but in their own self-interest?[51]

Sofia placed little faith in obtaining help from abroad. As the problem of the Russian Revolution began to engage the peacemakers at the Paris Conference in early 1919, she wrote a letter to Nikolai revealing the depth of her pessimism as she regarded the postwar world. "I am without doubt in a denunciatory mood," she warned Nikolai in February, "and *am inclined to think and say nothing complimentary about humanity* at the present time." Both revolutionary Russia and postwar Europe were in a state of collapse, she asserted, caused by "two extremes." The first was moral degeneration caused by total war, or what she termed "the masses' reversion to a state of natural wildness [*odichanie*] . . ., which inevitably gives birth to Bolshevism, however it is called, left or right." The second extreme was "utopianism of a most pernicious, 'nationalistic' principle, proclaimed by the dreamer [President Woodrow] Wilson as a slogan of freedom under the name of self-determination, but in essence constituting the very same bestial-bolshevik [*zverino-bol'shevistskii*] slogan, only in hidden form." Idealistic proclamations like Wilson's Fourteen Points, Sofia seems to imply, have the same destructive effect as war: the disintegration of great empires, the collapse of a civilized social order, and the decline of human decency. The months since the armistice, Sofia fumed, "have done more in the sense of destroying common human hopes and faith in the nearness of attaining at least some ideals than all the horrors of the preceding war." The certainty of progress and the moral attainments of Western civilization that she had been raised to believe in now rang hollow. Nowhere could she see "those high qualities of spirit, with which life must be built—and by 'nowhere' I mean both Europe and America." Overcome by angry disillusionment as a result of the West's reluctance to face the Communist threat head-on, Sofia confessed she found it difficult to continue: "*the hopelessness of the Sisyphean task creeps into one's heart.*"[52]

If the "Sisyphean task" facing Sofia in February 1919 referred to defeating the Communists, that cause seemed a bit less hopeless as winter turned to spring. Denikin's army in the south and Admiral Alexander Kolchak's in Siberia, though outnumbered, began to win important victories against an overextended Red Army. Prospects improved for the eventual unification of Denikin's and Kolchak's forces. Help finally arrived from abroad as well. Although the French proved to be unreliable allies after suddenly evacuating their forces from Odessa in April 1919, the arrival of military supplies and advisers promised by the British raised morale in Ekaterinodar.

As European assistance to the White movement grew, so did external pressure on its leaders, especially Denikin. In late May 1919 three representatives of the Russian Political Conference, an awkward coalition of former tsarist ministers and politicians created in 1918 in Paris to advocate for Russia's interests, arrived in Ekaterinodar from France. The visitors pressured Denikin to accept Kolchak, whose victories in eastern Russia impressed the Allies, as the supreme White leader. News of recent White victories, they claimed, along with increasing knowledge about the true nature of Bolshevism, had produced a "turning point" in Europe's relations toward Russia. But deep suspicions of the Whites as unrepentant reactionaries remained, the visiting Russians warned, deterring the British, French, and Americans from providing more aid.[53]

The Russian delegation from Paris met with a cool reception in Ekaterinodar. Members of the National Center and Denikin's Special Council felt that the Allies and the Political Conference treated the general and his army with disrespect. After all, the business of liberating Russia from the Communists was being done not in Paris, but on Russian soil; how dare politicians, comfortable and safe in the French capital, dictate to the general? Nikolai's proposal that Denikin send a delegation of his own representatives to Paris received the Council's unanimous approval. When General Denikin unexpectedly issued "Order No. 145" on May 30, recognizing Admiral Kolchak as the "Supreme Ruler of the Russian State and Supreme Commander of the Russian Armies," soldiers, civilians, and British military advisers in Ekaterinodar responded ecstatically, their hopes for victory now buoyed by the united anti-Red coalition. The next day General Dragomirov informed the Special Council that Denikin had approved Nikolai's proposal, and one week later Sofia, Nikolai, and the rest of Denikin's delegation left Ekaterinodar for Paris.[54]

In hindsight Denikin's mission to Paris appears doomed, occurring as it did when both Kolchak's military fortunes and Western interest in fighting Communism were waning. At the time, however, the idea had practical as well as political justifications. Communications between Kolchak and Denikin across the vast Russian territory that separated their forces were virtually impossible: their telegrams were being intercepted and their couriers killed by the Red Army. In Paris, Denikin believed, his delegation would be able to establish reliable telegraph

contact with Kolchak in Siberia, send the admiral a detailed report on
the military and political situation in the south, and receive his instructions in return. Denikin's representatives could also learn firsthand
about the European mood while communicating information about the
true situation on the ground in southern Russia, thus, everyone hoped,
solidifying Western support for the White cause.

The people Denikin selected for his mission did not bode well for
its success, however, since they mirrored the political differences that
riddled his Special Council and undermined its authority. The appointment of Dragomirov to lead the delegation would hardly assuage Allies'
concerns about anti-democratic tendencies within the Volunteer Army;
the British considered the general to be one of the most prominent members of Ekaterinodar's reactionary clique.[55] To emphasize the mission's
military purpose, Dragomirov was accompanied by a suite of three
colonels and two Cossacks. The rest of the delegation was made up of
civilians, including Nikolai, Denikin's most liberal adviser, along with
two other members of the Special Council who completely lacked
Nikolai's democratic sympathies. Konstantin Sokolov, a right-leaning
Kadet, directed the Volunteer Army's Propaganda Department, which
was notorious for communications that were both anti-Semitic and in-
effective.[56] Anatoly A. Neratov, a former assistant minister of foreign
affairs under the tsarist government, served as Denikin's acting foreign
minister; he is not known to have held any political views at all. Perhaps the most surprising choice for a delegation whose main objective
was military in nature was Sofia. According to Sokolov, "the Countess
was sent abroad by the National Center to aid N. I. Astrov and for contact with public-political circles."[57] His comment hints at how much
Nikolai relied on Sofia, and how others, including Denikin, regarded
the couple as an inseparable team. Fluent in French and English, known
in the West as a progressive philanthropist and the first female government minister, Sofia may also have seemed to be valuable to the delegation's efforts at influencing European public opinion in the Whites'
favor.

Departing on June 8/21 from the port of Novorossiisk on the Black
Sea, Sofia and Nikolai spent the entire summer of 1919 in Western Europe. Their experience at the first stop, Constantinople, foreshadowed
the disappointments the mission encountered in its efforts to influence
Western governments and public opinion to support the Whites. Neither Russian nor Allied representatives in Constantinople showed
much interest in their arrival.[58] While Dragomirov and Neratov paid

calls on Allied military representatives, the mission's civilians played tourist, visiting Hagia Sofia during Ramadan. Finally, a week after leaving Ekaterinodar, the delegation boarded a crowded French hospital ship carrying troops evacuated from Odessa and refugees of various nationalities. Dragomirov, Neratov, Nikolai, and Sofia received comfortable accommodations and dined with the ship's officers while the others made do in cabins below deck. The members of the mission used the leisurely journey to discuss their plans and objectives. Their main goal was still to establish contact with Kolchak, and the group approved Sokolov's draft report for Kolchak on conditions in southern Russia. The emissaries also agreed to contact officials and journalists in Paris in order to gain government and public support for the White cause.[59]

Another humiliating arrival awaited the delegation in Marseille, where French authorities scrutinized their credentials and detained them on the ship for a couple of days. Finally, Sofia and her companions reached Paris by train early on the morning of July 6, 1919. The mission's two Cossack NCOs, who donned their full regalia for the arrival—coats of scarlet and royal blue, silver cartridge pouches and daggers, high leather boots and immense fur hats—attracted considerable attention at the Gare de Lyon. In all other respects, however, the delegation met with a discouraging reception. No one from the Russian embassy or Political Conference met them at the station. Short notices in a few British and French newspapers announced the mission's arrival but mangled members' names and affiliations.[60]

Even more significant were the rapid changes that had taken place during their two-week journey. When Sofia and Nikolai left southern Russia in early June, the prospects for the White cause still seemed strong. By the time they arrived in Paris that moment had slipped away. As the fortunes of the White armies against the Reds seemed to brighten in one region, they dimmed in others. Denikin's forces were still advancing, but Kolchak's in Siberia had begun what became an irreversible retreat. In May the Allies seemed to be moving toward full, official recognition for Kolchak and the Omsk government as Russia's legitimate national government; but the farther Kolchak retreated, the more remote that hope became. Finally, as the delegation was sailing toward Paris, the Allies and Germany signed the Treaty of Versailles. With the Great War officially over, President Wilson and other Allied leaders began leaving for home. Whatever unity that had once existed in the Allied position on the "Russian question" was dissolving, and the momentum for a coordinated intervention in the Civil War on the side of the

Whites was waning. French, British, and American public opinion, never strongly in favor of a military crusade against the Communists, was even more opposed after the signing of the peace in June 28. Denikin's representatives arrived in Paris in time to watch the official celebration of the peace treaty on Bastille Day, an event that deeply wounded their patriotic feelings. No Russian troops were permitted to participate in the parade, and the celebration omitted any mention of how Russia's sacrifices on the Eastern Front had contributed to the Allied victory.[61]

Denikin's delegation completed its primary mission within a few days after arriving. Its report on conditions in southern Russia was sent to Kolchak in Omsk as a series of long telegrams; now they had time on their hands while waiting for Kolchak's reply. The first people they sought to influence were Russian representatives in Paris. They discovered a jumble of émigré organizations of every political hue and learned just how minimal the influence wielded by these self-appointed spokesmen for Russia actually was. The Russians whom Sofia and her companions met, whether on the left or right, were either hostile or skeptical toward the Denikin mission as well as incapable of advocating effectively for the anti-Communist cause.[62]

Mission members also pursued opportunities to communicate their message to European politicians and influence public opinion. The results were similarly discouraging. Neratov and Vasily Maklakov, head of the Political Conference, had a fruitless meeting with French Foreign Minister Stéphen Pichon. Dragomirov obtained an audience with Prime Minister Georges Clemenceau, who accused him and the delegation of "Germanophilia." Nikolai and Sofia met with several French politicians, including the former prime ministers Aristide Briand and Rene Viviani, the socialist Albert Thomas, and the journalist Joseph Reinach, famous for his defense of Dreyfus. Everyone they met listened attentively, Sokolov recalled, to their "firm speeches" about the Communist danger and the White cause, and responded with interest and even "amazement." But then the politicians began expressing their doubts about the anti-Communist struggle, bolstered by evidence of Soviet tenacity and news of Kolchak's retreat.[63] In a lengthy letter to Denikin, Nikolai admitted that the mission was having little effect. Their few meetings with politicians and journalists helped the Russians understand French politics but "changed nothing." Nikolai pointed to the refusal to give Russians a place in the July 14 victory parade as one indication of how the French government gave in to the unpopularity of the Whites in public opinion. It is truly tragic for us, he lamented, that the cause of helping Russia had fallen victim to internal political battles in the West. "Only we ourselves," he concluded, "can save our cause."[64]

As their second month in Paris began, the mission had still received no reply from Kolchak. By this time, having exhausted their chances of influencing the French, they redirected their hopes to Britain. Writing to Denikin from Paris, Nikolai predicted that Britain would continue its aid to the Whites, though under increasingly difficult conditions: although Winston Churchill remained staunchly anti-Communist, Prime Minister David Lloyd George's support for the Whites was lukewarm and vacillating.[65] In late July Sofia and Nikolai, together with Dragomirov and Neratov, crossed the English Channel. In contrast to their unsympathetic reception by members of the dysfunctional Political Conference in Paris, Nikolai and Sofia found a more like-minded group of Russian representatives in London in the Kadet-dominated Russian Liberation Committee. Organized in early 1919, the committee was run by the indefatigable Tyrkova-Williams with her son and husband. Its office on Fleet Street issued a steady stream of information for the British public about the sufferings of Russians under Bolshevism and White successes in the Civil War.[66] A meeting planned between Churchill and Dragomirov was cancelled at the last minute, however, and Sofia and Nikolai returned to Paris after only a week. As the summer passed, the members of the delegation grew increasingly anxious at being far from southern Russia, where the military situation was changing rapidly. European newspapers were publishing exciting news about Denikin's victories, but only one courier had arrived with official correspondence for the mission in six weeks. Isolated and impatient, the emissaries decided to return home without waiting for Kolchak's reply. Members of the Russian political community in Paris escorted the troublesome delegation to the railroad station to bid them farewell, not without a sigh of relief.[67]

Sofia and Nikolai were back in southern Russia by late August, returning directly to the town of Rostov, located north of Ekaterinodar. Rostov, the capital of the territory of the Don Cossacks, had become the new headquarters of Denikin's government when his army advanced toward Moscow. After two and a half months in Europe, Sofia and Nikolai felt like strangers in Russia, she wrote Miliukov, and needed time "to be reconnected with reality."[68] Any information the members of the mission could now convey seemed utterly irrelevant, so greatly had the Russian situation changed in their absence. Denikin listened politely to accounts of the delegation's European experiences and impressions but seemed to attach little significance to them. Reporting on their journey to fellow Kadets and members of the National Center in September, Sofia and Nikolai emphasized the conclusion Nikolai had expressed to Denikin from Paris: Europe will not help them, and "only we ourselves can save our cause."[69]

For a brief time in the summer and fall of 1919, it seemed as though Bolshevism's opponents might be able to win back their country on their own. The advancing southern White front extended from Rostov across Ukraine and central Russia. Denikin's forces seized major cities from the Red Army, including Kiev, and by early October they reached Orel, a mere two hundred miles south of Moscow. In the north General Nikolai Yudenich's White army advanced to the suburbs of Petrograd. Optimists began counting the days before Denikin marched triumphantly into Moscow and toppled the Communist regime.

All political groups now focused their attention on the military advance. Members of the Kadet Central Committee streamed into Rostov, exacerbating divisions in the party. "We cannot in any way come to agreement," Sofia reported to Miliukov, "for at heart the difference lies in *psychology*"—the willingness of some Kadets, she seems to imply, to compromise their principles.[70] Among the new arrivals was Tyrkova-Williams, a fervent advocate of imposing a military dictatorship over territory conquered by the Whites. Sofia and Nikolai disagreed, insisting on the necessity of establishing a civilian administration and winning over the population with concessions to their desires for land reform and social justice. The couple found greater support for their position in the left-leaning National Center. Meeting on October 7, members of the center's governing board optimistically discussed how to govern central Russia once it had been wrested from Soviet control. At the next meeting, Sofia announced, they would identify potential candidates for governor, mayor, and other civilian posts in Moscow.[71]

As Kadets, Cossacks, and opportunists streamed into the Volunteer Army's new headquarters, living conditions in the already strained provincial town worsened. Sofia and Nikolai shared a "tiny little apartment" in Rostov with fellow Kadet P. P. Yurenev and a host of temporary lodgers, Obolensky recalled, where "six to twelve people spent the night on beds, rearranged armchairs, or simply on the floor." The only large room served as a common dining room where Kadets came to eat and the National Center held its daily meetings. Vernadsky, Sofia's fellow assistant minister of education in 1917, arrived in Rostov shortly after she returned from Europe. Describing her as "animated and as always in such situations, superb," Vernadsky recorded how she regaled everyone with vivid stories about European politics and public opinion, and about Russia's ineffectual representatives in Paris.[72]

Sofia and Nikolai naturally rejoiced at the Volunteer Army's victories in the early fall of 1919. Normally cautious and pessimistic, Sofia assured Miliukov on October 10 that the capture of Moscow was not far off—"God willing."[73] But disturbing reports about the behavior of White troops in their newly occupied territories—summary executions, looting, rape, and attacks on Jews—undermined the couple's confidence in victory. "I was glad of the [military] success, but I did not believe in it," Nikolai wrote a few years later. His warnings to White authorities that moral corruption and "white Bolshevism" in the rear would bring defeat were mocked or ignored, he claimed.[74] Sofia was concerned that no one seemed to be paying attention to the atrocities committed by the Reds. "There is of course much that is very difficult and ugly in the rear of our [White] military successes," she conceded. But the leaders of the Volunteer Army were doing everything in their power to stop the anti-Jewish pogroms, she claimed. It was "anarchist elements" in the rear that were determined to "exterminate the Jewish tribe, and it is very difficult to fight against these awakened instincts of the crowd." Nevertheless, she insisted, "the Europeans cannot be allowed to pass over [Red atrocities] in silence." Europeans will write about pogroms against Jews "in a heartrending voice," she complained, "but they are silent or almost silent about what provoked these pogroms— about the *unbelievable* activity of the Cheka [*chrezvychaek*] in all the towns." She begged Miliukov, who was by now in London, to get information about Red atrocities published in the English press.[75]

Sofia's letter to Miliukov reflects the failure of Kadets to sustain their democratic commitment to civil rights for Jews, demonstrated in the Provisional Government's policies in 1917, under the conditions of civil war. Her complex and ambivalent attitudes toward Jews reflect those of other Kadets. On the one hand, she maintained friendships with people such as Maxim and Roza Vinaver and Liubov and Yakov Gurevich (whose father had converted to Christianity). But on the other hand, she regarded some Jews, like the "ingratiatingly insolent" Comrade Gordon (who arrested her), as personifications of the Jewish nature of Bolshevism. Sofia did not subscribe to the openly anti-Semitic views of some in her party, but she did share the Kadets' tendencies to rationalize the vicious pogroms against Jews carried out by Denikin's troops and to blame the "instincts" of the masses for them. She virtually excuses attacks on Jews by characterizing the violence as an understandable popular response to atrocities committed by the Communists, especially the Cheka, with their significant component of Jews; and she expresses bitter resentment over the greater attention Europeans seemed to give to White-inspired anti-Jewish pogroms than to the Cheka's crimes against Russians.[76]

Sofia's anger was no doubt influenced by devastating news she and Nikolai received from Moscow in late September. The Cheka finally succeeded in discovering the National Center's Moscow underground organization and arrested its leader, longtime Kadet Central Committee member Nikolai Shchepkin, along with dozens of Sofia and Nikolai's friends and fellow Kadets. Sixty-seven of them were shot. Although they did not belong to the National Center, Nikolai's brothers Vladimir and Alexander, his teenaged nephew Boris, and his elderly stepmother were among those arrested. Accused of being spies for Denikin, Nikolai's brothers and nephew were executed. Pavel, the sole surviving brother, managed to flee Moscow with his family but died of typhus on the road south to find Nikolai.[77]

The "Moscow catastrophe," as Nikolai later termed it, permanently scarred him and Sofia. The air of tragedy clinging to Nikolai the émigré, endearing him to some and irritating others, derived from a deep sense of guilt. To him there was only one conclusion to be drawn: the Communists killed his young nephew and all of his brothers, who were innocent of any anti-Soviet activity, solely because of their relationship to him. The tragedy had a different effect on Sofia: her opinion of Europeans sank even lower than it had after her discouraging experiences in Paris and London during the summer. Informing Miliukov in October of the "terrible extermination" of "our friends in Moscow," Sofia poured out her resentment at the "criminality" of European liberals, who say nothing while Russia's "best people" perish. "How the Titanic aroused indignation," she protested, "and how indifferent [they are] to the brutality of what is taking place now!"[78]

Sofia's resentment toward Russia's faithless European friends surely deepened later that fall, when Lloyd George suspended all aid to the anti-Communist forces. The White cause was doomed, the prime minister told the British on November 8, 1919; "I would rather leave Russia Bolshevik until she sees her way out of it than see Britain bankrupt. And that is the surest road to Bolshevism in Britain."[79] Lloyd George was correct about the Whites. Denikin's successes reached their peak in

September and early October but then began to wane. The hope of winning Moscow and Petrograd that Sofia expressed in her letter to Miliukov on October 10 was premature. On October 7, as she and the National Center in Rostov made plans for White governance of Moscow, the Red Army recaptured Orel. Soviet forces under Trotsky repelled Yudenich's advance on Petrograd, and his army disintegrated. By the end of October the Volunteer Army was in retreat all across its overextended front, overwhelmed by the superiority of the Red Army in troops and supplies. Refugees began streaming into Rostov, bringing panic and typhus. "How quickly everything is changing!" Vernadsky exclaimed at the end of November. "Kiev—Kharkov—Poltava are Bolshevik again, and I have ended up in some kind of new region. Where to go . . .? And how to live?"[80]

Fleeing Rostov before it fell to the Red Army became the top priority for its terrified residents. Sofia and Nikolai left Rostov on December 26 on one of the last trains, as looting, gunfire, and chaos seized the town. They traveled a hundred miles to Novorossiisk, the port from where they had embarked the previous June to seek Allied support in Europe. Corpses of victims of typhus and violence lay along the tracks, and roving anarchist bands threatened to derail the trains.[81] When Rostov fell on January 11, 1920, Novorossiisk became the final headquarters of the Volunteer Army. The Kadet leadership and National Center held their last meetings on Russian soil in the overcrowded port, now swollen with thousands of exhausted, starving refugees. Cossacks, army officers, politicians, and civilians, plagued by ubiquitous, typhus-bearing lice, desperately sought a precious place on an outgoing ship. On March 1, as Red forces advanced on Novorossiisk, Sofia and Nikolai boarded the *St. Nicholas*, bound for Constantinople, and left their homeland for what they knew in their hearts was forever.[82]

The "first woman of Russia" who stepped over gender boundaries in 1917 maintained her commitment to the liberal cause to the bitter end on the docks of Novorossiisk. She could have fled Russia at any time during the Civil War. She could have chosen to remain in France or England when the rest of Denikin's delegation returned. For two years she experienced great material hardship and endured exhausting trips by ship, train, freight car, and tarantass; the risk of being recognized and arrested; and the discord of the Kadets' contentious meetings. One of a tiny number of women in the liberal opposition's leadership, she surely felt isolated as well. Sofia's steadfast opposition to the Bolsheviks and her devotion to Nikolai help explain the physical and emotional stamina

Sofia, circa 1921. (pri-
vate collection)

this middle-aged woman, accustomed to wealth, comfort, and security, displayed throughout the war.

Yet after acting with boldness and independence in Petrograd's anti-Communist underground in late 1917, Sofia adopted a distinctly subordinate role during the Civil War. She attended countless meetings but seldom expressed her own views, subscribing unwaveringly to Nikolai's principles and positions. She served as his amanuensis and adviser, helping him draft memoranda and letters, and provided him with care and comfort. Nikolai's health, never robust in the best of times, was constantly in peril; and he lost what he loved most when the Communists took his beloved Moscow, his party fell apart, and his brothers died in the violence. From 1918 to his death, Sofia made providing him with unconditional political and personal support the primary focus of her life.

It is difficult to overstate the significance of this choice by a woman who until 1914 had lived in a female-dominated world. As a child she had lived in what she termed a matriarchy, dominated by two proud and strong-willed women, her mother and grandmother.[83] It took courage and determination for Sofia to claim her individuality and autonomy during her youth and early adulthood. After her brief marriage Sofia immersed herself in communities of other women—childhood friends, cousins, and her female coworkers at the Ligovsky People's House. There is no credible evidence of her romantic involvement with any man in the two decades following her divorce. When Sofia decided to link her fate to Nikolai's in 1918, she reproduced choices her mother had made decades earlier. After meeting the married Ivan Petrunkevich in 1879, Anastasia embraced the liberal principles he championed. Defying moral norms and the risk of losing her only child, she married him and devoted her life to his welfare and political cause. Like her mother, Sofia ignored both conventional moral norms and Nikolai's marital status. She followed Anastasia's example by forging a loving partnership in which the personal and the political were inseparable and her partner's reputation and well-being were paramount.[84]

Although Sofia gained the intimate companionship of a man she revered, the Civil War also brought her incalculable material and emotional loss. Fleeing Russia in 1920, she left friends and family, home and possessions, and the institution on the outskirts of St. Petersburg to which she had dedicated her life. Unlike many of her fellow Kadets, she left little record of her experiences and resisted the temptation to write her own interpretation of why everything went so wrong. Enough evidence remains, however, to reveal how large humanity's moral failings—those of Russians and Europeans alike—loomed in her explanation of the disaster. Sofia lost her faith in progress; it was replaced by a profound disillusionment with humanity that continued to darken her outlook in the decades that followed. War had turned her fellow Russians into "beasts" while Europeans watched indifferently from afar. Even principled liberals in the Kadet Party were not immune. The Civil War, in the words of the historian Oleg Budnitskii, was a "severe test for the theoretical and moral convictions of Russian liberals"—a test that in Sofia and Nikolai's experience, they failed.[85] The anti-Communist movement was tainted by reactionaries, militarists, and opportunists, and even friends like Miliukov made appalling moral choices. Sofia and Nikolai struggled with the ethics of supporting the White cause while abhorring its leaders' politics and conduct. Facing disunity and betrayal within the Kadet Party, they tried to remain loyal to liberalism's principles—individual freedom, reform, national unity, the rule of law, the primacy of reason over passion. Traveling across their ravaged country, they asserted their own humanity by condemning those brutalized by war. Observing how French and British politicians failed to appreciate the Communist menace, Sofia and Nikolai lost their faith in the West as a model for Russia's future.

11

"Our Bread Tastes Bitter in Foreign Lands"

Fleeing Novorossiisk as the Red Army shelled the port, Sofia joined an exodus of refugees from the revolution that ultimately numbered in the hundreds of thousands. They migrated to an archipelago of émigré colonies large and small extending from Paris, Berlin, and Belgrade to Harbin and San Francisco. Like many of her compatriots in the Russian diaspora, she settled in one island colony only to move to another, forced by economic necessity or the growing insecurity of living as a stateless person in interwar Europe. Sofia perceived her life in emigration as a personal, generational, and national tragedy. "Our generation," she reflected in 1939, experienced "the first great mass migration of modern times, with all of its hardships. . . . Wherever we went, we were considered undesirable aliens, with no right to work, no right to move . . . and last, but not least—we had to learn all the bitterness of the loss of one's own fatherland."[1]

The loss of their fatherland was both literal and metaphorical. The pain of separation was compounded by the catastrophe Sofia and her fellow émigrés saw occurring in Soviet Russia: dictatorship, repression, famine, and the destruction of the country's prerevolutionary culture and values. Although the years she spent in exile turned into decades, Sofia's grief at being severed from her Russian life never diminished.

Musing on the death of a friend from her years in Prague, she compared life in emigration to a barren desert. "The great tragedy for people who have lost their fatherland lies in the loss of the very *point* of their existence and the transformation of our lives into empty *existence*." Turning in horror from the "abyss" of a pointless life, she continued, "we . . . construct for ourselves the most varied defensive illusions, a kind of 'Potemkin village,' and immerse ourselves in the noise and in the bustle of life that externally fills the hours of the days as they hasten by, but does not nourish our hearts with life-giving water." In words that echo Dante's *Divine Comedy*, Sofia lamented, "our bread tastes bitter in foreign lands."[2]

Sofia may have sought to numb the pointlessness of émigré life by immersing herself in life's "noise and bustle," but what she constructed was no Potemkin village. On the contrary, she quickly adapted to the conditions of exile and reinvented herself more than once. Her adjustment to vastly changed financial circumstances is one example. Ksenia Denikina found her indifference toward the loss of her wealth remarkable. "Coming from a very distinguished and wealthy milieu," she wrote in her obituary of Sofia, "she not only adapted quickly to the wretched poverty of both the White movement and emigration, she simply began living on kopecks so naturally, it was as though she had never managed thousands, and if she sought out funds, it was only in order to help others."[3] From her arrival in Geneva at age fifty until she was in her eighties, Sofia earned her own living. Living extremely modestly herself, she also supported her elderly mother and scraped money together to send care packages to relatives and friends in Russia and Europe. Money was a constant worry for Sofia, but she never mourned the disappearance of her fortune.

Emigration transformed Sofia's personal life as well. After many years on her own, she now headed a household and lived within a mutually supportive, intimate family circle during most of her European years. Her elderly and often ailing parents found security and companionship under her roof. Writing from Prague, Anastasia described to a close friend the "energy and cheerfulness with which my daughter surrounds us both, and protects us from all kinds of life's thorns." Thanks to Sofia, Anastasia added in a well-meaning overstatement, their life together was a joyful one, and "we cannot complain of our fate at all."[4] In addition to caring for her mother and stepfather, Sofia exchanged the role she had fulfilled during the Civil War, as Nikolai's companion and political partner, for the more intimate relationship of spouse and, on occasion, nurse. She shed her reticence to let others glimpse her private life, and the entire émigré community considered her to be Nikolai's "civil wife" and recognized their union.

Finally, in emigration Sofia left politics to return to serving the needs of others. She stands out as one of the most creative and successful builders of "Russia Abroad"—the vigorous civil society that sustained the social and cultural life of émigrés in interwar Europe. Working at the League of Nations and later at the Tolstoy Foundation in New York, she also contributed to the construction of the modern international humanitarian regime for refugees in the early 1920s and during and after World War II. Wherever she settled, Sofia built networks of friends and collaborators to support her initiatives to aid refugees and émigrés.

Sofia left a comparatively rich body of private documents from this period, in contrast to the paucity of similar materials for her life during the revolution and Civil War. She stayed in regular contact with a number of close friends, such as the Denikins and her stepcousin Alexandra Petrunkevich, who preserved her letters and deposited them at Columbia and in other archives.[5] Many of these documents offer insights into the emotional complexity of Sofia's life in exile. Feelings of emptiness persisted despite an extremely busy schedule and tangible accomplishments. Loneliness coexisted alongside the supportive communities of friends and family she cultivated. In her final years, Sofia looked back on her life with both satisfaction and despair. Happy recollections of the people's house and a sense of pride in its positive influence dominate *On the Outskirts of Petersburg*, the memoir that she wrote in the United States in the late 1940s and allowed to be published after her death. At the same time, she confided enigmatically to Alexandra Petrunkevich in 1953, "I remember very little from the past with a light and happy heart." She goes on to confess that she recalled "much, much more that is painful, difficult and bad," the memory of which lay "like a heavy stone on my heart."[6] Sofia's life after she left Russia reveals the depths and contradictions of her character, as well as the despair and self-doubt that cast their shadow on this courageous and accomplished woman. Yet she did not sink under the weight of these feelings: instead she transformed her own pain into empathy and action on behalf of other refugees. Her insights into the grief born by involuntary migrants, expelled from their own nation and unwelcome in foreign lands, carry special resonance as her own experience replicated that of many other refugees in the twentieth century.

Sofia and Nikolai arrived in Constantinople in mid-March 1920, just when the city came under Allied military occupation. In addition to the challenges of imposing the peace settlement on the defeated Ottoman

Empire, the British, French, and American military authorities faced a humanitarian crisis of enormous proportions. Constantinople and its environs quickly filled with Armenians displaced by genocide, Kurds fleeing persecution, and a diverse and growing population of refugees created by the collapse of the anti-Bolshevik military campaigns in Russia: adults and children, White officers and Cossack cavalrymen, politicians and entertainers, social activists and black marketeers. The refugees aroused at least as much irritation as sympathy among Western observers. "The Russians are now invading Constantinople to such an extent that they attract everybody's attention, in spite of the cosmopolitan character of the city and the many additions since the war to its medley of races and Babel of tongues," the *Times* of London reported in April. In words that foreshadow the grudging reception Russians received in most countries of refuge, the correspondent complained that the "inter-Allied Passport Offices and the foreign Embassies and Consulates are beset by importunate Russians in quest of permits to continue their flight from Bolshevist barbarism to European civilisation." He railed against "the wiles of Russian versatility and persuasiveness" that the refugees allegedly employed "to overcome the repugnance of the Allies to admit any more destitute, or otherwise objectionable, Russians into their respective countries than they can possibly help." For Sofia and Nikolai, already embittered by the Allies' failure to provide meaningful support to the White cause during the Civil War, this kind of response to the plight of Russians fleeing the horrors of revolution and war surely deepened their disillusionment with European "civilisation."[7]

The refugees crowded into makeshift camps set up on the islands in the Sea of Marmara, where the typhus epidemic that plagued Russia during the Civil War continued to rage. British, American, and French humanitarian organizations provided some aid, while Russian organizations with experience dealing with refugees during World War I— the Red Cross, the Union of Towns, and the Union of Zemstvos—quickly reconstituted themselves. Linking up almost immediately upon their arrival with the Union of Towns, Sofia and Nikolai plunged into relief operations. These organizations, with their wealth of experience, access to Western and offshore Russian funds, and the administrative talents of people such as Sofia and Nikolai, constructed systems of emergency assistance to thousands of refugees in a remarkably short time.[8]

While committing themselves to relief work on behalf of fellow refugees, Sofia and Nikolai were not quite ready in 1920 to give up on efforts to influence Western policy toward Soviet Russia. In late June they left

Constantinople for Paris, the de facto capital of the Russian emigration, to join efforts to unite émigrés and inform Western public opinion about the devastating impact of Communist rule. There they reconnected with Kadet colleagues, attending frequent party meetings in Paris that wore Sofia out.[9] Hoping to awaken Europeans' conscience and sympathy, they brought along masses of materials about Russia's crisis, which they quickly translated into English and French. The couple stayed in Paris for only the month of July. After meeting an unnamed representative of a committee created by the British Parliament to gather information about Bolshevik Russia, they decided to seize the chance to influence British policy.[10] Arriving in London in early August, they testified several times before the "Committee to Collect Information on Russia," formed by Parliament in May 1920. Sofia told the committee the story of her trial and the testimony given in her defense by the worker Ivanov, which committee members interpreted as a bright ray of "comradeship and gratitude" amid the tragedy and terror experienced by British subjects as well as Russians during the revolution.[11] She and Nikolai also talked with anyone who would listen—"[with] parliamentary activists, with representatives of the clergy, charitable organizations, with workers' organizations, simply with people," and tried to get their "protest against the bloody atrocities" published. The response was discouraging. After listening to them, people "shook their heads, sighed, [and] uttered sympathetic words," Nikolai lamented; then they would declare "that it was impossible to print this material, for the demand for it had passed, the public was no longer interested, it wants to rest from the horrors of war and all kinds of cruelties."[12] The summer months Sofia and Nikolai spent in Paris and London turned out to be as unproductive in winning Western support as their trip there one year ago, as members of General Denikin's mission. Paris and London were no longer celebrating their victory in the Great War, but in the view of Sofia and Nikolai, Europeans still ignored Russia's sacrifices for the Allies during the war and its suffering under Soviet rule.

The couple did enjoy some brighter moments. In England they reunited with friends who knew and appreciated what they had endured, including Ariadna Tyrkova-Williams and her husband Harold and the Denikins, who had also found temporary refuge in England after fleeing to Constantinople from Novorossiisk. Ksenia Denikina's photos of Sofia and Nikolai in the Denikins' garden help to convey the comfort such reunions brought, when painful memories of war and defeat could be assuaged temporarily with a game of croquet and a cup of tea.

Nikolai in England, circa 1920–21. On the back: "At our house in England, 1920–21. N. I. holds a croquet mallet. He played with Nadya and me in our little garden. Ks. Denikina." (Columbia University Bakhmeteff Archive, S. V. Panina Collection, Box 6)

Sofia in England, circa 1920–21. On the back: "At our house, when we lived in England. 1920–21. Ks. Denikina." (Columbia University Bakhmeteff Archive, S. V. Panina Collection, Box 6)

Despite the company of friends, Nikolai soon sank into a state of profound depression—"psychic numbness," he called it—brought on by recollections of the deaths of his brothers, friends, and countless other victims of the Civil War. Emotionally vulnerable and weakened further by the London weather, he fell gravely ill with pneumonia and pleurisy, to which he had long been susceptible. He spent September in a London hotel and a nursing home, afterward moving with Sofia to rural Devonshire, where he was admitted to the Dartmoor Sanatorium— a private, cottage-like institution for the treatment of tuberculosis.

Sofia hardly left his bedside during the seven months they lived at the sanatorium.[13]

Nikolai's illness at first seemed to be something of a blessing in disguise. Writing to Tyrkova-Williams in early October, Sofia called the sanatorium "an idyll after the Russian hell." There in the deep English countryside, twenty miles from the nearest railroad, they listened to songbirds sing all day and owls hoot all night; ducks quacked and chickens cackled under their window. The tranquility and charm of the Devonshire countryside soon wore off, however, when autumn's rains, then winter's deep snows arrived. To Sofia's horror the sanatorium's English personnel continued to open the windows wide to provide plenty of fresh air to the patients. "We are freezing something awful," she told her friend in December; "it is almost impossible to write, for one has to do so in gloves."[14] Nikolai's condition would periodically improve, only to worsen again, causing Sofia great anxiety. Money was also a constant worry; the penniless couple survived at this time thanks to the charity of friends, and they wondered how they would make a living once Nikolai was well.[15]

Unable to speak English and forbidden by his doctors to write letters or sometimes even to read, Nikolai became completely dependent on Sofia. "I regret more than I can express," Sofia wrote Tyrkova-Williams, "that I cannot take part in the work to aid our refugees, but you yourself understand, that at present that is *completely* impossible." Nikolai was still bedridden, his condition grave, and "he would be completely helpless [without me] in an environment where not a single living soul speaks in any language other than English."[16]

Desperate to follow events and stay in contact with friends and party associates, Sofia read aloud from newspapers to Nikolai for hours a day and furiously wrote letters on his and her own behalf. "We here, in our total isolation, live from newspaper to newspaper and passionately await news from Constantinople, but so far we have no letters from there," Sofia wrote Ksenia. "As for the Russian political intrigues in Paris, we follow their chronicle with mental anguish and irritation."[17]

While Sofia and Nikolai were buried in the English countryside, the Communists won a decisive victory in the Russian Civil War by defeating Baron Peter Wrangel and the last of the White forces in November 1920. To make matters worse, in March 1921 the British signed a trade agreement with Soviet Russia, further demonstrating to Sofia and Nikolai the West's abandonment of the White cause. The news from Paris about the state of the Kadet Party was equally discouraging.

Miliukov now advocated a "new tactic": an anti-Communist alliance with the Socialist Revolutionary Party. His proposal once again threw the Kadets into turmoil and threatened to split it apart.[18]

Nikolai was finally well enough to leave Dartmoor Sanatorium in April 1921. After months of observing the upheavals in the Kadet Party from afar, he and Sofia were able to participate in the central committee meetings in Paris in May and June that led to its demise. Deeply opposed to Miliukov's "new tactic," Nikolai and Sofia, again acting as political partners, advocated a compromise position that they hoped would save the party. Though still convalescing, Nikolai threw himself body and soul into this last-ditch effort, while Sofia, who previously seldom spoke at party meetings, took an unusually active part in this dispute.[19] Their anti-Miliukov faction narrowly prevailed, but the victory proved to be a Pyrrhic one; for all intents and purposes, the Kadet Party ceased to exist after this. The demise of the party that had dominated the lives not only of Sofia and Nikolai but also of Sofia's parents plunged the entire extended family into dismay. Writing from New Haven, where Anastasia and Ivan had found a temporary home with his son Alexander, Sofia's mother filled her long letter to "my dear friends, Sofyushka and Nikolai Ivanovich" with exclamation marks as she bemoaned the "unexpected, and sad . . . and terrible" party split. Nikolai blamed "that rotting swamp of the Russian emigration with its hysterics, intrigues, scheming, [and] squabbles." Thus the first period of émigré life for Sofia and Nikolai, from their arrival in teeming Constantinople in March 1920 through the summer of 1921, deepened their disillusionment not only with Western politicians but also with their own.[20]

Yet these months were also constructive ones, for the isolation that Nikolai's illness imposed enabled the couple to put distance between themselves and the catastrophe they had experienced, and to gain perspective. Nikolai later called this period a time of reflection and renewal. The mutual dependence that bound the couple together also deepened. In him Sofia found someone who truly needed her, while Nikolai credited her with saving his life: "S. V. nursed me back to health and won me back from death," he wrote a few years later.[21]

In June 1921 Nikolai and Sofia moved from Paris to Geneva, headquarters of the League of Nations, where they lived for the next three years. The couple went there as the designated representatives to humanitarian and international organizations of the "Russian Zemstvo-Town Committee for Aid to Russian Citizens Abroad," or Zemgor. The committee was created in Paris in early 1921 out of the remnants of the wartime relief association of the same name, a federation of the Union of Zemstvos and the Union of Towns, and was recognized by émigré leaders as the main source of charitable assistance to Russian refugees.[22] By this time the refugee problem had become a crisis. Europe had barely begun to absorb the first wave of refugees when Wrangel's defeat unleashed another flood of tens of thousands into Constantinople. In February 1921 leaders of the Russian Red Cross and the International Committee of the Red Cross sent urgent appeals to the League of Nations to address the crisis.[23] The league, which began operations only in January 1920, responded cautiously, unwilling to commit itself to providing any direct aid but prepared to appoint a special high commissioner for Russian refugees—with the proviso that he should not be a Russian. An intergovernmental conference on the crisis in August 1921 confirmed this approach, and the post of high commissioner was offered to Fridtjof Nansen, the Norwegian Arctic explorer who already served successfully as high commissioner for repatriating prisoners of war.[24] After accepting the appointment in September, Nansen formed an advisory council composed of representatives of sixteen international and Russian organizations already involved in relief to Russian refugees, including Zemgor. As its representatives in Geneva, Sofia and Nikolai became original members of this council, joined by a physician, Iu. I. Lodyzhensky (1888–1978), representing the prerevolutionary Russian Red Cross, and a diplomat, K. N. Gulkevich (18??–1935), former Russian ambassador to Norway and Sweden, representing the Council of Russian Ambassadors.[25]

The creation of the Office of the High Commissioner for Russian Refugees at the League of Nations marks a major turning point in the history of international humanitarianism. For the first time nations collectively acknowledged a responsibility to address the urgent needs of a mass of people displaced by war. But it began operations with very limited responsibilities and powers. The league made it clear from the outset that it considered the crisis to be temporary and Nansen's position to be a short-term one.[26] The office's bureaucratic home was in the league's Commission on Social Questions, which also dealt with such issues as human trafficking and the opium trade (and also, oddly, Esperanto)—serious problems to be sure, but in the eyes of the Russians on the Advisory Council, hardly equivalent to the refugee crisis.[27] The league provided funds only for the office's administrative costs: governments and private relief organizations were expected to supply the money for aid. Guided by the reluctance of member governments to

take broad responsibility for the refugees, Nansen announced in September that his objectives included the following: taking a census of all
refugees in Europe; organizing the resettlement of refugees in any
country that would take them; encouraging and facilitating aid by governments and private organizations, but not at the league's expense;
unifying and coordinating the organizations providing relief; creating
a legal status and identity documents for refugees that national governments would accept; and developing plans for repatriating refugees.
His office, in other words, would address the crisis primarily by providing administrative direction, organizational support, and legal aid.[28]

Over the course of the three years they spent in Geneva, Sofia and
Nikolai grew frustrated with international humanitarianism in general
and the high commissioner in particular. As refugees themselves, they
along with the other Russians on the Advisory Council provided a voice
for their stateless and destitute fellows. But they struggled to make that
voice heard against what they considered to be member governments'
grudging acceptance of minimal responsibility and the league's refusal to provide sufficient funds. Nikolai complained that international
humanitarianism was "factory charity," controlled by "heartless, brisk
young people, very quick, very industrious, like traveling salesmen,
having nothing in common with charity."[29] Already concerned that
the famine crisis in Russia in 1921–22 would overshadow the refugees'
plight, he and Sofia grew alarmed as European governments moved
toward recognizing the Soviet regime. "My God," Sofia wrote to a friend
in May 1922, "[look at] all the repulsive monsters at every level of international European life, the crown of which is sparkling at Genoa"—a
reference to the international conference that had just ended, where
Western nations took steps to establish economic relations with Soviet
Russia. While Sofia voiced her criticisms in private letters, Nikolai regularly sent lengthy reports to Zemgor in Paris, in which he dissected all
the twists and turns of the league's policies and the shortcomings of the
high commissioner.[30]

The couple's disillusionment came from several sources. Their recent
harrowing experience of civil war and flight, combined with their inexperience with foreign affairs, made the diplomatic conventions that
governed the international bodies in Geneva look insincere. The slow
pace of intergovernmental policymaking and the miserly funds provided by the league and member nations looked like gross neglect of
refugees' urgent needs. The diplomat Gulkevich commented on their inexperience with international politics to fellow Russian diplomat M. I.

Girs at the end of 1921, noting how the "extremely well-meaning" Sofia and Nikolai, along with Red Cross representative Lodyzhensky, assigned "a naively touching significance" to their mission.[31] To be fair to the league and its members, the Council of Russian Ambassadors in Paris had considerable sums at its disposal, derived from former imperial and provisional government assets located abroad. But those funds were not as large as the legends about vast reserves of "Russian gold" led Europeans to believe, and they were insufficient to meet the needs of hundreds of thousands of refugees. Moreover, the conflicts in Paris between the Council of Ambassadors, which controlled the funds, and Zemgor and the Red Cross, which dispensed them, cast their shadow in Geneva, complicating the relations among the four Russians on Nansen's Advisory Council.[32]

Sofia and Nikolai also distrusted Nansen from the outset, regarding him as pro-Soviet. Just before becoming high commissioner for refugees, he directed the league's efforts to aid victims of the famine in Soviet Russia, where Nansen had cordial relations with Soviet officials and even honorary membership in the Moscow Soviet. Sofia and Nikolai were horrified by the sufferings of those starving in Russia but feared that a focus on famine relief by the league would strengthen the Soviet regime and work to the detriment of hungry and homeless refugees, for whom aid was already insufficient. While they had reservations about Nansen, they detested his Swiss assistant, Eduard Frick, who appeared to dominate the high commissioner and revealed his pro-Soviet sympathies through his indifference toward refugees and ill-informed hostility toward émigré organizations. After several months in Geneva, Sofia summed up the situation. "All the work with foreigners for Russia and Russians has many thorns," she reported, with the fate of the refugees in the hands of the "polar bear" Nansen and Frick, his "extremely brisk and clever escort." Nansen's dual role as head of refugee aid and aid to famine victims in Soviet Russia complicated the situation: "the refugee question suffers very much, for it drowns in the enormity of the famine question." In arguing with Nansen over his unforgivably lenient attitude toward the Soviet government, she pointed out, "we [the Russians on the council] spoil our relations with him in refugee affairs."[33] Not only Nansen and Frick, but the entire League of Nations, in Nikolai's view, regarded Russian refugees with "undisguised hostility" as "the past that will not return. We are not strange and not interesting [unlike the novel Communist state of Soviet Russia]. We are the fallen who will never get up."[34] For his part, Nansen, a well-intentioned man and a

scientist, not a politician, was confused and discouraged by the disagreements among the Russians on his own council and in Russian
émigré organizations that claimed to represent refugees.

Nevertheless, the high commissioner and his Advisory Council
could claim some successes. By May 1922 Offices of the High Commissioner were located in fourteen European countries. Nansen reported
to the league's council in July 1923 that virtually all of the Russian refugees in Constantinople had been evacuated and resettled.[35] The high
commissioner could also claim credit for solving an acute problem for
the stateless refugees: their lack of official, legal identity documents,
which made it extremely difficult for them to live, work, and travel. The
problem became urgent at the end of 1921, when the Soviet government
issued decrees that deprived virtually all Russians living abroad of citizenship. Nansen and his Advisory Council developed a proposal for a
special identity certificate for Russian refugees. The certificate came to
be known as the "Nansen passport." Reporting to Zemgor in Paris,
Nikolai claimed credit for getting the high commissioner to take into
account proposals submitted by émigré Russian jurists and to remove
the offensive term "refugee" from the title of the certificate.[36] At a
league conference in July 1922, European governments approved the
document and resolved to adopt it themselves or recognize it on their
territory. By September 1923, thirty-one countries had agreed to accept
the Nansen passport. The document had its limitations and could not
be said to give refugees full legal rights. Some countries, such as Czechoslovakia, issued their own identity papers to Russian refugees that were
more advantageous for work or travel. All the same, the Nansen passport eased the lives of refugees by regularizing their legal status.[37]

The issue of repatriation proved to be far more explosive. Upon arriving in Geneva in June 1921, Sofia and Nikolai were aghast to discover
that non-Russians, even ones working in humanitarian organizations,
believed that the best and only solution to the refugee crisis was to return them to Russia—a "malignant idea," Sofia wrote, that she and
Nikolai tried to expel from their "sheep heads."[38] Nansen, they discovered, also considered repatriating refugees to Soviet Russia to be the
best solution to the crisis since his office had insufficient funds to resettle
them permanently in Europe. He trusted the Soviet authorities to treat
returnees fairly, without reprisals. At the same time the high commissioner knew from his own visits to Russia in 1921 that sending refugees
back to a country where famine and epidemic disease still raged was
hardly a good idea. Nansen revived the issue of repatriation in 1922, to

the dismay of Sofia and Nikolai and against the energetic and unanimous opposition of Russian representatives in Geneva. The high commissioner argued that action was necessary because some groups of refugees, Cossacks in particular, now expressed a strong desire to return to their homeland; some were already doing so on their own.[39]

Originally dead set against repatriation, Sofia and Nikolai modified their position in the spring of 1923, causing a schism within the Russian minority on the Advisory Council and a nasty public uproar in the émigré community. The dispute between them and the Red Cross representative Dr. Lodyzhensky first erupted over an alternate version of a resolution on repatriation proposed by Sofia and Nikolai at a meeting of the council on April 20. They sought to address a dual problem: a "crisis" in Poland and Romania, whose governments were now moving to expel Russian refugees by force, and the desire on the part of some refugees to go back to Russia voluntarily. Their resolution called on Nansen to intercede on behalf of refugees in Poland and Romania and to negotiate with the Soviet government to gain immunity and guarantees for refugees who returned. As is often the case with resolutions, a quarrel that arose over differences in wording was rooted in both a disagreement over principle and personal antipathies. Lodyzhensky interpreted Sofia and Nikolai's version, which the council adopted, as an abandonment of the heretofore unanimous opposition by émigré organizations to repatriation under any circumstances. Sofia and Nikolai regarded their position as a necessary response to the dire situation of refugees in Poland and Romania and the need to gain the high commissioner's protection for those who truly wished to return home.[40]

The dispute demonstrates the émigré community's propensity for public squabbling and the antipathies that divided its leadership. Lodyzhensky communicated his outrage in angry letters to Sofia and Nikolai, copies of which he circulated to émigré leaders and organizations far and wide. Sofia and Nikolai ceased to exchange even a polite hello with him.[41] While Sofia privately criticized the doctor for misrepresenting their position, rejecting their efforts at reconciliation, and spreading lies, Nikolai publicly defended their position in the émigré press.[42] Zemgor passed a resolution supporting its representatives in Geneva and affirming their integrity. But the public quarrel accentuated Nikolai's flaws in the eyes of others. For the influential Tyrkova-Williams, who headed the Russian Refugee Relief Association in London, the controversy reinforced her already low opinion of him. Former Minister of War in the Provisional Government A. I. Guchkov wrote Gulkevich that "I have known [Nikolai] for a long time. . . . And in my entire life I have rarely met such a lying, two-faced and petty person. This episode with 'repatriation' fully reflects his physiognomy." The quarrel does not seem to have hurt Sofia's reputation, perhaps because of the broad respect she enjoyed, but also because of a perception that she followed Nikolai blindly. Sofia is an "excellent woman," Lodyzhensky wrote to a mutual friend, but "she is not free and not separable from N[ikolai] I[vanovich]. The latter belongs to the category of people whose quirks [*vyverty*] are so deep and whose reserve of civic courage in the face of foreigners so small that it is better to give up on him."[43]

Was Sofia really so subservient to Nikolai? What was the actual relationship between the couple by this time? The differences in the way each adjusted to life in emigration during these early years provide some insight. Nikolai immersed himself in the back-biting world of émigré politics and the discouraging work of trying to extract support for refugees from European governments still suffering from the Great War's economic and political fallout. He relied on Sofia for her expertise in foreign languages and at the typewriter. Prone to depression and illness, he depended on her for emotional support as well. By contrast, Sofia's mother described her in 1922 as "full of cheerfulness and life, as always. . . . I could not be more amazed by her energy and industriousness." Sofia embraced new opportunities and kept herself constantly occupied, remarking in many of her letters how extremely busy she was. She completed a two-year course of study to become a librarian and applied for a job at the library of the League of Nations in April 1924.[44] As she had throughout the revolution and Civil War, Sofia participated in the shark tank of Russian politics with evident reluctance, avoiding the public conflicts that her colleague Tyrkova-Williams relished. While serving as Nikolai's political secretary and supporting his political positions, she set an independent direction for her own life—one that was intentionally nonpolitical. Perhaps Sofia disagreed with Nikolai in private at times; but in the public arena she set aside any difference of opinion she may have had out of her intense personal loyalty to him.

After their exhausting, often dangerous travels during the Civil War, the couple enjoyed a measure of stability in the rooms they shared with Sofia's parents in a modest, cramped *pension* on Geneva's garden-like outskirts. Three surviving letters that Sofia sent Nikolai in October 1921, when he was in Paris on Zemgor business, offer a glimpse into a relationship that was both a political and a domestic partnership. She wrote him every day during his absence and sent him three telegrams as well. Her letters, which focus on her efforts on behalf of a trainload of Russian students stranded in the Balkans, indicate a relationship dominated by refugee affairs and intrigues within the émigré community. She addresses him formally as Nikolai Ivanovich, in the second person plural. While this sounds odd to modern ears, such formality of address was not uncommon between spouses of their generation and class. The letters close with a wish for his good health or a "friendly handshake" (*zhmu Vashu ruku*), and are signed "S. P." For all their business-like formality, the letters reveal the warmth and concern that lay at the foundation of the couple's relationship, in which Sofia assumed the role of guardian of Nikolai's health and well-being. "I hope that you . . . will have dinner every day, and not catch cold," she gently admonished him. "Today I will mentally be at your report and am very, very sorry that I won't hear it. I am afraid that you are very tired from the trip, and the meeting will be hard. . . . Don't linger in Paris, and return as soon as possible." "Are you well . . . and not too exhausted?" she asked two days later. The housekeeper thoroughly cleaned your room in your absence, she added, and then wrote him, "I eagerly await your return and am completely orphaned without you."[45]

Mutual affection and dependence bound all four members of Sofia's household. United by common memories, they could lend each other a sympathetic ear as they experienced deep nostalgia for Russia. For Nikolai it was intense memories of prerevolutionary Moscow, a city of ancient churches and a vibrant modern civic culture, whose destruction under Soviet rule he recounted in lectures and articles in the émigré press. For Sofia it was Marfino, the estate both she and her mother dearly loved. In May 1922, perhaps inspired by the arrival of spring in Geneva, Sofia penned a lyrical reminiscence. Remembering the billowing masses of lilac bushes that are one of Marfino's distinctive springtime features, she wrote how "the tender rays of the morning sun pour out joy over this flowering kingdom, and bees, drunk with the fragrance, hurry to it from all sides." While whistling swifts plied the air above, she reminisced, the "kingdom of flowers and colors, light and shade" found their perfect reflection in the estate's mirror-like lake below.[46]

The elderly Petrunkeviches relied completely upon Sofia; without her, Anastasia wrote in 1922, she and her husband "would have both been lost." Sofia's emotional support became all the more important when they received tragic news about relatives still in Russia, where

Ivan's youngest son and his wife died of typhus, his daughter was murdered, and his eldest son was imprisoned. Nikolai had long revered Ivan, regarding him as a political mentor and confidant. Sofia's mother in turn admired and appreciated Nikolai as an "excellent person, intelligent and sincere and at the same time an energetic and serious worker"; "the better we come to know him, the more we love and value him."[47] Like most émigrés they had very little money. Ivan depended entirely on remittances from his son Alexander, an internationally known but modestly paid professor at Yale University. Sofia supported herself and her mother by her earnings from Zemgor, typing, and translation. (She translated much of General Denikin's memoirs into French.) Her letters repeatedly express worry over making ends meet. Sofia also received a steady stream of appeals from friends, acquaintances, and complete strangers for information, advice, a recommendation, and money—a continual reminder of the difficulties endured by fellow refugees.[48]

Sofia's budget came under even greater strain when the opportunity arose in 1921 to send "Nansen" and "Hoover" parcels with food and clothing to friends and relatives in Soviet Russia through humanitarian channels. The easing of repression in Soviet Russia following the introduction of the New Economic Policy that year also made it possible for former coworkers at the people's house in Petrograd to correspond with Sofia. During most of that decade she was able to send them letters of her own, along with food parcels. Sofia carried these precious letters with her as she moved from Geneva to Prague and then across the Atlantic. Her decision to preserve this correspondence reveals the extent to which her self-identity depended on the people's house and her relationships with the women who formed its inner circle.[49]

Filled with expressions of sisterly love and longing, reverential admiration and gratitude, the letters reflect the enduring influence of Sofia's charisma on her friends, now intensified by nostalgia in the radically different conditions of the Soviet 1920s. They are filled with bittersweet memories of a shared mission and productive lives before the catastrophe of revolution. Alexandra, for example, writing on the occasion of the twentieth anniversary of the people's house, thanked Sofia for the "enormous beneficial influence you had on me—you cannot define or measure it."[50] Former visitors and neighbors, including even the occasional Communist, remembered her and her institution with respect and gratitude, Sofia's friends assured her. "I almost forgot to tell you about one typical thing," Alexandra wrote Sofia's mother in November 1923. "Recently I was told that a dog constantly hangs around Kuznetsk Market (near Nikolaev Street). All the traders feed it 'because this is Sofia Vladimirovna's dog.' Where they got the idea that it belonged to S. V. is unknown, but the fact itself is very touching."[51] Sofia's correspondents described their intimate gatherings over tea to commemorate anniversaries in the history of the people's house and recounted for her the empty pomp and rhetoric of the official celebrations, such as the one for its twentieth anniversary in 1923. They often remarked on the absence of "soul" in the institution after the revolution, using its spiritual decline as further proof of Sofia's unmatched and inspiring leadership.[52]

Sofia also heard directly from three working-class visitors who took considerable risks when they wrote to express their gratitude to a former enemy of the people and White supporter. The first letter arrived in 1925, addressed to "our dear, beloved Russian Woman, most ideal soul" from A. Golubev, who had been a "pupil" at the people's house from 1904 to 1907. Golubev expressed his longing for her to return home to her native Russia—for it must be sad, he commiserated, to live "in an alien land." Recently he went back to the Ligovsky People's House to find out how it had survived the revolution, he told her. Though still intact, it no longer had any soul. Please come back, he begged, and "if living here in the motherland is [financially] difficult, I will share my pay with you."[53]

Pavel Mikhailov, once a member of the circle of proletarian writers at the people's house, used the occasion of the institution's twenty-fifth anniversary in 1928 to tell Sofia how every year, one hundred "old Panintsy" gathered at Christmas to reminisce. Written with impeccable penmanship, his letter recounted how he was nineteen years old and deeply ashamed of his illiteracy when he first came to her institution. There he and others like him not only learned to read and write, but were "reeducated . . . in the spirit of a free school, which no longer exists anywhere." The institution's influence, he continued, may be seen not only in his own transformation but in the lives of many other former visitors "from the masses" who now held "responsible posts." Sofia may have smiled with amused pride when she read Mikhailov's comparison of the people's house to the elite lycée at Tsarksoe Selo in the time of Alexander I, which educated Pushkin and "a whole pleiade" of other talented people. The influence of the people's house, Mikhailov proclaimed, was much greater than the lycée's.[54]

Writing in 1936, when shrill warnings from the Kremlin about "wrecking" by foreign agents were fueling a wave of mass repressions, the third correspondent took an even greater personal risk in contacting

Sofia. But a stricken conscience outweighed his apprehension. The anonymous writer offered his thanks to "Sofia Vladimirovna, Divine, Ideal Woman of the Russian Land" for her services to "the Russian People and in general to the people of various nationalities, so broadly does the greatness of your soul extend." Punctuation fell by the wayside when he gave voice to his emotions and his longing for Sofia's return:

> Sofia Vladimirovna a grave rebuke lies on us that is on your pupils for "not preserving what we have" but if your pupils would protect you, and conditions stayed the same then I would think that it would not be harder for you to survive [here] than you survive there far away in an alien land. We have not forgotten you the memory of you is preserved our dear Sofia Vladimirovna. This is what I wrote, but I am afraid to sign it they say to have connections with abroad but you probably know there about the conditions here? I would like you to return to the motherland goodbye Sofia Vladimirovna.[55]

Whether written by friends or former visitors, the letters Sofia received from Soviet Russia in the 1920s and 1930s expressed a yearning to reconnect with the prerevolutionary past, regardless of their writers' attitudes toward the revolution. Her correspondents sought that connection in ideals they believed the people's house represented—freedom, friendship, unity. Though separated geographically and politically from all the "old Panintsy," Sofia herself embodied that longed-for continuity for them better than the building she had constructed, which had survived the revolution but lost its soul.

As her correspondents in Leningrad perceived, they still possessed one thing Sofia did not: their motherland. Sofia's letters to her friends in Leningrad do not seem to have survived, but since Alexandra's letters to her sometimes echo what Sofia wrote to her, they open an indirect window into Sofia's emotional life during her first decade of exile. The older woman's affectionate and reassuring words were often a response to Sofia's sadness over her separation from Russia, as well as her feelings of unworthiness and self-doubt. In two letters from late 1923, for example, Alexandra made reference to Sofia's expressions of disappointment with herself in letters of her own. "You can tell yourself that you sowed only good," Alexandra reassured her, "and thousands of people carry this good in their souls."[56] Don't think you are no longer able to serve your motherland, Alexandra advised her in 1925. You can still use your talents to serve Russia from abroad, and "convince people, and especially your fellow countrymen, of the necessity, for the benefit of the motherland and their own benefit, not to shun the renewed motherland." Try to understand Soviet Russia, obtain reliable information about it and disseminate that truthful information abroad, Alexandra urged, and "raise the younger generations to love their motherland." In letters that frequently comment on the changes produced by the revolution, Alexandra sought to come to terms with it herself. "You see," she wrote Sofia, "nothing can stop the growth of the masses or their striving to be equal participants in the life of the world." At other times, Alexandra offered Sofia sympathy rather than advice, assuring her that she understood the "lasting sorrow you carry with you, having been deprived of what is most dear—the motherland, one's native soil." There is nothing worse for someone such as you, Alexandra added, who loves the motherland with all her heart.[57]

Corresponding with her old friends provided Sofia with emotional support as she experienced the grief and tribulations of exile. It is not difficult to imagine the comfort Alexandra's words brought her as she adapted to émigré life, the disillusionment of working with Europeans on the refugee crisis, and the certainty that she would never see Russia again. She could express feelings to her distant correspondents that she doubtless needed to suppress as she attended to the physical, financial, and emotional demands of caring for her ailing, elderly parents and the sensitive, melancholy Nikolai.

As Alexandra had urged, Sofia did find another chance to serve her motherland—in Prague, the city that rivaled Paris as the capital of the émigré Russian community in interwar Europe. After a long visit there in early 1924 to explore employment opportunities, Sofia accepted a position as the paid founding director of the "Russian Hearth" (*Russkii ochag*), a community center for Prague émigrés, and held that position until late 1938. Sofia and Nikolai, along with her parents, moved from Geneva to Czechoslovakia in August 1924 and settled in the village of Roztoky u Prahy, situated just north of the city on a high bank of the Vltava River. Roztoky's rural surroundings, primitive conditions, and unpaved roads frequented by geese and ducks initially reminded Anastasia of a Russian village. The four moved into a six-room house with a big vegetable garden on the edge of the settlement, which they shared with another large family. When they arrived, their three rooms were barely furnished, and the house lacked electricity and running water.

But it was comfortable, Anastasia reassured a friend, and better than the living conditions that many impoverished émigrés had to endure. At least there was a large common dining room, she noted, which allowed them to avoid entertaining guests in their bedrooms, as some émigrés were forced to do. "So you see," Anastasia gamely concluded, "there are very good aspects to our new life; I can foresee that there will be difficult ones as well, but who doesn't have those? Especially in the Russian emigration, which lost everything, even the fatherland!"[58]

Six months later Anastasia's initial enthusiasm for her new home had waned. The house had all the inconveniences of a rural village and few of its charms. Anastasia and Ivan were ill for much of the winter. Soon after they arrived the house became extremely crowded. Anastasia, Ivan, Nikolai, and Sofia occupied the first floor with Nikolai's nephew Dmitry, Ivan's grandson Ivan, and Sofia's cousin Nadezhda Zurova, who had finally escaped from Petrograd after a spell of imprisonment for trying to leave illegally. Members of three other families lived on the second floor. At one time there were as many as twenty people sharing the house, yard, pump, and common dining room. In Geneva Sofia and her family had some help, but in Roztoky the residents did all the housework. Sofia, Nikolai, and her parents lived in the rickety house at least until Ivan died in 1928, a demise hastened, perhaps, by the bouts of flu and bronchitis that afflicted Anastasia and Ivan every winter.[59] Sofia and Nikolai commuted daily into Prague by tram. After three years in Geneva, Sofia found it challenging at first to live in Czechoslovakia, a "provincial European backwater."[60]

Despite the crowded and primitive conditions, the extended household shared the political beliefs, values, and experiences of the liberal émigré intelligentsia. Sofia became close friends with the matriarch of the family upstairs, Adelaida Vladimirovna Zhekulina (1866–1950), with whom she had worked on aid to refugees in Constantinople in 1920.[61] Before the revolution Zhekulina ran a well-known secondary school for girls that she founded in Kiev while also raising nine children (she gave birth to a total of twelve). Her membership in the Kadet Party placed Zhekulina on the Bolsheviks' list of enemies to be shot. She managed to flee Kiev in 1919, but her youngest son, nineteen-year-old Gleb, was taken hostage and killed. Arriving in Constantinople, Zhekulina established several elementary and secondary schools for refugee children, funded by the YMCA and a number of wealthy Americans. In early 1921 she succeeded in evacuating the teachers, students, and staff from Constantinople to the Czech town of Moravská Třebová, where her boarding school for Russian high school students thrived for the

next two decades. A successful fundraiser as well as a respected peda-
gogue, Zhekulina, like Sofia, held a number of leadership positions in
émigré educational, cultural, and relief organizations. According to her
grandson, she was so well-known in Czechoslovakia that its postal service unfailingly delivered letters addressed only to "Madame Zhekulina, Prague." He remembers her as a rather stout woman with a bit of a
waddle, expressive brown eyes, a cheerful manner, and an infectious
laugh. Her contemporaries also respected the sharp intellect that lay
behind her genial and upbeat manner. But when the residents gathered
every day around 5 p.m. for tea, it was the stately Countess Panina who
sat at the head of the table and presided over the samovar.[62] Zhekulina
and most of her family soon moved out of the house, but she and Sofia
continued to collaborate through the 1930s on their shared calling—
providing educational and cultural services to the children and youth
of Prague's Russian community.

Sofia's new institution, the Russian Hearth, was the brainchild of
Dr. Alice Garrigue Masaryk (1879–1966), daughter of the founder of independent Czechoslovakia and its first president, Dr. Tomáš Masaryk.
The institution was part of Czechoslovakia's broad-based and generous
aid program for Russian refugees, known as "Russian Action" (*Russkaia
aktsiia pomoshchi*, in Czech *Ruská pomocná akce*), which subsidized schools;
paid stipends to students, scholars, and prominent émigrés; and supported cultural institutions like the Hearth. In addition to its institutional donors—the Czechoslovakian government, President Masaryk's
chancellery, the Czechoslovakian Red Cross, the League of Nations, the
YMCA, and the Carnegie Endowment for International Peace—the
Hearth received donations from individual philanthropists, most no-
tably the wealthy Chicago industrialist Charles Crane (1858–1939) and
his son John (1899–1983), who were Russophiles and friends of Tomáš
Masaryk. Russian Action was unique: no other nation provided such
extensive support to the revolution's refugees. Historians differ over
the political reasons that motivated the new Czechoslovakian government in 1921 to allocate its scarce resources to Russian refugees, but
one major impetus came from the personal commitment of President
Masaryk and his family. Lovers of Russian culture, the Masaryks sympathized with the exiles' plight, for they had experienced persecution
and exile themselves as nationalists in the Austro-Hungarian Empire.[63]

Alice Masaryk was a teacher, sociologist, social worker, and friend
of Jane Addams from Chicago, where she had studied for several years.
Like Sofia, she had been a political prisoner: during World War I she
was arrested by the Austrian authorities and spent several months in a

Vienna prison.[64] Once Czechoslovakia became independent, the new president's daughter became the president of the Czechoslovakian Red Cross, a position she held until 1938, and established the country's first school of social work while also serving as her father's official hostess. Alice Masaryk and Sofia first met in Geneva in 1922, while Sofia was still involved with the League of Nations. Although Alice was six years younger, the two women bonded over their common experiences of exile and imprisonment and their shared commitment to social welfare. They began laying plans for an institution that would not only support young Russian refugees but also preserve "the torch and hearth of our culture," as Sofia explained to Zhekulina.[65] Sofia resettled in Prague in 1924 at Alice Masaryk's invitation. The personal friendship she developed with the Masaryks had its material as well as emotional advantages, as the family helped ease her legal and financial situation on more than one occasion well into the 1930s.

The Russian Hearth opened in November 1925. Sofia rented several rooms for it in the center of Prague—spacious and sunny quarters that accommodated a library, reading room, lecture and meeting rooms, and of course, a tearoom and snack bar. The center quickly attracted a large clientele, at first comprised primarily of students. Reporting to Alice Masaryk in 1928, Sofia enthused that the Hearth's premises were "always full, even overflowing," with young people who spent the entire day in its "warm, clean, and bright rooms."

> They leave only for lectures. They study here, breaking into groups and helping each other. They always have tea and something to eat in the tearoom. They spend their free time in intellectual pursuits, they sing in the choir, take part in the theater studio, or simply read. They support each other in the professional mutual aid organizations that have arisen thanks to the "Russian Hearth." We now have professional associations of doctors, agronomists, chemists, artists and many others.[66]

With its full calendar of concerts, lectures, and meetings, the aptly named Hearth became a center of Russian civil society in Prague and the colony's cultural home. It aligned with the original mission of Russian Action and also Zemgor, which supported a network of Russian schools in Czechoslovakia and other European countries: to resist the assimilation of young émigrés, or what was termed with horror as "denationalization," in the hope that they would soon be able to return to the motherland and use their education to rebuild it.[67]

Though small in scale compared to the Ligovsky People's House, the Hearth resembled it in several ways. As in St. Petersburg, Sofia was not only the center's director but its moral leader. At the same time she drew inspiration from other women, such as Adelaida Zhekulina and Alice Masaryk, as she had from Alexandra Peshekhonova in the 1890s, and relied on a mostly female staff, including her cousin Nadezhda Zurova, a veteran of the Ligovsky People's House, who worked at the Hearth as a librarian. Of course, Sofia had nowhere near the funds at her disposal that she was able to shower on the Ligovsky People's House as the heiress to the Panin fortune. But with leadership on the board of directors in the hands of her friends and patrons Alice Masaryk and John Crane, she exercised considerable autonomy through the 1920s and enjoyed access to government and private funds. To be sure, the Hearth was not exactly what Alexandra Peshekhonova had in mind when she advised Sofia in 1925 to use her talents to serve her country from exile and raise the younger generations to love their motherland. In Sofia's vision, the Hearth served the aim of preserving the mother-land's cultural, intellectual, and moral legacy in the younger generation until they were able to return. That motherland was the old, prerevolu-tionary Russia of liberal reforms and Pushkin, not Alexandra's new motherland of socialist revolution and radical poets like Mayakovsky. But the Hearth continued the mission of the Ligovsky People's House in other ways, by employing high culture, education, and community to enlighten the minds, better the souls, and cheer the lives of the iso-lated and marginalized—whether they were working-class men and women in a Petersburg slum or impoverished, despised exiles forced from their homeland by the revolution.

Sofia's first years of life in Prague were relatively happy ones. The Hearth provided her with the full, active public life she was accustomed to; it also gave her an outlet for her homesickness and patriotism. She distanced herself from the political factions in Paris and Geneva that carried on complex, endless quarrels over who lost Russia to the Com-munists. Prague was the emigration's academic and scholarly capital, dominated by intellectuals, professors, and social activists like herself. They created a separate world of their own schools, institutes, volun-tary associations, and community centers. Members of the colony from her generation engaged little to not at all with the affairs of their host country; Sofia was unusual among them in knowing some Czech.[68] In addition, the Czechoslovakian government remained an anti-Soviet ally in the eyes of émigrés by not recognizing the USSR until 1934, whereas Great Britain, France, and Germany all capitulated in the early

Sofia in Musco-
vite costume at
the "Evening of
Slavic Women,"
Prague, 1930. (pri-
vate collection)

to mid-1920s. Finally, thanks to her stable position at the Hearth, she, Nikolai, and Anastasia were able to move from Roztoky after Ivan Petrunkevich's death in 1928 to much better accommodations in the center of Prague.

Sofia was respected and beloved as a pillar of this insular community. She lent her administrative talents to numerous charitable and cultural associations, such as the Federation of Russian Aid Organizations for the Needy, which she founded in 1934. Her passionate commitment to preserving Russia's cultural legacy was felt in other émigré communities across the archipelago as well. In 1925 she became the chairperson of the annual festival known as the "Day of Russian Culture," a position she held until she left Czechoslovakia. Taking place

Sofia (*standing, sixth from right*) and Nikolai (*sitting, second from right*) with members of the
Russian community, Prague, 1929. (private collection)

every year on Pushkin's birthday, the event sought to unite the Russian
diaspora while reminding the rest of the world of the great contributions of Russian literature, art, and music. The first Day of Russian Culture took place in Prague on June 8, 1925; by 1928 it was celebrated by
the Russian communities in seventeen different countries, including
the United States and China.[69] Sofia occasionally visited other émigré
colonies to participate in the annual events. In 1933, for example, she
traveled to Riga and Revel (Tallinn) to lecture on Ivan Turgenev, the
novelist with the "blindingly white" hair whom she had met in Moscow decades before as a little girl, and whose story of tragic love in *Nest
of Gentlefolk* had captured her heart when she read it as a schoolgirl in
the Catherine Institute.[70]

Nikolai also created plenty of outlets for his talents and experience
in Prague. While still belonging to Zemgor, he largely shunned the
"swamp" of émigré politics and immersed himself in the Prague colony's
thriving academic life. A prolific, indefatigable writer, he published essays on the history of Moscow and Russian self-government, a 350-page
autobiography covering his life up to 1906, and a coauthored volume
on the Russian government during World War I for the series published
in the 1920s by the Carnegie Endowment for International Peace.[71] Like
Sofia he served on numerous committees and boards and filled his days

with meetings. While Sofia dedicated herself to preserving Russian culture abroad, Nikolai concentrated on preserving the record of its recent
turbulent and tragic history. His most important legacy is the Russian
Historical Archive Abroad, a rich repository of personal and official
papers from the era of the Russian Revolution and Civil War that he
helped establish and build. When the Red Army occupied Czechoslovakia in 1945, it removed the "Prague Archive," as it is known, to Moscow's
main state archive, where it remained off-limits to most researchers,
Russian and foreign, until the 1990s.[72]

As the 1930s began and the world slipped deeper into economic
crisis, the tenuous stability of Sofia's life in Prague began to dissolve.
The Czechoslovakian government ended its funding for Russian Action
in 1931, leaving the Hearth to rely on the generosity of the Masaryks
and the Cranes, and its own modest revenues. Sofia's salary as director
was reduced by half. The diminished resources forced the Hearth to
move twice to smaller quarters. As young émigrés completed their
education, established families of their own, and found jobs in Czechoslovakia or moved abroad, the number of visitors to the Hearth also diminished. Sofia remained its director until she left the country in 1938,
but her letters from the 1930s often express sadness over its decline and
pessimism about its future.[73]

Then her beloved mother died of cancer in April 1932, after four
weeks of great pain and suffering that Anastasia bore with courage and
patience. Although Sofia stayed with her day and night, Anastasia's
death was so sudden and terrible "that I am like a wounded beast that
cannot find a place for itself," she told her stepbrother Alexander.
Adding to her grief were the financial burdens of Anastasia's final illness and burial, which forced her to ask Alexander for help.[74] Sofia
found some comfort in writing about her great loss to friends and relatives who knew her mother. But the solace religion can provide eluded
her. "Now [Anastasia] lies beside Ivan Ilich," Sofia wrote, "and if I had
the grace of faith and I could believe that she is united with her beloved, it would not be so hard for me."[75]

This rare confession of her lack of religious faith provides further insight into how Sofia adapted to life outside of Russia. Other émigrés were sustained by their devotion to their Christian faith. Raised
in a devout home, Nikolai remained committed to the Russian Orthodox Church. Other previously nonreligious émigrés such as Tyrkova-
Williams turned to the church for spiritual comfort and support. But
the "grace of faith" was not bestowed on Sofia in emigration or earlier,

during the trials of the Civil War. A brief but revealing entry from late September 1919 that she jotted down in a notebook reinforces this impression. After the funeral mass in Rostov for Nikolai's slain brothers and the Moscow Kadets, she found comfort in the quiet church, illuminated by candles, and peace fell on her soul "like a life-giving dew." But the moment passed quickly, and her note ends with a cry of despair: "how far we still are from peace!" Nor could she believe any more in the prerevolutionary intelligentsia's secular faith in progress, which had once inspired her social activism; revolution and civil war had destroyed her belief in human reason and perfectibility.[76]

Two years later, in the summer of 1934, Sofia suffered an even greater blow—the death of Nikolai. Since he regularly fell ill with pneumonia and other respiratory diseases and then recovered, she refused to believe that this latest episode would be fatal. With Sofia constantly by his bedside, Nikolai hung on for four weeks until he finally succumbed on August 12 at 2 a.m.—a date and time Sofia carefully noted in his last pocket diary.[77] The loss of her cherished companion transformed the resilient, composed Sofia into an inconsolable widow. "Sofia Vladimirovna continues to be in a completely abnormal condition," wrote one acquaintance in Prague to Miliukov two weeks after Nikolai's death. "She's given up everything and sits for entire days at the grave. . . . I fear for her. Spiritually there is nothing for her to live for. The Hearth is dying, she's surrounded by people who are well beneath her level— how will she live?"[78] Sofia admitted to the Denikins that "it is so unbearably hard for me now that I cannot write at all. . . . My life is completely pointless now and necessary to no one." Although she received numerous condolence letters, which she lovingly preserved and excerpted in a special notebook, the tributes that Nikolai's friends and associates paid to him did little to diminish the pain of being left entirely alone. "Loneliness is a very terrible and difficult thing," she confessed to a friend in Paris three years later, "and I am growing used to it only with great difficulty." To make matters worse, the Russian Hearth seemed to be on its last legs, and "life here in general is getting more and more meager, in all respects."[79]

The situation in Prague grew even worse after Britain, France, and Italy signed the infamous Munich Agreement with Germany in September 1938, which allowed Hitler to annex parts of Czechoslovakia that bordered Germany. The failed effort to appease Hitler and avert another European war caused panic and turmoil in the country that had been Sofia's home for fourteen years. Writing in October to a friend in Switzerland, Sofia compared Czechoslovakia to a country at war. Its borders had been sealed, banks were closed, and railroads were at a standstill. Prague teemed with refugees and seethed with hostility toward foreigners. Unemployment soared, and the authorities were beginning to expel Russians. "Thus are great events reflected in the fates of little people," she mused. "Everything that is happening here now reminds me of our 1918, to my horror. I must confess that it is not a happy thing to live through this again." The conditions facing Czechoslovakia were so difficult, she continued, that she decided to give up the meagre government salary she still received as director of the Russian Hearth, even though the prospects of finding other work were very small.[80]

   In the midst of this crisis, Sofia suddenly received the necessary documentation for an American visa from Alexander Petrunkevich in New Haven. She hated to leave Prague but felt she had no alternative: "only in America will I be able to still make some kind of living."[81] Crowds of friends and colleagues assembled at the train station to say farewell when she departed for Paris in mid-December, the first stage of her journey to the United States.[82] One month later Sofia sailed from Le Havre for the New World. The new war that she had foreseen erupted in September 1939. It soon engulfed the European colonies of the Russian émigré archipelago and created another humanitarian crisis, one whose enormity no one at the League of Nations in 1921 could have ever imagined. Once again a refugee, Sofia brought to America the insight and compassion she had acquired for the plight of those who were rejected by their own nation and unwanted in those where they desperately sought asylum.

Epilogue

Sofia's ship sailed into New York harbor on a very cold day in late January 1939 after a week at sea. Among fellow passengers on the SS *Champlain* were hundreds of other European refugees, many of them Jews fleeing the advance of Nazism in Central and Eastern Europe. Other than noting Sofia's "senility" (she was sixty-seven years old when she arrived), the United States Immigration inspector found her to be in good health and permitted her to enter the country. For the third time since 1920 she faced the challenge of reinventing herself in a strange land. As a little girl she had imagined herself as a moccasin-wearing Indian and cherished a statue of young George Washington, but she never saw herself stepping onto American shores. Except for a long sojourn in France in the mid-1950s, Sofia lived in the United States for the remainder of her life. As she had during her years in Prague, she found work to support herself, causes to keep her engaged, and friends to connect her to the émigré community. She applied for a Social Security card in 1939 and became an American citizen in 1944. But the final years of her life were nomadic ones, and she continued to suffer the pain of her exile from Russia, her only true homeland.[1]

The émigré colony in New York City was the largest in the United States. It supported a thriving civil society of mutual aid societies, youth organizations, and religious institutions. Sofia's stepbrother's home in New Haven was a short train ride away. Sometimes called the "king of spiders," Alexander Petrunkevich (1875–1964) was one of the world's most eminent arachnologists. He was educated at the University of Moscow and the University of Freiburg, Germany, but settled in the United States in 1903 after marrying an American. His scientific accomplishments won him international renown and induction into the National Academy of Sciences in 1954. "Pete" was a famous and beloved figure at Yale, where he had taught since 1910. In a laboratory filled with dozens of live tarantulas, he held weekly social gatherings where he served strong Russian tea prepared on a Bunsen burner.[2] The widowed Alexander warmly welcomed his stepsister into his home and into the circle of other Yale professors of Russian origin, which included Sofia's old friend and fellow Kadet Michael Rostovtseff (1870–1952) and another historian, George Vernadsky (1887–1973), the son of the scientist who was her fellow assistant minister in the Provisional Government. Alexander also offered a rare link to her childhood and her mother, Anastasia, who had lived at Alexander's with Ivan in New Haven for a time after the revolution. But Sofia soon concluded that it was impossible for her to earn a living in New York, a city "not for someone of my years, and too exhausting"—and rather frightening as well. Nor did she wish to stay in New Haven and become dependent on her stepbrother. Like countless immigrants before her, Sofia decided to seek her fortune—or at least, a way to support herself—in California.[3]

Sofia lived in Los Angeles for about a year, making her home with the family of Dr. Gregory Altshuller, a physician and family friend whose father had been Nikolai's doctor during his final illness (and also one of Tolstoy's at Gaspra). After the cold and snow of winter on the East Coast, California's sunny climate and natural beauty enraptured her. She marveled at the city's markets, where Japanese vendors sold a dazzling array of fruit at prices so low that she was able to eat it every day, "despite my meager budget." She admired the small, charming one-story houses of Los Angeles, each with its own garden. Los Angeles is so vast that it is not like a city at all, she explained to friends in Paris; everyone has their own cars, and public buses carry only "proletarians like me."[4] Although making a living was a constant struggle, Sofia managed by giving private French lessons and by doing occasional translations. The enterprising countess also turned to handicrafts to supplement her income: for the Christmas holidays she made dolls dressed in Czech and Slovak national costumes, and at Easter she sold her handmade painted eggs. While not providing a steady source of income, her handicrafts found a ready market.[5]

Sofia was so intrigued by life in California that she wrote three short essays entitled "California Impressions," which she published in a Paris émigré newspaper in 1939. The first essay describes a performance she attended by the Negro Theatre Project, a New Deal program created to provide work to unemployed artists.[6] The musical, called "Run, Little Chillun'!," captivated and moved her. It opened a window into the dialect, life, and culture of African Americans, and she was impressed by the deep religiosity the musical depicted. But Sofia was skeptical toward another form of American religious expression she observed in Los Angeles, Christian revivalism. Her second feuilleton recounted a visit to the gigantic domed church built by Aimee Semple McPherson (1890–1944), where she heard the famous evangelist preach to a large audience. Unmoved by McPherson's reputed charisma, Sofia disdained the evangelist's flashy style of preaching and self-promotion, and she accused McPherson (unfairly) of neglecting the needy while collecting millions of dollars in donations. Her third sketch about California praised a patriotic women's group called "Pro America" for its stand against communism and fascism and its inspiring dedication to freedom and democracy. "I have seldom seen such unity of enthusiasm, energy, mind and discipline," she enthused, "in the pursuit of those cultural tasks that stand before every conscious citizen of a free country."[7] Additional exotic features of her new country were revealed when Sofia traveled in August 1939 to Arizona. Alexander Petrunkevich's daughter Anya lived with her husband, whom Sofia described as "a real cowboy," on a cattle ranch in the mountains near the Mexican border. The spectacular landscape reminded her of Crimea. While Alexander captured tarantulas and scorpions she hiked in the mountains, hoping not to encounter any rattlesnakes.[8]

The eruption of war in Europe the following month cast a deep shadow on Sofia's explorations of her new country. When she first heard about the war, she told friends in Paris, "my heart literally stopped in terror." Many of her oldest friends and closest relatives lived in France, and a beloved cousin had moved to Poland just a few months before the war broke out. Stranded on the West Coast, Sofia felt isolated and helpless; "I curse my fate that brought me to such distant parts, and I am oppressed by my uselessness."[9] Anxious to assist friends and family stranded by the war, she was initially determined to return to Europe. Instead she moved back East in the summer of 1940, where she threw herself into work for the Tolstoy Foundation.

Named after the author of *War and Peace*, the foundation was established in February 1939, when Sofia joined a group of prominent Russian-Americans in a meeting at the New York apartment of Boris Bakhmetev, Russia's last non-Communist ambassador to the United States. Its original purpose was to provide relief to Russian émigrés in prewar Europe threatened by the escalating economic turmoil, political uncertainty, and threat of war. While many of the other founders had lived in the United States for years, Sofia had just experienced in Prague the very humanitarian crisis that the Tolstoy Foundation was created to address. Her prestige within the Russian diaspora, prior work in refugee relief, and recent experiences in Prague after the Munich Agreement made her a compelling advocate for the new organization.

The president of the new foundation was the writer's youngest daughter. Alexandra Tolstoy (1884–1979) had lived with her ailing father at Sofia's Crimean estate in 1901–2, but the two women had never met before New York. Remaining in Russia after the October Revolution in order to preserve her father's literary and spiritual legacy, Alexandra Tolstoy endured imprisonment and repression. She finally left the USSR in 1929. After two years in Japan she moved to the United States in 1931, where she eked out a living by lecturing and egg farming. The two women may have been introduced to each other in 1939 by a mutual friend, a nurse named Tatiana Shaufus (1891–1986), who knew Sofia from Prague; in addition to working for a Russian refugee aid committee there, Shaufus nursed Nikolai during his final illness. Like Sofia, she left Czechoslovakia for the United States in 1938.

With its headquarters in New York City, the foundation's governing board and honorary members included such prominent Russian-Americans as the composer Sergei Rachmaninoff (1873–1943), director of the Boston Symphony Orchestra Serge Koussevitzky (1874–1951), and aviation pioneer Igor Sikorsky (1889–1972). Alexandra Tolstoy also recruited a number of Americans with Russian experience, such as Dr. Ethan Colton, who had worked for the YMCA twenty years earlier. Former president Herbert Hoover, the director of the American Relief Agency's famine assistance in Russia in the early 1920s, agreed to serve as the foundation's honorary chairman. An assortment of White Russian aristocrats and Ivy League professors of Russian origin joined bankers and members of the city's social elite on the governing board,

adding luster to the new organization's solid social and financial credentials. In 1941 the foundation expanded its reach when it received
the gift of Reed Farm, a seventy-five-acre estate with a large house and
several outbuildings located near the town of Nyack on the Hudson
River, north of New York. The foundation still conducts modest activities there today.[10]

Although Sofia left New York for California soon after the creation
of the foundation, she worked on its behalf by giving lectures to potential American and Russian-American donors there. In one titled "The
Russian Emigration in Europe," which she gave in 1939, she described
to her Russian-speaking audience the strong communities that émigrés built in Europe even while they suffered legal disenfranchisement
and hostility from their reluctant hosts. As a country of immigrants, the
United States drew no distinction between natives and the foreign-born,
she reminded her audience with sincerity if not complete accuracy; America opened its doors to all, while other countries regard the immigrant as
an internal enemy who steals the very bread from the mouths of "true"
citizens.[11]

Fundraising is disheartening work, Sofia discovered. The outbreak
of war in Europe gave rise to a host of other, more "fashionable" causes,
and "Russians do not show to advantage." Stranded in exotic California, far from friends and relatives in Europe, she felt useless and
powerless—"an extremely detestable condition."[12] Yet for reasons that
are unclear, she stayed in California until mid-1940. When she finally
moved back to New York City in the fall, she rented a room in Alexandra
Tolstoy's apartment on Riverside Drive. Although working at the Tolstoy Foundation gave her a sense of purpose, Sofia still chafed at being
distant from Europe and felt even more cut off after the United States
entered the war at the end of 1941. As she had in the 1920s, she sent aid
parcels to friends and relatives, but she still felt frustrated at not being
able to do more.[13]

During the war the foundation concentrated its modest resources on
sending aid to Russian émigrés and prisoners of war who were trapped
in Europe. Once the war ended, its activities increased significantly. It
joined the United Nations, European and American governments, and
other private agencies in the massive effort of assisting the millions of
people who filled the camps in Europe and the Middle East for displaced
persons. Under the leadership of the able Tatiana Shaufus, the foundation established resettlement offices in Europe and South America for
refugees from the Soviet Union and built institutions for those too

elderly to move to a new country. Back in New York Sofia handled the huge volume of letters the foundation received from people seeking aid, lost relatives, or just an outlet for their suffering. After the war she moved to the foundation's Reed Farm, whose dormitories, farming operations, and cultural activities provided a temporary home in the late 1940s and early 1950s for thousands of former residents of European refugee camps of diverse nationalities.[14] Sofia took particular care to welcome them. One of them remembers Sofia as a kindly though "majestic" figure who wore a long grey dress in the style of the turn of the century and helped the immigrants learn English.[15] In the small cottage she shared with three other women, Sofia met almost every evening with an orphaned boy from Persia, whom she tutored in English and other subjects. When Ariadna Tyrkova-Williams arrived from France in 1951, Sofia was at the New York dock to greet her.[16]

While her work with the Tolstoy Foundation made her feel useful, it also reinforced her feelings of despair and frustration. So many people wrote directly to Sofia to beg for help that she felt herself drowning in letters: "I am overwhelmed by both an awareness of my own lack of means and, most of all, by the immeasurable human grief and unhappiness," she lamented in 1946.[17] The harrowing stories she heard from former slave laborers, prisoners of war, and other victims of both Nazi and Soviet violence not only revealed the extent of suffering caused by World War II, but also reminded her of the violence and inhumanity she had witnessed firsthand in Russia in the aftermath of World War I. What is more, the governments of Western nations and agencies like the United Nations Relief and Rehabilitation Administration were making the same mistakes, she believed, as the Allies and the League of Nations after the Russian Revolution. The Yalta Conference in February 1945, where Stalin, Churchill, and Roosevelt began laying plans for a postwar Europe, demonstrated the same willingness to appease the Soviet regime, failure to appreciate its true nature, and unwarranted trust in its good faith. The handling of refugee resettlement, Sofia charged, was "criminal and idiotic"; the Western nations largely acquiesced to Soviet demands for the repatriation of POWs and refugees to the USSR, where they ended up in the Gulag.[18] The advent of the Cold War brought additional disillusionment, as Sofia despaired over Americans' lack of understanding of the important differences between the USSR and Russia, whose prerevolutionary history and culture she had dedicated herself to preserving. "As always they lump us all together," she commented bitterly.[19]

Sofia with her step-brother Professor Alexander Petrunkevich circa 1950. (private collection)

The victims of World War II who appealed to Sofia for aid may not have realized that the onetime heiress had to earn her own living. In addition to giving private lessons, translating, and doing secretarial work for the Tolstoy Foundation, Sofia became the paid assistant on a new project—a biography Alexandra Tolstoy was writing of her famous father. The work of researching, typing, and editing the book added income and considerable intellectual stimulation to Sofia's life, along with occasional irritation at Alexandra Tolstoy's temperamental personality.[20] In 1953, when the biography was finally published, Alexandra offered Sofia the position of director of a new home for the elderly at Reed Farm. Now eighty-two years old, Sofia declined. She was delighted to learn, however, that her secretarial work qualified her for Social Security, and she was thrilled with her new monthly pension—of fifty dollars.[21]

Sofia never possessed a home of her own during her years in the United States. She spent the summer months in New Haven with Alexander and the rest of the year in the cottage she shared at Reed Farm. She occasionally returned to New York City to stay with her niece (actually, the granddaughter of a cousin) Evgenia Lehovich and her husband Dmitry. During these visits she would take care of the two Lehovich children, who later remembered their aristocratic babysitter's youthful and energetic manner, musical voice, and playfulness. One time, they recall, she blew up a big white balloon, drew a face on it, and batted it around the room while talking in a funny voice.[22] Sofia enjoyed listening to the New York Philharmonic on the radio and visiting the Metropolitan Museum of Art. She even ventured into American cuisine: her papers include a recipe she jotted down for a casserole made with canned fish, canned cream of mushroom soup, and a crust of crumbled potato chips; another recipe was for a "salmon loaf" made with Bisquick and topped with—what else?—cream of mushroom soup.[23]

Like many Russian émigrés of her background and generation, Sofia harbored ambivalent feelings about the United States. She admired the women of "Pro America," perhaps because their dedication to developing citizenship in a free democracy reminded her of her own goals at the Ligovsky People's House. But the strong pragmatic tendencies in American life contrasted sharply with the idealism of the prerevolutionary Russian intelligentsia. Americans may have much good in them, she wrote a friend soon after arriving, but there is also a great deal that is "half-baked."[24] Written in New Haven in the late 1940s, her memoir about the Ligovsky People's House explicitly compares Russian selflessness with American materialism and individualism. Americans were also superficial, Sofia seemed to think. Take the ubiquitous word "okay": it is an American expression that means nothing, she wrote in "California Impressions," "and at the same time means everything, which you can use with the same success in the most diverse instances of life."[25] Despite Sofia's sympathy for the plight of displaced people and her celebration of the United States as the land of immigrants, she found the postwar influx of Puerto Ricans hard to accept: their "wild and primitive customs," she complained to her cousin in France, were making them "the plague of New York."[26] It is not surprising that Sofia found it difficult to like America's individualistic ethos, restless tempo, and ethnic diversity. She had spent almost two decades before coming to the United States in the insular, self-absorbed, and largely homogeneous communities of the Russian diaspora, collaborating with friends and associates who shared the values and experiences of her generation. After spending a year in southern California, where she seems to have enjoyed discovering aspects of America's diverse culture, Sofia returned without regret to familiar Russian enclaves in New Haven, New York, and Reed Farm.

Sofia's postwar letters also repeatedly express her longing to leave the United States and join her beloved cousins and old friends in Paris. You will find me easy to live with, she wrote Tatiana Osorgina in 1952 in response to the younger woman's invitation; "with all of my deficiencies you may be certain that, first of all, I have no pretenses whatever and am always satisfied with everything, and second, I never 'take offense,' that quality is absolutely foreign to me."[27] In the meantime she continued to spend her modest savings on countless parcels to relatives and friends in war-ravaged Europe, sending them clothing, shoes, bedding, vitamins, medicines, and small luxuries like coffee well into the 1950s.[28] A number of factors delayed her departure, including a bout of Ménière's disease, characterized by deafness and vertigo, and the immense task of organizing her personal papers for donation to Columbia University. Her dream of returning to Europe finally materialized when her ocean liner arrived in France on September 1, 1954. Sofia spent more than a year in Ste.-Geneviève-des-Bois, a Russian émigré colony outside Paris, but by the end of 1955 she was back in the United States.

Her surviving letters offer no insight into the reasons why she did not stay in Europe permanently, as she had once intended. Perhaps by this time America felt as much or as little like home as anywhere else. Two world wars had forced Sofia to seek a new home, livelihood, and purpose in a foreign country. Every place she lived felt distant from the memories she cherished of St. Petersburg, her people's house, and its dedicated circle of loving coworkers and soulmates. She was already advanced in years when the second exile in 1939 placed an ocean between her and lifelong friends, the graves of loved ones, and ties to her homeland. "I understand," she told a friend after the war, "that I exchanged hell for paradise when I left Prague, but for me there can be no paradise without those whom I loved, and my heart is tied inseparably to the Russian soil and to the soil of Olshansky Cemetery," where Nikolai and her parents were buried.[29]

Despite feeling displaced and disillusioned, Sofia adapted well to her second involuntary exile. Already proficient in English, she did not face the language barrier that complicates the lives of many refugees. Despite her age she managed to find work that, while sometimes insecure or ill paid, provided her with economic independence and the ability to help others. She discovered exotic landscapes, cultural curiosities, and interesting new social phenomena in her adopted country. It was painful, to be sure, to be separated from the people and places in

Europe that she loved. But living in America made it possible for her to renew relationships with friends similarly swept across the Atlantic by war and revolution, such as Anton and Ksenia Denikin, George Vernadsky and Michael Rostovtseff in New Haven, and her old Kadet comrade Ariadna Tyrkova-Williams. They shared not only her prerevolutionary values but also her experience of Russia's catastrophe. She created new social networks in the Russian community in America as well and formed affectionate bonds with her arachnologist stepbrother, the young Lehovich family, and Alexandra Tolstoy. These relationships, along with good health and her characteristic energy, kept Sofia active and independent right up to the last two months of her life.

In late April 1956, several months after returning from France, Sofia suffered a stroke that paralyzed the right side of her body and rendered her unable to speak. She was taken to New York's Roosevelt Hospital, where at first it seemed that she might recover. But as the weeks passed, she slipped in and out of consciousness. Friends and family worried not only about her worsening chances of recovery but also her mounting hospital bills. Although she worked continually from the time she arrived in the United States, Sofia managed to save very little and spent much of what she earned on assistance to friends and relatives. When Alexandra Tolstoy announced that the foundation could not assume all the responsibility for her friend's hospital costs, relatives raised enough in donations to cover her care for a few months. After contracting pneumonia, Sofia died on June 13, 1956, two months shy of her eighty-fifth birthday. At the requiem mass celebrated at the Russian Orthodox Church of Christ the Savior in New York City, friends placed three red roses in her coffin and an icon of the Kazan Mother of God in her hands. Her funeral took place at Reed Farm a few days later on a hot, sunny Saturday, after which she was buried at the nearby cemetery of the Novo-Diveevo Russian Orthodox Convent.[30]

Outside of a small circle of loving friends and relatives, the death of this once highly respected social reformer and political pioneer attracted little notice. In her beloved St. Petersburg, now Leningrad, a few surviving coworkers from the Ligovsky People's House, such as the theater director Gaideburov, would have remembered her. If they heard about her death, they may have mourned her in private; but in Khrushchev's Russia it was still dangerous to mention former enemies of the people in any way other than to condemn them. In the Russian diaspora Sofia had outlived most of her fellow Kadets and other leading representatives of her generation. A few friends who shared Sofia's experience of

Sofia's grave, Novo-Diveevo Cemetery, Spring Valley, New York, November 2013. The two graves to the right behind hers are Tatiana Shaufus's and Alexandra Tolstoy's. (photograph by the author)

revolution and exile published obituaries in the émigré press in New York City and Paris. Full of praise for this "remarkable," "amazing" Russian woman, their tributes dwelled on the paradoxes of Sofia's life. She was the fabulously wealthy aristocrat who once had so many estates, she jokingly told Tyrkova-Williams, that she could not remember them all; but for the last three decades of her life, she eked out a modest living by her own labors. She was the countess whose personal qualities—unstinting generosity, devotion to the cultural advancement of common folk, and a warm, natural way of interacting with people across the social divide—belied her august origins. To Sofia's eulogists, this descendant of tsarist ministers who dedicated her life and fortune to advancing democratic principles was a symbol of prerevolutionary Russia at its

best and of the progress it would have made had not war and revolution derailed the course of reform.[31]

But Sofia Panina was much more than a symbol; she was an active
agent of the changes that swept across the social, cultural, and political
landscape of late imperial and revolutionary Russia. One of those
changes was the emancipation of women. While she never called herself a feminist, Sofia followed her mother's example in fighting for autonomy in her personal life. She eagerly pursued the unprecedented
opportunities for social advancement and influence that opened for
women during her lifetime. From being a star pupil in a sheltered
school for privileged girls, she evolved into an intellectually curious
student and a social reformer who rejected stereotypes of female benevolence. To be sure, Sofia's wealth and social connections enabled her to
enjoy a degree of independence out of reach for most women. Nonetheless the contributions she made to creative and progressive social reform
before 1914—higher education for women, cultural advancement for
working women and men, support for young women in danger of falling
into prostitution—demonstrate the major role that women of her generation played in producing the thriving civil society that emerged in
urban Russia in the late nineteenth and early twentieth centuries. With
the outbreak of war in 1914 Sofia translated this experience into supporting Russia's war effort on the home front. When the fall of the
monarchy in February 1917 made women's demands for equality attain-
able, she lent her reputation and influence to the cause of cajoling the
country's new all-male leadership to grant women their rights. Entering
city and national government in 1917, Sofia became one of the most
notable representatives in Russia and beyond of women's new status as
full citizens.

Sofia's life also paralleled the evolution of the liberal intelligentsia of
late imperial and revolutionary Russia. Her life exemplifies the support
for social progress and political reform that came even from the aristocracy, the class with the greatest stake in maintaining the old regime.
The Kadet Party, founded by Sofia's stepfather and financed by her
mother, included other titled aristocrats, such as Prince Obolensky,
Prince Shakhovskoy, and Prince Pavel Dolgorukov, as well as members
of the hereditary nobility. They downplayed their class identity and
privileged status to fight for democracy and civil rights against monarchists on the right and socialists on the left. The price many of them
paid was high. Sofia's mother defied her powerful Panin in-laws and
lost custody of her daughter in defense of justice and the rule of law.

Others, like Shakhovskoy and Dolgorukov, paid with their lives. Sofia suffered imprisonment and prosecution and might have met a harsher fate had her trial not been the first conducted by the inexperienced Petrograd Revolutionary Tribunal.

Sofia and Nikolai, Ivan and Anastasia, and other leaders of the Kadet Party based their Russian brand of liberalism on the principle that politics should be above class. Disregarding their own privileged status and the inequalities of Russia's stratified society, they imagined a future democratic state founded on civic, not economic, equality. They also sought to subordinate party affiliation to what they imagined to be the common good. From the very beginning of the liberal movement, when her stepfather tried to forge an alliance with terrorists in the late 1870s, they tried to implement their faith in shared goals by reaching across ideological divisions. Sofia enacted her own liberal faith in such alliances long before she herself entered politics, when she sheltered and supported socialists and dissidents like Tolstoy at the people's house and on her estates. In 1917 her own ministerial positions in the coalition Provisional Government were products of Kadet efforts to find common ground with parties on the left, and her willingness to enter that government demonstrates her commitment to these liberal hopes.

Thanks to her philanthropic work, Sofia had more actual experience than most liberals in interacting with people from different class and ideological backgrounds. At her people's house she observed firsthand how working women and men aspired to better themselves. She saw how they eagerly seized the opportunities to write their own poetry, have fun at a dance or a movie, attend a lecture on history or biology, or bring the family to drink tea and listen to Sunday readings of Pushkin and Tolstoy. The Ligovsky People's House convinced her of the possibility of a shared culture and cross-class cooperation in pursuit of common goals. She believed that just as she had emancipated herself, its working-class visitors longed for their own fulfillment as individuals and citizens and would follow her well-intentioned lead toward an enlightened, westernized future for Russia.

She was right—until war and revolution proved her wrong and brought profound disillusionment to a woman whose optimism and resilience had previously sustained her through disappointment and adversity in her personal life. Sofia's experiences in 1917 and the Civil War betrayed her faith in the working people she thought she knew. The women and men who came to her people's house, it turned out, were not like the masses at large. Horrified by the drunken, wanton behavior of Petrograd crowds and the inhumanity she witnessed during the Civil War, Sofia does not seem to have understood war's devastating impact on her fellow Russians. A parallel betrayal came out of Sofia's brief career in the anti-Bolshevik movement—an irreversible disillusionment with the West, once the model of Russia's future for liberals, now revealed to be a faithless, unprincipled former ally. The years in emigration, when she worked to ease the sorrows of fellow refugees, only accentuated the loss of the confidence Sofia once had in the possibility of social progress and her faith in the West as a source of virtue. Toward the end of her life she confessed to having lost all faith in the "'enlightenment' of humanity"—a striking admission from a woman who had committed her life to this very cause.[32]

At the same time Sofia never ceased to look for continuities as she experienced the great disruptions of twentieth-century history. In exile she overcame economic hardship and moral disillusionment by recommitting herself to serving others. Still believing in the ability of one person to make a positive difference, she contributed to humanitarian projects in Europe and the United States to help those whose lives had also been ruined by war and revolution. She threw herself into the construction of a thriving civil society in the Russian diaspora that would ensure the survival of the prerevolutionary culture and principles she valued. Courageous and resilient, she never succumbed to adversity. Not only in exile but throughout her entire life, Sofia demonstrated a remarkable capacity to reinvent herself while remaining true to her most cherished values—generosity, honesty, and loyalty to friends and country.

Notes

Introduction

1. The Russian Social Democratic Workers' Party (RSDWP) was the pre-revolutionary predecessor to the Communist Party. The State Duma was Russia's first national parliament, introduced in the midst of the 1905 Revolution.

2. See the 1991 booklet by the director of the institution, Kim Nikolaevich Izmailov: *Novye zaboty starogo kluba* (Moscow: Vsesoiuznyi nauchno-metodicheskii tsentr narodnogo tvorchestva i kul'turno-prosvetitel'noi raboty, 1991).

3. She died in 1956 in New York City and is buried in the Russian cemetery in Spring Valley, New York.

4. The copy was painted in 1989 by Iu. V. Belov.

5. The conference presentations were published as M. Iu. Sorokina, comp., *Mysliashchie miry rossiiskogo liberalizma: Grafinia Sof'ia Vladimirovna Panina (1871–1956). Materialy Mezhdunarodnogo nauchnogo kollokviuma, Moskva, 29–31 maia 2011 g.* (Moscow: Dom russkogo zarubezh'ia im. Aleksandra Solzhenitsyna, 2012).

6. Quotations from "Such Is Life," a speech she gave in California in 1939, in English; manuscript in Columbia University, Bakhmeteff Archive, S. V. Panina Collection (hereafter, BAR Panina), Box 14, Subject File Panina's Arrest, 1917 (1), 2.

7. For example, Laurie S. Stoff, *They Fought for the Motherland: Russia's Women Soldiers in World War I and the Revolution* (Lawrence: University Press of Kansas, 2006); Melissa K. Stockdale, "'My Death for the Motherland Is Happiness': Women, Patriotism, and Soldiering in Russia's Great War, 1914–1917," *American Historical Review* 109, no. 1 (February 2004): 78–116; Rochelle Goldberg Ruthchild, *Equality and Revolution: Women's Rights in the Russian Empire, 1905–1917* (Pittsburgh: University of Pittsburgh Press, 2010).

8. Louise Bryant, *Six Red Months in Russia: An Observer's Account of Russia before and during the Proletarian Dictatorship* (New York: George H. Doran, 1918), 122.

9. Letter from Sofia Panina to Alexandra Petrunkevich, New Haven, September 23, 1953; La Contemporaine (formerly Bibliotèque de Documentation Internationale Contemporaine, hereafter BDIC), F delta rés 892, Fond Alexandra Petrounkévich, chemise 3.

10. Jill Lepore, "Historians Who Love Too Much: Reflections on Micro-history and Biography," *The Journal of American History* 88, no. 1 (June 2001): 129–30.

11. Vladimir Lehovich, "Crimean Notes: A Glimpse into Family Matters" (unpublished manuscript, Lehovich Family Collection), 29–30.

12. Bryant, *Six Red Months*, 123.

Chapter 1. A Fairy-Tale Childhood

1. S. V. Panina, "Moi gorod," BAR Panina, Box 6, 2.

2. Untitled, undated reminiscences, in Russian, of her mother and her childhood, unsigned but in Sofia's hand, are hereafter referred to as Panina, "My Childhood." Lehovich Family Collection.

3. David L. Ransel, *The Politics of Catherinian Russia: The Panin Party* (New Haven: Yale University Press, 1975), 9.

4. On Peter and Nikita Panin, see ibid., 45–46, 64–70, 108–9, 198–99, 248–49.

5. Richard S. Wortman, *The Development of a Russian Legal Consciousness* (Chicago: University of Chicago Press, 1976), 170–71. Dugino was burned to the ground in 1917. Panin descendant Michael Ignatieff describes it in his family memoir *The Russian Album: A Family Saga of Revolution, Civil War, and Exile* (London: Penguin Books, 1988).

6. Of the five Orlov brothers, Grigory (Empress Catherine's lover) and Ivan died childless. Alexei had one surviving daughter who never married and left her wealth to the Church. Fedor had no legitimate children. The fifth brother, Vladimir, had three daughters: one who had no surviving children; another who had only one son and heir, Vladimir Orlov-Davydov; and Sofia, who married Nikita Petrovich Panin and had ten children, five of whom survived to adulthood. E. P. Karnovich, *Zamechatel'nyia bogatstva chastnykh lits v Rossii. Ekonomichesko-istoricheskoe izsledovanie* (The Hague: Europe Printing, 1965 [St. Petersburg, 1874]), 305, 309–10, 338–39. The disposition of Sofia Orlova-Panina's fortune after her death in 1844 is not entirely clear. Her three daughters do not seem to have married, and her sons, Victor and Alexander, seem to have been her only heirs. When Alexander died in 1850, his estate seems to have reverted to his brother. Rossiiskii gosudarstvennyi arkhiv drevnikh aktov (hereafter RGADA), f. 1274 (Panin and Bludov Collection), op. 1, d. 1321, ll. 3–4.

7. The bequest is mentioned in the inventory of Panin family documents in Institut literatury Rossiiskoi akademii nauk (Pushkinskii dom) (hereafter PD), f. 223 (Panina Collection), No. 38b, l. 110b.

8. Wortman, *The Development of a Russian Legal Consciousness*, 173.

9. RGADA, f. 1274, op. 1, d. 3316, contains the decree by the Orthodox Church giving Victor Panin permission to marry his second cousin.

10. Nikolai Semenov, "Graf Viktor Nikitich Panin. Kharakteristicheskii ocherk po rasskazam, moim zapiskam i vospominaniiam," *Russkii arkhiv* 12 (1887): 542–44. The harshly critical entry on V. N. Panin in the *Brokgauz-Efron Encyclopedia* illustrates the man's unenviable reputation in the late nineteenth century as a pedant, formalist, and reactionary.

11. Wortman, *The Development of a Russian Legal Consciousness*, 175–76, 195.

12. D. C. B. Lieven, *The Aristocracy in Europe, 1815–1914* (New York: Columbia University Press, 1993), 44–45. Other estimates of the number of serfs Panin owned on the eve of the abolition of serfdom in 1861 range from 12,000 to 21,000 adult male souls. Wortman, citing archival sources, gives the number of serfs as "over 12,000"; Wortman, *The Development of a Russian Legal Consciousness*, 169. Semenov states that he owned "up to" 21,000 souls; Semenov, "Graf Viktor Nikitich Panin," 542.

13. By comparison, slightly more than 3 percent of Russian serf owners owned more than five hundred serfs in 1858. Peter Kolchin, *Unfree Labor: American Slavery and Russian Serfdom* (Cambridge, MA: Belknap Press of Harvard University Press, 1987), 54.

14. Semenov, "Graf Viktor Nikitich Panin," 542. According to Semenov, who knew Panin, he allocated a portion of his annual income to a special fund designated for charity. On government salaries in the nineteenth century, see P. A. Zaionchkovskii, *Pravitel'stvennyi apparat samoderzhavnoi Rossii v XIX v.* (Moscow: Mysl', 1978), 77–79. Provincial prosecutors and judges in Panin's ministry received salaries in the range of 800 rubles a year.

15. PD, f. 223, No. 38 (b); this is an inventory of Panin family papers, evidently the contents of the administrative office of the family's holdings and personal documents, dating back as far as 1862; the inventory was made sometime after 1900. In it eleven estates are named, e.g., on l. 80b.

16. According to Victor Panin's will, dated May 19, 1867; RGADA, f. 1274, op. 1, d. 1316, ll. 1–3.

17. I. A. Golyshev, *Bogoiavlenskaia sloboda Mstera Vladimirskoi gubernii, Viaznikovskogo uezda: Istoriia eia, drevnosti, statistika i etnografiia* (Vladimir, 1865), 5–7.

18. Aleksandr Akinyshin and Oleg Lasunskii, *Voronezhskoe dvorianstvo v litsakh i sud'bakh* (Voronezh: Petrovskii skver, 1994), 144–46.

19. Semenov, "Graf Viktor Nikitich Panin," 542.

20. PD, f. 223, No. 38 (b) l. 110b.

21. As Vladimir's widow, Anastasia was entitled to one-seventh of his immovable property, with his daughter inheriting the remainder. William G. Wagner, *Marriage, Property, and Law in Late Imperial Russia* (Oxford: Clarendon Press, 1994), 228–33.

22. Victor Panin's will, RGADA, f. 1274, op. 1, d. 1316, ll. 1–3. The same will, with a codicil from 1870 and a new designation of executors made in 1873, was probated on May 24, 1874; RGADA, f. 1274, op. 1, d. 1321, ll. 51–56.

23. V. I. Nemirovich-Danchenko, "Amerika v Rossii," *Russkaia mysl'* 1882, no. 1:318–55; no. 2:268–301; no. 4:115–46; no. 8:85–113; no. 10:73–109; no. 12:219–36.

24. G. N. Ul'ianova, "Mal'tsovy: Dvesti let na rossiiskom rynke," in *Mal'tsovskii mir: Nauchnyi sbornik*, vyp. 1, ed. Andrei Anatol'evich Bauer (Kirov: Kirovskii istoriko-kraevedcheskii muzei, Kaluzhskoi oblasti, 1999), 6–13; I. N. Zhinzhikova, "Rodoslovnaia Mal'tsovykh," in *S. I. Mal'tsov i istoriia razvitiia Mal'tsovskogo promyshlennogo raiona*, ed. V. V. Krasheninnikov (Briansk: Brianskoe oblastnoe izdatel'stvo "Grani," 1994), 14–15.

25. V. G. Khokhlov and M. M. Datskov, "Sergei Ivanovich Mal'tsov—predprinimatel', patriot, chelovek," in *S. I. Mal'tsov*, 22–24; G. N. Ul'ianova, "Vzgliady Sergeia Ivanovicha Mal'tsova po obshchestvennym voprosam," in ibid., 31; Ul'ianova, "Mal'tsovy," 13–15.

26. Lieven, *Aristocracy in Europe*, 44–45; Ul'ianova, "Vzgliady Sergeia Ivanovicha Mal'tsova," 33–34; Khokhlov and Datskov, "Sergei Ivanovich Mal'tsov," 24–26.

27. Now primarily the provinces of Briansk and Kaluga.

28. Ul'ianova, "Mal'tsovy," 16–19.

29. Maria Sergeevna Urusova, "Souvenirs d'enfance de Marie Serguévna Ouroussow (née vers 1844, + 1904), ('Monia') née Maltzev, épouse de Léonide Dmtrievitch, Prince Ouroussow, No. 382/333 de la Généalogie Ouroussow De Plechko," 33, 46–48, Lehovich Family Collection.

30. In a pamphlet written around 1858, he argued that "history and the experience of other nations prove positively the irrevocable harm" of universal land ownership. Maltsov's resistance to reform contributed to sparking unrest among workers at his Liudinovo ironworks in 1861 and again in 1865. Ul'ianova, "Mal'tsovy," 15–16, 20–24; Ul'ianova, "Vzgliady Sergeia Ivanovicha Mal'tsova po obshchestvennym voprosam," 33–37.

31. Urusova, "Souvenirs d'enfance," 4, 33, 50.

32. Ibid., 32.

33. Prince Serge Ouroussow, "Noirs Oiseaux de L'Adversité, par Le Prince Serge Ouroussow (Mémoires)," book I, "L'Ermite de Simeis," Lehovich Family Collection.

34. A. F. Tiutcheva, *Pri dvore dvukh imperatorov*, vol. 2, *Dnevnik 1855–1882*, ed. S. V. Bakhrushin (Moscow: izd. M. i I. Sabashnikovykh, 1929), 185–86; Lydia Wassiltschikow, *Verschwundenes Russland. Die Memoiren der Fürstin Lydia Wassiltschikow 1886–1919*, ed. Tatiana Metternich, trans. Karl-Otto Czernicki and Friderike Czernicki (Vienna: Verlag Fritz Molden, 1980), 33.

35. Wassiltschikow, *Verschwundenes Russland*, 35.

36. Maria Sergeevna Urusova, "Souvenirs de notre grand'mère maternelle Marie Serguéevna, Princesse Ouroussow, ('Monia') née Maltzow. Souvenirs des années (1867–1878)," 17, Lehovich Family Collection.

37. Ibid., 13.

38. Letters written in 1856, 1857, and 1859 from Vladimir Panin to his mother, Bakhmeteff Archive, Columbia University, Panin Family Collection, Box 2.

39. Urusova, "Souvenirs de notre grand'mère," 17; Boris Losskii, "Eshche o grafine S. V. Paninoi," *Russkaia mysl'*, no. 4097 (October 19–25, 1995): 16.

40. Documents dated 1864–71 in an inventory of Panin family papers mention the burial of Evgeniia and Nataliia Panin in 1864 and the purchase of gravesites and monuments for them; PD, f. 223 No. 38b ll. 5, 8.

41. Urusova, "Souvenirs de notre grand'mère," 17–18.

42. Georgii I. Vasil'chikov, "Grafinia S. V. Panina, posledniaia vladelitsa Marfina," *Nashe nasledie* 29–30 (1994): 77.

43. Wassiltschikow, *Verschwundenes Russland*, 33. Vladimir Panin's sister Olga was the grandmother of Lidia Vasilchikova (Lydia Wassiltschikow).

44. M. M. Gorinov, "O date rozhdeniia S. V. Paninoi: Poiski v arkhivakh," in Sorokina, *Mysliashchie miry rossiiskogo liberalizma: Grafinia Sof'ia Vladimirovna Panina*, 31.

45. Urusova, "Souvenirs de notre grand'mère," 41–42.

46. Ibid., 54. Family letters from 1873 refer continually to concerns about Sofia's and Natasha's appearance, health, and development. Letters from Anastasia Panina to her mother-in-law Natalia Pavlovna Panina, April–August 1873, in BAR Panin, Box 3, and letters from Leonilla Komarovskaya (née Panina) to her mother Natalia Pavlovna Panina, May–June 1873; BAR Panin, Box 1.

47. Letters from Anastasia Panina to Natalia Pavlovna Panina of May 22 and 31, 1873, in BAR Panin, Box 3.

48. Urusova, "Souvenirs de notre grand'mère," 58–60.

49. Ibid.," 69–72; Panina, "My Childhood."

50. Letter from Leonilla Komarovskaya to Natalia Pavlovna Panina, Marfino, August 6, 1873, in BAR Panin, Box 1; Wassiltschikow, *Verschwundenes Russland*, 33–34.

51. Panina, "My Childhood."

52. Panina, "Moi gorod," 2; letter from Sofia Panina to Alexandra Petrunkevich, Reed Farm, August 5, 1950, BDIC, F delta rés 892, folder 1.

53. Panina, "My Childhood."

54. Panina, "Moi gorod," 1–2.

55. Panina, "My Childhood."

56. An authoritative biographical dictionary of Russian revolutionaries, compiled in the 1920s and early 1930s, lists two Zhitetskys: a teacher and exiled revolutionary named Irodion Alexeevich, born in 1851, and a Pavel Nikolaevich, also the son of a priest but born a generation earlier, in 1836. Vserossiiskoe obshchestvo politicheskikh katorzhan i ssyl'no-poselentsev, *Deiateli revoliutsionnogo dvizheniia v Rossii: Bio-bibliograficheskii slovar'*, vol. 2, *Semidesiatye gody*, vyp. 3, comp. A. A. Shilov and M. G. Karnaukhova (Moscow, 1931), 422. The compilers of the dictionary associate the older and more respectable Pavel Zhitetsky with Anastasia Panina, not Irodion Alexeevich, but it appears that this is an error. Pavel Nikolaevich, a teacher of literature at prestigious Kiev educational institutions, belonged to a Ukrainian association, "Hromada," and was regarded by the Kiev police as politically unreliable. But eventually he became a professor at St. Petersburg University, a famous linguist, and a member of the Academy of Sciences. The younger and more radical Irodion Alexeevich seems a much more likely candidate as Sofia's teacher. Sofia herself calls him Rodion Alexeevich in her "My Childhood" and calls him a "prominent, staunch radical Ukrainophile." In her stepfather's memoirs, her tutor is identified as I. A. Zhitetsky. Ivan Il'ich Petrunkevich, *Iz zapisok obshchestvennogo deiatelia. Vospominaniia*, ed. A. A. Kizevetter. *Arkhiv russkoi revoliutsii* 21 (1934), 102.

Chapter 2. The Battle for Sofia

1. Panina, "Moi gorod," 2–3.

2. Ibid., 5.

3. Gosudarstvennyi arkhiv Rossiiskoi federatsii (hereafter GARF), f. 102, op. 3D 1882, d. 741, "O pomeshchenii docheri Anastasii Petrunkevich (po pervomu muzhu Grafini Paninoi) v odin iz institutov vedomstva Imperatritsy Marii," ll. 23, 25. Evidently the major-general felt sympathy for Anastasia and her daughter. As he reported to his superior, he allowed Anastasia to take Sofia to the institute herself, instead of with a police escort.

4. At 16,000 rubles per year, the allowance compares quite favorably to the official salary of 12,000 rubles paid to members of the State Council, for example. Zaionchkovskii, *Pravitel'stvennyi apparat*, 86–88.

5. Tsentral'nyi gosudarstvennyi istoricheskii arkhiv S-Peterburga (hereafter TsGIA SPb.), f. 254, Peterburgskoe gubernskoe pravlenie, op. 1, tom 1, d. 4266, "Po raportu S-Peterburgskoi Dvorianskoi opeki kasatel'no raz"iasneniia voprosa o vozbuzhdennom opekunsheiiu vdovoiu Grafineiu Anastasieiu Paninoi prerekanii, kasatel'no lichnogo sostava opekunskogo upravleniia, 19 IV 1879–31 dek. 1881," l. 50b–6. In an effort to save his industrial empire from bankruptcy, Sergei Maltsov turned his thirty-odd enterprises into a joint stock company in 1875. He was required by imperial order to distribute shares to his estranged wife and children. Khokhlov and Datskov, "Sergei Ivanovich Mal'tsov," 29; Ul'ianova, "Mal'tsovy."

6. TsGIA SPb., f. 254, op. 1, tom 1, d. 4266, ll. 3, 5, 7.

7. Ibid., ll. 3, 5–7, l. 170b. Anastasia spent 19,500 rubles on Sofia's maintenance in 1877, and slightly more than 24,000 rubles in 1878.

8. This action resulted from a report delivered by the minister of justice to Alexander II, who instructed the Senate to issue the decree; ibid., l. 1.

9. Ibid., ll. 70b–80b.

10. Ibid., ll. 3–4, 9–10, and 17–20.

11. In its documents on the case the St. Petersburg Board of Guardians identified only Anastasia's overspending and opposition to another guardian as the reasons for the intensified scrutiny she came under beginning in 1879. But the police file on the custody dispute between Anastasia and Countess Natalia Panina contains detailed reports on Anastasia's politically suspect activities and connections beginning a few years earlier. GARF, f. 102, op. 3D 1882, d. 741, esp. ll. 15–17.

12. Anastasia was enough of a radical to merit her own entry in the early Soviet biographical dictionary of revolutionaries. The entry, doubtless relying on claims made in the police file, notes her "wide acquaintance" with students and revolutionaries in Kiev, the financial assistance she gave to participants in student demonstrations, and the carpentry workshop she supported where revolutionaries worked. Keeping her under surveillance in both Kiev and Moscow, the police subjected her more than once to interrogation and searches between 1879 and 1882; "she was considered politically unreliable, although she could not be brought to account due to the absence of sufficient evidence." According to this source, she remained under police observation up to 1905. *Deiateli revoliutsionnogo dvizheniia v Rossii*, vol. 2, vyp. 3, 1138–39.

13. Petrunkevich, "Iz zapisok," 45.

14. Ibid., 41.

15. A summary of Petrunkevich's political activity is in GARF, f. 102, op. 3D 1882, d. 741, ll. 9–100b. In his memoirs Ivan admits to sheltering "illegals" on his estate from the police; "Iz zapisok," 98.

16. F. A. Petrov, "Iz istorii obshchestvennogo dvizheniia v period vtoroi revoliutsionnoi situatsii v Rossii. Revoliutsionery i liberaly v kontse 1870-kh godov." *Istoriia SSSR* 1 (1981): 144–51; Petrunkevich, "Iz zapisok," 101.

17. Petrunkevich, "Iz zapisok," 101–2. It is not clear whether police knew about the December 3 meeting. Their summary reports on Anastasia's and Ivan's political activity do not mention it; GARF, f. 102, op. 3D 1882, d. 741, ll. 9–220b. But according to one historian the police generally knew from informers that liberals and revolutionaries were meeting in Kiev in December 1878; Petrov, "Iz istorii obshchestvennogo dvizheniia," 149.

18. Petrunkevich, "Iz zapisok," [7]; I. V. Gessen, *V dvukh vekakh: Zhiznennyi otchet* (Berlin: Speer & Schmidt, 1937), 181.

19. Panina, "My Childhood"; emphasis in the original.

20. Petrunkevich, "Iz zapisok," 102–3, 106–9, 115–20; Petrov, "Iz istorii obshchestvennogo dvizheniia," 146–47; GARF, f. 102, op. 3D 1882, d. 741, ll. 12–130b.

21. Information about Ivan's first marriage comes from Petrunkevich's descendant Nikolai A. Shlippenbakh, in a personal communication to the author, September 9, 2009; and also from Ivan's son Alexander Petrunkevich, who is the subject of a two-part article by Eugene Kinkead. On Ivan's divorce, see Kinkead, "Profiles: Arachnologist. 2," *The New Yorker*, April 29, 1950, 43.

22. Petrunkevich, "Iz zapisok," 115–20.

23. Kinkead, "Arachnologist 2," 43. Ivan merely claims in his memoirs that they divorced "by mutual consent." Petrunkevich, "Iz zapisok," 160.

24. Petrunkevich, "Iz zapisok," 122–23, 132–36. Ivan's sentence of exile from his home province and the capital city continued, but the government allowed him to choose to live in one of three cities—Yaroslavl, Vladimir, or Smolensk.

25. Anastasia received 6,000 rubles from her father, another 6,000 in income from property left directly to her by her husband, and the allowance from Countess Natalia Panina for Sofia's support, which had now almost doubled to 30,000 rubles; GARF, f. 102, op. 3D 1882, d. 741, ll. 160b–17.

26. There are nineteen letters from Anastasia Panina to Natalia Panina beginning on April 30/May 12, 1873, and ending June 7, 1874, written from St. Petersburg, Marfino, Geneva, Villeneuve, Nice, and Paris. BAR Panin, Box 3.

27. Panina, "Moi gorod," 9; the emphasis is hers.

28. Wassiltschikow, *Verschwundenes Russland*, 31, 34.

29. Alexander Polovtsov, Sofia's father-in-law, claims that Countess Natalia Panina swore him to secrecy when she recounted episodes to him from the Panin family's history; A. A. Polovtsov, *Dnevnik gosudarstvennogo sekretaria A. A. Polovtsova: v 2-kh tomakh*, ed. Peter Andreevich Zaionchkovskii, vol. 2, *1887–1892 gg.* (Moscow: Nauka, 1966), 330.

30. Polovtsov, *Dnevnik A. A. Polovtsova*, 291–92.

31. TsGIA SPb., f. 254, op. 1, tom 1, d. 4266, l. 21.

32. Petrunkevich, "Iz zapisok," 142, 155–56.

33. Kinkead, "Arachnologist 2," 43.

34. GARF, f. 102, op. 3D 1882, d. 741, l. 17.

35. Petrunkevich, "Iz zapisok," 156–59.

36. A. A. Tolstaia, *Zapiski freiliny. Pechal'nyi epizod iz moei zhizni pri dvore* (Moscow: Entsiklopediia rossiiskikh dereven', 1996), 65–67.

37. GARF, f. 102, op. 3D 1882, d. 741, ll. 17ob–18; the two senators appointed by Alexander II remained the trustees of Sofia's capital.

38. Ibid., ll. 18ob–20; Petrunkevich, "Iz zapisok," 158–60.

39. Countess Panina sent her petition from Baden-Baden; GARF, f. 102, op. 3D 1882, d. 741, ll. 1–20b. Back in St. Petersburg, her two daughters and sons-in-law used their contacts to put pressure on the minister and emperor to act in the family's favor; Petrunkevich, "Iz zapisok," 160–61.

40. GARF, f. 102, op. 3D 1882, d. 741, ll. 6–60b; emphasis in the original.

41. Ibid., ll. 60b–8.

42. Ibid., ll. 3–40b. The minister's report to Alexander never mentions Anastasia's arguments; he briefly summarizes the history of decisions about custody over Sofia, then supports Natalia Panina's request.

43. Vasil'chikov, "Grafinia S. V. Panina," 77; Wassiltschikow, *Verschwundenes Russland*, 34.

44. Petrunkevich, "Iz zapisok," 161.

45. Panina, "My Childhood."

46. Petrunkevich, "Iz zapisok," 162. Anastasia spent the first year (1882–83) that Sofia was in school living in St. Petersburg with Ivan's children, instead of with him in Smolensk, so that she could see her daughter and monitor her health and well-being. The gendarmes continued to follow Anastasia and to open letters between her and Ivan. Finally in 1883 Ivan was allowed to move to any town except Moscow or St. Petersburg. He and Anastasia moved to Tver, north of Moscow, in June 1883; they lived there until 1890.

47. Panina, "Moi gorod," 7.

48. Ibid., 5; ellipsis in original.

49. Ibid., 8.

50. Ibid., 6.

51. Wassiltschikow, *Verschwundenes Russland*, 33, 35.

52. Panina, "Moi gorod," 8.

Chapter 3. "The Richest Marriageable Girl in Russia"

1. *Entsiklopediia Brokgauz-Efron* (St. Petersburg, 1894), s.v. "Instituty zhenskie." Of the thirty institutes in the 1890s, one-third of them were located in St. Petersburg. Quarenghi designed many of St. Petersburg's most familiar and iconic buildings during the late eighteenth and early nineteenth centuries, including Smolny Institute. The building now houses the periodicals and music departments of the Russian National Library.

2. Panina, "Moi gorod," 4.

3. Ibid.; TsGIA SPb, f. 3, Petrogradskoe uchilishche ordena Sv. Ekateriny, op. 2, d. 335, "Ob otchete za 1882 g.," l. 910b.

4. TsGIA SPb, f. 3, op. 3, d. 335, ll. 510b, 70–80; N. S. Kartsov, *Neskol'ko faktov iz zhizni S.-Peterburgskogo uchilishcha ordena sv. Ekateriny. Ko dniu ego stoletnogo iubileia. Sostavleno, po porucheniiu soveta instituta, inspektorom klassov N. S. Kartsovym* (St. Petersburg, 1898), 32.

5. Panina, "Moi gorod," 6–7.

6. *Istoricheskii ocherk stoletnei deiatel'nosti S-Peterburgskogo uchilishcha ordena sv. Ekateriny* (St. Petersburg, 1902), 203–7.

7. Ibid., 201–3, 207–11.

8. M. K. Tenisheva, *Vpetchatleniia moei zhizni* (Leningrad: Iskusstvo, 1991), 67–69. For more on criticism of the institutes see Richard Stites, *The Women's Liberation Movement in Russia: Feminism, Nihilism and Bolshevism, 1860–1930*, rev. ed. (Princeton: Princeton University Press, 1990), 4–6.

9. Anna Bek and Anne Dickason Rassweiler, *The Life of a Russian Woman Doctor: A Siberian Memoir, 1869–1954* (Bloomington: Indiana University Press, 2004), 30.

10. S. A. Anikieva, *Vospominaniia byvshei institutki o S.-Peterburgskom Ekaterininskom institute* (St. Petersburg, 1899), 44–47.

11. *Entsiklopediia Brokgauz-Efron* (St. Petersburg, 1894), s.v. "Instituty zhenskie."

12. Kartsov, *Neskol'ko faktov*, 47–49.

13. Komitet Obshchestva dlia dostavleniia sredstv Vysshim zhenskim kursam v S.-Peterburge, *S.-Peterburgskie Vysshie zhenskie kursy za 25 let. 1878–1903. Ocherki i materialy* ([St. Petersburg], 1903), 205.

14. Bek, *The Life of a Russian Woman Doctor*, 25–32.

15. Sofia's school notebooks are in PD, f. 223, op. 1, d. 32.

16. TsGIA SPb., f. 3, op. 1, d. 2659, ll. 2, 4, 25–26, 29–30, 41, 51, 120. Sofia also received her certification as a "domestic instructress," or governess, which seems an unlikely career option for the young heiress.

17. Panina, "Moi gorod," 7–8; emphasis in the original.

18. Petrunkevich, "Iz zapisok," 188.

19. In 1886 Ivan was allowed to move from Tver back to his estate in the Ukrainian province of Chernigov, where he was immediately re-elected to the zemstvo. The government reacted by forbidding him to live in any of the five Ukrainian provinces as well as St. Petersburg or Moscow, whereupon Ivan and Anastasia moved back to Tver. They never returned to Ukraine. Petrunkevich, "Iz zapisok," chapters 8 and 9.

20. This leaf from the Bakunin family album includes a handwritten partial identification of the people in the photo. The same photo is in BDIC, Fond Alexandra Petrounkévitch, F delta rés 892, chemise 2, in which all ten individuals are identified. They are, from left to right: Ivan Mikhailovich Petrunkevich (the son of Mikhail Ilich) [sitting on chair on extreme left]; Sofia [sitting on grass, in profile]; Liubov Petrunkevich [née Vulf] (Mikhail Ilich's wife); Mikhail Ilich's two daughters, Aleksandra [with pince-nez and guitar] and Anna (who became a singer with the professional surname of Ian-Ruban); Mikhail Ilich Petrunkevich [standing behind his daughters Aleksandra and Anna]; Sofia's mother Anastasia [seated, reading book]; Ivan Petrunkevich's son Vladimir [sitting on

grass]; Sofia's stepfather Ivan [standing behind his wife]; and Pavel Ivanovich Novgorodtsev, a family friend.

21. Quotations from Wassiltschikow, *Verschwundenes Russland*, 32–33. Also on the Panin mansion: Anatolii Ivanov, "Smes' kovrov i nadushennoi pudry," *Sankt-Peterburgskie vedomosti*, September 4, 2004, 5; Lydia Wassiltchikoff, "'Vanished Russia.' Memoirs of Lydia Princess ('Dilka') Wassiltchikoff, re-written and heavily edited by her daughter Tatiana Metternich," Hoover Institution Archives, Lydia Wassiltchikow Collection, 30; and Varvara Petrovna Volkova (née Geiden), [Recollections], BDIC, F delta rés 892, chemise 9. On Sofia's travels, see the expense report for Sofia Panina for April 1–July 1, 1889, in RGADA f. 1274, op. 1, d. 1328, l. 16.

22. Losskii, "Eshche o grafine S. V. Paninoi."

23. Letter from Sofia Panina to Varvara Petrovna Geiden (Volkova), St. Petersburg, November 6, 1889, in GARF, f. 887, op. 1, d. 391, l. 40b.

24. I. A. Murav'eva, *Vek moderna: Panorama stolichnoi zhizni* (St. Petersburg: izd. "Pushkinskogo fonda," 2004), 49.

25. Ibid., 56–57. Volkova, [Recollections]; Varya was one of the young women who took dancing classes at Countess Panina's.

26. A note left with the baby girl gave only her first name and patronymic (Mikhailovna, daughter of Mikhail). According to her son, Nadezhda bore a striking physical resemblance to Catherine the Great. Alexander Polovtsoff, "Vospominaniia," typescript memoir dated 1934 in Alexandre Polovtsoff Papers, Sterling Library, Yale University, mss. #403, Box 5, folder 2, 19–21.

27. Galina Prokhorenko, "Sanovnik, metsenat i kollektsioner Aleksandr Aleksandrovich Polovtsov," *Nashe nasledie* 77 (2006), http://www.nasledie -rus.ru/podshivka/7708hp; B. V. Anan'ich, *Bankirskie doma v Rossii, 1860–1917 gg.: Ocherki istorii chastnogo predprinimatel'stva* (Leningrad: Nauka, 1991), 21n60; Polovtsoff, "Vospominaniia," 25–28; Murav'eva, *Vek moderna*, 57.

28. Polovtsoff, "Vospominaniia," 43–51.

29. Polovtsov, *Dnevnik A. A. Polovtsova*, 273; Alexandre Polovtsoff Papers, mss. #403, Sterling Library, Yale University, Box 5, folder 1, notebook with handwritten notes for his autobiography.

30. S. Iu. Vitte, *The Memoirs of Count Witte*, trans. and ed. Sidney Harcave (Armonk, NY: M. E. Sharpe, 1990), 199; Volkova, [Recollections], pages 2–20b; and Losskii, "Eshche o grafine S. V. Paninoi."

31. Polovtsov, *Dnevnik A. A. Polovtsova*, 268–69.

32. Nadine Wonlar-Larsky, *The Russia That I Loved* (London: The Women's Printing Society, n.d.), 55, 72–73.

33. *S-Peterburgskie vedomosti*, April 26 (May 8), 1890, 2; similar or identical short notices appeared in *Peterburgskii listok*, *Pravitel'stvennyi vestnik*, *Novoe vremia*, and *Birzhevye vedomosti*.

34. For example, Natalia Dumova, *Konchilos' vashe vremia* (Moscow: Iz-datel'stvo politicheskoi literatury, 1990), 145.

35. Polovtsov, *Dnevnik A. A. Polovtsova*, 277, 294.

36. Ibid., 289.

37. Polovtsoff Papers, notebook with handwritten notes for his autobiography, 73.

38. RGADA, f. 1274, op. 1, d. 1328, Panin family bookkeepers' accounts for 1889.

39. Letter from Sofia Panina to Varvara Petrovna Geiden (Volkova), London, July 3/15, 1890, in GARF, f. 887, op. 1, d. 391, ll. 5–60b.

40. Polovtsoff, "Vospominaniia," 52, 54.

41. Polovtsov, *Dnevnik A. A. Polovtsova*, 425–26; Polovtsoff, "Vospominaniia, 52–53." Although Alexander Jr. describes his experiences in famine relief at some length in his autobiography, he fails to note that Sofia accompanied him.

42. Letter from Sofia Panina to Varvara Petrovna Geiden (Volkova), Gaspra, September 16, 1893, in GARF, f. 887, op. 1, d. 391, 11 16–180b.

43. Letter from Sofia Panina to Varvara Petrovna Geiden (Volkova), Marfino, June 7, 1894, in GARF, f. 887, op. 1, d. 391, l. 190b.

44. Letter from Sofia Panina to Varvara Petrovna Geiden (Volkova), Gaspra, September 16, 1893, in GARF, f. 887, op. 1, d. 391, l. 170b.

45. Letter from Sofia Panina to Varvara Petrovna Geiden (Volkova), St. Petersburg, December 17, 1895, in GARF, f. 887, op. 1, d. 391, ll. 29–290b.

46. Earlier that year Sofia had been presented to the young Empress Alexandra, whom she found to be beautiful and diligent but excruciatingly shy. Letter from Sofia Panina to Varvara Petrovna Geiden (Volkova), St. Petersburg, February 27, 1896, in GARF, f. 887, op. 1, d. 391, l. 39.

47. Letter from Sofia Panina to Varvara Petrovna Geiden (Volkova), St. Petersburg, May 18, 1896, in GARF, f. 887, op. 1, d. 391, ll. 470b–48.

48. In the St. Petersburg city directory for 1895 Sofia Polovtsova is listed separately for the first time, living at the same address as her grandmother; *Ves' Peterburg na 1896 g.* (St. Petersburg, 1895). The city directory for 1896 lists her as both Sofia Polovtsova and Sofia Panina, and still living with the elderly Countess Panina; *Ves' Peterburg na 1897 g.* (St. Petersburg, 1896). Varvara Volkova states that Sofia's grandmother "proved herself excellently" after Sofia left Alexander, and she also hints that Alexander may have attempted to go through Varvara in order to reconcile with Sofia in 1895; Volkova, [Recollections]. Unfortunately the file for Sofia's divorce is missing from the Holy Synod archive. Its listing in the inventory indicates only the date and official grounds for the divorce; Rossiiskii gosudarstvennyi istoricheskii arkhiv, f. 796, op. 177, d. 2583.

49. Wagner, *Marriage, Property and Law*, chapter 2; Mikhail Mikhailovich Artsybashev, *Nash brakorazvodnyi protsess* (St. Petersburg, 1908), 1–16. Barbara Alpern Engel's excellent analysis of divorce in the late imperial era confirms the liberalizing climate for marital separations initiated by women, but she focuses primarily on the peasantry and working class: *Breaking the Ties That Bound: The Politics of Marital Strife in Late Imperial Russia* (Ithaca: Cornell University Press, 2011).

50. Alexander's homosexuality is the explanation for the divorce offered by Prince George Vasilchikov (Vassiltchikov), a relative of Sofia's who also knew Alexander, in a letter to this author dated October 7, 1997. The same reason is given by a colleague of Alexander's at the Ministry of Foreign Affairs, who refers to the "noisy and unattractive history of the divorce"; G. N. Mikhailovskii, *Zapiski. Iz istorii Rossiiskogo vneshnepoliticheskogo vedomstva. 1914–1920*, vol. 1,

Avgust 1914–oktiabr' 1917 (Moscow: Mezhdunarodnye otnosheniia, 1993), 201.
Both Vasilchikov and Mikhailovskii use the term "homosexual" or "homosexual inclinations" when discussing Alexander. The word homosexual is an
anachronism for the late nineteenth century, however, since it was not yet in
use in Russian. The terms that were in use in Russia in the 1890s included *mu-
zhelozhstvo, sodomskii grekh,* and *pederastiia.*

51. Alexander does mention Sofia briefly in the notebook for his autobiography in the Polovtsoff Papers.

52. Dan Healey, *Homosexual Desire in Revolutionary Russia: The Regulation of
Sexual and Gender Dissent* (Chicago: University of Chicago Press, 2001), 92–94.
See also Alexander Poznansky, "The Tchaikovsky Myths: A Critical Reassessment," in *Tchaikovsky and His Contemporaries: A Centennial Symposium,* ed. Alexandar Mihailovic (Westport, CT: Greenwood Press, 1999), 81–82.

53. Letter from Sofia Panina to Varvara Petrovna Geiden (Volkova), St.
Petersburg, March 26, 1896, in GARF, f. 887, op. 1, d. 391, ll. 40–45.

54. Letter from Sofia Panina to Varvara Petrovna Geiden (Volkova), Ham-
burg, July 23, 1897, in GARF, f. 887 op. 1 d. 391, l. 950b.

55. Until 1904 a spouse found guilty of adultery was prohibited from remarrying. Alexander Polovtsov married his second wife in that year.

56. A. Tyrkova-Vil'iams, *Na putiakh k svobode* (New York: Izdatel'stvo imeni
Chekhova, 1952), chap. 1.

57. Letter from Sofia Panina to Varvara Petrovna Geiden (Volkova), Baden-
Baden, July 16/28, 1896, in GARF, f. 887, op. 1, d. 391, ll. 53–56.

58. *S.-Peterburgskie Vysshie zhenskie kursy,* 219–20.

59. Bek, *The Life of a Russian Woman Doctor,* 32.

60. Elizaveta D'iakonova, *Dnevnik russkoi zhenshchiny: Dnevniki, literaturnye
etiudy, stat'i* (Moscow: Mezhdunarodnyi universitet, 2006), 253.

61. Ibid., esp. 238–42; Stites, *The Women's Liberation Movement,* 168–74.

62. Letters from Sofia Panina to Varvara Petrovna Geiden (Volkova), March
26, 1896, and May 18, 1896, St. Petersburg, in GARF, f. 887, op. 1, d. 391, ll. 40–45
and 46–490b.

63. Letter from Sofia Panina to Varvara Petrovna Geiden (Volkova), May
18, 1896, ll. 480b–49.

64. Alexandra was a member of the graduating class of 1896, but her
diploma is dated February 24, 1897. BDIC, F delta rés 892, chemise 1; Natalia
Aleksandrovna Vetvenitskaia, *Spisok okonchivshikh kurs na S-Peterburgskikh
vysshikh zhenskikh kursakh 1882–1889 gg., 1893–1911 gg.* ([St. Petersburg],
n.d.), 52.

65. The documents related to Sofia's admission and withdrawal are in
TsGIA SPb., f. 113, Vysshie zhenskie kursy (Bestuzhevskie), op. 1, d. 1387,
"Vybyvshie do okonchaniia. [Letter] P." Although other sources assert that
Sofia graduated, the archival record shows definitively that she withdrew from
the Bestuzhev Courses before graduating.

66. *S.-Peterburgskie Vysshie zhenskie kursy,* 220–21, 225.

67. D'iakonova, *Dnevnik russkoi zhenshchiny,* 275.

68. Letter from Sofia Panina to Varvara Petrovna Geiden (Volkova), St. Petersburg, February 17, 1897, in GARF, f. 887, op. 1, d. 391, l. 85.

69. Samuel D. Kassow, *Students, Professors and the State in Tsarist Russia* (Berkeley: University of California Press, 1989), 87; http://ru.wikipedia.org /wiki/Vetrova,_Mariia_Fedos'evna.

70. Kassow, *Students, Professors and the State*, 88–104.

71. Letter from Sofia Panina to Varvara Petrovna Geiden (Volkova), Mashuk, August 26, 1899, in GARF, f. 887, op. 1, d. 391, ll. 122–23.

72. *S.-Peterburgskie Vysshie zhenskie kursy*, 223–24, 254–55, 258.

73. Grevs helped organize the fundraising that ransomed Sofia out of prison in December 1917, and he went in person to the prison to escort her home when she was released. Rostovtseff, who later joined the Kadet Party along with Sofia, became a close friend of hers after she moved to the United States in 1939.

74. Letter from Sofia Panina to Varvara Petrovna Geiden (Volkova), Baden-Baden, July 28, 1896, in GARF, f. 887, op. 1, d. 391, l. 59.

75. Panina, "Moi gorod," 1.

Chapter 4. The People's House

1. S. V. Panina, "Na peterburgskoi okraine [On the outskirts of Petersburg]," *Novyi zhurnal* 48 (1957): 163. The two women were not previously acquainted, and Sofia does not explain why Alexandra came to her for assistance on her project.

2. On the Ligovsky People's House and its place within the context of international progressive philanthropy, see Adele Lindenmeyr, "Building a Civil Society One Brick at a Time: People's Houses and Worker Enlightenment in Late Imperial Russia," *Journal of Modern History* 84, no. 1 (March 2012): 1–39.

3. In 1922 Alexandra wrote a short autobiography she titled "Moe detstvo [My childhood]," which she sent to Sofia. Handwritten and typed versions are in BAR Panina, Box 7, and also in Rossiiskii institut istorii iskusstv (hereafter RIII), Kabinet rukopisei, f. 32, op. 1, ed. khr. 126, l. 1.

4. On urban schoolteachers like Alexandra, see Christine Ruane, *Gender, Class, and the Professionalization of Russian City Teachers, 1860–1914* (Pittsburgh: University of Pittsburgh Press, 1994).

5. *Peterburgskii listok*, April 13 (26), 1903, 3; Panina, "Na peterburgskoi okraine," 48:165.

6. The census district in 1900 was the second precinct of Alexander Nevsky district. Its dominant industries were metal and woodworking, clothing and footwear, food processing, construction, and especially transport. *S.-Peterburg po perepisi 15 dekabria 1900 goda*, vol. 2, *Raspredelenie naseleniia po zaniatiiam* (SPb: Tip. Shredera, 1903), 4–5, 8–11, 21–23, 35. On the literacy rates and social origins of the population in this district, see *S.-Peterburg po perepisi 15 dekabria 1900 goda*, vol. 1, *Chislennost' i sostav naseleniia po polu, vozrastu, mestu rozhdeniia (v S.-Peterburge ili vne ego), vremeni poseleniia v S.-Peterburge, semeinomu sostoianiiu, gramotnosti, sosloviiu, veroispovedaniiu i rodnomu iazyku* (SPb: Tip. Shredera, 1903), 17, 20–23, 31–33, 37, 43–49.

7. Letter from Sofia Panina to Varvara Petrovna Geiden (Volkova), St. Petersburg, December 12/17, 1895, in GARF, f. 887, op. 1, d. 391, l. 30.

8. *"Evropa da i tol'ko."* Letter from Sofia Panina to Varvara Petrovna Geiden (Volkova), Mashuk, June 25, 1896, in ibid., ll. 52–520b.

9. Panina, "Na peterburgskoi okraine," 48:166.

10. Sofia narrates this history of the people's house in her speech at the tenth anniversary celebration, printed in *Otchet Ligovskogo narodnogo doma za pervoe desiatiletie, 1903–1913 gg.* (St. Petersburg, 1914), 13–15, and in "Na peterburgskoi okraine," 48:166–68. The same narrative is borne out in her letters to Varya Volkova from the mid- to late 1890s, which document the gradual evolution of the project from Sunday readings to more ambitious activities.

11. Patricia Herlihy, *The Alcoholic Empire: Vodka and Politics in Late Imperial Russia* (Oxford: Oxford University Press, 2002), chap. 2. On the origins and development of people's houses in Russia, see *Narodnyi dom: Sotsial'naia rol', organizatsiia, deiatel'nost' i oborudovanie Narodnogo doma. S prilozheniem bibliografii, tipovykh planov, primernogo ustava i pervoi vserossiiskoi ankety o narodnykh domakh* (Petrograd: Tipografiia B. M. Vol'fa, 1918).

12. Daniel T. Rodgers, *Atlantic Crossings: Social Politics in a Progressive Age* (Cambridge, MA: Belknap Press of Harvard University Press, 1998). Sofia's visit to Toynbee Hall is recorded in its Visitors' Book; London Metropolitan Archives: Records of Toynbee Hall, A/TOY/17/2 Visitors' Book 1885–c. 1920. Another Russian visitor that year was the socialist feminist Alexandra Kollontai, who signed the Toynbee Hall Visitors' Book on June 19. I am indebted to Dr. Katharine Bradley for this information.

13. Sofia's letters to Varya Volkova about her trip to England in 1899, for example, do not mention her visit to Toynbee Hall or comment on English philanthropy; letters from Sofia Panina to Varvara Petrovna Geiden (Volkova), Mashuk, August 26, 1899, and St. Petersburg, November 9, 1899, in GARF, f. 887, op. 1, d. 391.

14. For example, writing to a friend about a visit to a scientific museum for the working class in Berlin, she noted its relatively cultured visitors and stated that she "did not discover any Americas" during her visit. Letter from Sofia Panina to Lidia Yakovleva, Berlin, June 24, 1911, in RIII, f. 32, op. 1, ed. khr. 121, ll. 21–23.

15. Panina, "Na peterburgskoi okraine," 48:169–70. Sofia exaggerated the novelty of the people's house; her "symbiosis" may be found throughout Britain, America, and Europe in the contemporary movement to provide the poor with "rational recreation." See, for example, Peter Bailey, *Leisure and Class in Victorian England: Rational Recreation and the Contest for Control, 1830–1885* (London: Routledge and K. Paul, 1978).

16. Letter from Sofia Panina to Varvara Petrovna Geiden (Volkova), St. Petersburg, February 27, 1896, in GARF, f. 887 op. 1, d. 391, ll. 360b–370b.

17. Letter from Sofia Panina to Varvara Petrovna Geiden (Volkova), Lotarevo, August 22, 1896, in GARF, f. 887 op. 1, d. 391, ll. 61–64.

18. Letters from Sofia Panina to Varvara Petrovna Geiden (Volkova), St. Petersburg, February 27, 1896; Lotarevo, August 22, 1896; and St. Petersburg, December 16, 1896, in GARF, f. 887 op. 1, d. 391, ll. 360b–370b, ll. 61–64, and l. 750b.

19. Letter from Sofia Panina to Varvara Petrovna Geiden (Volkova), Mashuk,

July 1, 1899, in ibid., l. 1190b; a reference to the parable of the talents, told in the Gospels of Matthew and Luke.

20. The 1900 St. Petersburg directory is the first to list Sofia, now heir to the Panin properties, as a property owner; *Ves' Peterburg na 1900 god* (St. Petersburg, 1899), s.v. Panina gr. Sof. Vlad. Her newly purchased properties in the area near Ligovskaya Street are first listed with her name in the 1901 city directory, which gives information for 1900; *Ves' Peterburg na 1901 god* (St. Petersburg, 1900), s.v. Panina gr. Sof. Vlad.

21. Walter Besant, *All Sorts and Conditions of Men* (Oxford: Oxford University Press, 1997).

22. E. S., "Ligovskii narodnyi dom gr. S. V. Paninoi," *Teatral'naia Rossiia*, March 5, 1905, 149; see also Elena Adamenko, "V Ligovskii narodnyi dom mog priiti liuboi izvozchik—za znaniiami," *Chas pik*, May 15, 1996, 14.

23. V. F. Aleksandrovskii, *Narodnyi dom kievskogo obshchestva gramotnosti v g. Kieve. Kratkii ocherk istorii sooruzheniia narodnogo doma* (Kiev, 1902).

24. Sofia first submitted her petition, dated April 24, 1901, to the municipal administration; by June 2 the city commandant (*gradonachal'nik*) had approved it; TsGIA SPb, f. 513, Peterburgskaia gorodskaia uprava, op. 133, d. 97, 1901–11, ll. 1–5. In late 1903 the city gave final approval to the building's status as a small theater, with a permitted capacity of seven hundred for plays and more than nine hundred for concerts, dances, and other events. Fire safety in the building appears to have been the municipal government's only major concern; TsGIA SPb, f. 513, op. 133, d. 97.

25. The police dossier on Sofia contains no expression of concern about the people's house before 1905. GARF, f. 102, op. DOO 1902, d. 992, "O grafine Sof'i Vladimirovny Paninoi [1902–1907]," ll. 4–5, 11–12.

26. Panina, "Na peterburgskoi okraine," 48:171.

27. Tyrkova-Vil'iams, *Na putiakh k svobode*, 393–95.

28. Anastasia is barely mentioned in standard works on the movement that became the Kadet Party. Although she possessed considerable wealth, it is Ivan, not Anastasia, who is identified as playing the leading role in raising funds for the illegal newspaper in Shmuel Galai, *The Liberation Movement in Russia, 1900–1905* (Cambridge: Cambridge University Press, 1973), 116. Anastasia may have been a source of intellectual as well as financial support to her husband. One friend remarked on the difference in both temperament and wit between Ivan and Anastasia when he compared her letters—"masterpieces of a kind, like the letters of Madame de Sévigné" (the seventeenth-century French aristocrat whose letters to her daughter are famous for their insightful descriptions and observations)—to Ivan's "long, intelligent, but somehow colorless" letters. V. I. Vernadskii, *Dnevniki 1917–1921. Oktiabr' 1917–ianvar' 1920*, ed. M. Iu. Sorokina (Kiev: Naukova dumka, 1994), 156 (entry for September 15/28, 1919).

29. Letter from A. S. Petrunkevich to A. V. Peshekhonova, St. Petersburg, April 6, 1913, in Gosudarstvennyi muzei istorii Sankt-Peterburga. Rukopisno-dokumental'nyi fond. Opis' fonda Ligovskii narodnyi dom. Doc. #11. Affectionate letters that Alexandra wrote to Anastasia in emigration after the revolution reflect the schoolteacher's warm relations with Sofia's mother. BAR Panina, Box 7, folder Peshekhonova.

30. Larissa Broitman and Arsenii Dubin, *Ulitsa Chaikovskogo* (Moscow-St. Petersburg: Tsentroligraf, 2003), 149–56. St. Petersburg city directories indicate Sofia purchased the property on Sergievskaya Street in 1901, but the Panin mansion remained her listed address until the directory for 1909.

31. A contemporary newspaper report puts the cost of construction at around 400,000 rubles; *Peterburgskii listok*, April 8, 1903, 3. At this time one ruble was worth $.50.

32. *Otchet Ligovskogo narodnogo doma za pervoe desiatiletie, 1903–1913 gg.*, 13.

33. The building's floor plans are in TsGIA SPb., f. 513, op. 133, d. 97, ll. 75a–75g.

34. E. Ponomareva, "Ligovskii narodnyi dom grafini S. V. Paninoi v Peter-burge," *Trudovaia pomoshch'* (March–April 1906), 412–13; Adamenko, "V Ligov-skii narodnyi dom mog priiti liuboi izvozchik." According to Adamenko, the paintings were removed from the Ligovsky People's House after the 1917 Revo-lution and eventually ended up in the Hermitage and the Russian Museum, where they remain. Sofia's Italian marble statues continued to adorn its corridors.

35. *Otchet Ligovskogo narodnogo doma za pervoe desiatiletie*, 37–38; "Otchet Ligovskoi uchebnoi masterskoi s 20-go avgusta 1903 g. po 1-oe iiunia 1913 g. (10-ti letnii)," TsGIA SPb., f. 219, Ligovskii narodnyi dom, op. 1, ed. khr. 35.

36. E. S., "Ligovskii narodnyi dom gr. S. V. Paninoi."

37. *Otchet Ligovskogo narodnogo doma za pervoe desiatiletie*, 68. In 1913, for ex-ample, the Sunday readings attracted a total of more than twenty-six thousand visits, an average of more than eight hundred per event. The complete list of topics is on pages 79–86.

38. V. Anisimov, "Kratkii ocherk Ligovskogo narodnogo doma," in *Ekho otvetnoe: Literaturnyi sbornik, posviashchennyi 10-letiiu L[igovskikh] V[echernikh] K[lassov]* (St. Petersburg, 1913), 5.

39. A. V. Peshekhonova, "Iz zhizni odnoi besplatnoi biblioteki," *Bibliotekar'* 3 (1913): 173–82; *Otchet Ligovskogo narodnogo doma za pervoe desiatiletie*, 25–26. On popular reading tastes and the campaign for "good" literature, see Jeffrey Brooks, *When Russia Learned to Read: Literacy and Popular Literature, 1861–1917* (Princeton: Princeton University Press, 1985), chap. 9; Laura Engelstein, *The Keys to Happiness: Sex and the Search for Modernity in Fin-de-Siècle Russia* (Ithaca: Cornell University Press, 1992), chap. 10; for similar trends in Germany, see Lynn Abrams, *Workers' Culture in Imperial Germany: Leisure and Recreation in the Rhineland and Westphalia* (London: Routledge, 1992), 145–53.

40. S. V. Panina, "Iskusstvo v narodnoi auditorii," *Trudy Vserossiiskogo s"ezda khudozhnikov: Dekabr' 1911–ianvar' 1912* (St. Petersburg, 1912), vol. 5, 2.

41. *Otchet Ligovskogo narodnogo doma (5-yi god). S 1-go iiunia 1907 g. po 1-oe iiunia 1908 g.* (St. Petersburg, 1908), 27–28; Panina's letters to Lidia Yakovleva, RIII, f. 32, op. 1, ed. khr. 121.

42. *Otchet Ligovskogo narodnogo doma. (5-yi god)*, 38–40; *Otchet Ligovskogo narodnogo doma. (8-oi god). S 1-go iiunia 1910 g. po 1–3 iiunia 1911 g.* (St. Peters-burg, 1911), 40–41.

43. *Otchet Ligovskogo narodnogo doma. (5-yi god)*, 31. For a list of plays per-formed during the first ten years, see *Otchet Ligovskogo narodnogo doma za pervoe desiatiletie*, 90–93. On Gaideburov, see Simon Dreiden, "Stranitsy bol'shoi

zhizni," in Nadezhda Fedorovna Skarskaia and P. P. Gaideburov, *Na stsene i v zhizni. Stranitsy avtobiografii* (Moscow, 1959), 8–9. Gaideburov's recollections of the Ligovsky People's House are in P. P. Gaideburov and Simon Dreiden, *Literaturnoe nasledie. Vospominaniia, stat'i, rezhisserskie eksplikatsii, vystupleniia* (Moscow: Vserossiiskoe teatral'noe obshchestvo, 1977), 187–204. James Van Geldern discusses the importance of Gaideburov's theater at the Ligovsky People's House in *Bolshevik Festivals, 1917–1920* (Berkeley: University of California Press, 1993), 119–21.

44. Average attendance at the movies in 1907–8 was 978, while attendance at the Sunday and holiday readings fell that year to an average of 562. In 1910–11 the people's house showed twelve movies, with an average attendance of 801. *Otchet Ligovskogo narodnogo doma. (5-yi god)*, 35–37; *Otchet Ligovskogo narodnogo doma. (8-oi god)*, 41. Coworkers' disapproval of films is suggested by the complete absence of any mention of them in the tenth anniversary report of the people's house.

45. The report for 1907–8 praised "the beginning of the formation of a kernel of civic consciousness among students in the evening classes. This is especially valuable and positive data, giving a token of certainty that the House's work is going along the right path." *Otchet Ligovskogo narodnogo doma. (5-yi god)*, 5. A well-known representative of the intellectually ambitious worker of this period is Semen Kanatchikov; *A Radical Worker in Tsarist Russia: The Autobiography of Semën Ivanovich Kanatchikov*, ed. and trans. Reginald E. Zelnik (Stanford: Stanford University Press, 1986).

46. TsGIA SPb, f. 219, op. 1, d. 5, "Otchet [uchenicheskogo literaturnogo kruzhka] s 15 apr. 1908 goda po 25 apr. 1909 goda." *Otchet Ligovskogo narodnogo doma (8-oi god)*, 7–8, 11; *Otchet Ligovskogo narodnogo doma za pervoe desiatiletie*, 17–18; A. A. Briantsev and Aleksandra Noevna Gozenpud, *Vospominaniia, stat'i, vystupleniia, dnevniki, pis'ma* (Moscow: Vserossiiskoe teatral'noe obshchestvo, 1979), 57; V. Torskii, "Samodeiatel'nost' uchashchikhsia v Ligovskikh vechernikh klassakh," in *Ekho otvetnoe*, 11–15; "K kharakteristike deiatel'nosti Ligovskogo narodnogo doma," in *Ekho otvetnoe*, 39–42.

47. For the institution's fees, see *Otchet Ligovskogo narodnogo doma za pervoe desiatiletie*, 69. Sofia's subsidies fluctuated from month to month. Generally she provided whatever was necessary to cover the shortfall between monthly income and the costs of running the institution, and she made additional contributions whenever the building needed major repairs or improvements. Her monthly contribution increased sharply from mid-1915, when she began to support a military hospital at the people's house. TsGIA SPb, f. 219, op. 1, d. 6, Otchety LND nach. Dek. 1909 okonch. 1917 g. This file contains monthly and annual financial reports from December 1909 to the end of 1916. On the Council, see TsGIA SPb., f. 219, op. 1, d. 14, ll. 1, 12–120b; d. 3, ll. 5–6.

48. BAR Panina, Box 14, folder "Narodnyi dom." Entitled "Financial Statute," the unsigned, undated document states that "I" leave to the people's house an unspecified sum of capital, to be administered by the St. Petersburg municipal government, the interest from which must be given to the institution's governing council, comprised of a "guardian or guardianess" elected by the council and approved by the city government, two representatives of the

city government, and the heads of all the departments of the institution. At the annual meetings of the institution, all the coworkers and all adult student-visitors should have the right to vote, according to this document.

49. Of the sixty-four coworkers in 1913, forty were women and twenty-four were men; of the twenty-two who were volunteers, all but two were women. Thirty-two had been at the people's house for more than five years, and six of them had worked there for more than ten. Most of the positions that women occupied at the people's house were unpaid, while most of the positions men held were paid. *Otchet Ligovskogo narodnogo doma za pervoe desiatiletie*, 69. Such a strong female presence was also typical in the settlement house movement: Katharine Bentley Beauman, *Women and the Settlement Movement* (London: Radcliffe Press, 1996); Martha Vicinus, *Independent Women: Work and Community for Single Women, 1850–1920* (Chicago: University of Chicago Press, 1985), esp. chap. 6.

50. *Ves' Peterburg na 1909 god. Adresnaia i spravochnaia kniga S-Peterburga* (St. Petersburg, 1908); *Ves' Peterburg na 1915 god. Adresnaia i spravochnaia kniga S-Peterburga* (St. Petersburg, 1914). Elizaveta Popova's death in late 1930 is reported in a letter from Alexandra to Sofia, dated November 24/December 7 [1930]; Alexandra's death in April 1932 is described in Nadezhda Yalozo's letter to Sofia, dated April 7, 1932; both letters are in BAR Panina, Box 7, folder Peshekhonova.

51. Letter from S. Kislinskaia to Sofia Panina, April 6, 1913, in RIII, f. 32, op. 1, ed. khr. 123, l. 7; letter from Liudmila F. Grammatchikova to Sofia Panina, December 28, 1922, BAR Panina, Box 7, folder Peshekhonova.

52. *Otchet Ligovskogo narodnogo doma za pervoe desiatiletie*, 3–13, 62–67.

53. "Kniga glubokoi priznatel'nosti," PD, f. 223; excerpts in *Otchet Ligovskogo narodnogo doma za pervoe desiatiletie*, 9–12.

54. Reprinted in Jane Addams and Victoria Brown, *Twenty Years at Hull-House: With Autobiographical Notes* (Boston: Bedford/St. Martin's, 1999), chap. 6; see also Louise W. Knight, *Citizen: Jane Addams and the Struggle for Democracy* (Chicago: University of Chicago Press, 2005), Part 2, on the evolution of her religious and social views.

55. Adele Lindenmeyr, "Public Life, Private Virtues: Women in Russian Charity, 1762–1914," *Signs: Journal of Women in Culture and Society* 18, no. 3 (1993): 562–91; Brenda Meehan-Waters, *Holy Women of Russia: The Lives of Five Orthodox Women Offer Spiritual Guidance for Today* ([San Francisco]: HarperSan Francisco, 1993).

56. See, for example, Seth Koven, *Slumming: Sexual and Social Politics in Victorian London* (Princeton: Princeton University Press, 2004), chap. 3.

57. On the ethos of charity and Russian women, see Lindenmeyr, "Public Life, Private Virtues." On Muriel Lester, see Seth Koven, *The Matchgirl and the Heiress* (Princeton: Princeton University Press, 2014), esp. chap. 3.

58. Letter from Sofia Panina to Varvara Petrovna Geiden (Volkova), St. Petersburg, April 15, 1898, in GARF, f. 887 op. 1, d. 391, l. 109.

59. Letter from Sofia Panina to Varvara Petrovna Geiden (Volkova), Mashuk, July 1, 1899, in ibid., l. 119ob.

60. Letter from Sofia Panina to Varvara Petrovna Geiden (Volkova), Mashuk, July 8, 1897, in ibid., ll. 930b–94.

61. Letters from Sofia Panina to Lidia Yakovleva from July 8, 1912; April 14, 1913; and November 22, 1913, in RIII, f. 32, op. 1, ed. khr. 121, ll. 19–20.

62. Living as an émigré in Switzerland, Sofia received an unsigned letter dated April 15, 1923, in honor of the twentieth anniversary of the Ligovsky People's House. "Dedicated to a dear friend," it is an allegory titled "A Fairy Tale," in which Sofia is depicted as a bright star sent to earth to dispel darkness, bring love, and lead people to the light. BAR Panina, Box 14, folder Ligovskii Narodnyi Dom, Soviet Period.

Chapter 5. The "Red Countess"

1. T. P. Bondarevskaia, A. Ia. Velikanova, and F. M. Suslova, *Lenin v Peterburge-Petrograde: Mesta zhizni i deiatel'nosti v gorode i okrestnostiakh 1890–1920* (Leningrad: Lenizdat, 1977), 130–33. One worker who attended the meeting was the Bolshevik D. I. Grazkin, who describes it in his memoir, *Za temnoi noch'iu den' vstaval* (Moscow: Izdatel'stvo politicheskoi literatury, 1975), 87–90. According to these sources, the meeting was attended by about three thousand people, which seems impossible in a theater with fewer than one thousand seats. The painting is by V. Zhilin, titled "V. I. Lenin's Speech at the People's House of Countess S. V. Panina in 1906." The poster, the work of M. Sokolov, depicts an ecstatic but oddly modern-looking crowd in the theater. It may be viewed at http://www.sovietposters.ru/pages_rus/831.htm.

2. Panina, "Na peterburgskoi okraine," 48:172.

3. Panina, "Na peterburgskoi okraine," 49:191–92.

4. Laurie Bernstein, *Sonia's Daughters: Prostitutes and Their Regulation in Imperial Russia* (Berkeley: University of California Press, 1995), 9.

5. *Otchet Ligovskogo narodnogo doma. (5-yi god)*, 3.

6. In December 1907 the Department of Police asked the St. Petersburg City Commandant's office to draw up a "most detailed" report about the people's house, including information on all the meetings that had taken place there since 1904. GARF, f. 102, op. DOO 1902, d. 992, "O grafini Sof'i Vladimirovnoi Paninoi, 1902–1907," l. 18; the report, on ll. 22–220b, lists those meetings officially permitted by the city commandant's office that had "the most revolutionary tendency." Obviously, it does not include meetings that the city commandant did not permit or know about.

7. *Otchet Ligovskogo narodnogo doma (8-oi god)*, 3–4.

8. TsGIA SPb., f. 569, Kantseliariia petrogradskogo gradonachal'nika, op. 13, d. 10592, ll. 106–10. The lecture was scheduled for March 2, 1914; according to the outline submitted to the police in advance, Sofia discussed the zemstvos' impact on agriculture, education, and public health, but not their political significance.

9. *Otchet Ligovskogo narodnogo doma (6-i god). S 1-go iiunia 1908 g. po 1-oe iiunia 1909 g.* (St. Petersburg, 1909), 16. After the introduction of the Stolypin land reform in 1906, which allowed peasants to claim a share of communally held land

as private property, urban migrants who maintained ties to their villages flooded the office out of concern that the new law would deprive them of their rights to communal land.

10. A list of the topics of all lectures for the first ten years is in *Otchet Ligovskogo narodnogo doma za pervoe desiatiletie*, 75–79.

11. *Otchet Ligovskogo narodnogo doma. (5-yi god)*, 13–15.

12. *Otchet Ligovskogo narodnogo doma. (8-oi god)*, 14–16.

13. TsGIA SPb., f. 569, op. 3, d. 1059g., l. 107.

14. TsGIA SPb, f. 569, op. 13, d. 1059g, ll. 1–20.

15. *Otchet Ligovskogo narodnogo doma. (8-oi god)*, 15; *Otchet Ligovskogo narodnogo doma za pervoe desiatiletie*, 22–23.

16. Alexander Kerensky, *Russia and History's Turning Point* (New York: Duell, Sloan and Pearce, 1965), 44; Richard Abraham, *Alexander Kerensky: The First Love of the Revolution* (New York: Columbia University Press, 1987), 25.

17. The first time was in November 1905, for a conspiratorial meeting of the St. Petersburg Social Democratic Party. He came again in February 1906, for an all-city party conference. *Lenin v Peterburge-Petrograde*, 129–30; Adamenko, "V Ligovskii narodnyi dom mog priiti liuboi izvozchik."

18. Mikhail Petrovich Efremov, "Avtobiografiia," manuscript dated July 7, 1932, in Rossiiskaia gosudarstvennaia biblioteka (RGB), Otdel rukopisi, 369.386.2. Ilya Sadofyev, another aspiring worker-poet, joined the workers' literary circle after the 1905 Revolution; he ended up being exiled to Siberia just before World War I, due, he claims, to his affiliation with the Bolsheviks: Il'ia Ivanovich Sadof'ev, "Raskopki pamiati—avtobiografiia," RGB, Otdel rukopisi, 154.5.12. Evdokimova's autobiography is in Gosudarstvennyi muzei politicheskoi istorii Rossii, f. VI, No. 622. I am grateful to Liudmila Bulgakova for this information.

19. GARF, f. 102, op. DOO 1902, d. 992, l. 260b.

20. "Podpol'naia rabota v gody imperialisticheskoi voiny v Petrograde," *Krasnaia letopis'* 2/3 (1922): 116–43; P. Ia. Zavolokin, *Sovremennye rabochekrest'ianskie poety v obraztsakh i avtobiografiiakh s portretami* (Ivanovo-Voznesensk: Osnova, 1925), 26–28. On Mashirov-Samobytnik, see Mark D. Steinberg, *Proletarian Imagination: Self, Modernity, and the Sacred in Russia, 1910–1925* (Ithaca: Cornell University Press, 2002), 304–5.

21. *Otchet Ligovskogo narodnogo doma. (8-oi god)*, 6; emphasis in the original.

22. *Otchet Ligovskogo narodnogo doma za pervoe desiatiletie*, 39. Sofia's reference to a "hidden truth" might be an allusion to a common popular belief that the privileged classes conspired to keep the poor from finding out about laws that granted them justice and land.

23. *The White Slave Trade. Transactions of the International Congress on the White Slave Trade, Held in London on the 21st, 22nd and 23rd of June, 1899, at the Invitation of the National Vigilance Association* (London: Office of the National Vigilance Association, 1899), 8; L. A. Bogdanovich, *Bor'ba s torgovlei zhenshchinami i "Rossiiskoe obshchestvo zashchity zhenshchin"* (Moscow, 1903); Bernstein, *Sonia's Daughters*, 161–66, 192–93; Philippa Lesley Hetherington, "Victims of the Social Temperament: Prostitution, Migration, and the Traffic in Women from Late

Imperial Russia and the Soviet Union, 1890–1935," PhD dissertation, Harvard University, 2014, chap. 2.

24. Leo Tolstoy, *Resurrection*, translated by Vera Traill (New York: New American Library, 1984), 16.

25. "Ligovka: Boskhovo gul'bishche," in Dmitrii Gubin, Lev Lur'e, and Igor' Poroshin, *Real'nyi Peterburg: O gorode s tochki zreniia nedvizhimosti i o nedvizhimosti s tochki zreniia istorii* (St. Peterburg: Limbus Press, 1999), 80–85.

26. *Rossiiskoe obshchestvo zashchity zhenshchin v 1900 i 1901 g.* (St. Petersburg, 1902); *Rossiiskoe obshchestvo zashchity zhenshchin v 1909 g.* (St. Petersburg, 1910); *Rossiiskoe obshchestvo zashchity zhenshchin v 1913 godu* (Petrograd, 1914).

27. *Rossiiskoe obshchestvo zashchity zhenshchin v 1900 i 1901 g.*, 30.

28. PD, f. 223, No. 53, copies of monthly, annual and ten-year reports on the hostel with Sofia's comments and questions.

29. *Rossiiskoe obshchestvo zashchity zhenshchin v 1909 g.*, 12–13.

30. Bernstein, *Sonia's Daughters*, 273, 278–90; Hetherington, "Victims of the Social Temperament," 189–97. Two thirds of the congress's 293 participants were women, of whom 58 were affiliated with feminist organizations.

31. Reporter for the printers' union newspaper, quoted in Bernstein, *Sonia's Daughters*, 219.

32. Ibid., 219–29. Complete congress proceedings are in *Trudy pervogo Vserossiiskogo s"ezda po bor'be s torgom zhenshchinami i ego prichinami, proiskhodivshego v S-Peterburge s 21 po 25 aprelia 1910 g.*, 2 vols. (St. Petersburg, 1911–12).

33. Letter from Sofia Panina to Lidia Yakovleva dated February 25 [no year], in RIII, f. 32, op. 1, ed. khr. 121, ll. 58–60; ellipsis in original. The speech she gave seems to have taken place at the people's house.

34. Sofia's speech and the debate that followed it are in *Trudy pervogo Vserossiiskogo s"ezda po bor'be s torgom zhenshchinami*, 1:233–45.

35. *Rossiiskoe obshchestvo zashchity zhenshchin v 1913 godu*, 86–87; Elizabeth Waters, "Victim or Villain? Prostitution in Post-revolutionary Russia," in *Women and Society in Russia and the Soviet Union*, ed. Linda Edmondson (Cambridge: Cambridge University Press, 1992), 171.

36. Ruthchild, *Equality and Revolution,* chaps. 3 and 4.

37. Letter from Sofia Panina to Varvara Petrovna Geiden (Volkova), St. Petersburg, March 26, 1896, in GARF, f. 887, op. 1, d. 391, ll. 42–42ob. Sofia is listed as a member in the society's annual reports for 1895–96, 1896–97, and 1897–98. *Godovoi otchet Russkogo zhenskogo vzaimno-blagotvoritel'nogo obshchestva za 1895–96 god* (St. Petersburg, 1897), 76; *Godovoi otchet Russkogo zhenskogo vzaimno-blagotvoritel'nogo obshchestva za 1896–1897 god* (St. Petersburg, 1898), 85; *Godovoi otchet Russkogo zhenskogo vzaimno-blagotvoritel'nogo obshchestva za 1897–1898 god* (St. Petersburg, 1899), 172. Thereafter she ceased to be a member. I am grateful to Rochelle Ruthchild for this information.

38. Although Sofia attended the first Russian congress on women's rights that was held in 1908, she remained a silent observer, even at its sessions on philanthropy and women's education. *Trudy pervogo Vserossiiskogo zhenskogo s"ezda pri Russkom zhenskom obshchestve v S.-Peterburge 10–16 dekabria 1908 goda* (St. Petersburg, 1909), 915.

39. On Bebel, see the letter from Sofia Panina to Varvara Petrovna Geiden (Volkova), Baden-Baden, July 28, 1896, in GARF, f. 887, op. 1, d. 391, l. 60; on Braun, see the letter from Sofia Panina to Lidia Yakovleva, July 13, 1910, in RIII, f. 32, op. 1, ed. khr. 121, ll. 19–20. The dearth of surviving correspondence between Sofia and feminist acquaintances such as Tyrkova-Williams and Miliukova makes it difficult to determine the extent to which she shared their feminist convictions.

40. Letter from Natalia Nordman to Sofia Panina, April 24, 1910, in PD, f. 223, No. 16. Repin's inscription on his 1913 drawing of Sofia is in PD, f. 223, "Kniga glubokoi priznatel'nosti," l. 13; emphasis in the original.

41. Obituary in *Moskovskiia vedomosti*, January 18, 1844, 48.

42. Letters from Sofia Panina to Lidia Yakovleva from Marfino, July 13, 1910, and July 8, 1912, RIII, kabinet rukopisei, f. 32, op. 1, ed. khr. 121, ll. 19–20, 24–26.

43. *Izvestiia Moskovskoi gubernskoi zemskoi upravy*, vol. 12 (Moscow, 1912), 33; *Otchet o deiatel'nosti Marfinskogo zemskogo uchastkogo popechitel'stva o bednykh za 1911 g.* (Moscow, 1912).

44. Sofia told Lidia Yakovleva how much she loved Gaspra in a letter of June 24, 1911, and a postcard dated April 14, 1913, RIII, kabinet rukopisei, f. 32, op. 1, ed. khr. 121, ll. 21–23, 31.

45. A. A. Galichenko, *Gaspra* (Simferopol: Biznes-Inform, 2005), 14–29.

46. V. S. Il'in, *Istoriia vozniknoveniia, organizatsiia i deiatel'nost' Stepnoi biologicheskoi stantsii imeni gr. S. V. Paninoi*, in Otd. Botaniki, no. 1, supplement, *Trudy Petrogradskogo obshchestva estestvoispitatelei* 46 (1916). I am indebted Archil F. Dondua of St. Petersburg University for the information about Sofia's involvement with the St. Petersburg Imperial Society of Natural Science Researchers.

47. Letter from Tolstoy to V. G. Chertkov, Gaspra, September 14, 1901, in L. N. Tolstoi, *Polnoe sobranie sochinenii. Seriia tret'ia. Pis'ma* (Moscow: Gosudarstvennoe izdatel'stvo khudozhestvennoi literatury, 1954), 73:245.

48. Letters from Tolstoy to S. N. Tolstoy, Gaspra, end of October, 1901 (unsent) and November 6, 1901, in ibid., 73:157–58. See also *L. N. Tolstoi. Entsiklopediia*, comp. and ed. N. I. Burnasheva (Moscow: Prosveshchenie, 2009), 374–75.

49. Letter from Sofia Panina to Varvara Petrovna Geiden (Volkova), St. Petersburg, January 10, 1896, in GARF, f. 887, op. 1, d. 391, ll. 32–35.

50. *Otchet Ligovskogo narodnogo doma (8-oi god)*, 4.

51. TsGIA SPb., f. 569, op. 13, d. 10592, ll. 57–61.

52. I. I. Iukina and Iu. E. Guseva, *Zhenskii Peterburg* (St. Petersburg: Aleteiia, 2004), 238.

53. Ivan Stoliarov, *Zapiski russkogo krest'ianina* (Paris: Institut d'études slaves, 1986), 122–47. I am grateful to Timothy Mixter for this reference.

54. GARF, f. 102, Departament politsii, 6 deloproizvodstvo, 1916, d. 27, "Raznye zaprosy po pamiatnym listkam i kartochkam," ll. 115–16. The police first noted oppositionist sentiments among the peasants and teachers living on Sofia's estate in Voronezh during the 1905 revolution; the report also mentions Shcherbachenko. GARF, f. 102, op. DOO 1902, d. 992, ll. 26–26ob.

55. GARF, f. 102, 1916, d. 27, ll. 116–17. The original reads: "deiatel'nost'

otdelov 'Nar. Doma' gr. Paninoi za 11 let sushchestvovaniia ne vozbuzhdala somnenii v politicheskoi blagonadezhnosti." The reference to the institution's eleven years of existence suggests that the original police report was written in 1914 and reproduced in this file; in addition, since the file is about Sofia, not her institution, the reference is presumably to her political reliability, not the institution's. The report erroneously states that there was evidence that Sofia was related to the "émigré anarchist Prince Krapotkin [sic]." Characterized as "very rich" in a 1911 police file, Sofia was described as a "public activist with liberal leanings, siding with the party 'People's Freedom'"; GARF, f. 102, Obshchii otdel, 1911, d. 276, "S otvetami na rozysknye tsirkuliary," ll. 150b–16.

56. Vasil'chikov, "Grafinia S. V. Panina," 83; Wassiltschikow, *Verschwundenes Russland*, 36–37.

57. "Kniga glubokoi priznatel'nosti," PD, f. 223, l. 43.

58. Letter dated May 4, 1913, and signed A., in RIII, f. 32, op. 1, ed. khr. 123, ll. 11–12.

59. Aleksei Kapralov, "Ligovskii narodnyi dom: Vospominaniia blagodarnogo vospitannika," *Russkaia mysl'*, July 24, 1956, 7.

60. Letter from Alexandra Peshekhonova to Sofia Panina, [Petrograd], November 17 [1923], in BAR Panina, Box 7, folder Peshekhonova.

61. BAR Panina, Box 7, Peshekhonova folders; Box 8, Letters from the USSR, 1921–26 folder; Box 14, folder Narodnyi dom.

Chapter 6. Sofia Goes to War

1. Kerensky quoted in Allan K. Wildman, *The End of the Russian Imperial Army*, vol. 1, *The Old Army and the Soldiers' Revolt (March–April 1917)* (Princeton: Princeton University Press, 1980), 80. See also Robert B. McKean, *St. Petersburg between the Revolutions: Workers and Revolutionaries, June 1907–February 1917* (New Haven: Yale University Press, 1990), chap. 10. Boris Kolonitskii points out, however, that patriotic, pro-Serbia demonstrations had been taking place in the capital since at least July 13: *"Tragicheskaia erotika." Obrazy imperatorskoi sem'i v gody pervoi mirovoi voiny* (Moscow: Novoe literaturnoe obozrenie, 2010), 77–78.

2. Richard S. Wortman, *Scenarios of Power: Myth and Ceremony in Russian Monarchy*, vol. 2, *From Alexander II to the Abdication of Nicholas II* (Princeton: Princeton University Press, 2000), 510–11; Kolonitskii, *"Tragicheskaia erotika,"* 78–80.

3. Tyrkova-Williams quoted in Arkadii Borman, *A. V. Tyrkova-Vil'iams po ee pis'mam i vospominaniiam syna* (Louvain, 1964), 111–12. On the question of elite and popular support for the war during its first months, see Melissa Kirschke Stockdale, *Mobilizing the Russian Nation: Patriotism and Citizenship in the First World War* (Cambridge: Cambridge University Press, 2016), chap. 1; Josh Sanborn, "The Mobilization of 1914 and the Question of the Russian Nation: A Reexamination," *Slavic Review* 59, no. 2 (Summer 2000): 267–89; and Joshua A. Sanborn, *Drafting the Russian Nation: Military Conscription, Total War, and Mass Politics, 1905–1925* (DeKalb: Northern Illinois University Press, 2003), 29–31.

4. Letter from Sofia Panina to Lidia Yakovleva, Marfino, August 7, 1914, RIII, f. 32, op. 1, ed. khr. 121, l. 38.

5. Peter Gatrell, *Russia's First World War: A Social and Economic History* (Harlow, England: Pearson-Longman, 2005), 22–23, 245–46.

6. Ibid., 22–23, 67–68, 73.

7. TsGIA SPb, f. 219, op. 1, d. 27, "Otchet po upravleniiu nar. domom Gr. S. V. Paninoi za iiun', iiul', avgust, sentiabr', oktiabr', noiabr' i dekabr' 1917 g. i ianvar' 1918," ll. 14, 39 (pay sheets for April 1917). On women in the British and French labor force during World War I, see Gail Braybon, *Women Workers in the First World War: The British Experience* (London: Croom Helm, 1981); Claire A. Culleton, *Working-Class Culture, Women and Britain, 1914–1921* (New York: St. Martin's Press, 2000); Margaret H. Darrow, *French Women and the First World War: War Stories of the Home Front* (Oxford: Berg, 2000), chap. 6.

8. On the British Women's Auxiliary Army Corps, see Susan R. Grayzel, *Women's Identities at War: Gender, Motherhood, and Politics in Britain and France during the First World War* (Chapel Hill: University of North Carolina Press, 1999), 198–202. On the similar use of women in the Austrian and German armies, see Maureen Healy, *Vienna and the Fall of the Habsburg Empire: Total War and Everyday Life in World War I* (Cambridge: Cambridge University Press, 2004), 204–9, and Bianca Schönberger, "Motherly Heroines and Adventurous Girls: Red Cross Nurses and Women Army Auxiliaries in the First World War," in *Home/Front: The Military, War, and Gender in Twentieth-Century Germany*, ed. Karen Hagemann and Stefanie Schiller-Springorum (Oxford: Berg, 2002), 87–114. On Russian women soldiers, see Stoff, *They Fought for the Motherland*, and Stockdale, "'My Death for the Motherland Is Happiness.'"

9. Iukina and Guseva, *Zhenskii Peterburg*, 235; Borman, *A. V. Tyrkova-Vil'iams*, 112–17. On Russian nurses during World War I, see Laurie S. Stoff, *Russia's Sisters of Mercy and the Great War: More Than Binding Men's Wounds* (Lawrence: University Press of Kansas, 2015).

10. Panina, "Na peterburgskoi okraine," 49:189; McKean, *St. Petersburg between the Revolutions*, 319.

11. Between June 1, 1915, and June 1, 1916, for example, her subsidies to the people's house, including the infirmary, amounted to more than 104,000 rubles; for the same period in 1916–17 her contributions exceeded 120,000 rubles. When converted into current US dollars, the subsidies for these two years alone amount to a fortune—more than $2.6 million. The only other sources of revenue besides Sofia's subsidies to keep the people's house in operation were proceeds from sales at the cafeteria and tearoom. TsGIA SPb, f. 219, op. 1, d. 29, "Tablitsa denezhnogo oborota za 1913–1918 gg." The infirmary's official name was the "Sixteenth Petrograd City Infirmary for the Wounded in the People's House of Countess S. V. Panina," and Sofia was its Guardian (*popechitel'nitsa*) as well as its financial supporter. It was administered by the Petrograd municipal authorities under the auspices of the All-Russian Union of Towns, which contributed only a token amount to the infirmary for nurses' aides and medical orderlies. TsGIA SPb, f. 569, op. 14, d. 42, l. 17. On military infirmaries in Petrograd, see B. B. Dubentsov and V. A. Nardova, *Peterburgskaia gorodskaia duma 1846–1918* (St. Petersburg: Liki Rossii, 2005), 268.

12. Over the course of the war the state treasury paid out 4.92 billion rubles in aid to the wives and families of soldiers. Gatrell, *Russia's First World War*, 81n8.

13. Liudmila Bulgakova, "Privilegirovannye bedniaki: Pomoshch' soldatskim sem'iam v gody pervoi mirovoi voiny," in *Na puti k revoliutsionnym potriaseniiam: Iz istorii Rossii vtoroi poloviny XIX–nachala XX veka*, ed. V. S. Diakin and I. P. Palkina (St. Petersburg: Nestor-Historia, 2001), 429–34; quotation from 431. See also I. P. Pavlova, *Sotsial'noe popechenie v Rossii v gody pervoi mirovoi voiny* (Krasnoiarsk: Krasnoiarskii gosudarstvennyi agrarnyi universitet, 2003), 8–12, 19–20. On Austria and Britain, see Healy, *Vienna*, 193–97; and Susan Pedersen, "Gender, Welfare, and Citizenship in Britain during the Great War," *American Historical Review* 95, no. 4 (October 1990): 983–1006. The Austrian system of state allowances for soldiers' families was also introduced in a 1912 law. Healy points out that because the system delegated responsibility for distributing the allowances to the same municipal agencies that distributed poor relief, it confused the state subsidies with charity.

14. *Peterburgskaia gorodskaia duma 1846–1918*, 263–64; N. Aleksandrovskii, "Deiatel'nost' Petrogradskikh gorodskikh popechitel'stv o bednykh po okazaniiu pomoshchi prizvannykh na deistvitel'nuiu voennuiu sluzhbu," *Prizrenie i blagotvoritel'nost' v Rossii* 1914, no. 6–7 (August–September): 643–58; P. Litvinov, "Raskhod Petrogradskikh gorodskikh popechitel'stv o bednykh na prizrenie semei nizhnikh chinov, prizvannykh na voinu," *Prizrenie i blagotvoritel'nost' v Rossii* 1914, no. 8–9–10 (October–November–December): 985–98. On the history of the guardianship system, see Adele Lindenmeyr, "A Russian Experiment in Voluntarism: The Municipal Guardianships of the Poor, 1894–1914," *Jahrbücher für Geschichte Osteuropas* 30, no. 3 (1982): 429–51.

15. Kniaz' V. A. Obolenskii, *Moia zhizn' i moi sovremenniki* (Paris: YMCA, 1988), 504.

16. *Otchet 13-go Gorodskogo popechitel'stva o bednykh v Petrograde 2, 3 i 4-go uch. Aleksandro-Nevskoi chasti. Za 1913 god. Shestoi god deiatel'nosti popechitel'stva* (Petrograd, 1914); *Otchet 13-go Gorodskogo popechitel'stva o bednykh. Za 1914 god.* (Petrograd, 1915), 7–9.

17. *Otchet 13-go Gorodskogo popechitel'stva o bednykh. Za 1914 god*, 3, 14–15.

18. Ibid., 7, 9. The guardianship's lengthy and detailed report for 1914 makes no mention of involvement by volunteers from the Ligovsky People's House in war relief until after the first disbursements of state aid had been completed in late August.

19. Ibid., 5, 15–21.

20. Ibid., 5, 24–60. The other commissions, several of which were headed by coworkers from the people's house, were in charge of cafeterias, housing, employment, statistical information, finances, and fundraising. The new bureau included the officers of the organization, the chairpersons and secretaries of the eight new commissions, and three members of the guardianship, elected by the council. Two of its secretaries, Nadezhda Yalozo and Yulia Beliaevskaya, had worked with Sofia from the earliest days of the people's house. Yalozo and Beliaevskaya also became members of the newly expanded council, which included several of Sofia's other long-time collaborators: her friend Lidia Yakovleva, her

cousin Nadezhda Zurova, Liudmila Grammatchikova, and Alexander Briantsev, who was the assistant to the director of the people's house theater.

21. Gr. S. Panina, "Obshchestvennaia rabota v gorodskikh popechitel'stvakh
(Doklad, chitannyi 1 fevralia 1916 goda na sobranii, ustroennom Rossiiskoi
ligoi ravnopraviia zhenshchin)," *Prizrenie i blagotvoritel'nost' v Rossii* 1916,
no. 1–2 (January–February): 6.

22. The late historian V. R. Leikina-Svirskaya recalled to this author how
she worked during the war for the Petrograd municipal guardianships when
she was a student at the progressive Vyborg Commercial School.

23. Letter from Sofia Panina to Lidia Yakovleva, June 18, 1915, RIII, f. 32,
op. 1, ed. khr. 121, ll. 42–43; Panina, "Na peterburgskoi okraine," 49:191.

24. Quoted in Stockdale, "'My Death for the Motherland is Happiness,'"
87. On the mobilization of the home front for war, see Adele Lindenmeyr,
Christopher Read, and Peter Waldron, eds., *The Experience of War and Revolution*, book 2 of *Russia's Home Front in War and Revolution, 1914–1922* (Bloomington: Slavica, 2016); Stockdale, *Mobilizing the Russian Nation*, chap. 4.

25. Obolenskii, *Moia zhizn'*, 506–7; D. V. Nadsadnyi, "Pomoshch' bezhentsam v Petrograde vo vremia pervoi mirovoi voiny: Deiatel'nost' gorodskogo
samoupravleniia i Vserossiiskogo soiuza gorodov pomoshchi bol'nym i
ranenym voinam (1914–1917 gg.)," *Izvestiia rossiiskogo gosudarstvennogo pedagogicheskogo universiteta imeni A. I. Gertsena* 162 (2013): 32.

26. "Obshchee sobranie chlenov Vserossiiskogo soiuza uchrezhdenii, ob-
shchestv i deiatelei po obshchestvennomu i chastnomu prizreniiu," *Prizrenie i
blagotvoritel'nost' v Rossii* 1916, no. 5 (May): 438.

27. Obolenskii, *Moia zhizn'*, 505.

28. Wildman, *The End of the Russian Imperial Army*, 83–89; quote on 93.

29. Orlando Figes and Boris Kolonitskii, *Interpreting the Russian Revolution:
The Language and Symbols of 1917* (New Haven: Yale University Press, 1999),
chap. 1; Kolonitskii, "*Tragicheskaia erotica.*"

30. I. I. Tolstoi, *Dnevnik 1906–1916* (St. Petersburg: Evropeiskii dom, 1997),
577.

31. Panina, "Obshchestvennaia rabota," 5–6.

32. On press censorship during the war, see Stockdale, *Mobilizing the Russian Nation*, chap. 2.

33. "Na obshchestvennoi rabote," *Rech'*, April 22, 1916, 3. I am grateful to
Tony Heywood for this reference.

34. Tolstoi, *Dnevnik*, 682, 690–93. On the February 1916 municipal elections,
see *Peterburgskaia gorodskaia duma 1846–1918*, 288–303.

35. McKean, *St. Petersburg between the Revolutions*, 320, 339–41; *Peterburgskaia gorodskaia duma 1846–1918*, 279–83; Kolonitskii, "*Tragicheskaia erotica*,"
132–33.

36. TsGIA SPb, f. 219, op. 1, d. 29, "Tablitsa denezhnogo oborota za 1913–
1918 gg."

37. McKean, *St. Petersburg between the Revolutions*, 343–46; *Peterburgskaia
gorodskaia duma 1846–1918*, 309. Berlin and Vienna began to experience similar
shortages, especially from 1916, sowing social tensions and protests among
working-class women. See Belinda J. Davis, *Home Fires Burning: Food, Politics*

and Everyday Life in World War I Berlin (Chapel Hill: University of North Carolina Press, 2000), and Healy, *Vienna*, chap. 1.

38. Letter from Sofia Panina to Lidia Yakovleva, August 10, 1916, RIII, f. 32,
op. 1, ed. khr. 121, l. 48.

39. Letter from Sofia Panina to Liubov Ya. Gurevich, September 17, 1916,
PD 20.035/CXXXVIb3, ll. 3–30b.

40. Letter from Sofia Panina to Lidia Yakovleva, October 22, 1916, RIII, f. 32,
op. 1, ed. khr. 121, ll. 50–51.

41. Kondratiev's reminiscences are in "Podpol'naia rabota v gody imperialisticheskoi voiny v Petrograde," 120–21, and Mashirov-Samobytnik's are in
ibid., 133–34.

42. Panina, "Obshchestvennaia rabota," 11.

43. Melissa Kirschke Stockdale, *Paul Miliukov and the Quest for a Liberal Russia, 1880–1918* (Ithaca: Cornell University Press, 1996), 222–26.

Chapter 7. Revolution in Petrograd

1. Portions of this chapter first appeared in Adele Lindenmeyr, "'The First
Woman in Russia': Countess Sofia Panina and Women's Political Participation
in the Revolutions of 1917," *Journal of Modern Russian History and Historiography*
9, no. 1 (2016): 159–82. Out of 767 deputies elected to the Constituent Assembly,
only 10, or 1.3 percent, were female, and all were members of either the Bolshevik or the Socialist Revolutionary (SR) party. L. G. Protasov, "Zhenshchina i
Vserossiiskoe uchreditel'noe sobranie," in *Ot muzhskikh i zhenskikh k gendernym
issledovaniiam. Materialy mezhdunarodnoi nauchnoi konferentsii, 20 aprelia 2001
goda,* ed. P. P. Shcherbinin (Tambov: Tambovskii gosudarstvennyi universitet,
2001), 52–53. The absence of women is also reflected in a 1993 biographical dictionary of politicians of the revolutionary and Civil War period. Among the
more than three hundred entries, only thirteen are women—a statistic that
goes unmentioned by the editors. All but two of the female entries—Sofia and
Tyrkova-Williams—are socialists. *Politicheskie deiateli Rossii 1917: Biograficheskii
slovar',* ed. P. V. Volobuev (Moscow: Bol'shaia rossiiskaia entsiklopediia, 1993).

2. "Famous Women of the World," pamphlet published under the auspices
of the Pepsin Syrup Co., Monticello, IL, s.n. but circa 1920, in the collection of
the Historical Society of Pennsylvania, Pam CT 3202.F36 1920. The text reads:
"The first woman to hold a high cabinet position in any country of the world is
the Countess Sophie Panin, of Petrograd. She was a Minister of State in the new
Russian revolutionary government. She was Assistant Minister of Social Tutelage and administers the charitable and social institutions of the country. She
is still a woman much below middle age, and though of noble birth her sympathies are with the masses. Her specialty has been the study of the law as it
pertains to the rights of the common people." The source of this information,
seriously out of date by 1920, is not given.

3. N. N. Sukhanov and Joel Carmichael, *The Russian Revolution 1917: Eyewitness Account* (New York: Harper and Brothers, 1962), 3.

4. Barbara Alpern Engel, "Not by Bread Alone: Subsistence Riots in Russia
during World War I," *The Journal of Modern History* 69, no. 4 (December 1997): 697.

5. Wildman, *The End of the Russian Imperial Army*, chap. 4; McKean, *St. Petersburg between the Revolutions*, 460–70; *Peterburgskaia gorodskaia duma 1846–1918*, 315.

6. Dmitrii Ivanovich Demkin, "Petrogradskaia gorodskaia duma v pervye dni smuty: Iz vospominaniia," *Russkaia letopis'* 6 (1924): 146–47. On the situation at the Tauride Palace on February 27 and relations between rebellious soldiers and the State Duma, see R. Sh. Ganelin et al., *Pervaia mirovaia voina i konets Rossiiskoi imperii*, vol. 3, *Fevral'skaia revoliutsiia* (St. Petersburg: Liki Rossii, 2014), 233–49.

7. Tyrkova-Williams recorded Sofia's actions and words on that day in her diary; A. Tyrkova, "Petrogradskii dnevnik," in *Zven'ia: Istoricheskii al'manakh*, vyp. 2, ed. A. I. Dobkin et al. (Moscow: Feniks-Atheneum, 1992), 327.

8. Quoted in Figes and Kolonitskii, *Interpreting the Russian Revolution*, 42.

9. Natalia Dumova, the leading Soviet-era historian of the Kadet Party, claims that Sofia supported a monarchy for Russia during 1917 but provides no evidence of her position; *Konchilos' vashe vremia*, 34. Sofia's letters to Varya Volkova in the 1890s reveal that the few occasions in the 1890s when she had direct contact with the monarchy—her presentation to the painfully shy Empress Alexandra and her attendance at the coronation of Alexandra and Nicholas—left her distinctly unimpressed.

10. According to Petrograd city authorities 1,224 individuals were killed or wounded during the last week of February and first week of March, but E. N. Burdzhalov estimates the number of victims at two thousand; *Russia's Second Revolution: The February 1917 Uprising in Petrograd*, ed. and trans. Donald J. Raleigh (Bloomington: Indiana University Press, 1987), 337–38.

11. G. I. Vasil'chikov, "Lotarevskaia 'Kniga sudeb,'" *Nashe nasledie* 39 (1997): 65.

12. V. M. Kruchkovskaia, *Tsentral'naia gorodskaia duma Petrograda v 1917 g.* (Leningrad: Nauka, 1986), 20; *Izvestiia Petrogradskoi gorodskoi dumy*, No. 3–4 (Petrograd, 1917), 141; I. I. Mil'chik, "Petrogradskaia tsentral'naia gorodskaia duma v fevrale-oktiabre 1917 g.," *Krasnaia letopis'* 2 (1927): 191–92. Sofia and Tyrkova-Williams were brought into the council's charity committee, Miliukova into the education committee. The other women co-opted that day by the council were Olga N. Nechaeva, a leader of the Kadet Party in the capital (education committee), feminist physicians P. N. Shishkina-Iavein (sanitary committee) and A. N. Shabanova (hospital committee), Elena Depp (charity committee), and Alexandra Brunner (fundraising committee for military needs).

13. Ruthchild, *Equality and Revolution*, 1–2, 226–29; O. A. Khasbulatova, *Opyt i traditsii zhenskogo dvizheniia v Rossii (1860–1917)* (Ivanovo: Ivanovskii gosudarstvennyi universitet, 1994), 108; I. I. Iukina, *Russkii feminizm kak vyzov sovremennosti* (St. Petersburg: Aleteiia, 2007), 419–21.

14. Panina, "Na peterburgskoi okraine," 49:190–91.

15. *Prizrenie i blagotvoritel'nost' v Rossii* 1917, no. 1 (January); no. 2–3 (February–March); no. 5 (May).

16. Bulgakova, "Privilegirovannye bedniaki," 464–65; *Prizrenie i blagotvoritel'nost' v Rossii* 1917, no. 5 (May): 151–52. On the activities of soldiers' wives throughout the country, see Sarah Badcock, "Women, Protest, Revolution: Soldiers' Wives in Russia during 1917," *International Review of Social History* 49, no. 1 (2004): 47–70.

17. Barbara Evans Clements, *Bolshevik Feminist: The Life of Alexandra Kollontai* (Bloomington: Indiana University Press, 1979), 112.

18. *Prizrenie i blagotvoritel'nost' v Rossii* 1917, no. 5 (May): 152–53.

19. E. I. Tovarkovskaya of the 19th Guardianship, quoted in Bulgakova, "Privilegirovannye bedniaki," 465; Obolenskii, *Moia zhizn'*, 522–23.

20. Panina, "Na peterburgskoi okraine," 49:190.

21. Davis, *Home Fires Burning*, chaps. 8 and 9. Fed up with standing in endless food lines, poor women and youths rioted in Vienna for several days in May 1916; Healy, *Vienna*, 82–84.

22. Panina, "Na peterburgskoi okraine," 49:192.

23. William G. Rosenberg, *Liberals in the Russian Revolution: The Constitutional Democratic Party, 1917–1921* (Princeton: Princeton University Press, 1974), 13. The Kadets drew their leaders mostly from professional and intellectual circles, especially in the fields of law and academia. Their rank-and-file support came from Russia's middle strata of local government workers, teachers, doctors, and lawyers—the people with whom Sofia had collaborated in her social work since the 1890s. Ibid., 20–24.

24. Konstitutsionno-demokraticheskaia partiia, Tsentral'nyi komitet, *Protokoly Tsentral'nogo komiteta i zagranichnykh grupp Konstitutsionno-demokraticheskoi partii, 1905–seredina 1930-kh gg.*, ed. Shmuel Galai and D. B. Pavlov, vol. 3, *Protokoly Tsentral'nogo komiteta Konstitutsionno-demokraticheskoi partii, 1915–1920 gg.* (Moscow: ROSSPEN, 1998), 37; Konstitutsionno-demokraticheskaia partiia, *Vestnik Partii narodnoi svobody* (hereafter VPNS) 1917, no. 2 (May 18), 11; Rosenberg, *Liberals*, 131–32. Sofia received 169 votes out of 223 cast.

25. B. F. Dodonov, E. D. Grin'ko, and O. V. Lavinskaia, eds., *Zhurnaly zasedanii Vremennogo pravitel'stva*, vol. 2, *mai–iiun' 1917 goda* (Moscow: ROSSPEN, 2002), 131. On the April crisis and creation of the first coalition, see Stockdale, *Paul Miliukov*, 252–55, and Rosenberg, *Liberals*, chap. 4. On Shakhovskoy, see the introduction to D. I. Shakhovskoi, "Pis'ma o bratstve," in *Zven'ia*, vyp. 2, 174–75.

26. On her political career, see A. M. Karabanova, "A. V. Tyrkova—zhenshchina-lider Kadetskoi partii: Osobennosti sotsializatsii i politicheskoi kar'ery," in *Zhenshchina v rossiiskom obshchestve* 3–4 (2005): 60–72; V. V. Shelokhaev, "Ariadna Vladimirovna Tyrkova," *Voprosy istorii* 11–12 (1999): 67–81; Shelokhaev, "Ariadna Vladimirovna Tyrkova: 'Sotsialisty sdelali iz moego otechestva ogromnoe opytnoe pole dlia svoikh dogm i teorii,'" in *Rossiiskii liberalizm: Idei i liudi*, ed. A. A. Kara-Murza (Moscow: Novoe izdatel'stvo, 2004), 515–26.

27. Obolenskii, *Moia zhizn'*, 448.

28. *Encyclopedia of Russian Women's Movements*, ed. Norma Corigliano Noonan and Carol Nechemias (Westport, CT: Greenwood Press, 2001), s.v. Women's Military Congress (August 1–4 1917); Iukina and Guseva, *Zhenskii Peterburg*, 163.

29. S. Gogel', "Ministerstvo gosudarstvennogo prizreniia," *Prizrenie i blagotvoritel'nost' v Rossii* 1917, no. 6–7 (August–September): 481–82; emphasis in original.

30. *Zhurnaly zasedanii Vremennogo pravitel'stva*, vol. 2, 146, 183, 187–88, 235, 238.

31. C. Howard Hopkins, *John R. Mott, 1865–1955: A Biography* (Grand Rapids, MI: William B. Eerdmans, 1979), 506. I am grateful to Matthew Miller for this reference.

32. Sofia Panina, "Moi pisaniia," Lehovich Family Collection, 7–10.

33. Ibid.

34. Ibid.; Rosenberg, *Liberals*, 174–75. The Provisional Government cabinet approved Sofia's request to resign on July 12, 1917. B. F. Dodonov and E. D. Grin'ko, eds., *Zhurnaly zasedanii Vremennogo pravitel'stva*, vol. 3, *iiul'–avgust 1917 goda* (Moscow: ROSSPEN, 2004), 89.

35. BAR Panina, Box 14, folder "Events at one of S. V. Panina's estates, 1917 (Marfino)."

36. Peasants from villages adjoining the estate first harassed Boris and Lili, then locked them up in the village school. Supporters of the Viazemskys managed to persuade the enraged (and drunk) peasants to let Lili go free and to send Boris to the war front instead of killing him on the spot. But after Boris was taken to the nearest railroad station, he was murdered by a group of soldiers on their way to the front. Vasil'chikov, "Lotarevskaia 'Kniga sudeb,'" 80.

37. Two assistant ministers of education were appointed at the cabinet meetings in August: the eminent scientist Vernadsky, a friend of Oldenburg (August 1), and Sofia (August 14); *Zhurnaly zasedanii Vremennogo pravitel'stva*, vol. 3, 221, 289. See also Rosenberg, *Liberals*, 191–92.

38. Appointed on July 24, Oldenburg resigned on September 25. He was succeeded by the left liberal physician Sergei Salazkin, who served until he was arrested on October 26. Volobuev, *Politicheskie deiateli Rossii 1917*, s.v. Ol'denburg Sergei Fedorovich and Salazkin Sergei Sergeevich.

39. Daniel T. Orlovsky, "The Provisional Government and Its Cultural Work," in *Bolshevik Culture: Experiment and Order in the Russian Revolution*, ed. Abbott Gleason, Peter Kenez, and Richard Stites (Bloomington: Indiana University Press, 1985), 46. Based on the minutes of the meetings of the Provisional Government, it appears that Sofia did not attend any cabinet meetings from her appointment as assistant minister of education in mid-August to the final meetings in late October 1917; *Zhurnaly zasedanii Vremennogo pravitel'stva*, vol. 3, and B. F. Dodonov and E. D. Grin'ko, eds., *Zhurnaly zasedanii Vremennogo pravitel'stva*, vol. 4, *sentiabr'–oktiabr' 1917 goda* (Moscow: ROSSPEN, 2004).

40. His notation reads: "Vernulas' Panina. Marfino dlia M. N. Pr." Vernadskii, *Dnevniki 1917–1921*, 14 (diary entry for October 11 [1917]).

41. Mil'chik, "Petrogradskaia tsentral'naia gorodskaia duma," 192.

42. On the August 20 elections, see *Vestnik Partii narodnoi svobody 1917*, no. 17–18 (September 7): 11; Mil'chik, "Petrogradskaia tsentral'naia gorodskaia duma," 192–93; *Peterburgskaia gorodskaia duma 1846–1918*, 320–21, 324. The temporary city council was elected on June 19 by the deputies of the district city councils (*raionnye dumy*), created shortly after the February Revolution. Sofia, though elected in the general election in August, was not among the ten women, including Tyrkova-Williams and Kollontai, who were elected to the temporary council in June. The composition of the temporary council elected in June signaled the decline of the Kadets, who won 47 seats compared to the Socialist Revolutionaries' 54 seats (the Mensheviks obtained 40 and the Bolsheviks

37). *Peterburgskaia gorodskaia duma 1846–1918*, 321; "Vremennaia tsentral'naia duma," *Novoe vremia*, June 21/July 4, 1917, 4.

43. Obolenskii, *Moia zhizn'*, 536. For the list of council deputies elected on August 20, see *Peterburgskaia gorodskaia duma 1846–1918*, 526–28. Among the Bolshevik deputies were M. I. Kalinin, future president of the USSR, Z. I. Lilina-Radomyslskaya (Grigorii Zinovev's wife), D. Z. Manuilsky, L. B. Kamenev, Ya. M. Sverdlov, and M. S. Uritsky. Mil'chik states that Grigory Zinovev was also elected, but his name is not on the list in *Peterburgskaia gorodskaia duma 1846–1918*, 526–28.

44. Mil'chik, "Petrogradskaia tsentral'naia gorodskaia duma," 193–94; Obolenskii, *Moia zhizn'*, 536–37.

45. Obolenskii, *Moia zhizn'*, 536–37; *Peterburgskaia gorodskaia duma 1846–1918*, 332.

46. Obolenskii, *Moia zhizn'*, 536–37.

47. Mil'chik, "Petrogradskaia tsentral'naia gorodskaia duma," 197–98; *Peterburgskaia gorodskaia duma 1846–1918*, 322–23, 328–30, quotation on 322.

48. *Zhurnaly Petrogradskoi gorodskoi dumy* (Petrograd, 1917), no. 77, zasedanie 11 sentiabria 1917 goda, 9; no. 90, zasedanie 20 oktiabria 1917, 2.

49. *Peterburgskaia gorodskaia duma 1846–1918*, 530; Kruchkovskaia, *Tsentral'naia gorodskaia duma Petrograda*, 131.

50. Vernadskii, *Dnevniki 1917–1921*, 28 (diary entry for October 24–25, 1917).

51. Mil'chik, "Petrogradskaia tsentral'naia gorodskaia duma," 195–96.

52. Ibid., 199–201; *Peterburgskaia gorodskaia duma 1846–1918*, 334–39.

53. *Zhurnaly Petrogradskoi gorodskoi dumy*, no. 93, zasedanie 25 oktiabria 1917 goda, 3; Kruchkovskaia, *Tsentral'naia gorodskaia duma Petrograda*, 89–94.

54. The above account is based on the council's report on its October 25 meeting in *Zhurnaly Petrogradskoi gorodskoi dumy*, no. 93, zasedanie 25 oktiabria 1917 goda, 3–9; the recollections of Mil'chik, "Petrogradskaia tsentral'naia gorodskaia duma," 201–3, and Obolenskii, *Moia zhizn'*, 553–57; and *Peterburgskaia gorodskaia duma 1846–1918*, 339–43. Sofia's declaration is in Mil'chik, "Petrogradskaia tsentral'naia gorodskaia duma," 202.

55. Mil'chik, "Petrogradskaia tsentral'naia gorodskaia duma," 202–3. See also Kruchkovskaia, *Tsentral'naia gorodskaia duma Petrograda*, 93–95.

56. Obolenskii, *Moia zhizn'*, 554, 556.

57. John Reed, *Ten Days That Shook the World* (London: Penguin Classics, 1977), 106. Sergei Eisenstein's 1927 film, which is based on Reed, depicts virile, stalwart revolutionary sailors easily turning back the council representatives, caricatured as pompous or ineffectual intellectuals and aristocrats.

Chapter 8. Sofia Goes Underground

1. Sofia describes her arrest and interrogation in two short, autobiographical manuscripts in her handwriting, held in the Lehovich Family Collection. Although both are undated, they seem to have been written sometime during the 1920s. The first is titled "Moi pisaniia" and signed S. P.; it is slightly more than twelve handwritten pages. The second, untitled and unsigned, is in two

parts of two and four handwritten pages. In addition to a similar account of the events of November 28, it contains her recollections of the subsequent murders of the two Kadet leaders arrested with her, F. F. Kokoshkin and A. I. Shingarev, and is hereafter cited as "Kokoshkin and Shingarev."

2. On the deteriorating and dangerous conditions in Petrograd after the October Revolution, see Mary McAuley, *Bread and Justice: State and Society in Petrograd, 1917–1922* (Oxford: Clarendon Press, 1991), and Tsuyoshi Hasegawa, *Crime and Punishment in the Russian Revolution: Mob Justice and Police in Petrograd* (Cambridge: Harvard University Press, 2017), chap. 6.

3. Alexander Rabinowitch, *The Bolsheviks in Power: The First Year of Soviet Rule in Petrograd* (Bloomington: Indiana University Press, 2007), chap. 1; quotation on 28–29.

4. Panina, "Such Is Life," 3.

5. Ibid.

6. A great many of the memoirs written by Kadets about 1917 were published in two émigré periodicals that were created precisely for the purpose of explaining the revolution: *Arkhiv russkoi revoliutsii*, edited by Kadet I. V. Gessen and published annually in Berlin from 1921 to 1937; and the Kadet newspaper published in Paris, *Poslednie novosti* (1920–40), which was edited by former party leader Miliukov.

7. Panina, "Such Is Life," 5. The autobiographical documents in which she recounts the events of 1917 include this speech, delivered in Los Angeles in 1939; the second part of the memoir, written in 1948 and published posthumously as "Na peterburgskoi okraine: revoliutsiia," *Novyi zhurnal* 49 (1957): 189–203; and the two handwritten manuscripts "Moi pisaniia" and "Kokoshkin and Shingarev."

8. Quotation from Panina, "Kokoshkin and Shingarev," 1.

9. Vladimir Nabokov, "Vremennoe pravitel'stvo: Vospominaniia," *Arkhiv russkoi revoliutsii* 1 (1922): 87–88, 91; Mil'chik, "Petrogradskaia tsentral'naia gorodskaia duma," 203–4; S. An-skii, "Posle perevorota 25-go oktiabria 1917 g.," *Arkhiv russkoi revoliutsii* 8 (1923): 43–55.

10. Though widespread, the rumors that the women soldiers had been raped and tortured were incorrect, according to Stockdale, "'My Death for the Motherland Is Happiness,'" 110. Tyrkova-Williams was one of three city council members who visited the battalion's camp outside Petrograd, interviewed the women soldiers about their treatment, and found rumors of sexual violence against them unfounded; Stoff, *They Fought for the Motherland*, 160.

11. Nabokov, "Vremennoe pravitel'stvo: Vospominaniia," 91.

12. Obolenskii, *Moia zhizn'*, 558. On relations among committee members, see also Nabokov, "Vremennoe pravitel'stvo: Vospominaniia," 88–89.

13. Mil'chik, "Petrogradskaia tsentral'naia gorodskaia duma," 208; *Zhurnal Petrogradskoi gorodskoi dumy*, no. 123, zasedanie 20 noiab. 1917 g. The Bolsheviks held elections for a new municipal council on November 27–28, the outcome of which produced a Bolshevik-dominated body. The old council continued to meet occasionally in various locations underground at least until mid-January; Rabinowitch, *The Bolsheviks in Power*, 56–57, 70.

14. Rosenberg, *Liberals*, 264–65, 270, 275–77; N. G. Dumova, *Kadetskaia kontrrevoliutsiia i ee razgrom (oktiabr' 1917–1920 gg.)* (Moscow: Nauka, 1982), 40; Borman, *A. V. Tyrkova-Vil'iams*, 143.

15. Nabokov, "Vremennoe pravitel'stvo. Vospominaniia," 94–95; Panina, "Moi pisaniia," 10.

16. A. Dem'ianov, "Zapiski o podpol'nom Vremennom pravitel'stve," *Arkhiv russkoi revoliutsii* 7 (1922), 46. Vernadsky mentions Sofia's involvement in party and government meetings numerous times in diary entries during November 1917; the meetings were often at her home. Vernadskii, *Dnevniki 1917–1921*, 29–36, 40, 43, 47. According to Nabokov, the Kadet Central Committee began meeting at Sofia's on October 26 and met for the next 10–15 days, some days at her house, other days at the home of V. A. Stepanov, another committee member; Nabokov, "Vremennoe pravitel'stvo: Vospominaniia," 87.

17. Nabokov, "Vremennoe pravitel'stvo: Vospominaniia," 89.

18. Obolenskii, *Moia zhizn'*, 563, 565.

19. Dem'ianov, "Zapiski o podpol'nom Vremennom pravitel'stve," 34–36, 40–41. Demianov explains that the assistant ministers had met regularly in the last months of the Provisional Government in the "Little Council of Ministers," which he had chaired; this was the body he called together after the October coup. Another source is M. Fleer, "Vremennoe pravitel'stvo posle oktiabria," *Krasnyi arkhiv*, 1924, No. 6, 197–98. Though hostile to the underground body's anti-Soviet activities, Fleer's account is based on the minutes of its meetings and other archival documents. The Little Council also held at least one joint meeting with the Committee for the Salvation of the Fatherland and the Revolution, since Sofia and a few of the council's other members belonged to both bodies. Members of the Little Council were condescending toward the committee, Demianov recalls, and viewed themselves as more knowledgeable about politics; Dem'ianov, "Zapiski o podpol'nom Vremennom pravitel'stve," 46.

20. Nabokov, "Vremennoe pravitel'stvo: Vospominaniia," 90–91; Dem'ianov, "Zapiski o podpol'nom Vremennom pravitel'stve," 34, 36–37.

21. Fleer, "Vremennoe pravitel'stvo posle oktiabria," 205–7; Dem'ianov, "Zapiski o podpol'nom Vremennom pravitel'stve," 47–49.

22. Dem'ianov, "Zapiski o podpol'nom Vremennom pravitel'stve," 49.

23. Vernadskii, *Dnevniki 1917–1921*, 43 (entry for November 14 [1917]).

24. Dem'ianov, "Zapiski o podpol'nom Vremennom pravitel'stve," 39; Rosenberg, *Liberals*, 265; Panina, "Such Is Life," 4.

25. Dem'ianov, "Zapiski o podpol'nom Vremennom pravitel'stve," 35; Rosenberg, *Liberals*, 265n; Sofia claims to have been the "soul" of the strike in "Such Is Life," 5. Obolensky's account of the origins of the boycott is contradictory. He gives considerable credit to the Committee for the Salvation of the Fatherland and the Revolution; at its first meeting, he states, the idea was raised (he does not say by whom) of contacting the assistant ministers and through them obtaining the committee's control over civil servants. Through its members who were also assistant ministers—most prominently, Sofia—the committee then proceeded to organize the civil servants' "sabotage." But he also states that the idea for a boycott arose "by itself" (*sama soboi*), from the civil servants

themselves. He recalls meeting one man who introduced himself as the representative of the employees of the State Bank, who proposed an agreement between themselves and the Committee for the Salvation of the Fatherland and the Revolution to honor only money orders and drafts on government funds that were counter-signed by the committee. Obolenskii, *Moia zhizn'*, 557, 559–60. Dumova, citing Obolensky, states that Sofia proposed giving civil servants instructions to ignore any orders issued by Soviet authorities and to follow only those that came from designated representatives of the Provisional Government. Dumova, *Kadetskaia kontrrevoliutsiia*, 30–31. According to yet another source, the Petrograd City Council played a key role; at its evening session on October 27, a group of representatives of the government bureaucracy, including civil servants of the Ministry of Education, announced that they were willing to participate in "sabotage" against the new regime and were ready to refuse to work; Kruchkovskaia, *Tsentral'naia gorodskaia duma Petrograda*, 100–101.

26.   Fleer, "Vremennoe pravitel'stvo posle oktiabria," 207–8. Fleer also accuses the ministers of siphoning funds from the state treasury to fund anti-Bolshevik resistance under the pretext of making inflated allocations to local governments for the purchase of firewood; ibid., 203–5.

27.   Ibid., 204, 208–9; Panina, "Such Is Life," 4. Sofia's signed order to the officials is in the trial dossier in GARF, f. R-1074, op. 1, d. 10, 28 noiab. 1917–30 dek. 1917, "Delo Paninoi. Protokol Zasedaniia revoliutsionnogo tribunala, 10 dekabria 1917 goda," l. 11.

28.   GARF, f. R-1074, op. 1, d. 10, l. 1. Rogalsky identified himself as a commissar of education in his deposition; ibid., l. 6. He is identified as assistant commissar of education in L. Kin, "Sud nad gr. S. V. Paninoi," *Vechernyi zvon*, December 11, 1917. The date of his visit is not indicated in any of the documents, but it must have occurred between November 16 and 26. The file on Sofia's trial does not contain an actual arrest order, making it impossible to say with certainty when her arrest was ordered and by whom. But the documents support the inference that the order came from the Investigative Commission on November 26, 1917, after it heard Rogalsky's report.

29.   *Novaia rech'*, November 28/December 10, 1917.

30.   Rosenberg, *Liberals*, 271; Panina, "Kokoshkin and Shingarev," 1.

31.   Volobuev, *Politicheskie deiateli Rossii 1917*, s.v. Panina; *VPNS*, 1917, no. 26–27 (November 23), 6–9. The Kadet Central Committee decided at its meeting on October 1, 1917, to put Sofia on its candidate list for the Petrograd elections to the Constituent Assembly in the seventh position, in place of A. A. Kornilov, a long-time local party leader; Konstitutsionno-demokraticheskaia partiia, Tsentral'nyi komitet, *Protokoly Tsentral'nogo komiteta i zagranichnykh grupp Konstitutsionno-demokraticheskoi partii, 1905–seredina 1930-kh gg.*, vol. 3, *Protokoly Tsentral'nogo komiteta Konstitutsionno-demokraticheskoi partii, 1915–1920 gg.*, 405–6. The Bolsheviks won twelve of the city's eighteen electoral districts, dominating working-class districts, while the Kadets took the other six districts. Rabinowitch, *The Bolsheviks in Power*, 62–69, 415–16n31.

32.   Borman, *A. V. Tyrkova-Vil'iams*, 140–41; the quote is from a note she wrote in June 1919 and so undoubtedly was colored by the defeats her party and the anti-Bolshevik cause experienced after November 1917.

33. Protasov, "Zhenshchina i Vserossiiskoe uchreditel'noe sobranie," 52–53.

34. Panina, "Moi pisaniia," 2. Other Kadets were less sanguine; see N. I. Astrov, "Proobraz Russkoi tragedii," *Poslednie novosti*, January 18, 1925, 2; Rosenberg, *Liberals*, 277–78.

35. Panina, "Moi pisaniia," 2–4; ellipses are in the original. The temperature that day was -10 degrees Celsius, according to one diarist; Zinaida Gippius, "Chernye tetradi," in *Zven'ia*, vyp. 2, 26.

36. Oleg Budnitskii, *Russian Jews between the Reds and the Whites, 1917–1920*, trans. Timothy J. Portice (Philadelphia: University of Pennsylvania Press, 2012), 62, 106. According to Leonard Schapiro, thousands of Jews joined the Bolshevik party during 1917, and they "abounded" in the lower-level ranks of the party apparatus, especially in its secret police agencies; "The Role of Jews in the Russian Revolutionary Movement," *Slavonic and East European Review* 40, no. 94 (December 1961): 148–67. See also Budnitskii, *Russian Jews*, chaps. 2 and 3.

37. Panina, "Moi pisaniia," 2, 4.

38. Ibid., 5.

39. Ibid., 6, 10–11. Sofia's home was put under surveillance, which yielded two more arrests as other Kadets arrived during the day for more meetings— Dolgorukov and V. F. Konstantinov, the former assistant minister of communication. Kn. Pavel Dmitrievich Dolgorukov, *Velikaia razrukha* (Madrid, 1964), 57–59.

40. Panina, "Moi pisaniia," 12, ellipsis in the original; Dolgorukov, *Velikaia razrukha*, 60.

41. Dolgorukov, *Velikaia razrukha*, 60. In fact, Shingarev was not elected to the Constituent Assembly, although due to his national prominence in the party it was widely assumed that he had won a seat; L. G. Protasov, *Liudi Uchreditel'nogo sobraniia: Portret v inter'ere epokhi* (Moscow: ROSSPEN, 2008), 30, 41–42.

42. Panina, "Moi pisaniia," 11–13; Panina, "Kokoshkin and Shingarev," 2–20b; F. Rodichev, "Vospominaniia o kniaze Pavle Dmitrieviche Dolgorukove," in N. I. Astrov, V. F. Zeeler, and P. N. Miliukov, eds., *Pamiati pogibshikh: [sbornik]* (Paris, 1929), 225–26.

43. *Izvestiia*, November 28, 1917; Obolenskii, *Moia zhizn'*, 569; Rabinowitch, *The Bolsheviks in Power*, 74–76. Around the country elections to the assembly ran far behind schedule, enabling only a small number of delegates to arrive in Petrograd by November 28. Lenin seized on this as a reason to delay the opening of the assembly, and on November 26 he issued a decree requiring at least four hundred delegates (about half of the total) to be present in Petrograd in order for the assembly to open. That opening took place on January 5, 1918. Rabinowitch, *The Bolsheviks in Power*, 71–72.

44. GARF, f. R-1074, op. 1, d. 10, ll. 12–14.

45. At the meeting that night Trotsky characterized the pro-assembly demonstration earlier that day as a counter-revolutionary armed uprising planned by the Kadets' Central Committee. Rabinowitch, *The Bolsheviks in Power*, 76. A typewritten copy of the decree, dated November 28, 1917, at 10:30 p.m., is in the archival file on Sofia's trial; GARF, f. R-1074, op. 1, d. 10, l. 3. Although the decree states that it is effective from the "moment of its signing," in fact it was

applied retroactively to Dolgorukov, Kokoshkin, and Shingarev, who had been arrested hours earlier. Dumova erroneously implies that the three were arrested after and as a result of the Council of People's Commissars decree, instead of before it; *Kadetskaia kontrrevoliutsiia*, 57.

46. GARF, f. R-1074, op. 1, d. 10, l. 16. The fate of the missing 93,000 rubles is unclear. Some sources state that the funds were deposited in a foreign bank. The ministry employees involved either did not know where the money was deposited or never revealed the location. In her memoirs Sofia only states that she instructed the officials to deposit the money in a bank in the name of the Constituent Assembly. Panina, "Na peterburgskoi okraine," 49:192.

47. Panina, "Such Is Life," 4.

48. Ibid., 3, 5; emphasis in the original.

49. Panina, "Na peterburgskoi okraine," 49:193.

50. Ibid., 193-94; Panina, "Such Is Life," 5-6.

51. Panina, "Na peterburgskoi okraine," 49:193; Panina, "Such Is Life," 6.

52. TsGIA SPb., f. 569, op. 13, d. 1331, 1915.

53. *Narodnyi dom*, iii-iv.

54. Quoted by Sofia in "Na peterburgskoi okraine," 49:195-96. The information that Sofia was not allowed visitors in prison is from *Nash vek*, December 10/22, 1917.

55. *VPNS*, 1917, no. 29-30 (December 14), 8-10, published the protests from the Ligovsky People's House, residents of the surrounding district, and numerous public organizations. *Nash vek* also reported and printed the protests in every issue during the first week of December. Newspaper clippings about the arrest and trial and protests (letters to the editor, etc.) are also in Russkaia natsional'naia biblioteka, Otdel rukopisei, f. 423 (Lbovskii, A. N.).

56. M. Gor'kii, "Nesvoevremennye mysli," *Novaia mysl'*, December 6/19, 1917, 1.

57. Excerpted in *VPNS*, 1917, no. 31 (December 28), 10.

58. Quotations from Panina, "Na peterburgskoi okraine," 49:195. The letters and clippings are in BAR Panina, Box 14, folders "Sofia's Arrest" (1 and 2).

59. GARF, f. R-1074, op. 1, d. 10, l. 16-17; Ia. Ia. Gurevich, "Delo grafini S. V. Paninoi v revoliutsionnom tribunale," *Russkoe bogatstvo* no. 11-12 (November-December 1917): 286.

60. Panina, "Na peterburgskoi okraine," 49:196.

Chapter 9. Enemy of the People

1. The Petrograd Revolutionary Tribunal was established in accordance with a Soviet decree published on November 24 that called on local soviets to establish revolutionary tribunals and investigative commissions. Rex A. Wade and Alex G. Cummins, eds., *Documents of Soviet History*, vol. 1, *The Triumph of Bolshevism, 1917-1919* (Gulf Breeze, FL: Academic International Press, 1991), 52-53, 62-64, 73-75; D. S. Karev, *Sudoustroistvo* (Moscow: Iuridicheskoe izdatel'stvo, 1948), 107-8, 115-16. A second decree on December 19 set out detailed instructions for the tribunals. Meanwhile, the establishment of the Cheka on

December 7 created another, potentially more powerful counterrevolutionary agency whose jurisdiction overlapped with the tribunals.

2. An earlier version of this chapter was published as Adele Lindenmeyr, "The First Soviet Political Trial: Countess Sofia V. Panina before the Petrograd Revolutionary Tribunal," *The Russian Review* 60, no. 4 (October 2001): 505–25.

3. *Nash vek,* December 5/17, 1917, 3, cols. 6–7.

4. "Sud bol'shevikov nad gr. S. V. Paninoi," *Novaia petrogradskaia gazeta,* December 12, 1917; Kin, "Sud nad gr. S. V. Paninoi"; Gurevich, "Delo grafini S. V. Paninoi."

5. I. Zhukov, "Revoliutsionnyi tribunal (vospominaniia pervogo predse-datelia Tribunala)," *Rabochii sud* 22 (1927): 1755–56.

6. Kin, "Sud nad gr. S. V. Paninoi." Stuchka was soon replaced as commis-sar of justice by the Left SR member Isaac Shteinberg, who was much more le-nient toward political opponents; Rabinowitch, *The Bolsheviks in Power,* 84–85.

7. Bessie Beatty, *The Red Heart of Russia* (New York: Century, 1918), 295.

8. Zhukov, "Revoliutsionnyi tribunal." Zhukov's chagrin over his botched first trial is suggested by the fact that he devotes only one sentence to it in this memoir.

9. Quoted from the version of Zhukov's speech in the trial transcript from GARF, f. R-1074, op. 1, d. 10, l. 20. Despite accusations from other communists of arrogance and willingness to exceed his authority, Zhukov rose quickly to occupy important positions, first in the Cheka, then in various economic commissariats. He became commissar of local industry in the RSFSR but was arrested and shot in 1937. GARF, f. 336, op. 1, d. 156, "Sledstvennoe delo po obvineniiu predsedatel'ia rev. tribunala Zhukova v presvyshenii dannykh emu polnomochii i zloupotreblenii po dolzhnosti 6 [16] dek. 1917–21 fevr. 1918"; E. V. Ershova, "Pervyi protsess Petrogradskogo revtribunala v 1917 godu," in *Neizvestnye stranitsy istorii Verkhnevol'zhia: Sbornik nauchnykh trudov* (Tver: Tverskoi gosudarstvennyi universitet, 1994), 96n.

10. Beatty, *The Red Heart of Russia,* 296.

11. GARF, f. R-1074, op. 1, d. 10, l. 20.

12. Gurevich, "Delo grafini S. V. Paninoi," 291.

13. Kin, "Sud nad gr. S. V. Paninoi." Kin's recounting of this scene in *Vechernyi zvon* is the most detailed and colorful. The transcript tersely reports, "A scream from the public. A fit of hysteria in one of those present (an old man, they say, one of the workers at Panina's People's House). They take him out of the hall." GARF, f. R-1074, op. 1, d. 10, l. 21.

14. Accounts of Ivanov's speech differ in both their length and wording. This reconstruction is based on the reports of the speech found in the trial tran-script, Gurevich's article, and the newspapers *Verchernyi zvon* (which Gurevich termed the best) and *Novaia petrogradskaia gazeta.*

15. Foma Railian, "Intelligentsiia pered sudom 'Tribunala,'" *Novaia petro-gradskaia gazeta,* December 12, 1917, 1. No other account of the trial suggests that Ivanov's appearance was planned in advance. But according to one source, Ivanov had given the court a note before the trial stating his desire to speak; "Sud bol'shevikov."

16. Kin, "Sud nad gr. S. V. Paninoi"; Panina, "Na peterburgskoi okraine," 49:197. Versions of Naumov's speech vary even more than those of Ivanov's. Unsympathetic observers described it as rambling and incoherent; Sofia called it "nonsense." This account of Naumov's speech is based on the trial transcript (GARF, f. R-1074, op. 1, d. 10, ll. 210b–22) and *Izvestiia*, the official newspaper of the Central Executive Committee of the Soviets; "Zasedanie Revoliutsionnogo tribunala. Delo gr. Paninoi," *Izvestiia*, December 12, 1917.

17. Panina, "Na peterburgskoi okraine," 49:192. Accounts of the trial differ on the nature of these funds. According to the trial transcript and one newspaper account, Sofia stated that the money belonged to civil servants in her ministry and that she acted in order to guarantee them their wages: GARF, f. R-1074, op. 1, d. 10, l. 22; "Sud bol'shevikov." According to Kin in *Vechernyi zvon*, however, Sofia stated that she took the funds for safekeeping because they were contributions from the people.

18. The longest report of Rogalsky's speech is in the trial transcript, on which this account is based; GARF, f. R-1074, op. 1, d. 10, l. 22.

19. Gurevich, "Delo grafini S. V. Paninoi," 295. Sofia's words quoted in Kin, "Sud nad gr. S. V. Paninoi."

20. Panina, "Na peterburgskoi okraine," 49:198; Kin, "Sud nad gr. S. V. Paninoi." Gurevich's protest note is in GARF, f. R-1074, op. 1, d. 10, l. 24.

21. GARF, f. R-1074, op. 1, d. 10, l. 23.

22. "V Voenno-revoliutsionnom tribunale. Delo gr. S. V. Paninoi," *Volia naroda*, December 12, 1917.

23. Kin, "Sud nad gr. S. V. Paninoi," 3.

24. For example, the articles by P. Gerasimov, "Voprosy partiinoi zhizni. III. Na skam'e podsudimykh," *VPNS*, 1917, no. 31 (December 28), 1, 3–4; and A. Tyrkova, "Kogo sudili?" in ibid., 4–6. See also Rosenberg, *Liberals*, 281–82.

25. Harold Williams, "Farcical Trial of Countess Panin," *New York Times*, December 26, 1917, 2.

26. "A Bolshevist Trial," *Times*, January 31, 1918, 5.

27. It seems probable that it was not the central Soviet government but the Petrograd Soviet, dominated by hardline Bolsheviks and headed from late November by Zinoviev, that played the leading role in Sofia's arrest and trial. Fierce conflicts between Bolsheviks and their coalition partner, the Left SRs, divided the Council of People's Commissars, especially over the issues of how to deal with political opponents. The Left SRs opposed harsh repressions and wholesale arrests. Rabinowitch, *The Bolsheviks in Power*, chap. 3, esp. 84–85.

28. "Zasedanie Revoliutsionnogo tribunala," *Izvestiia*, December 12, 1917, which emphasizes certain aspects and incidents of the trial, especially the accusatory speeches by Naumov and Rogalsky and Kramarov's disrespect toward the tribunal, but barely mentions others, such as Ivanov's defense.

29. Maxim Litvinov and Ivy Litvinov, *The Bolshevik Revolution: Its Rise and Meaning* (London: British Socialist Party, 1919), 33. I am grateful to Seth Koven for the reference.

30. John Reed, "How the Russian Revolution Works," *The Liberator* 1, no. 6 (August 1918): 16–17; Bryant, *Six Red Months*, 194–96.

31. Beatty, *The Red Heart of Russia*, 301; Albert Rhys Williams, *Journey into Revolution, Petrograd 1917–1918* (Chicago: Quadrangle Books, 1969), 163–65. Soviet historians echoed their judgment that the trial showed the tribunal to be both fair and humane; Dumova, *Kadetskaia kontrrevoliutsiia*, 65–66; D. L. Golinkov, *Krushenie antisovetskogo podpol'ia v SSSR*, 2 vols., 3rd ed. (Moscow: Politizdat, 1980), 1:77–79; K. I. Kozlova and V. S. Orlov, "Pervoe zasedanie narodnogo revtribunala," *Voprosy istorii* 10 (1977): 211–15.

32. Panina, "Such Is Life," 6.

33. Ibid., 7; Panina, "Na peterburgskoi okraine," 49:198–99.

34. The actual letter appears not to have survived, but it is quoted in full in Gurevich, "Delo grafini S. V. Paninoi," 297–98.

35. Ibid.

36. GARF, f. R-1074, op. 1, d. 10, ll. 25–29. It proved very difficult to raise the funds through donations, since banks were closed and Bolsheviks were conducting house searches to confiscate valuables from the wealthy. In order to raise the needed sum as quickly as possible, Sofia's friends and supporters obtained the cooperation of the Committee to Obtain Funds for the Petersburg Higher Women's Courses, which advanced them the money; although they pledged to pay back the advance, the committee was never reimbursed in full. Panina, "Na peterburgskoi okraine," 49:199–200.

37. Panina, "Na peterburgskoi okraine," 49:198–200.

38. Ibid., 200–201.

39. Panina, "Kokoshkin and Shingarev," 2–3. On the rising incidence of "drunken pogroms" in Petrograd during the winter of 1917–18, see Hasegawa, *Crime and Punishment in the Russian Revolution*, chap. 6.

40. Her concern was no doubt deepened by the letter Shingarev wrote her on December 21. The only good news he had read in the newspapers, he commented despondently, was her release from prison. Everything else was "sad and loathsome. I feel such pain for Russia and the Russian people." Letter from A. I. Shingarev to Sofia Panina, December 21, 1917, in BAR Panina, Box 5, folder Shingarev. On her visits to him in prison, see also A. I. Shingarev, *Kak eto bylo. Dnevnik A. I. Shingareva. Petropavlovskaia krepost', 27.XI.17–5.I.18* (Moscow, 1918), 44.

41. Panina, "Kokoshkin and Shingarev," 3.

42. Ibid., 3–3ob.

43. Rabinowitch, *The Bolsheviks in Power*, 106, 112–25.

44. Panina, "Kokoshkin and Shingarev," 3–4. Ellipsis in the original.

45. Ibid., 4–4ob.

46. A. S. Izgoev, "Piat' let v Sovetskoi Rossii (Obryvki vospominanii i zametki)," *Arkhiv russkoi revoliutsii* 10 (1923): 26.

47. Letter from Sofia Panina to Liubov Yakovlevna Gurevich, Moscow, January 24, 1918, in PD, 20.035/CXXXVIb3, ll. 5–6. George Vasilchikov claims that Sofia told him a very different story: after being escorted from Petrograd to the Finnish border by an honor guard composed of visitors to the Ligovsky People's House, she managed to get from Finland to England, from where she traveled to the south of Russia. The story is dramatic but inaccurate; for one, it omits the

period she spent in Moscow from January to August 1918, which is confirmed by numerous sources. Vasil'chikov, "Grafinia S. V. Panina," 82.

48. Panina, "Kokoshkin and Shingarev," 1.

Chapter 10. Fighting the Bolsheviks

1. Peter Holquist, *Making War, Forging Revolution: Russia's Continuum of Crisis, 1914–1921* (Cambridge: Harvard University Press, 2002), 143.

2. Tyrkova-Williams left Petrograd in December 2017 for Moscow and then left for England in March 1918. She spent the rest of 1918 and half of 1919 in London, returning to southern Russia in late summer 2019 before leaving for good in March 1920.

3. Losskii, "Eshche o grafine S. V. Paninoi"; Vladimir Sysoev, *Tat'iana Alekseevna Bakunina-Osorgina: Illiustrirovannyi biograficheskii ocherk* (Tver: Presto, 2005), 11–21, 32. Sofia briefly worked with Bakunin in 1917 in the Ministry of State Welfare, where he served also as an assistant minister.

4. Dolgorukov, *Velikaia razrukha*, chap. 5; Roza Georgievna Vinaver, "Vospominaniia," typescript dated January 1944, in Roza Georgievna Vinaver Collection, Hoover Institution Archives, 100. The Moscow Cheka either did not know she was there or did not consider her a threat. Her name, for example, is not found in its collection about the Moscow anti-Communist movement: *Krasnaia kniga VChK*, vol. 2, 2nd ed. (Moscow: Izdatel'stvo politicheskoi literatury, 1989); and in its summary report on the formation of the National Center the Moscow Cheka assigned Nikolai a leading role but did not identify Sofia among its members; ibid., 38–40.

5. Mauricio Borrero, *Hungry Moscow: Scarcity and Urban Society in the Russian Civil War, 1917–1921* (New York: Peter Lang, 2003), chaps. 3 and 7. See also William J. Chase, *Workers, Society and the Soviet State: Labor and Life in Moscow, 1918–1929* (Urbana: University of Illinois Press, 1987).

6. See Article 2, paragraph 23 and Article 2, paragraph 65 of the 1918 Soviet Constitution. On the deprivation of rights of previously privileged social groups under Bolshevik power, see Douglas Smith, *Former People: The Final Days of the Russian Aristocracy* (New York: Farrar, Straus and Giroux, 2012), chap. 8; Golfo Alexopoulos, *Stalin's Outcasts: Aliens, Citizens, and the Soviet State, 1926–1936* (Ithaca: Cornell University Press, 2003), chap. 1.

7. Dmitrii Meisner, *Mirazhi i deistvitel'nost': Zapiski emigranta* (Moscow: Novosti, 1966), 170.

8. The story is accepted as true by Dumova in *Kadetskaia kontrrevoliutsiia i ee razgrom*, 150, and "Istoriia v litsakh. Grafinia, sozdavshaia Narodnyi dom," *Rabotnitsa* 11 (1994): 16–17. Dumova adds a postscript to the story in her 1994 article: the little suitcase had been taken by an old peasant, who hid it in his hut until the hungry years of the 1930s, when he unsuccessfully tried to sell one piece of jewelry and landed behind bars; "Countess Panina's treasure," she claims, "has been kept in the Russian state treasury" ever since.

9. On the meeting with Alexandra, see letter from Alexandra Peshekhonova to Sofia Panina, [Leningrad], June 12 [1925], BAR Panina, Box 7, Arranged Correspondence, folder Peshekhonova. On the reception Sofia received when

she visited, see the letter from Lidia L. Vasil'chikova to Ilarion Sergeevich Vasil'chikov, Kharaks [near Gaspra, Crimea], May 30, 1918, in Ilarion Sergeevich Vasil'chikov and G. I. Vasil'chikov, *To, chto mne vspomnilos'—Vospominaniia kniazia Ilariona Sergeevicha Vasil'chikova: Iz arkhiva sem'i Vasil'chikovykh* (Moscow: "Olma-Press," 2002), 174. On Marfino's condition, see letter from Anastasia Petrunkevich to Roza Georgievna Vinaver, Geneva, December 7 and 8, 1921, in GARF, f. 5839, op. 1, ed. khr. 57, l. 43. The children's colony was replaced by a rest home for Moscow artisans in 1923. Then from 1930 to 1941 it was the "Red Pilot" sanatorium for the military, and ever since Marfino, owned today by the Russian Ministry of Defense, has served as a sanatorium for military officers.

10. Letter from Ivan Petrovich Karkhlin to Sofia Panina, Riga, December 6, 1921, Lehovich Family Collection.

11. "Moskovskie organizatsii 1917–1918," typed manuscript, signed "N. I. Astrov" and edited in his hand, in BAR Panina, Box 10, folder Astrov, Nikolai Ivanovich; Rosenberg, *Liberals*, 289–93.

12. Astrov, "Moskovskie organizatsii," 14–17; Rosenberg, *Liberals*, 314.

13. On the May 1918 Kadet meeting, see Astrov, "1918 god," BAR Panina, Box 11, folder Panina Manuscripts by N. I. Astrov, 1–3; and Vinaver, "Vospominaniia," 101. On the Moscow Kadets and the internal conflicts within the Kadet Party in 1918, see Rosenberg, *Liberals*, chap. 9, and V. V. Shelokhaev, *Konstitutsionno-demokraticheskaia partiia v Rossii i emigratsii* (Moscow: ROSSPEN, 2015), 620–27.

14. Letter from Sofia Panina to M. M. Vinaver, dated June 28, 1918; no place given—probably Moscow; typescript copy in YIVO, Elias Tcherikower Archives, Maxim Vinaver Papers, microfilm roll 63, file 766a, folio [frame] 63871.

15. Astrov, "1918 god," 5–6; L. A. Krol', *Za tri goda: Vospominaniia, vpechatleniia i vstrechi* (Vladivostok: Tip. T-va izd. Svobodnaia Rossiia, 1921), 48.

16. Astrov, "1918 god," 9–10. Rosenberg, *Liberals*, 297–98. Nikolai's writings on the Civil War period mention consulting Sofia on political issues and including her in decisions a number of times.

17. Rosenberg, *Liberals*, 298.

18. Nikolai mentions that the National Center received funds from foreigners and established contact from the very beginning with "representatives of the Allies." Astrov, "1918 god," 11–12, 15–16, 19–20; Astrov, "Moskovskie organizatsii," 18–19. On Lockhart's relations with various anti-communist movements, see Rabinowitch, *The Bolsheviks in Power*, 156–57, 319.

19. Draft of letter by Sofia Panina to Mark Veniaminovich Vishniak, September 23, 1934, in BAR Panina, Box 5.

20. N. I. Astrov, *Vospominaniia* (Paris: YMCA Press, 1940), Part 1.

21. A summary of Nikolai's professional and political career is in an unpublished autobiography in BAR Panina, Box 13, folder Astrov, Nikolai Ivanovich (biographical). On his role in the Union of Towns, see V. M. Shevyrin, "N. I. Astrov kak lider i istoriograf Vserossiiskogo soiuza gorodov," *Rossiia i sovremennyi mir* 2 (2003): 203–24.

22. Shingarev, *Kak eto bylo*, 31.

23. Kn. Grigorii N. Trubetskoi, *Gody smut i nadezhd 1917–1919* (Montreal:

[Éditions R.U.S.], 1981), 76–77; Tyrkova-Williams quoted in Borman, *A. V. Tyrkova-Vil'iams*, 180, 187.

24. V. A. Obolenskii, "Astrov kak chelovek. Okonchatel'naia redaktsiia," undated typescript in GARF, f. 5913, op. 1, d. 1129, ll. 1, 3–5. Another friend characterized Nikolai as a skeptic and a pessimist; P. D. Dolgorukov, "Obshchestvennaia deiatel'nost' N. I. Astrova v emigratsii," unpublished ms, Prague 1934, BAR Panina, Box 6, folder Dolgorukov, Petr Dmitrievich.

25. S. V. Bakhrushin, quoted in L. F. Pisar'kova, "Gorodskie golovy Moskvy (1863–1917)," *Otechestvennaia istoriia* 2 (1997): 15.

26. "Vypiski iz pisem. Pamiati N. I. A.," BAR Panina, Box 13, folder Astrov, Nikolai Ivanovich, biographical. She also filled a school notebook with excerpts from condolence letters from friends that describe him as "noble," "selfless," "kind," "intelligent," and "fair"; the notebook is in ibid.

27. Nikolai's reminiscences of the Civil War period refer several times to her decision to accompany him on his travels. N. I. Astrov, "Grazhdanskaia voina," typescript in BAR Panina Box 9, quote on 50. Most references to Sofia in this manuscript are carefully crossed out, evidently by Sofia, since the annotations are in her handwriting.

28. Rabinowitch, *The Bolsheviks in Power*, 314ff.

29. Rosenberg, *Liberals*, 315–16; Astrov, "Grazhdanskaia voina," 1–3.

30. Astrov, "Grazhdanskaia voina," 7.

31. Ekaterina Vasilievna Astrova is listed in the Moscow city directories for 1903, 1909, 1913, and 1916 as residing in a house owned by Nikolai; in 1916, however, he is listed as residing at another apartment, paid for by the Moscow City Council. The couple apparently had no children. I am grateful to Galina Ulianova for this information.

32. Astrov, "Grazhdanskaia voina," 4–6.

33. The identity document is in GARF, f. 5913, op. 1, d. 1, and reads, "Sostoit li ili sostoial v brake: kholost." The daughter of friends of Sofia and Nikolai in Prague once asked her mother why "Aunt Sonya" was not called "Madame Astrova." Nikolai had never divorced his wife in Moscow, her mother explained. Introduction by Katy Jacobs, granddaughter of Sofia's friend Dr. I. N. Altshuller, to Grafinia Sofia Vladimirovna Panina, "Pamiati Druga," *Slovo/Word* 47 (2005); http://magazines.russ.ru/slovo/2005/47/gr31.html.

34. Astrov, "Grazhdanskaia voina," 8.

35. Ibid., 9.

36. Ibid., 10–14. Nikolai does not explain whether the couple used their real identities with the Germans or how they managed to gain their approval to proceed to Kiev.

37. P. N. Miliukov, K. M. Anderson, and N. I. Kanishcheva, *Dnevnik P. N. Miliukova. 1918–1921* (Moscow: ROSSPEN, 2005), 131 (entry dated August 29/September 11 [1918]); Astrov, "Grazhdanskaia voina," 14, 23.

38. Miliukov, *Dnevnik*, 136, 138–39 (entry dated September 3/16 [1918]); Astrov, "Grazhdanskaia voina," 15–24.

39. Astrov, "Grazhdanskaia voina," 25–26; letter from Sofia Panina to Pavel N. Miliukov, Rostov n/D, October 10/23, 1919, in BAR Miliukov, Box 2; manuscript written in Sofia's hand dated London, July 26/August 8, 1920, titled "My

article about Dr. K. A. Mikhailov, located in Burtsev's 'Obshchee delo' SP,'" in BAR Panina, Box 11, folder Minor Manuscripts by S. V. Panina.

40. Brian Boyd, *Vladimir Nabokov: The Russian Years* (Princeton: Princeton University Press, 1990), 136-49.

41. Astrov, "Grazhdanskaia voina," 27.

42. Ibid., 32-34; GARF, f. 5913, op. 1, d. 50, "Tezisy doklada N. I. Astrova na soveshchanii v Gaspre i ego zapisi vystuplenii razlichnykh lits na tom zhe soveshchanii," [October 2, 1918].

43. Astrov, "Grazhdanskaia voina," 35.

44. Ibid., 36.

45. Miliukov, *Dnevnik*, 183 (entry dated October 19/November 1, 1918).

46. Astrov, "Grazhdanskaia voina," 50-52. The quotation, found on page 50, is crossed out but legible.

47. GARF, f. 5913, op. 1, d. 265, "Zhurnaly zasedanii pravleniia Natsio-nal'nogo tsentra (Kopii i chernovye zapisi N. I. Astrova. Nachalo: 23 ianv. 1919 g. okonch. 19 ianv. 1920)"; ibid., d. 262, "Zhurnaly zasedanii obshchikh sobranii Natsional'nogo tsentra," ll. 23-24.

48. Astrov, "Grazhdanskaia voina," 50; Dimitry V. Lehovich, *White against Red: The Life of General Anton Denikin* (New York: Norton, 1974), 298, 492. Nikolai edited Denikin's five-volume history of the Civil War in the early 1920s. Ksenia, in turn, organized and cataloged Sofia's voluminous archive at Columbia after Sofia's death.

49. GARF, f. 5913, op. 1, d. 262, "Zhurnaly zasedanii obshchikh sobranii Natsional'nogo tsentra," minutes of meeting No. 11, January 31/February 13, 1919, ll. 39-43.

50. Miliukov, *Dnevnik*, 187 (entry dated October 21/November 3 [1918]).

51. GARF, f. 5913, op. 1, d. 262, "Zhurnaly zasedanii obshchikh sobranii Natsional'nogo tsentra."

52. GARF, f. 5913, op. 1, d. 751, "Pis'ma i telegrammy S. V. Paninoi N. I. Astrovu," l. 10-100b. This is an excerpt from a letter written in Sofia's hand though unsigned, dated February 21/March 6, 1919. "Gr. S. V. Paninoi" is written in pencil in Nikolai's handwriting, and the passages that are in italics are underlined in pencil in the original.

53. The Political Conference bombarded Ekaterinodar with letters and tele-grams explaining the tenuous nature of Allied support for the anti-communist cause and begging Denikin to recognize Kolchak. See, for example, the letter from V. A. Maklakov in Paris to the National Center, dated May 2 [N.S.], but received only on May 12 [O.S.], or more than three weeks after it was sent: "Iz perepiski V. A. Maklakova s Natsional'nym tsentrom v 1919 g.," *Krasnyi arkhiv* 36 (1929): 3-30.

54. N. I. Astrov, "Priznanie Gen. Denikinym Adm. Kolchaka. Prikaz 30 maia 1919 goda.—No. 145. (Iz vospominanii i dokumentov)," *Golos minuvshago na chuzhoi storone* 3, no. 1 (1926): 203-17.; K. N. Sokolov, *Pravlenie Generala Deni-kina (iz vospominanii)* (Sofia: Rossiisko-bolgarskoe knigoizdatel'stvo, 1921), 129-36.

55. From a memorandum written by General Staff Intelligence at British headquarters in Constantinople on conditions in Ekaterinodar, April 1919,

issued by General Staff "Intelligence," British Salonika Force, Constantinople, No. 4063 "I," dated May 10, 1919. The National Archives, Foreign Office 608/207, ff. 271–75.

56. Sokolov vigorously defends his record as head of the Propaganda Department and denies charges of anti-Semitism in *Pravlenie Generala Denikina*, chap. 5. See Holquist, *Making War*, chap. 7, and Budnitskii, *Russian Jews*, chap. 7, on the use of anti-Semitic propaganda by Denikin's government.

57. Quotation about Sofia in Sokolov, *Pravlenie Generala Denikina*, 141. The delegation also included a secretary, A. A. Raevskii, from the chancellery of the Special Council; Dragomirov's personal secretary and a translator; another colonel; and a "financial consultant," I. A. Geiman.

58. Ibid., 142. On the day of their arrival, June 23, 1919 [N.S.], British GHQ Constantinople sent a telegram to the Directorate of Military Intelligence in London stating that the British military headquarters in Constantinople had no knowledge of this mission or its delegates and inquiring whether there was any objection to General Dragomirov's party proceeding to Paris. At the request of British Military Intelligence in Constantinople, the British delegation in Paris asked the Russian embassy there and the Political Conference about the mission, but neither had heard of it. The British delegation in Paris finally advised Military Intelligence in Constantinople to allow Dragomirov and his party to proceed, but by then the mission had already landed in France. The National Archives, Foreign Office 608/199/31: Missions. General Denikin's Mission to Paris; Views of General Dragomirov on Military Situation in Russia 1919. It is noteworthy that none of the telegrams sent between Constantinople, Paris, and London speculates about the motives behind sending the mission, its goals, or its composition.

59. Sokolov, *Pravlenie Generala Denikina*, 143–46. Members disagreed on how energetically their outreach activities should be: while Dragomirov advocated restraint, Nikolai pushed for a more activist course.

60. The London *Times* identified Sofia as "Countess Panin, who was the first woman minister in Russia, having been in charge of the Public Health under Prince Lvoff and M. Kerensky"; "New Russian Mission," *Times*, July 7, 1919, 14. *Le Temps* identified Nikolai as a professor of law at the University of Moscow, "Count Panin" as the former mayor of Moscow, and his wife, Countess Panine, as "minister of education at the beginning of the Russian Revolution." "La mission Denikine à Paris," *Le Temps*, July 6, 1919, 2.

61. Sokolov, *Pravlenie Generala Denikina*, 151.

62. Ibid., 149–50, 153–54.

63. Ibid., 150–51.

64. Letter from N. I. Astrov to Anton Iv. Denikin, Paris, July 5–10/18–23, 1919, in BAR Panina, Box 1, folder Astrov, N. I.

65. Before arriving in London Nikolai told Ivan and Anastasia that while he had given up on the French, he still hoped for assistance from Britain and the United States; letter from N. I. Astrov to I. I. and A. S. Petrunkevich, Paris, July 18, 1919, in BAR Panina, Box 1, folder Astrov, N. I. Sofia informed Tyrkova-Williams of their plans to travel to London in a letter from Paris dated July 4/17, 1919, in BAR Tyrkova-Williams, Box 2.

66. Charlotte Alston, "The Work of the Russian Liberation Committee in London," *Slavonica* 14, no. 1 (2008): 6–17.

67. Sokolov, *Pravlenie Generala Denikina*, 158. Dragomirov telegraphed Kolchak on August 20 [N.S.], explaining that due to the rapidly changing military situation in southern Russia, the mission was leaving Paris before receiving his answer to their report. GARF, f. 5913, op. 1, d. 54, ll. 47–49.

68. Letter from Sofia Panina to Pavel N. Miliukov, October 10/23, 1919. Their route and means of transportation from Paris back to southern Russia are unknown.

69. Vernadskii, *Dnevniki 1917–1921*, 141 (diary entry for September 11[/24], [1]919) and 153 (diary entry for September 14[/27], [1919]).

70. Letter from Sofia Panina to Pavel N. Miliukov, October 10/23, 1919; emphasis in original.

71. GARF, f. 5913, op. 1, d. 265, "Zhurnaly zasedanii pravleniia Natsional'nogo tsentra," l. 64.

72. Obolenskii, *Moia zhizn'*, 693; Vernadskii, *Dnevniki 1917–1921*, 141, 153; quotation on 153.

73. Letter from Sofia Panina to Pavel N. Miliukov, October 10/23, 1919.

74. N. I. Astrov, "Iz pis'ma," typed manuscript with revisions in Sofia's handwriting, dated Geneva 1923, in BAR Panina, Box 9, Arranged Manuscripts, folder Astrov N. I., 1918–1921, 3–4.

75. Letter from Sofia Panina to Pavel N. Miliukov, October 10/23, 1919, and postscript dated October 11/24, 1919; emphasis in the original.

76. Budnitskii condemns the Kadets for their "appalling lack of action" in combatting pogroms and anti-Semitic propaganda and for supporting those who blamed the entire Jewish people for the revolution; *Russian Jews*, chap. 7.

77. N. I. Astrov, "Moskovskaia katastrofa i smert' moikh brat'ev," BAR Panina, Box 9. His stepmother spent several weeks in prison before being released.

78. Letter from Sofia Panina to Pavel N. Miliukov, October 10/23, 1919.

79. Quoted in Evan Mawdsley, *The Russian Civil War* (Boston: Unwin and Allen, 1987), 130. Lloyd George's speech had a devastating impact on morale in Rostov; C. E. Bechhofer Roberts, *In Denikin's Russia and the Caucasus, 1919–1920* (New York: Arno Press, 1971), 121–22.

80. Vernadskii, *Dnevniki 1917–1921*, 191 (entry for November 30/December 13, [1]919).

81. Astrov, "Iz pis'ma," 4; Dolgorukov, "Obshchestvennaia deiatel'nost' N. I. Astrova v emigratsii," 1. Roberts, who made the trip from Rostov to Novorossiisk in March, describes the horrendous scenes along the route; *In Denikin's Russia*, 195–96.

82. Dolgorukov, "Obshchestvennaia deiatel'nost' N. I. Astrova," 1.

83. Panina, "Moi gorod," 2.

84. A report from 1904 by the political police alleges the existence of "intimate relations" between Sofia and Prince Leonid Viazemsky, who collaborated with her in founding the people's house. The report provides no evidence of how the police obtained the information, although the same allegation is

repeated in a police report of December 23, 1907. GARF, f. 102, op. DOO 1902,
d. 992, ll. 12 [1904] and 26 [1907]. The liaison seems unlikely. More than twenty
years older than Sofia, Viazemsky was married to her cousin Missy, and Sofia
was close to the entire family.

85. Budnitskii, *Russian Jews*, 275.

Chapter 11. "Our Bread Tastes Bitter in Foreign Lands"

1. Panina, "Such Is Life," 2.

2. "N. G. Ia.," handwritten manuscript, unsigned but in Sofia's writing, undated; emphasis in the original. The subject is the recent death of Natalia Gri-
gorevna Yashvil, whom Sofia knew in Prague. BAR Panina Box 11, folder
Minor Manuscripts. Dante addresses the pain of exile in *Paradiso*, XVII (55–60),
where Cacciaguida, his great-great-grandfather, warns him what to expect:
"You shall leave everything you love most: this is the arrow that the bow of
exile shoots first. You are to know the bitter taste of others' bread, how salty it
is, and know how hard a path it is for one who goes ascending and descending
others' stairs."

3. Kseniia Denikina, "V N. Iorke skonchalas' Grafinia Sof'ia Vladimirovna
Panina," *Novoe russkoe slovo*, June 15, 1956, 1.

4. Letter from Anastasia Petrunkevich to Roza Georgievna Vinaver, Roztoky, Czechoslovakia, February 16, 1925; GARF, f. 5839, op. 1, ed. khr. 57,
l. 83ob.

5. Sofia's and Nikolai's post-revolutionary correspondence with fellow émigrés and others fills boxes 1–5 and 7–8 in the Panina Collection at Columbia
University's Bakhmeteff Archive. Other holdings there with significant correspondence from Sofia include the Rodichev, Denikin, and Tyrkova-Williams Collections. Also invaluable for understanding Sofia during the émigré period of
her life are her letters to Alexandra Petrunkevich and Tatiana Osorgina, in BDIC.

6. Letter from Sofia Panina to Alexandra Petrunkevich, September 23, 1953.

7. "A Russian Exodus," *Times*, April 19, 1920, 18.

8. Marc Raeff, *Russia Abroad: A Cultural History of the Russian Emigration,
1919–1939* (New York: Oxford University Press, 1990), 29–30. Nikolai claims
credit for reviving the Union of Towns in Constantinople in an unpublished
autobiographical manuscript in BAR Panina, Box 13, folder Astrov, Nikolai
Ivanovich (biographical). Nikolai also traveled to Crimea to help organize aid
to refugees gathering there. Baron Peter Nikolaevich Wrangel, who replaced
Denikin as commander-in-chief of the White forces in April 1920, was making a
last stand against the Bolsheviks. Writing a few years later, he states that he
"looked upon Wrangel's efforts without hope." Astrov, "Iz pis'ma," 5.

9. "Just think," Sofia complained, "four Kadet meetings in one week!"
Letter from Sofia Panina to Ariadna Tyrkova-Williams, Paris, July 29, 1920, in
the British Library, H. W. Williams Papers, vol. III, f. 224.

10. Astrov, "Iz pis'ma," 5–6. In this manuscript Nikolai states that he was in
Constantinople until the end of June, and he does not mention Sofia's whereabouts; but in the untitled autobiographical manuscript in BAR Panina, Box 13,
he states that he left Constantinople with Sofia in July 1920 for Paris.

11. Sofia's story about her trial was included in Alfred Emmott, *Interim Report of the Committee to Collect Information on Russia* (London: His Majesty's Stationery Office, 1920), 13. Sofia's and Nikolai's British Certificates of Registration for Aliens, issued on January 1, 1921, give August 2, 1920, as the date of their entry into the United Kingdom, and also the same previous address, a Paris hotel. GARF, f. 5913, op. 1, d. 1 (Astrov), d. 1085 (Panina).

12. Astrov, "Iz pis'ma," 6.

13. Ibid.; letters from Sofia Panina to Anton Denikin, London, September 3 and 21, 1920, in BAR Panina, Box 5, folder S. V. Panina.

14. Letters from Sofia Panina to Ariadna Tyrkova-Williams, Dartmoor Sanatorium, October 5, 1920, and December 15, 1920; BAR Tyrkova-Williams, Box 2.

15. Although the sources of the funds on which Sofia and Nikolai lived during 1920–21 are not known, they received some help from the Williamses. In a letter dated November 18, 1921, Sofia thanks Tyrkova-Williams profusely for "last year's help and support," mentioning specifically her hospitality and the use of a "little house in Ealing." BAR Tyrkova-Williams, Box 2. Nikolai mentions their worries about earning a living in his letter to Ksenia Denikina, January 31, 1921, in BAR Panina, Box 1.

16. Letter from Sofia Panina to Ariadna Tyrkova-Williams, Dartmoor Sanatorium, December 15, 1920; emphasis in the original.

17. Letter from Sofia Panina to Ksenia Denikina, Dartmoor Sanitorium, November 26, 1920, in BAR Panina, Box 5, folder S. V. Panina.

18. Rosenberg, *Liberals*, 445–54.

19. According to the minutes, Sofia spoke at some length about Miliukov's new tactic and party unity at the May 30, 1921, meeting of the Central Committee; she also spoke briefly at the climactic meeting on June 2; Protokol No. 4, Soveshchaniia chlenov TsK partii narodnoi svobody, zasedanie 30 maia 1921, ll. 121–23, and Protokol No. 6, Soveshchaniia chlenov TsK partii narodnoi svobody, dnevnoe zasedanie 2 iiunia 1921, in the Archive of the Constitutional Democratic Party, Box 1, Hoover Institution.

20. Letter from Anastasia Petrunkevich to Sofia Panina and Nikolai Astrov, New Haven, February 4/20, 1920, in BAR Panina, Box 5; Astrov, "Iz pis'ma," 7.

21. Astrov, "Iz pis'ma," 6. Before giving this manuscript of Nikolai's to Columbia, Sofia carefully crossed out this sentence.

22. The Soviet government disbanded the original Zemgor in 1918. Refugees who had been local government leaders revived the Union of Zemstvos and the Union of Towns, and the two organizations were combined to create the Rossiiskii Zemsko-gorodskoi komitet pomoshchi rossiisskim grazhdanam za granitsei (RZGK or Zemgor) in January 1921. RZGK was registered officially in the Paris prefecture as Le Comité des Zemstvos et Villes [or Municipalités] Russes de Secours aux Citoyens Russes à l'Etranger. It had its headquarters in Paris. On the appointment of Nikolai and Sofia as its representatives, see Astrov, "Iz pis'ma," 6, and a document from Le Comité des Zemstvos et Villes Russes de Secours aux Citoyens Russes à l'Étranger, Paris, May 27, 1921, which certifies Nikolai's appointment as its official representative in Switzerland before the Red Cross and International Bureau of Labor, adding, "Il sera assisté dans sa

tache par la Comtesse Sophie Panine," in GARF, f. 5913, op. 1, d. 1; also see a certificate that "La Comtesse Sophie Panine, membre du Comité Central de l'Union des Villes de la Russie est chargée par le Comité Central de se rendre à Genève comme Representante du Comité," Constantinople, May 23, 1921, in GARF, f. 5913, op. 1, d. 1085.

23. The Soviet government forced the prerevolutionary Russian Red Cross to close in 1918 and replaced it with the Soviet Red Cross Society. Leaders of the "old" Russian Red Cross reconstituted it in Paris in February 1921. Using the organization's prerevolutionary assets located abroad, the old Red Cross took an active role in refugee relief. The International Committee of the Red Cross (ICRC) recognized it until late 1921, when it changed its recognition to the Soviet Red Cross.

24. Copies of these letters and a memorandum from the Russian Red Cross, sent to members of the League of Nations Council, are in the National Archives, Foreign Office, 371/6865, ff. 105–15. The first letter, dated January 10, 1921, from the General Council of the Russian Red Cross Abroad, urgently requests the Council of the League of Nations to come to the aid of the refugees by providing funds and evacuating the refugees from Constantinople. The letter from the ICRC, dated January 12, 1921, and addressed to the League's secretary-general, Sir Eric Drummond, states that the ICRC supports the request of the Russian Red Cross. Gustav Ador, president of the ICRC and Switzerland's representative to the League of Nations, also wrote the council in February 1921 to urge its involvement and recommend the creation of a special commission. On the establishment of the position of high commissioner, see also Claudena M. Skran, *Refugees in Inter-War Europe: The Emergence of a Regime* (Oxford: Clarendon Press, 1995), chap. 3; and Z. S. Bocharova, *Russkie bezhentsy: Problemy rasseleniia, vozvrashcheniia na Rodinu, uregulirovaniia, pravogo polozheniia (1920–1930-e gody); Sbornik dokumentov i materialov* (Moscow: ROSSPEN, 2004), 8–10.

25. Created in Paris in February 1921, the council was comprised primarily of the Provisional Government's ambassadors. It assumed the role of defending the interests of Russian citizens abroad and control over Russian government funds and property located abroad. Other organizations represented on the Advisory Council were the International Committee of the Red Cross and the League of Red Cross Societies, the YMCA, the Save the Children Fund, and the Jewish Colonization Association.

26. Originally concerned only with aid to Russian refugees, the office broadened its responsibilities later in the 1920s to include Armenian and other Near Eastern refugee populations. By 1930 it had virtually ceased to give any attention to Russians, but the needs of refugee populations from Germany and Spain in the 1930s kept the office in business until World War II.

27. See Nikolai's report to Zemgor of October 6, 1922, reprinted in Bocharova, *Russkie bezhentsy*, 108.

28. Bocharova, *Russkie bezhentsy*, 11–12.

29. Astrov, "Iz pis'ma," 7.

30. Letter from Sofia Panina to Adelaida Zhekulina, May 12, 1922, quoted in Z. S. Bocharova, "'Vozrashchivat' dobrye plody svoego neutolimnogo truda':

Deiatel'nost' S. V. Paninoi i N. I. Astrova v Lige natsii," in *Mysliashchie miry rossiiskogo liberalizma: Grafinia Sof'ia Vladimirovna Panina*, 80–81. Nikolai's reports are located in the Zemgor Collection at the Leeds Russian Archive, University of Leeds, Great Britain.

31. Bocharova, *Russkie bezhentsy*, 11.

32. Oleg Budnitskii, "Soveshchanie rossiiskikh poslov v Parizhe i Zemgor: Den'gi i politika (1921–1925)," *Cahiers du Monde russe* 46, no. 4 (October–December 2005): 699–718.

33. Letter from Sofia Panina to Ksenia Denikina, Geneva, October 11, 1921, in BAR Panina, Box 5, folder S. V. Panina. Nikolai's report to Zemgor of November 8, 1921, also excoriates Nansen and Frick for their pro-Soviet sympathies, obstructionism, and lack of sympathy toward the refugees; Bocharova, *Russkie bezhentsy*, 79–90.

34. Nikolai's report to Zemgor, November 8, 1921, in Bocharova, *Russkie bezhentsy*, 89.

35. Bocharova, *Russkie bezhentsy*, 12.

36. Nikolai's report to Zemgor of October 6, 1922, in Bocharova, *Russkie bezhentsy*, 109.

37. Skran, *Refugees in Inter-War Europe*, chap. 4; Bocharova, *Russkie bezhentsy*, 13–19. On the deficiencies of the Nansen passport, see Elena Chinyaeva, *Russians outside Russia: The Émigré Community in Czechoslovakia, 1918–1938* (Munich: R. Oldenbourg Verlag, 2001), 76–78.

38. Letter from Sofia Panina to Ksenia Denikina, Geneva, June 19, 1921. See Nikolai's report to the Zemgor's General Assembly of July 5, 1921, about the "sharp protest" he and Sofia made against those such as Gustav Ador, head of the ICRC, who favored repatriation; reprinted in Bocharova, *Russkie bezhentsy*, 73–74.

39. Nikolai's report to Zemgor, October 6, 1922, in Bocharova, *Russkie bezhentsy*, 110–19.

40. Documents illuminating the different sides of the dispute, including the versions of the original resolution, copies of the letters between Lodyzhensky and Sofia and Nikolai, and their letters to Tyrkova-Williams are located in the H. W. Williams Papers, vol. VII, Add. Mss. 54442, 1923, ff. 146–277, in the British Library, Manuscripts Department.

41. Untitled, unsigned summary of the dispute and the state of refugees affairs at the League of Nations, dated October 9, 1923, probably written by Ariadna Tyrkova-Williams, in the H. W. Williams Papers, vol. VII, Add. Mss. 54442, f. 277. For other examples, see documents 21–23 in Bocharova, *Russkie bezhentsy*, 183–86.

42. Letter from Sofia Panina to Ariadna Tyrkova-Williams, Geneva, May 18, 1923, in the H. W. Williams Papers, vol. VII, Add. Mss. 54442, ff. 167–68. Nikolai published his defense in the Berlin émigré newspaper *Rul'*.

43. Untitled memorandum dated October 9, 1923, unsigned but evidently written by Tyrkova-Williams, about her recent trip to Geneva and the controversy over repatriation, in the H. W. Williams Papers, vol. VII, Add. Mss. 54442, ff. 276–77; letter from A. I. Guchkov to K. N. Gul'kevich, Paris, June 21, 1923,

reprinted in Bocharova, *Russkie bezhentsy*, 202–3; letter from Iu. I. Lodyzhensky to A. V. Zhekulina, quoted in Bocharova, "Vzrashchivat' dobrye plody," 82.

44. Draft of a letter from Anastasia Petrunkevich to Alexandra Peshekhonova, August 3, 1922, in BAR Panina, Box 7. Describing herself as "overloaded with work," Sofia told Ksenia that she never finished her day before 1 a.m.; letter from Sofia Panina to Ksenia Denikina, February 12, 1923, in BAR Panina, Box 5, folder S. V. Panina. Sofia completed the course of study at the École d'Études sociales pour Femmes in Geneva and worked at the Geneva Public and University Library. Her application for the job at the league was unsuccessful because the position was canceled. BAR Panina, Box 14, folder "Panina as a Librarian."

45. Dated Geneva, October 4, 5, and 6, 1921, the letters are in GARF, f. 5913, op. 1, d. 751, ll. 1–6; there are also three telegrams she sent him in Paris during this same time. I am grateful to the late Sergei Dundin for finding these letters. A fourth letter from Sofia to Nikolai, dated Geneva, March 23, 1923, is similar to the ones from 1921; it is located in the Zemgor Collection, Leeds Russian Archive, folder 63.

46. "Siren' [Lilacs]," handwritten manuscript dated Geneva, May 14, 1922, Lehovich Family Collection.

47. Letters from Anastasia Petrunkevich to Roza Georgievna Vinaver, Geneva: May 5, 1921, September 13, 1922, and August 15, 1923, in GARF, f. 5839, op. 1, ed. kh. 57; letter from Anastasia Petrunkevich to Alexander Petrunkevich, Geneva, December 10, 1921, in Alexander I. Petrunkevich Papers, Yale University, New Haven, Sterling Memorial Library, Historical Manuscripts and Archives Department, Series I, Box 2, folder 35.

48. Letter from Ivan Petrunkevich to Alexander Petrunkevich, Geneva, November 25, 1921, in BAR Panina, Box 5; letter from Sofia Panina to Ksenia Denikina, Geneva, November 30, 1922. BAR Panina, Box 7, contains numerous letters asking for aid, such as one from three disabled veterans addressed to "Your Excellency" (*Vashe Siiatel'stvo*), dated February 7, 1924.

49. The earliest surviving letter to Sofia is dated October 27, 1921, and was written collectively by "your ancient and old friends," in response to a letter she sent. The letters are primarily from Alexandra Peshekhonova and the younger Nadezhda Yalozo. Other women who had worked with Sofia at the people's house sent occasional letters, while Alexandra sent letters to Sofia's mother and her cousin, Nadezhda Zurova, as well as to Sofia. For the first few years Sofia used the pseudonym "Carmen Bastino," with an address in Vevey, Switzerland; Mademoiselle Bastino was a Swiss governess who had worked for the Bakunins in Russia before the revolution (letter from Sofia Panina to Fedor Rodichev, Dartmoor Sanatorium, January 25, 1921, in BAR Rodichev, Box 3, folder Panina Sofiia Vladimirovna, v. p., 1920–21). After she moved to Prague in 1924 her correspondents seem to have written directly to her. The correspondence continued more or less regularly up to April 1932, when Alexandra died at the age of eighty, although Sofia received a trickle of letters and postcards from Nadezhda Yalozo during the 1930s; the last letters date from 1937. The letters are in BAR Panina, Box 7, folder Arranged Correspondence Peshekhonova, and Box 8, folders (2) Letters from USSR, 1927–1936. There are also two

letters, written in 1924, and several postcards from the 1930s in the Lehovich Family Collection.

50. Letter from Alexandra Peshekhonova to Sofia Panina, [Petrograd], April 12, [1923], in BAR Panina, Box 7, Arranged Correspondence Peshekhonova.

51. Letter from Alexandra Peshekhonova to Anastasia Petrunkevich, [Petrograd], November 7, 1923, in BAR Panina, Box 7, Arranged Correspondence Peshekhonova.

52. The authorities allowed Sofia's letter of greeting and congratulations to the institution and her former coworkers to be read only at a private gathering, after the official ceremony. Materials related to the twentieth-anniversary celebration at the people's house in 1923, including the formal congratulatory address sent to Sofia by coworkers and former visitors to the institution, are in BAR Panina, Box 14, folder Narodnyi Dom.

53. Letter from A. Golubev to Sofia Panina, Petrograd, June 7, 1925, in BAR Panina, Box 16, folder Narodnyi Dom.

54. Letter from Pavel Mikhailovich Mikhailov to Sofia Panina, Leningrad, April 15, 1928, in Bar Panina, Box 8, folder Letters from USSR, 1927-1936.

55. Anonymous letter to Sofia Panina, np, March 4, 1936, BAR Panina, Box 8, folder Letters from USSR, 1927-1936. Golubev, Mikhailov, and the anonymous correspondent probably obtained Sofia's address from Alexandra or another former coworker of the people's house.

56. Letters from Alexandra Peshekhonova to Sofia Panina, [Petrograd], November 17, [1923], and December 25, 1923, in BAR Panina, Box 7, Arranged Correspondence Peshekhonova; quotation from the letter of December 25.

57. Letters from Alexandra Peshekhonova to Sofia Panina, [Leningrad], August 23, [1925], and March 14, 1927, BAR Panina, Box 7, Arranged Correspondence Peshekhonova.

58. Letter from Anastasia Petrunkevich to Roza Georgievna Vinaver, Roztoky u Prahy, August 31, 1924, GARF, f. 5839, op. 1, ed. kh. 57, ll. 78-80.

59. Letters from Anastasia Petrunkevich to Roza Georgievna Vinaver, Roztoky, February 16, 1925, and April 21, 1926, GARF, f. 5839, op. 1, ed. kh. 57, ll. 81-83, 88; V. Iu. Voloshina, "Roztokskaia russkaia koloniia. Nachalo prazhkogo perioda emigratsii S. V. Paninoi," in *Mysliashchie miry rossiiskogo liberalizma*, 72-77.

60. Letter from Sofia Panina to Fedor Rodichev, Roztoky, December 4, 1924, in BAR Rodichev, Box 3, folder Panina Sofia Vladimirovna, Geneva and Prague, 1923-25.

61. Sofia expresses her deep admiration for Zhekulina in S. V. Panina, "Pamiati A. V Zhekuliny," *Novyi zhurnal* 24 (1950): 214-19.

62. A. B. Evreinov, *Cheshskaia rapsodiia. Dni minuvshie v sobytiiakh, portretakh, razmyshleniiakh* (Biisk: IITs BPGU im. V. M. Shukshina, 2004), 7-9, 24-25. See also Anastasiia Koprshivova, "Adelaida Vladimirovna Zhekulina: Prazhskaia vol'ter'ianka k 150-letiiu," http://www.ruslo.cz/index.php/anonsy/item/448-adelaida-vladimirovna-zhekulina-prazhskaya-volteryanka-k-150-letiyu.

63. Chinyaeva, *Russians outside Russia*; E. P. Serapionova, *Rossiiskaia emigratsiia v Chekhoslovatskoi respublike (20-30-e gody)* (Moscow: Institut slavianovedeniia i

balkanistiki Rossiiskoi akademii nauk, 1995); and *Russkaia aktsiia pomoshchi v Chekhoslovakii: Istoriia, znachenie, nasledie. K 90-letiiu nachala Russkoi aktsii pomoshchi v Chekhoslovakii*, ed. Lukash Babka and Igor' Zolotarev (Prague: Národní knihovna CR-Slovanská knihovna, 2012).

64. Ruth Crawford Mitchell, comp., *Alice Garrigue Masaryk, 1879–1966: Her Life as Recorded in Her Own Words and by Her Friends*, ed. Linda Vlasak, introduction by René Wellek (Pittsburgh: University of Pittsburgh, University Center for International Studies, 1980).

65. Letter from Sofia Panina to Adelaida Zhekulina, April 2, 1922, quoted in Zoia Sergeevna Bocharova, "Deiatel'nost' pravitel'stva ChSR po uregulirovaniiu pravovogo polozheniia russkikh emigrantov," in *Russkaia aktsiia pomoshchi v Chekhoslovakii*, 16.

66. Letter from Sofia Panina to Alice Masaryk, December 3, 1928, quoted in Tania Chebotareva, "'Na chuzhom piru nezvannye gosti': iz istorii 'Russkogo ochaga' v Prage," *Russkaia aktsiia pomoshchi*, 129.

67. Raeff, *Russia Abroad*, chap. 3; Elizabeth White, "'The Struggle against Denationalisation': The Russian Emigration in Europe and Education in the 1920s," *Revolutionary Russia* 6, no. 2 (2013): 128–46.

68. Raeff, *Russia Abroad*, chaps. 2 and 3, esp. 42–44.

69. V. Iu. Voloshina, *Uchenyi v emigratsii: Problemy sotsial'noi adaptatsii uchenykh-emigrantov skvoz' prizmu "personal'noi istorii"* (Omsk: Izd-vo omskogo gosudarstvennogo universiteta, 2010), 194–95.

70. Sofia's handwritten draft of her lecture on Turgenev is in the Lehovich Family Collection, while the mention of meeting Turgenev is in Panina, "Moi gorod," 2.

71. Pavel P. Gronsky and Nikolai I. Astrov, *The War and the Russian Government: The Central Government* (New Haven: Yale University Press, 1929); Nikolai wrote the second half of the volume, on wartime municipal government and the All-Russian Union of Towns.

72. Dolgorukov, "Obshchestvennaia deiatel'nost' N. I. Astrova v emigratsii," 4.

73. For example, Letter from Sofia Panina to Tatiana Osorgina, [Prague], May 16, 1937, in BDIC, Fonds Ossorguine, F delta rés 841 (3), chemise 2.

74. Letter from Sofia Panina to Alexander Petrunkevich, [Prague], April 24, 1932, Alexander I. Petrunkevich Papers, Box 2, folder 37; also letter from Sofia Panina to Fedor Rodichev, Prague, April 30, 1932, in BAR Rodichev, Box 3, folder Panina Sofiia Vladimirovna, Prague, 1932.

75. Letter from Sofia Panina to Fedor Rodichev, Prague, April 30, 1932.

76. BAR Panina, Box 11, folder Notes by S. V. Panina on Kadet Party, September–October 1919, note from September 24, 1919. On Tyrkova-Williams's turn to religion and the church in emigration, see N. I. Kanishcheva, "Predislovie," in *Nasledie Ariadny Vladimirovny Tyrkovoi: Dnevniki. Pis'ma*, comp. N. I. Kanishcheva (Moscow: ROSSPEN, 2012), 20.

77. Nikolai's pocket diary for 1934 is in the Lehovich Family Collection.

78. Letter from E. K. Kuskova-Prokopovich to P. N. Miliukov, Kurvilla Sonnhof, Jáchimov, Czechoslovakia, August 27, 1934, GARF, f. 5856, op. 1, d. 210.

79. Letter from Sofia Panina to Ksenia and Anton Denikin, Prague, August

28, 1934, BAR Panina, Box 5; "Vypiski iz pisem"; letter from Sofia Panina to Tatiana Osorgina, [Prague], May 16, 1937, BDIC, F delta rés 841 (3), chemise 2.

80.   Letter from Sofia Panina to Alexandra Rodicheva, Prague, October 18, 1938, BAR Rodichev, Box 3, folder Panina S. V., v. p. 1938–51.

81.   Ibid.

82.   Linaida Davydova, "Grafinia Sof'ia Panina. Chekhoslovakiia— priviazannost' i gorech' utrat," http://www.ruslo.cz/index.php/component /k2/item/474-grafinya-sofya-panina-chekhoslovakiya-privyazannost-i -gorech-utrat; postcard from Sofia Panina to Tatiana Osorgina, Paris, December 15, 1938, in BDIC, F delta rés 841 (3), chemise 2.

Epilogue

1.   "List or Manifest of Alien Passengers for the United States Immigrant Inspector for the Port of Arrival, SS Champlain, Arriving at Port of New York January 26, 1939," 130; Ancestry.com. *New York, Passenger Lists, 1820–195*, http:// search.ancestrylibrary.com/cgi-bin/sse.dll?indiv=1&db=nypl&h=1005290903. Sofia's Social Security card and US passport are in the Lehovich Family Collection. For her naturalization certificate, see *U.S. Naturalization Record Indexes, 1791–1992*; https://www.ancestrylibrary.com/interactive/1629/31197 _145630-06335.

2.   Obituary of Professor Alexander Petrunkevich, *New York Times*, March 10, 1964.

3.   Letter from Sofia Panina to Alexandra Rodicheva, Los Angeles, September 10, 1939, in BAR Rodichev, Box 3, folder Panina S. V., v. p. 1938–51.

4.   Ibid.; letter from Sofia Panina to Tatiana Osorgina and Emilia Bakunina, Los Angeles, September 5, 1939, in BDIC, F delta rés 841 (3), chemise 2; quotation from this letter.

5.   Letter from Sofia Panina to Tatiana Osorgina and Emilia Bakunina, Los Angeles, January 9, 1940, in BDIC, F delta rés 841 (3), chemise 2; letter from Sofia Panina to Irene Ourousoff, Los Angeles, February 11, 1940, Lehovich Family Collection.

6.   On the Federal Theatre Project and this play, see http://www.blackpast .org/aah/federal-theatre-project-negro-units.

7.   "Kaliforniiskiia vpechatleniia," 1939 g., BAR Panina, Box 11.

8.   Letter from Sofia Panina to Tatiana Osorgina and Emilia Bakunina, Los Angeles, September 5, 1939.

9.   Ibid.

10.   Aleksandra Tolstaia, *Doch'* (London, Ontario: Zaria, 1979), 486–87; Paul B. Anderson, "The Tolstoy Foundation," *Russian Review* 17, no. 1 (January 1958): 60–66.

11.   S. P. "Russkaia emigratsiia v Evrope," typed manuscript, dated in pencil 1939, in BAR Panina, Box 14, folder Emigration, Europe, 3. Another lecture was the one she titled "Such Is Life" and gave to an English-speaking audience in Los Angeles in 1939.

12.   Letter from Sofia Panina to Tatiana Osorgina and Emilia Bakunina, Los Angeles, January 9, 1940.

13. Letters from Sofia Panina to Tatiana Osorgina, New York, May 5, 1940, and February 26, 1941, in BDIC, F delta rés 841 (3), chemise 2; and to Ariadna Tyrkova-Williams, New Haven, June 18, 1941, and June 3, 1942, in BAR Tyrkova-Williams, Box 2.

14. Tolstoy Foundation (U.S.), *Tolstoy Foundation, Inc.: History, Aims and Achievements* (New York: The Foundation, 1976).

15. Private communication to the author from Professor Marina Ledkovsky, Christmas Season 2002–3, New York. Dr. Ledkovsky arrived at the Tolstoy Farm from Europe in 1951.

16. Letters from Sofia Panina to Alexandra Petrunkevich, Reed Farm, February 11, 1952, December 9, 1955, and February 8, 1956, in BDIC, F delta rés 892, chemise 3; Borman, 310.

17. Letter from Sofia Panina to Ariadna Tyrkova-Williams, New Haven, April 24, 1946, in BAR Tyrkova-Williams, Box 2.

18. Letter from Sofia Panina to Ariadna Tyrkova-Williams, New Haven, March 30, 1949, in ibid.

19. Letter from Sofia Panina to Alexandra Petrunkevich, Reed Farm, August 5, 1950, in BDIC, F delta rés 892, chemise 3.

20. Letter from Sofia Panina to Tatiana Osorgina, New Haven, May 18, 1947, in BDIC, F delta rés 841 (3), chemise 2; letter from Sofia Panina to Irene Ourousoff, Reed Farm, April 24, 1952, Lehovich Family Collection. Alexandra Tolstoy's biography of her father is *Otets: Zhizn' L'va Tolstogo* (New York: Izdatel'stvo imeni Chekhova, 1953).

21. Letter from Sofia Panina to Alexandra Petrunkevich, New Haven, September 23, 1953, in BDIC, F delta rés 892, chemise 3.

22. Lehovich, *Crimean Notes*, 29–30, and personal communications to the author.

23. Undated, handwritten document in the Lehovich Family Collection.

24. Letter from Sofia Panina to Alexandra Rodicheva, New York City, December 29, 1940, in BAR Rodichev, Box 3, folder Panina S. V.

25. Panina, "Kaliforniiskie vpechatleniia."

26. Letter from Sofia Panina to Irene Ourousoff, Reed Farm, March 18, 1956, Lehovich Family Collection.

27. Letter from Sofia Panina to Tatiana Osorgina, Reed Farm, Valley Cottage, New York, February 28, 1952, in BDIC, F delta rés 841 (3), chemise 2.

28. Letters from Sofia Panina to Alexandra Petrunkevich, New Haven, September 23, 1953, and New York, June 4, 1954, in BDIC, F delta rés 892, chemise 3.

29. Undated letter from Sofia Panina to Alexandra Rodicheva, n.p., n.d., but with notation in ink, "after second world war," in BAR Rodichev, Box 3, folder Panina S. V.

30. Information about Sofia Panina's final illness is from a letter from Mrs. P. Baranoff to Alexandra Petrunkevich, New York City, June 17, 1956, in BDIC, F delta rés 892, chemise 3, and letters to Alexander Petrunkevich from Alexandra Tolstoy, Dmitry Lehovich, and others in the Alexander I. Petrunkevich Papers, Box 1, folders 13 and 14.

31. Denikina, "V N. Iorke skonchalas' Grafinia Sof'ia Vladimirovna Panina"; Ek[aterina] Kuskova, "Gr. Sof'ia Vladimirovna Panina," *Russkaia mysl'*, 1956, 917 (June 26): 2; Kuskova, "Grafinia S. V. Panina," *Novoe russkoe slovo*, June 27, 1956; Ariadna Tyrkova-Vil'iams, "Zamechatel'naia russkaia zhenshchina," *Novoe russkoe slovo*, June 21, 1956, reprinted in *Russkaia mysl'*, 1956, 917 (June 26): 2, 7.

32. Letter from Sofia Panina to Alexandra Petrunkevich, Reed Farm, August 5, 1950.

Bibliography

Archival Sources

Russian Federation

Gosudarstvennyi arkhiv Rossiiskoi federatsii, Moscow.
  F. 102, Departament politsii, 3-e deloproizvodstvo, 1881, 1882 (A. S. Petrun-
    kevich, I. I. Petrunkevich); 1902 (S. V. Panina).
  F. 102, Departament politsii, 4-e deloproizvodstvo, 1906, 1908, 1910, 1913.
  F. 102, Departament politsii, 6-e deloproizvodstvo, 1915, 1916.
  F. 102, Obshchii otdel, 1881, 1882 (I. I. Petrunkevich); 1898, 1899, 1900, 1902,
    1908, 1910, 1911, 1913 (S. V. Panina).
  F. 336, op. 1, d. 156 [Investigation of Ivan Zhukov].
  F. 629, A. V. Tyrkova.
  F. 887, Geideny, Volkovy. Op. 1, d. 391; letters from Sofia Vladimirovna
    Panina to Varvara Petrovna Volkova (née Geiden).
  F. R-1074, op. 1, Revoliutsionnyi tribunal pri Petrogradskom sovete rabo-
    chikh i krasnoarmeiskikh deputatov.
  F. R-5839, I. I. Petrunkevich.
  F. R-5856, P. N. Miliukov.
  F. R-5913, N. I. Astrov.
Gosudarstvennyi muzei istorii Sankt-Peterburga, St. Petersburg.
  Rukopisno-dokumental'nyi fond. Opis' fonda Ligovskii narodnyi dom.
Institut russkoi literatury Rossiiskoi akademii nauk (Pushkinskii dom), St.
    Petersburg.
  F. 223, S. V. Panina.
Rossiiskii gosudarstvennyi arkhiv drevnikh aktov, Moscow.
  F. 1274, Panin and Bludov.
Rossiiskaia gosudarstvennaia biblioteka, Moscow.
  Otdel rukopisei.
  F. 154. 5.12, Il'ia Ivanovich Sadof'ev, "Raskopki pamiati."
  F. 218, kart. 1339, d. 1 [Bakunin Family Photographs].
  F. 358, N. A. Rubakin.
  F. 369.386.2, Mikhail Petrovich Efremov, "Avtobiografiia."
Rossiiskii gosudarstvennyi istoricheskii arkhiv, St. Petersburg.
  F. 796, Holy Synod.
Rossiiskii institut istorii iskusstv, St. Petersburg.
  Kabinet rukopisei, F. 32, P. P. Gaideburov and N. F. Skarskaia.

Rossiiskaia natsional'naia biblioteka, St. Petersburg.
    Otdel rukopisi, F. 423, Lbovskii, A. N.
Tsentral'nyi gosudarstvennyi arkhiv kinofotofonodokumentov g. S-Peterburga,
    St. Petersburg.
Tsentral'nyi gosudarstvennyi istoricheskii arkhiv S-Peterburga, St. Petersburg.
    F. 3, Petrogradskoe uchilishche ordena Sv. Ekateriny.
    F. 113, Vysshie zhenskie kursy (Bestuzhevskie).
    F. 219, Ligovskii narodnyi dom.
    F. 254, Peterburgskoe gubernskoe pravlenie.
    F. 513, Peterburgskaia gorodskaia uprava.
    F. 536, Petrogradskoe dvorianskoe deputatskoe sobranie.
    F. 569, Kantseliariia petrogradskogo gradonachal'nika.

United States

Columbia University, New York, Rare Book and Manuscript Library, Bakh-
    meteff Archive.
    Collections: S. V. Panina, Panin Family, A. M. Petrunkevich, P. N. Miliukov,
        F. I. Rodichev, A. I. Denikin, and A. V. Tyrkova-Williams.
Hoover Institution Archives, Stanford University.
    Archive of the Constitutional Democratic Party.
    Lydia Wassiltschikow Collection.
    Roza Georgievna Vinaver Collection.
Lehovich Family Collection, Washington, D. C.
Yale University, New Haven, Sterling Memorial Library, Historical Manuscripts
    and Archives Department.
    Alexander I. Petrunkevich Papers.
    Alexander Polovtsoff Papers.
YIVO, New York.
    Elias Tcherikower Archives, Maxim Vinaver Papers.

Great Britain

British Library, London.
    Manuscripts Department: H. W. Williams Papers.
    Slavonic and East European Collection: Ariadna Tyrkova-Williams Collection.
Leeds University Library Special Collections, Zemgor Archive.
The National Archives, Foreign Office.
    Materials on the British Military Mission to General Anton Denikin in the
        Russian Civil War: Files 608/199, 608/206, and 608/207.
    Political Departments: General Correspondence, Russia: Files 371/5420 and
        371/6865.

France

La Contemporaine, Université Paris Nanterre (formerly Bibliothèque de Docu-
    mentation Internationale Contemporaine, cited as BDIC).
Fond Alexandra Petrounkévitch: F delta rés 892.
Fonds Ossorguine: F delta rés 841.

Writings by Sofia V. Panina

Published Writings

"Iskusstvo v narodnoi auditorii." *Trudy Vserossiiskogo s"ezda khudozhnikov: Dekabr' 1911–ianvar' 1912.* Vol. 5. St. Petersburg, 1912.

"Na peterburgskoi okraine [On the outskirts of Petersburg]." *Novyi zhurnal* 48 (1957): 163–96; 49 (1957): 189–203. Longer manuscript version, typewritten with handwritten corrections, signed S. Panina, dated New Haven, CT, U.S.A., 1948, in BAR Panina, Box 6.

Narodnyi dom: Sotsial'naia rol', organizatsiia, deiatel'nost' i oborudovanie Narodnago doma. S prilozheniem bibliografii, tipovykh planov, primernogo ustava i pervoi vserossiiskoi ankety o narodnykh domakh. Introduction by Sofia Panina. Petrograd: Tipografiia B. M. Vol'fa, 1918.

"Obshchestvennaia rabota v gorodskikh popechitel'stvakh (Doklad, chitannyi 1 fevralia 1916 goda na sobranii, ustroennom Rossiiskoi ligoi ravnopraviia zhenshchin)." *Prizrenie i blagotvoritel'nost' v Rossii* 1916, no. 1–2 (January–February), cols. 3–16.

"Pamiati A. V Zhekuliny." *Novyi zhurnal* 24 (1950): 214–19.

"Pamiati druga." *Slovo/Word* 47 (2005); http://magazines.russ.ru/slovo/2005 /47/gr31.html.

Panina, S. V., Gr., and P. P. Gaideburov. "Iskusstvo v narodnoi auditorii." *Russkaia shkola* 5–6 (May–June 1914): 150–73.

Major Unpublished Writings

"Countess Sophie Vladimirovna Panin." Autobiographical sketch, undated but after 1939. Unsigned but in Sofia's hand, in English. Lehovich Family Collection.

"Kaliforniiskiia vpechatleniia." Typewritten manuscript. Written in Sofia's hand in ink on page 1: "Moi fel'etony napechatannye v 'Posl. Novosti' v 1939 g. S. P." Copies in BAR Panina, Box 11 and BAR Denikin, Box 2.

["Kokoshkin and Shingarev"]. Two untitled, undated manuscripts unsigned but written in Sofia's hand, in Russian, describing the arrests and detention of herself, Andrei Shingarev, and Fedor Kokoshkin, and the murders of Shingarev and Kokoshkin. Some variations exist between the two manuscripts. Lehovich Family Collection.

"Moi gorod." Unsigned, undated manuscript in two versions (one handwritten, the other typewritten with corrections). BAR Panina, Box 6.

"Moi pisaniia." Undated handwritten manuscript, signed S. P. Lehovich Family Collection.

["My Childhood"]. Untitled, undated reminiscences, in Russian, of her mother and her childhood, unsigned but in Sofia's hand. Lehovich Family Collection.

"Ob Alise Massaryk—docheri prezidenta Chekho-Slovakii." Undated manuscript, handwritten and typewritten versions. BAR Panina, Box 6.

"Russkaia emigratsiia v Evrope." Typewritten, hand-corrected text of public lecture in Russian, signed S. P. and dated 1939. BAR Panina, Box 14.

"Siren' (Vospominaniia o 'Marfine')." Manuscript dated Geneva, May 14, 1922, in two versions (one handwritten, the other typewritten), signed S. Panina. Lehovich Family Collection.

"Such Is Life." Typewritten, hand-corrected text. Written in Sofia's hand on page 1: "Publichnyi doklad v Los Angeles'e v 1939." BAR Panina, Box 14. Slightly different version, signed S. P., in BAR Denikin, Box 2.

Unpublished Biographical and Autobiographical Manuscripts

Lehovich, Vladimir. "Crimean Notes: A Glimpse into Family Matters." Lehovich Family Collection.

Ouroussow, Prince Serge. "Noirs Oiseaux de L'Adversité, par Le Prince Serge Ouroussow (Mémoires)." Book I, "L'Ermite de Simeis." Typed manuscript. Lehovich Family Collection.

Peshekhonova, Alexandra. "Moe detstvo." Handwritten and typed versions are in BAR Panina, Box 7, and also Rossiiskii institut istorii iskusstv, Kabinet rukopisei, f. 32, op. 1, ed. khr. 126.

Polovtsoff, Alexander. "Vospominaniia." Typescript memoir dated 1934, Alexandre Polovtsoff Papers, Sterling Library, Yale University, mss. #403, Box 5, folder 2.

Urusova, Maria Sergeevna. "Souvenirs d'enfance de Marie Serguévna Ouroussow (née vers 1844, + 1904), ('Monia') née Maltzev, épouse de Léonide Dmtrievitch, Prince Ouroussow, No. 382/333 de la Généalogie Ouroussow De Plechko." Lehovich Family Collection.

———. "Souvenirs de notre grand'mère maternelle Marie Serguéevna, Princesse Ouroussow, ('Monia') née Maltzow. Souvenirs des années (1867–1878)." Lehovich Family Collection.

Vassiltchikov, George. Letters to the author, Rolle, Switzerland, June 30, 1997; July 10, 1997; August 26, 1997; October 7, 1997; October 8, 1997; October 26, 1997; December 22, 1997; and January 7, 1998.

Volkova, Varvara Petrovna, née Geiden. [Recollections]. Undated notes of a conversation with Alexandra Petrunkevich. BDIC, F delta rés 892, chemise 9.

Wassiltchikoff, Lydia. "'Vanished Russia.' Memoirs of Lydia Princess ('Dilka') Wassiltchikoff, rewritten and heavily edited by her daughter Tatiana Metternich. Published in Vienna by Molden under the title 'Verschwundenes Russland.'" Hoover Institution Archives, Lydia Wassiltschikow Collection.

Published Primary Sources

Addams, Jane, and Victoria Brown. *Twenty Years at Hull-House: With Autobiographical Notes*. Boston: Bedford/St. Martin's, 1999.

Aleksandrovskii, V. F. *Narodnyi dom kievskogo obshchestva gramotnosti v g. Kieve. Kratkii ocherk istorii sooruzheniia narodnogo doma*. Kiev, 1902.

Anikieva, S. A. *Vospominaniia byvshei institutki o S.-Peterburgskom Ekaterininskom institute*. St. Petersburg, 1899.

An-skii, S. "Posle perevorota 25-go oktiabria 1917 g." *Arkhiv russkoi revoliutsii* 8 (1923): 43–55.

Artsybashev, Mikhail Mikhailovich. *Nash brakorazvodnyi protsess*. St. Petersburg, 1908.

Astrov, N. I. "Priznanie Gen. Denikinym Adm. Kolchaka. Prikaz 30 maia 1919 goda.—No. 145. (Iz vospominanii i dokumentov)." *Golos minuvshago na chuzhoi storone* 3, no. 1 (1926): 203–17.

———. "Proobraz russkoi tragedii." *Poslednie novosti*. January 18, 1925.

———. *Vospominaniia*. Paris: YMCA Press, 1940.

Astrov, N. I., Vladimir Feofilovich Zeeler, and P. N. Miliukov. *Pamiati pogibshikh: [sbornik]*. Paris, 1929.

Beatty, Bessie. *The Red Heart of Russia*. New York: Century, 1918.

Bek, Anna Nikolaevna, and Anne Dickason Rassweiler. *The Life of a Russian Woman Doctor: A Siberian Memoir, 1869–1954*. Bloomington: Indiana University Press, 2004.

Bogdanovich, L. A. *Bor'ba s torgovlei zhenshchinami i "Rossiiskoe obshchestvo zashchity zhenshchin."* Moscow, 1903.

Borman, Arkadii. *A. V. Tyrkova-Vil'iams po ee pis'mam i vospominaniiam syna*. Louvain, 1964.

Briantsev, A. A., and Aleksandra Noevna Gozenpud. *Vospominaniia, stat'i, vystupleniia, dnevniki, pis'ma*. Moscow: Vserossiiskoe teatral'noe obshchestvo, 1979.

Bryant, Louise. *Six Red Months in Russia: An Observer's Account of Russia before and during the Proletarian Dictatorship*. New York: George H. Doran, 1918.

Dem'ianov, A. "Zapiski o podpol'nom Vremennom pravitel'stve." *Arkhiv russkoi revoliutsii* 7 (1922): 34–52.

Demkin, Dmitrii Ivanovich. "Petrogradskaia gorodskaia duma v pervye dni smuty: Iz vospominaniia." *Russkaia letopis'* 6 (1924): 141–58.

D'iakonova, Elizaveta. *Dnevnik russkoi zhenshchiny: Dnevniki, literaturnye etiudy, stat'i*. Moscow: Mezhdunarodnyi universitet, 2006.

Dobkin, A. I., A. B. Roginskii, N. G. Okhotin, and M. Iu. Sorokina, eds. *Zven'ia: Istoricheskii al'manakh*. Vyp. 2. Moscow: Feniks-Atheneum, 1992.

Dodonov, B. F., and E. D. Grin'ko, eds. *Zhurnaly zasedanii Vremennogo pravitel'stva*. Vol. 3, *iiul'–avgust 1917 goda*. Moscow: ROSSPEN, 2004.

———. *Zhurnaly zasedanii Vremennogo pravitel'stva*. Vol. 4, *sentiabr'–oktiabr' 1917 goda*. Moscow: ROSSPEN, 2004.

Dodonov, B. F., E. D. Grin'ko, and O. V. Lavinskaia, eds. *Zhurnaly zasedanii Vremennogo pravitel'stva*. Vol. 2, *mai–iiun' 1917 goda*. Moscow: ROSSPEN, 2002.

Dolgorukov, Kniaz' Pavel Dmitrievich. *Velikaia razrukha*. Madrid, 1964.

Ekho otvetnoe: Literaturnyi sbornik, posviashchennyi 10-letiiu L[igovskikh] V[echernikh] K[lassov]. St. Petersburg, 1913.

Emmott, Alfred. *Interim Report of the Committee to Collect Information on Russia*. London: His Majesty's Stationery Office, 1920.

Fleer, M. "Vremennoe pravitel'stvo posle oktiabria." *Krasnyi arkhiv* 1924 (6): 195–221.

Gaideburov, P. P., and Simon Dreiden. *Literaturnoe nasledie. Vospominaniia, stat'i, rezhisserskie eksplikatsii, vystupleniia*. Moscow: Vserossiiskoe teatral'noe obshchestvo, 1977.

Gessen, I. V. *V dvukh vekakh: Zhiznennyi otchet*. Berlin: Speer & Schmidt, 1937.

Gippius, Zinaida. "Chernye tetradi." In *Zven'ia: Istoricheskii al'manakh*, vyp. 2, 11–173, edited by A. I. Dobkin et al. Moscow: Feniks-Atheneum, 1992.

Godovoi otchet Russkogo zhenskogo vzaimno-blagotvoritel'nogo obshchestva za 1895–96 god. St. Petersburg, 1897.

Godovoi otchet Russkogo zhenskogo vzaimno-blagotvoritel'nogo obshchestva za 1896–1897 god. St. Petersburg, 1898.

Godovoi otchet Russkogo zhenskogo vzaimno-blagotvoritel'nogo obshchestva za 1897–1898 god. St. Petersburg, 1899.

Golyshev, I. A. *Bogoiavlenskaia sloboda Mstera Vladimirskoi gubernii, Viaznikov-skogo uezda: Istoriia eia, drevnosti, statistika i etnografiia*. Vladimir, 1865.

Gor'kii, M. "Nesvoevremennye mysli." *Novaia mysl'*. December 6 (19), 1917.

Grazkin, D. I. *Za temnoi noch'iu den' vstaval*. Moscow: Izdatel'stvo politicheskoi literatury, 1975.

Gurevich, Ia. Ia. "Delo grafini S. V. Paninoi v revoliutsionnom tribunale." *Russkoe bogatstvo* no. 11–12 (November–December 1917): 283–98.

Il'in, V. S. *Istoriia vozniknoveniia, organizatsiia i deiatel'nost' Stepnoi biologicheskoi stantsii imeni gr. S. V. Paninoi*. In Otd. Botaniki, no. 1, supplement, *Trudy Petrogradskogo obshchestva estestvoispitatelei* 46 (1916).

Istoricheskii ocherk stoletnei deiatel'nosti S-Peterburgskogo uchilishcha ordena sv. Ekateriny. St. Petersburg, 1902.

Izgoev, A. S. "Piat' let v Sovetskoi Rossii (Obryvki vospominanii i zametki)." *Arkhiv russkoi revoliutsii* 10 (1923): 5–55.

"Iz perepiski V. A. Maklakova s Natsional'nym tsentrom v 1919 g." *Krasnyi arkhiv* 36 (1929): 3–30.

Izvestiia Moskovskoi gubernskoi zemskoi upravy. Vol. 12. Moscow, 1912.

Izvestiia Petrogradskoi gorodskoi dumy. No. 3–4. Petrograd, 1917.

Kanatchikov, Semen. *A Radical Worker in Tsarist Russia: The Autobiography of Semën Ivanovich Kanatchikov*, edited and translated by Reginald E. Zelnik. Stanford: Stanford University Press, 1986.

Kapralov, Aleksei. "Ligovskii narodnyi dom: Vospominaniia blagodarnogo vospitannika." *Russkaia mysl'*. July 24, 1956.

Karnovich, E. P. *Zamechatel'nye bogatstva chastnykh lits v Rossii. Ekonomichesko-istoricheskoe izsledovanie*. The Hague: Europe Printing, 1965 [St. Petersburg, 1874].

Kartsov, N. S. *Neskol'ko faktov iz zhizni S.-Peterburgskogo uchilishcha ordena sv. Ekateriny. Ko dniu ego stoletnogo iubileia. Sostavleno, po porucheniiu soveta insti-tuta, inspektorom klassov N. S. Kartsovym*. St. Petersburg, 1898.

Kerensky, Alexander. *Russia and History's Turning Point*. New York: Duell, Sloan and Pearce, 1965.

Kin, L. "Sud nad gr. S. V. Paninoi." *Vechernyi zvon*. December 11, 1917.

Komitet Obshchestva dlia dostavleniia sredstv Vysshim zhenskim kursam v S.-Peterburge. *S.-Peterburgskie Vysshie zhenskie kursy za 25 let. 1878–1903. Ocherki i materialy*. [St. Petersburg], 1903.

Konstitutsionno-demokraticheskaia partiia, Tsentral'nyi komitet. *Protokoly Tsentral'nogo komiteta i zagranichnykh grupp Konstitutsionno-demokraticheskoi partii, 1905–seredina 1930-kh gg. V 6 tomakh*, edited by Shmuel Galai and D. B. Pavlov. Vol. 3. *Protokoly Tsentral'nogo komiteta Konstitutsionno-demokraticheskoi partii, 1915–1920 gg.* Vol. 4. *Protokoly zagranichnykh grupp Konstitutsionno-demokraticheskoi partii, mai 1920 g–iiun' 1921 g.* Vol. 5. *Protokoly zagranichnykh grupp Konstitutsionno-demokraticheskoi partii, iiun'–dekabr' 1921 g.* Moscow: ROSSPEN, 1997–98.

Konstitutsionno-demokraticheskaia partiia. *Vestnik Partii narodnoi svobody.* Petrograd, 1917.

Krasnaia kniga VChK. 2 vols. 2nd ed. Moscow: Izdatel'stvo politicheskoi literatury, 1989.

Krol', L. A. *Za tri goda: Vospominaniia, vpechatleniia i vstrechi.* Vladivostok: Tip. T-va izd. Svobodnaia Rossiia, 1921.

Litvinov, M. M., and Ivy Litvinov. *The Bolshevik Revolution: Its Rise and Meaning.* London: British Socialist Party, 1919.

Meisner, Dmitrii. *Mirazhi i deistvitel'nost': Zapiski emigranta.* Moscow: Novosti, 1966.

Mikhailovskii, G. N. *Zapiski. Iz istorii Rossiiskogo vneshnepoliticheskogo vedomstva. 1914–1920.* Vol. 1, *Avgust 1914–oktiabr' 1917.* Moscow: Mezhdunarodnye otnosheniia, 1993.

Mil'chik, I. I. "Petrogradskaia tsentral'naia gorodskaia duma v fevrale-oktiabre 1917 g." *Krasnaia letopis'* 2 (1927): 189–218.

Miliukov, P. N., K. M. Anderson, and N. I. Kanishcheva. *Dnevnik P. N. Miliukova, 1918–1921.* Moscow: ROSSPEN, 2005.

Nabokov, Vladimir. "Vremennoe pravitel'stvo: Vospominaniia." *Arkhiv russkoi revoliutsii* 1 (1922): 9–96.

Nemirovich-Danchenko, V. I. "Amerika v Rossii." *Russkaia mysl'* 1882, no. 1: 318–55; no. 2: 268–301; no. 4: 115–46; no. 8: 85–113; no. 10: 73–109; no. 12: 219–36.

Obolenskii, Kniaz' V. A. *Moia zhizn' i moi sovremenniki.* Paris: YMCA, 1988.

Otchet 13-go Gorodskogo popechitel'stva o bednykh v Petrograde 2, 3 i 4-go uch. Aleksandro-Nevskoi chasti. Za 1913 god. Shestoi god deiatel'nosti popechitel'stva. Petrograd, 1914.

Otchet 13-go Gorodskogo popechitel'stva o bednykh. Za 1914 god. Petrograd, 1915.

Otchet Ligovskogo narodnogo doma (5-yi god). S 1-go iiunia 1907 g. po 1-oe iiunia 1908 g. St. Petersburg, 1908.

Otchet Ligovskogo narodnogo doma (6-i god). S 1-go iiunia 1908 g. po 1-oe iiunia 1909 g. St. Petersburg, 1909.

Otchet Ligovskogo narodnogo doma. (8-oi god). S 1-go iiunia 1910 g. po 1–3 iiunia 1911 g. St. Petersburg, 1911.

Otchet Ligovskogo narodnogo doma za pervoe desiatiletie, 1903–1913 gg. St. Petersburg, 1914.

Otchet o deiatel'nosti Marfinskogo zemskogo uchastkogo popechitel'stva o bednykh za 1911 g. Moscow, 1912.

Peshekhonova, A. V. "Iz zhizni odnoi besplatnoi biblioteki." *Bibliotekar'* 3 (1913): 173–82.

Petrunkevich, Ivan Il'ich. *Iz zapisok obshchestvennogo deiatelia. Vospominaniia,* edited by A. A. Kizevetter. *Arkhiv russkoi revoliutsii* 21 (1934).

"Podpol'naia rabota v gody imperialisticheskoi voiny v Petrograde." *Krasnaia letopis'* 2/3 (1922): 116–43.

Polovtsov, A. A. *Dnevnik gosudarstvennogo sekretaria A. A. Polovtsova v 2-kh tomakh,* edited by Peter Andreevich Zaionchkovskii. Vol. 2, *1887–1892 gg.* Moscow: Nauka, 1966.

Ponomareva, E. "Ligovskii narodnyi dom grafini S. V. Paninoi v Peterburge." *Trudovaia pomoshch'* (March–April 1906): 411–16.

Prizrenie i blagotvoritel'nost' v Rossii. Petrograd, 1914–17.

Railian, Foma. "Intelligentsiia pered sudom 'Tribunala.'" *Novaia petrogradskaia gazeta.* December 12, 1917.

Reed, John. "How the Russian Revolution Works." *The Liberator* 1, no. 6 (August 1918): 16–21.

———. *Ten Days That Shook the World.* London: Penguin Classics, 1977.

Roberts, C. E. Bechhofer. *In Denikin's Russia and the Caucasus, 1919–1920.* New York: Arno Press, 1971.

Rossiiskoe obshchestvo zashchity zhenshchin v 1900 i 1901 g. St. Petersburg, 1902.

Rossiiskoe obshchestvo zashchity zhenshchin v 1909 g. St. Petersburg, 1910.

Rossiiskoe obshchestvo zashchity zhenshchin v 1913 g. Petrograd, 1914.

S., E. "Ligovskii narodnyi dom gr. S. V. Paninoi." *Teatral'naia Rossiia.* March 5, 1905.

S.-Peterburg po perepisi 15 dekabria 1900 goda. Vol. 1, *Chislennost' i sostav naseleniia po polu, vozrastu, mestu rozhdeniia (v S.-Peterburge ili vne ego), vremeni poseleniia v S.-Peterburge, semeinomu sostoianiiu, gramotnosti, sosloviiu, veroispovedaniiu i rodnomu iazyku.* Vol. 2, *Raspredelenie naseleniia po zaniatiiam.* St. Petersburg: Tip. Shredera, 1903.

Semenov, Nikolai. "Graf Viktor Nikitich Panin. Kharakteristicheskii ocherk po rasskazam, moim zapiskam i vospominaniiam." *Russkii arkhiv* 12 (1887): 537–66.

Shakhovskoi, D. I. "Pis'ma o bratstve." In *Zven'ia: Istoricheskii al'manakh,* vyp. 2, 174–318, edited by A. I. Dobkin et al. Moscow: Feniks-Atheneum, 1992.

Shingarev, A. E. *Kak eto bylo. Dnevnik A. I. Shingareva. Petropavlovskaia krepost', 27.XI.17–5.I.18.* Moscow, 1918.

Skarskaia, Nadezhda Fedorovna, and P. P. Gaideburov. *Na stsene i v zhizni. Stranitsy avtobiografii.* Moscow: Iskusstvo, 1959.

Sokolov, K. N. *Pravlenie Generala Denikina (iz vospominanii).* Sofia: Rossiisko-bolgarskoe knigoizdatel'stvo, 1921.

Stoliarov, Ivan. *Zapiski russkogo krest'ianina.* Paris: Institut d'études slaves, 1986.

"Sud bol'shevikov nad gr. S. V. Paninoi." *Novaia petrogradskaia gazeta.* December 12, 1917.

Sukhanov, N. N., and Joel Carmichael. *The Russian Revolution 1917: Eyewitness Account.* New York: Harper and Brothers, 1962.

Tenisheva, M. K. *Vpetchatleniia moei zhizni.* Leningrad: Iskusstvo, 1991.

Tiutcheva, A. F. *Pri dvore dvukh imperatorov.* Vol. 2, *Dnevnik 1855–1882,* edited by S. V. Bakhrushin. Moscow: Izd. M. i I. Sabashnikovykh, 1929.

Tolstaia, A. A. *Zapiski freiliny. Pechal'nyi epizod iz moei zhizni pri dvore.* Moscow: Entsiklopediia rossiiskikh dereven', 1996.

Tolstaia, Aleksandra. *Doch'.* London, Ontario: Zaria, 1979.

———. *Otets: Zhizn' L'va Tolstogo.* New York: Izdatel'stvo imeni Chekhova, 1953.

Tolstoi, I. I. *Dnevnik 1906–1916.* St. Petersburg: Evropeiskii dom, 1997.

Tolstoi, L. N. *Polnoe sobranie sochinenii. Seriia tret'ia. Pis'ma.* Vol. 73. Moscow: Gosudarstvennoe izdatel'stvo khudozhestvennoi literatury, 1954.

Tolstoy Foundation (U.S.). *Tolstoy Foundation, Inc.: History, Aims and Achievements.* New York: The Foundation, 1976.

Trubetskoi, Kn. Grigorii N. *Gody smut i nadezhd 1917–1919.* Montreal: [Éditions R.U.S.], 1981.

Trudy pervogo Vserossiiskogo s"ezda po bor'be s torgom zhenshchinami i ego prichinami, proiskhodivshego v S-Peterburge s 21 po 25 aprelia 1910 g., 2 vols. St. Petersburg, 1911–12.

Trudy pervogo Vserossiiskogo zhenskogo s"ezda pri Russkom zhenskom obshchestve v S.-Peterburge 10–16 dekabria 1908 goda. St. Petersburg, 1909.

Tyrkova, A. "Petrogradskii dnevnik." In *Zven'ia: Istoricheskii al'manakh,* vyp. 2, 319–39, edited by A. I. Dobkin et al. Moscow: Feniks-Atheneum, 1992.

Tyrkova-Vil'iams, A. *Na putiakh k svobode.* New York: Izdatel'stvo imeni Chekhova, 1952.

"V Voenno-revoliutsionnom tribunale. Delo gr. S. V. Paninoi." *Volia naroda.* December 12, 1917.

Vasil'chikov, Ilarion Sergeevich, and G. I. Vasil'chikov. *To, chto mne vspomnilos' — Vospominaniia kniazia Ilariona Sergeevicha Vasil'chikova: Iz arkhiva sem'i Vasil'chikovykh.* Moscow: "Olma-Press," 2002.

Vernadskii, V. I. *Dnevniki 1917–1921. Oktiabr' 1917–ianvar' 1920,* edited by M. Iu. Sorokina. Kiev: Naukova dumka, 1994.

Ves' Peterburg na 1896 g. St. Petersburg, 1895.

Ves' Peterburg na 1897 g. St. Petersburg, 1896.

Ves' Peterburg na 1900 god. St. Petersburg, 1899.

Ves' Peterburg na 1901 god. St. Petersburg, 1900.

Ves' Peterburg na 1909 god. Adresnaia i spravochnaia kniga S-Peterburga. St. Petersburg, 1908.

Ves' Peterburg na 1915 god. Adresnaia i spravochnaia kniga S-Peterburga. St. Petersburg, 1914.

Vetvenitskaia, Natalia Aleksandrovna. *Spisok okonchivshikh kurs na S-Peterburgskikh vysshikh zhenskikh kursakh 1882–1889 gg., 1893–1911 gg.* [St. Petersburg], n.d.

Vitte, S. Iu. *The Memoirs of Count Witte,* translated and edited by Sidney Harcave. Armonk, NY: M. E. Sharpe, 1990.

Wassiltschikow, Lydia. *Verschwundenes Russland. Die Memoiren der Fürstin Lydia Wassiltschikow 1886–1919,* edited by Tatiana Metternich, translated by Karl-Otto Czernicki and Friderike Czernicki. Vienna: Verlag Fritz Molden, 1980.

The White Slave Trade. Transactions of the International Congress on the White Slave Trade, Held in London on the 21st, 22nd and 23rd of June, 1899, at the Invitation of the National Vigilance Association. London: Office of the National Vigilance Association, 1899.

Williams, Albert Rhys. *Journey into Revolution: Petrograd, 1917–1918.* Chicago: Quadrangle Books, 1969.

Wonlar-Larsky, Nadine. *The Russia That I Loved.* London: The Women's Printing Society, n.d.

"Zasedanie Revoliutsionnogo tribunala. Delo gr. Paninoi." *Izvestiia*. December 12, 1917.

Zavolokin, P. Ia. *Sovremennye raboche-krest'ianskie poety v obraztsakh i avtobiografiiakh s portretami*. Ivanovo-Voznesensk: Osnova, 1925.

Zhukov, I. "Revoliutsionnyi tribunal (vospominaniia pervogo predsedatelia Tribunala)." *Rabochii sud* 22 (1927): 1755–56.

Zhurnaly Petrogradskoi gorodskoi dumy. Petrograd, 1917.

Secondary Sources

Abraham, Richard. *Alexander Kerensky: The First Love of the Revolution*. New York: Columbia University Press, 1987.

Abrams, Lynn. *Workers' Culture in Imperial Germany: Leisure and Recreation in the Rhineland and Westphalia*. London: Routledge, 1992.

Adamenko, Elena. "V Ligovskii narodnyi dom mog priiti liuboi izvozchik—za znaniiami." *Chas pik*. May 15, 1996.

Akinyshin, Aleksandr, and Oleg Lasunskii. *Voronezhskoe dvorianstvo v litsakh i sud'bakh*. Voronezh: Petrovskii skver, 1994.

Alexopoulos, Golfo. *Stalin's Outcasts: Aliens, Citizens, and the Soviet State, 1926–1936*. Ithaca: Cornell University Press, 2003.

Alston, Charlotte. "The Work of the Russian Liberation Committee in London." *Slavonica* 14, no. 1 (2008): 6–17.

Anan'ich, B. V. *Bankirskie doma v Rossii, 1860–1917 gg.: Ocherki istorii chastnogo predprinimatel'stva*. Leningrad: Nauka, 1991.

Anderson, Paul B. "The Tolstoy Foundation." *Russian Review* 17, no. 1 (January 1958): 60–66.

Badcock, Sarah. "Women, Protest, Revolution: Soldiers' Wives in Russia during 1917." *International Review of Social History* 49, no. 1 (2004): 47–70.

Bailey, Peter. *Leisure and Class in Victorian England: Rational Recreation and the Contest for Control, 1830–1885*. London: Routledge and K. Paul, 1978.

Beauman, Katharine Bentley. *Women and the Settlement Movement*. London: Radcliffe Press, 1996.

Bernstein, Laurie. *Sonia's Daughters: Prostitutes and Their Regulation in Imperial Russia*. Berkeley: University of California Press, 1995.

Bocharova, Z. S. *Russkie bezhentsy: Problemy rasseleniia, vozvrashcheniia na Rodinu, uregulirovaniia, pravovogo polozheniia (1920–1930-e gody); Sbornik dokumentov i materialov*. Moscow: ROSSPEN, 2004.

Bondarevskaia, T. P., A. Ia. Velikanova, and F. M. Suslova. *Lenin v Peterburge-Petrograde: Mesta zhizni i deiatel'nosti v gorode i okrestnostiakh 1890–1920*. Leningrad: Lenizdat, 1977.

Borrero, Mauricio. *Hungry Moscow: Scarcity and Urban Society in the Russian Civil War, 1917–1921*. New York: Peter Lang, 2003.

Boyd, Brian. *Vladimir Nabokov: The Russian Years*. Princeton: Princeton University Press, 1990.

Braybon, Gail. *Women Workers in the First World War: The British Experience*. London: Croom Helm, 1981.

Broitman, Larissa, and Arsenii Dubin. *Ulitsa Chaikovskogo*. Moscow-St. Petersburg: Tsentroligraf, 2003.

Brooks, Jeffrey. *When Russia Learned to Read: Literacy and Popular Literature, 1861–1917*. Princeton: Princeton University Press, 1985.

Budnitskii, Oleg. *Russian Jews between the Reds and the Whites, 1917–1920*, translated by Timothy J. Portice. Philadelphia: University of Pennsylvania Press, 2012.

———. "Soveshchanie rossiiskikh poslov v Parizhe i Zemgor: Den'gi i politika (1921–1925)." *Cahiers du Monde russe* 46, no. 4 (October–December 2005): 699–718.

Bulgakova, Liudmila. "Privilegirovannye bedniaki: Pomoshch' soldatskim sem'iam v gody pervoi mirovoi voiny." In *Na puti k revoliutsionnym potriaseniiam: Iz istorii Rossii vtoroi poloviny XIX–nachala XX veka*, edited by V. S. Diakin and I. P. Palkina, 429–93. St. Petersburg: Nestor-Historia, 2001.

Burdzhalov, E. N. *Russia's Second Revolution: The February 1917 Uprising in Petrograd*, edited and translated by Donald J. Raleigh. Bloomington: Indiana University Press, 1987.

Chase, William J. *Workers, Society and the Soviet State: Labor and Life in Moscow, 1918–1929*. Urbana: University of Illinois Press, 1987.

Chinyaeva, Elena. *Russians outside Russia: The Émigré Community in Czechoslovakia, 1918–1938*. Munich: R. Oldenbourg Verlag, 2001.

Clements, Barbara Evans. *Bolshevik Feminist: The Life of Alexandra Kollontai*. Bloomington: Indiana University Press, 1979.

Culleton, Claire A. *Working-Class Culture, Women and Britain, 1914–1921*. New York: St. Martin's Press, 2000.

Darrow, Margaret H. *French Women and the First World War: War Stories of the Home Front*. Oxford: Berg, 2000.

Davis, Belinda J. *Home Fires Burning: Food, Politics and Everyday Life in World War I Berlin*. Chapel Hill: University of North Carolina Press, 2000.

Dubentsov, B. B., and V. A. Nardova. *Peterburgskaia gorodskaia duma 1846–1918*. St. Petersburg: Liki Rossii, 2005.

Dumova, N. G. "Istoriia v litsakh. Grafinia, sozdavshaia Narodnyi dom." *Rabotnitsa* 11 (1994): 16–17.

———. *Kadetskaia kontrrevoliutsiia i ee razgrom (oktiabr' 1917–1920 gg.)*. Moscow: Nauka, 1982.

———. *Konchilos' vashe vremia*. Moscow: Izdatel'stvo politicheskoi literatury, 1990.

Encyclopedia of Russian Women's Movements. Edited by Norma Corigliano Noonan and Carol Nechemias. Westport, CT: Greenwood Press, 2001.

Engel, Barbara Alpern. *Breaking the Ties That Bound: The Politics of Marital Strife in Late Imperial Russia*. Ithaca: Cornell University Press, 2011.

———. "Not by Bread Alone: Subsistence Riots in Russia during World War I." *The Journal of Modern History* 69, no. 4 (December 1997): 696–721.

Engelstein, Laura. *The Keys to Happiness: Sex and the Search for Modernity in Fin-de-Siècle Russia*. Ithaca: Cornell University Press, 1992.

Ershova, E. V. "Pervyi protsess Petrogradskogo revtribunala v 1917 godu." In *Neizvestnye stranitsy istorii Verkhnevol'zhia: Sbornik nauchnykh trudov*, edited by T. G. Leont'eva, 88–102. Tver: Tverskoi gosudarstvennyi universitet, 1994.

Evreinov, A. B. *Cheshskaia rapsodiia. Dni minuvshie v sobytiiakh, portretakh, razmyshleniiakh*. Biisk: IITs BPGU im. V. M. Shukshina, 2004.

Figes, Orlando, and Boris Kolonitskii. *Interpreting the Russian Revolution: The Language and Symbols of 1917.* New Haven: Yale University Press, 1999.

Galai, Shmuel. *The Liberation Movement in Russia, 1900–1905.* Cambridge: Cambridge University Press, 1973.

Galichenko, A. *Gaspra.* Simferopol: Biznes-Inform, 2005.

Ganelin, R. Sh., S. V. Kulikov, A. B. Nikolaev, and V. V. Polikarpov. *Pervaia mirovaia voina i konets Rossiiskoi imperii.* Vol. 3, *Fevral'skaia revoliutsiia.* St. Petersburg: Liki Rossii, 2014.

Gatrell, Peter. *Russia's First World War: A Social and Economic History.* Harlow, England: Pearson-Longman, 2005.

Golinkov, D. L. *Krushenie antisovetskogo podpol'ia v SSSR.* 2 vols. 3rd ed. Moscow: Politizdat, 1980.

Grayzel, Susan R. *Women's Identities at War: Gender, Motherhood, and Politics in Britain and France during the First World War.* Chapel Hill: University of North Carolina Press, 1999.

Gronsky, Pavel P., and Nikolai I. Astrov. *The War and the Russian Government: The Central Government.* New Haven: Yale University Press, 1929.

Gubin, Dmitrii, Lev Lur'e, and Igor' Poroshin. *Real'nyi Peterburg: O gorode s tochki zreniia nedvizhimosti i o nedvizhimosti s tochki zreniia istorii.* St. Petersburg: Limbus Press, 1999.

Hasegawa, Tsuyoshi. *Crime and Punishment in the Russian Revolution: Mob Justice and Police in Petrograd.* Cambridge: Harvard University Press, 2017.

Healey, Dan. *Homosexual Desire in Revolutionary Russia: The Regulation of Sexual and Gender Dissent.* Chicago: University of Chicago Press, 2001.

Healy, Maureen. *Vienna and the Fall of the Habsburg Empire: Total War and Everyday Life in World War I.* Cambridge: Cambridge University Press, 2004.

Herlihy, Patricia. *The Alcoholic Empire: Vodka and Politics in Late Imperial Russia.* Oxford: Oxford University Press, 2002.

Hetherington, Philippa Lesley. "Victims of the Social Temperament: Prostitution, Migration, and the Traffic in Women from Late Imperial Russia and the Soviet Union, 1890–1935." PhD diss., Harvard University, 2014.

Holquist, Peter. *Making War, Forging Revolution: Russia's Continuum of Crisis, 1914–1921.* Cambridge: Harvard University Press, 2002.

Hopkins, C. Howard. *John R. Mott, 1865–1955: A Biography.* Grand Rapids, MI: William B. Eerdmans, 1979.

Ignatieff, Michael. *The Russian Album: A Family Saga of Revolution, Civil War, and Exile.* London: Penguin Books, 1988.

Iukina, I. I. *Russkii feminizm kak vyzov sovremennosti.* St. Petersburg: Aleteiia, 2007.

Iukina, I. I., and Iu. E. Guseva. *Zhenskii Peterburg.* St. Petersburg: Aleteiia, 2004.

Ivanov, Anatolii. "Smes' kovrov i nadushennoi pudry." *Sankt-Peterburgskie vedomosti.* September 4, 2004.

Izmailov, Kim Nikolaevich. *Novye zaboty starogo kluba.* Moscow: Vsesoiuznyi nauchno-metodicheskii tsentr narodnogo tvorchestva i kul'turno-prosvetitel'noi raboty, 1991.

Kanishcheva, N. I., comp. *Nasledie Ariadny Vladimirovny Tyrkovoi: Dnevniki. Pis'ma.* Moscow: ROSSPEN, 2012.

Karabanova, A. M. "A. V. Tyrkova—zhenshchina-lider Kadetskoi partii: Osobennosti sotsializatsii i politicheskoi kar'ery." *Zhenshchina v rossiiskom obshchestve* 3–4 (2005): 60–72.

Karev, D. S. *Sudoustroistvo*. Moscow: Iuridicheskoe izdatel'stvo, 1948.

Kassow, Samuel D. *Students, Professors and the State in Tsarist Russia*. Berkeley:
University of California Press, 1989.

Khasbulatova, O. A. *Opyt i traditsii zhenskogo dvizheniia v Rossii (1860–1917)*. Ivanovo: Ivanovskii gosudarstvennyi universitet, 1994.

Khokhlov, V. G., and M. M. Datskov. "Sergei Ivanovich Mal'tsov—
predprinimatel', patriot, chelovek." In *S. I. Mal'tsov i istoriia razvitiia Mal'tsovskogo promyshlennogo raiona*, edited by V. V. Krasheninnikov, 22–30. Briansk:
Brianskoe oblastnoe izdatel'stvo "Grani," 1994.

Kinkead, Eugene. "Profiles: Arachnologist. 1." *The New Yorker*. April 22, 1950.

———. "Profiles: Arachnologist. 2." *The New Yorker*. April 29, 1950.

Knight, Louise W. *Citizen: Jane Addams and the Struggle for Democracy*. Chicago:
University of Chicago Press, 2005.

Kolchin, Peter. *Unfree Labor: American Slavery and Russian Serfdom*. Cambridge,
MA: Belknap Press of Harvard University Press, 1987.

Kolonitskii, Boris. *"Tragicheskaia erotika": Obrazy imperatorskoi sem'i v gody pervoi
mirovoi voiny*. Moscow: Novoe literaturnoe obozrenie, 2010.

Koven, Seth. *The Matchgirl and the Heiress*. Princeton: Princeton University
Press, 2014.

———. *Slumming: Sexual and Social Politics in Victorian London*. Princeton:
Princeton University Press, 2004.

Kozlova, K. I., and V. S. Orlov. "Pervoe zasedanie narodnogo revtribunala."
Voprosy istorii 10 (1977): 211–15.

Kruchkovskaia, V. M. *Tsentral'naia gorodskaia duma Petrograda v 1917 g*. Leningrad: Nauka, 1986.

L. N. Tolstoi. Entsiklopediia. Compiled and edited by N. I. Burnasheva. Moscow:
Prosveshchenie, 2009.

Lehovich, Dimitry V. *White against Red: The Life of General Anton Denikin*. New
York: Norton, 1974.

Lepore, Jill. "Historians Who Love Too Much: Reflections on Microhistory and
Biography." *The Journal of American History* 88, no. 1 (June 2001): 129–44.

Lieven, D. C. B. *The Aristocracy in Europe, 1815–1914*. New York: Columbia University Press, 1993.

Lindenmeyr, Adele. "Building a Civil Society One Brick at a Time: People's
Houses and Worker Enlightenment in Late Imperial Russia." *Journal of
Modern History* 84, no. 1 (March 2012): 1–39.

———. "The First Soviet Political Trial: Countess Sofia V. Panina before the
Petrograd Revolutionary Tribunal." *The Russian Review* 60, no. 4 (October
2001): 505–25.

———. "'The First Woman in Russia': Countess Sofia Panina and Women's
Political Participation in the Revolutions of 1917." *Journal of Modern Russian
History and Historiography* 9, no. 1 (2016): 159–82.

———. "Public Life, Private Virtues: Women in Russian Charity, 1762–1914."
Signs: Journal of Women in Culture and Society 18, no. 3 (1993): 562–91.

———. "A Russian Experiment in Voluntarism: The Municipal Guardianships of the Poor, 1894–1914." *Jahrbücher für Geschichte Osteuropas* 30, no. 3 (1982): 429–51.

Lindenmeyr, Adele, Christopher Read, and Peter Waldron, eds. *The Experience of War and Revolution*. Book 2 of *Russia's Home Front in War and Revolution, 1914–1922*. Bloomington: Slavica, 2016.

Losskii, Boris. "Eshche o grafine S. V. Paninoi." *Russkaia mysl'*, no. 4097 (October 19–25, 1995): 16.

Mawdsley, Evan. *The Russian Civil War*. Boston: Unwin and Allen, 1987.

McAuley, Mary. *Bread and Justice: State and Society in Petrograd, 1917–1922*. Oxford: Clarendon Press, 1991.

McKean, Robert B. *St. Petersburg between the Revolutions: Workers and Revolutionaries, June 1907–February 1917*. New Haven: Yale University Press, 1990.

Meehan-Waters, Brenda. *Holy Women of Russia: The Lives of Five Orthodox Women Offer Spiritual Guidance for Today*. [San Francisco]: HarperSan Francisco, 1993.

Mitchell, Ruth Crawford, comp. *Alice Garrigue Masaryk, 1879–1966: Her Life as Recorded in Her Own Words and by Her Friends*, edited by Linda Vlasak, with an introduction by René Wellek. Pittsburgh: University Center for International Studies, University of Pittsburgh, 1980.

Murav'eva, I. A. *Vek moderna: Panorama stolichnoi zhizni*. St. Petersburg: izd. "Pushkinskogo fonda," 2004.

Nadsadnyi, D. V. "Pomoshch' bezhentsam v Petrograde vo vremia pervoi mirovoi voiny: Deiatel'nost' gorodskogo samoupravleniia i Vserossiiskogo soiuza gorodov pomoshchi bol'nym i ranenym voinam (1914–1917 gg.)." *Izvestiia rossiiskogo gosudarstvennogo pedagogicheskogo universiteta imeni A. I. Gertsena* 162 (2013): 30–38.

Orlovsky, Daniel T. "The Provisional Government and Its Cultural Work." In *Bolshevik Culture: Experiment and Order in the Russian Revolution*, edited by Abbott Gleason, Peter Kenez, and Richard Stites, 39–56. Bloomington: Indiana University Press, 1985.

Pavlova, I. P. *Sotsial'noe popechenie v Rossii v gody pervoi mirovoi voiny*. Krasnoiarsk: Krasnoiarskii gosudarstvennyi agrarnyi universitet, 2003.

Pedersen, Susan. "Gender, Welfare, and Citizenship in Britain during the Great War." *American Historical Review* 95, no. 4 (October 1990): 983–1006.

Petrov, F. A. "Iz istorii obshchestvennogo dvizheniia v period vtoroi revoliutsionnoi situatsii v Rossii. Revoliutsionery i liberaly v kontse 1870-kh godov." *Istoriia SSSR* 1 (1981):144–55.

Pisar'kova, L. F. "Gorodskie golovy Moskvy (1863–1917)." *Otechestvennaia istoriia* 2 (1997): 3–19.

Poznansky, Alexander. "The Tchaikovsky Myths: A Critical Reassessment." In *Tchaikovsky and His Contemporaries: A Centennial Symposium*, edited by Alexandar Mihailovic, 75–91. Westport, CT: Greenwood Press, 1999.

Prokhorenko, Galina. "Sanovnik, metsenat i kollektsioner Aleksandr Aleksandrovich Polovtsov." *Nashe nasledie* 77 (2006). http://www.nasledie-rus.ru/podshivka/7708.php.

Protasov, L. G. *Liudi Uchreditel'nogo sobraniia: Portret v inter'ere epokhi*. Moscow: ROSSPEN, 2008.

———. "Zhenshchina i Vserossiiskoe uchreditel'noe sobranie." In *Ot muzhskikh i zhenskikh k gendernym issledovaniiam: Materialy mezhdunarodnoi nauchnoi konferentsii, 20 aprelia 2001 goda*, edited by P. P. Shcherbinin, 46–54. Tambov: Tambovskii gosudarstvennyi universitet, 2001.

Rabinowitch, Alexander. *The Bolsheviks in Power: The First Year of Soviet Rule in Petrograd*. Bloomington: Indiana University Press, 2007.

Raeff, Marc. *Russia Abroad: A Cultural History of the Russian Emigration, 1919–1939*. New York: Oxford University Press, 1990.

Ransel, David L. *The Politics of Catherinian Russia: The Panin Party*. New Haven: Yale University Press, 1975.

Rodgers, Daniel T. *Atlantic Crossings: Social Politics in a Progressive Age*. Cambridge, MA: Belknap Press of Harvard University Press, 1998.

Rosenberg, William G. *Liberals in the Russian Revolution: The Constitutional Democratic Party, 1917–1921*. Princeton: Princeton University Press, 1974.

Ruane, Christine. *Gender, Class, and the Professionalization of Russian City Teachers, 1860–1914*. Pittsburgh: University of Pittsburgh Press, 1994.

Russkaia aktsiia pomoshchi v Chekhoslovakii: Istoriia, znachenie, nasledie. K 90-letiiu nachala Russkoi aktsii pomoshchi v Chekhoslovakii. Edited by Lukash Babka and Igor' Zolotarev. Prague: Národní knihovna CR-Slovanská knihovna, 2012.

Ruthchild, Rochelle Goldberg. *Equality and Revolution: Women's Rights in the Russian Empire, 1905–1917*. Pittsburgh: University of Pittsburgh Press, 2010.

Sanborn, Joshua A. *Drafting the Russian Nation: Military Conscription, Total War, and Mass Politics, 1905–1925*. DeKalb: Northern Illinois University Press, 2003.

———. "The Mobilization of 1914 and the Question of the Russian Nation: A Reexamination." *Slavic Review* 59, no. 2 (Summer 2000): 267–89.

Schapiro, Leonard. "The Role of Jews in the Russian Revolutionary Movement." *Slavonic and East European Review* 40, no. 94 (December 1961): 148–67.

Schönberger, Bianca. "Motherly Heroines and Adventurous Girls: Red Cross Nurses and Women Army Auxiliaries in the First World War." In *Home/Front: The Military, War, and Gender in Twentieth-Century Germany*, edited by Karen Hagemann and Stefanie Schiller-Springorum, 87–114. Oxford: Berg, 2002.

Serapionova, E. P. *Rossiiskaia emigratsiia v Chekhoslovatskoi respublike, 20–30-e gody*. Moscow: Institut slavianovedeniia i balkanistiki Rossiiskoi akademii nauk, 1995.

Shelokhaev, V. V. "Ariadna Vladimirovna Tyrkova." *Voprosy istorii* 11–12 (1999): 67–81.

———. "Ariadna Vladimirovna Tyrkova: 'Sotsialisty sdelali iz moego otechestva ogromnoe opytnoe pole dlia svoikh dogm i teorii.'" In *Rossiiskii liberalizm: Idei i liudi*, edited by A. A. Kara-Murza, 515–26. Moscow: Novoe izdatel'stvo, 2004.

———. *Konstitutsionno-demokraticheskaia partiia v Rossii i emigratsii*. Moscow: ROSSPEN, 2015.

Shevyrin, V. M. "N. I. Astrov kak lider i istoriograf Vserossiiskogo soiuza gorodov." *Rossiia i sovremennyi mir* 2 (2003): 203–24.

Skran, Claudena M. *Refugees in Inter-War Europe: The Emergence of a Regime*. Oxford: Clarendon Press, 1995.

Smith, Douglas. *Former People: The Final Days of the Russian Aristocracy.* New York: Farrar, Straus and Giroux, 2012.

Sorokina, M. Iu., comp. *Mysliashchie miry rossiiskogo liberalizma: Grafinia Sof'ia Vladimirovna Panina (1871–1956). Materialy Mezhdunarodnogo nauchnogo kollokviuma, Moskva, 29–31 maia 2011 g.* Moscow: Dom russkogo zarubezh'ia im. Aleksandra Solzhenitsyna, 2012.

Steinberg, Mark D. *Proletarian Imagination: Self, Modernity, and the Sacred in Russia, 1910–1925.* Ithaca: Cornell University Press, 2002.

Stites, Richard. *The Women's Liberation Movement in Russia: Feminism, Nihilism and Bolshevism, 1860–1930.* Rev. ed. Princeton: Princeton University Press, 1990.

Stockdale, Melissa Kirschke. *Mobilizing the Russian Nation: Patriotism and Citizenship in the First World War.* Cambridge: Cambridge University Press, 2016.

———. "'My Death for the Motherland is Happiness': Women, Patriotism, and Soldiering in Russia's Great War, 1914–1917." *American Historical Review* 109, no. 1 (February 2004): 78–116.

———. *Paul Miliukov and the Quest for a Liberal Russia, 1880–1918.* Ithaca: Cornell University Press, 1996.

Stoff, Laurie S. *Russia's Sisters of Mercy and the Great War: More Than Binding Men's Wounds.* Lawrence: University Press of Kansas, 2015.

———. *They Fought for the Motherland: Russia's Women Soldiers in World War I and the Revolution.* Lawrence: University Press of Kansas, 2006.

Sysoev, Vladimir. *Tat'iana Alekseevna Bakunina-Osorgina: Illiustrirovannyi biograficheskii ocherk.* Tver: Presto, 2005.

Thompson, John M. *Russia, Bolshevism, and the Versailles Peace.* Princeton, NJ: Princeton University Press, 1967.

Ul'ianova, G. N. "Mal'tsovy: Dvesti let na rossiiskom rynke." In *Mal'tsovskii mir: Nauchnyi sbornik*, vyp. 1, edited by Andrei Anatol'evich Bauer, 6–13. Kirov: Kirovskii istoriko-kraevedcheskii muzei, Kaluzhskoi oblasti, 1999.

———. "Vzgliady Sergeia Ivanovicha Mal'tsova po obshchestvennym voprosam." In *S. I. Mal'tsov i istoriia razvitiia Mal'tsovskogo promyshlennogo raiona*, edited by V. V. Krasheninnikov, 31–38. Briansk: Brianskoe oblastnoe izdatel'stvo "Grani," 1994.

Van Geldern, James. *Bolshevik Festivals, 1917–1920.* Berkeley: University of California Press, 1993.

Vasil'chikov, Georgii I. "Grafinia S. V. Panina, posledniaia vladelitsa Marfina." *Nashe nasledie* 29–30 (1994): 76–83.

———. "Lotarevskaia 'Kniga sudeb.'" *Nashe nasledie* 39 (1997): 58–87.

Vicinus, Martha. *Independent Women: Work and Community for Single Women, 1850–1920.* Chicago: University of Chicago Press, 1985.

Volobuev, P. V. *Politicheskie deiateli Rossii 1917: Biograficheskii slovar'.* Moscow: Bol'shaia rossiiskaia entsiklopediia, 1993.

Voloshina, V. Iu. *Uchenyi v emigratsii: Problemy sotsial'noi adaptatsii uchenykh-emigrantov skvoz' prizmu "personal'noi istorii."* Omsk: Izd-vo omskogo gosudarstvennogo universiteta, 2010.

Vserossiiskoe obshchestvo politicheskikh katorzhan i ssyl'no-poselentsev. *Deiateli revoliutsionnogo dvizheniia v Rossii: Bio-bibliograficheskii slovar'.* Vol. 2,

Semidesiatye gody, vyp. 3, compiled by A. A. Shilov and M. G. Karnaukhova. Moscow, 1931.

Wade, Rex A., and Alex G. Cummins, eds. *Documents of Soviet History*. Vol. 1, *The Triumph of Bolshevism, 1917–1919*. Gulf Breeze, FL: Academic International Press, 1991.

Wagner, William G. *Marriage, Property, and Law in Late Imperial Russia*. Oxford: Clarendon Press, 1994.

Waters, Elizabeth. "Victim or Villain? Prostitution in Post-revolutionary Russia." In *Women and Society in Russia and the Soviet Union*, edited by Linda Edmondson, 160–77. Cambridge: Cambridge University Press, 1992.

White, Elizabeth. "'The Struggle against Denationalisation': The Russian Emigration in Europe and Education in the 1920s." *Revolutionary Russia* 6, no. 2 (2013): 128–46.

Wildman, Allan K. *The End of the Russian Imperial Army*. Vol. 1, *The Old Army and the Soldiers' Revolt (March–April 1917)*. Princeton: Princeton University Press, 1980.

Wortman, Richard S. *The Development of a Russian Legal Consciousness*. Chicago: University of Chicago Press, 1976.

———. *Scenarios of Power: Myth and Ceremony in Russian Monarchy*. Vol. 2, *From Alexander II to the Abdication of Nicholas II*. Princeton: Princeton University Press, 2000.

Zaionchkovskii, P. A. *Pravitel'stvennyi apparat samoderzhavnoi Rossii v XIX v.* Moscow: Mysl', 1978.

Zhinzhikova, I. N. "Rodoslovnaia Mal'tsovykh." In *S. I. Mal'tsov i istoriia razvitiia Mal'tsovskogo promyshlennogo raiona*, edited by V. V. Krasheninnikov, 12–18. Briansk: Brianskoe oblastnoe izdatel'stvo "Grani," 1994.

Index